CALIFORNIA
WATERFALLS

California Waterfalls Second Edition
Printing History:
First edition—1997
Second edition—May 2000

5 4 3 2 1 0

All interior photos by Ann Marie Brown except:
pp. 61, 79, 263, 265, 287, 321 (right), 334 by Roger Hooper
pp. 197, 318, 321 (left) by Bill Rhoades
pp. 95, 98, 101 by Dee Randolph
p. 439 by Justin Cunningham
p. 20 by Jeff Patty

Front cover photo: Pfeiffer Falls, Big Sur © Cheyenne Rouse
Cartography: Ann Pettit

ISBN: 1-57354-070-6
ISSN: 1090-0985

Published by
Avalon Travel Publishing, Inc.
5855 Beaudry St.
Emeryville, CA 94608 USA

Printed in the United States of America

Please send all comments, corrections, additions,
amendments, and critiques to:

California Waterfalls Second Edition
Foghorn Outdoors
Avalon Travel Publishing, Inc.
5855 Beaudry Street
Emeryville, CA 94608 USA
e-mail: info@travelmatters.com
www.travelmatters.com

Distributed in the United States and Canada by Publishers Group West

FOGHORN ☒ OUTDOORS

CALIFORNIA
WATERFALLS

Second Edition

Ann Marie Brown

CONTENTS

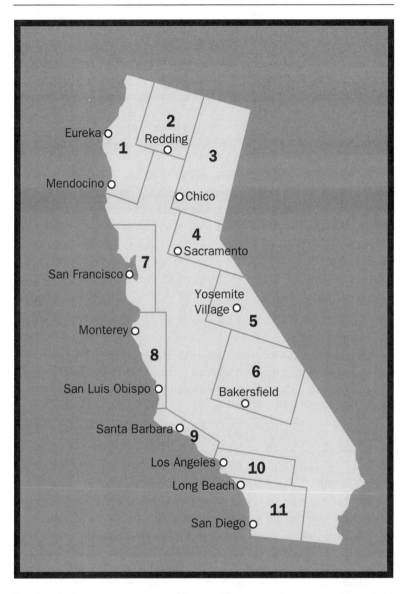

Eureka
Redding
Mendocino
Chico
Sacramento
San Francisco
Yosemite Village
Monterey
San Luis Obispo
Bakersfield
Santa Barbara
Los Angeles
Long Beach
San Diego

INTRODUCTION

There's magic in waterfalls. In the space where rock meets water, resulting in the steep descent of a river or stream, something occurs that is far richer than just a geologic irregularity. You can see it in the faces of people watching a waterfall. A star-filled sky can be compelling, a snow-capped mountain range can be awe-inspiring, an after-storm rainbow can stop you in your tracks, but only a waterfall can make you feel like you've fallen in love.

Some scientists explain this phenomena by pointing out that fast-flowing water ejects ionized particles into the air, supercharging the atmosphere with energy. Others say that because our human bodies are mostly water, and water is the lifeblood of the earth, we have a natural affinity with free-flowing rivers and streams. I take a less systematic approach. I believe that humans are innately drawn to natural beauty, and that despite our efforts to control the goings-on of every inch of our planet, we are still thrilled to see beauty that is created without, or in spite of, human intervention... Beauty that is caused by elements as random (and fickle) as rainfall, snowmelt, and the meandering course of water over rock.

It seems we humans cannot contain our delight at finding a river or stream that appears to fall from the sky. Perfectly responsible adults get downright giddy at the base of a plummeting cataract. Children forget about the miles of trail you forced them to walk when faced with a shimmering cascade. As my friend said when I took her on a waterfall hunt: "Oh, I see. We get to visit all of God's art museums."

I've spent several years wandering around the state of California, following the courses of rivers and streams in mountainous areas and praying for rain. The results of my research are found in this book, including all the facts you need to visit California's finest falls, whether you go by car, bicycle, or on foot, and whether you carry a 40-pound backpack or a diaper bag for your newborn baby. Inside these pages you'll find waterfalls from the beaches to the mountains to the desert, ranging in height from 15 feet to 2,425 feet, that are easy, moderate, and difficult to reach. Some are world-famous, and others are secret, hidden spots, far from the madding crowd. Some have luscious swimming holes; some occur in streams and rivers that are laden with hungry trout. All of them are places you'll want to visit again and again.

In your travels, please remember to take care of this beautiful land. I wish you many inspiring days in the outdoors.

—Ann Marie Brown

HOW TO USE THIS BOOK

This book is organized geographically, and it is divided into 11 chapters according to the major waterfall regions of California. Use the locator map on page 5 to determine which region you want to read about, then turn to the more detailed map of the region within each chapter. The regional maps are numbered, and the numbers correspond to the waterfall stories in each chapter.

You can also use the index to locate the names of cities, towns, parks, streams, rivers, and waterfalls, then turn to the corresponding pages in the book.

For each waterfall listing, the following information is included:

First, the **waterfall name** and **map number.** Waterfalls with more than one common name have all their names listed. A waterfall listed as a "falls" on a national forest or topographical map but not given a name has been named after its stream or a prominent nearby landmark.

Underneath the waterfall name is the **park or preserve** in which the fall is located, and its general location (closest highway and town).

Next to the waterfall name and location, you'll see a graphic icon rating each waterfall from 6 to 10. This is my subjective rating of the relative beauty of the fall, which takes into account the entire trip— trail conditions, scenery, setting, and overall view.

| Good | Great | Excellent | Spectacular | Top 20 in State |

Next, **access and difficulty** are listed. Access can be one or more of the following:

Hike-in—accessible by a day-hike on an established trail
Backpack—accessible by a backpacking trip on an established trail
Scramble—requires some off-trail travel to reach
Bike-in—accessible by bicycle
Wheelchair—accessible by wheelchair
Drive-to—accessible by car

Occasionally more than one option for accessing the fall is listed, such as a backpacking trip from two possible trailheads, or a trip where you can bike in or hike in. Roundtrip mileages are given for all hiking, backpacking, scrambling, or biking trips.

Difficulty is either "easy," "moderate," or "strenuous." An easy rating is generally suitable for children. A moderate rating denotes a longer hike, or a trail with a fair ascent. A strenuous rating denotes a challenging trail that includes long miles or steep ascents, or an off-trail scramble that is difficult and potentially treacherous. Be sure to choose your waterfall trips based on your abilities.

Trailhead elevation is listed, and an approximation of the **total one-way elevation gain or loss.** For trails that are "up" to the waterfall and "down" on the return, the elevation change is listed as a gain. For trails that are "down" to the waterfall and "up" on the return, the elevation change is listed as a loss. For trails that are both "up" and "down" in both directions, the elevation change is listed as gain/loss.

Below "Elevation" you'll find **"Best Season,"** which is my recommendation of the best months of the year for viewing each waterfall. As a general rule, waterfalls at low elevations should be visited in winter and spring, during the rainy season. Waterfalls at high elevations are usually only accessible in summer and early fall, when there is no snow on the ground. Remember that waterfalls are subject to the vagaries of weather, so the best months will vary greatly from year to year. Phone the parks for updated information about waterfall flow before your trip.

Finally, at the end of each waterfall story are **"Trip notes,"** which describe any fee, map, and permit information you may need, and the address and phone number of the managing agency for the waterfall. **"Directions"** tell you how to get to the waterfall's trailhead from the nearest major town.

Please remember that park fees can change at any time. So can trails, trail signs, and trail conditions. Always contact the managing agency for the park before making a long trip to see a waterfall—one phone call can give you the latest scoop on stream flow, road conditions, storm and fire damage, and trail alterations.

And most important of all, please exercise great caution. Many people are killed or injured each year from climbing on or around the slippery rock by waterfalls. It's an unnecessary tragedy. Always stay on trails wherever possible, and obey all warning signs about swift currents, slick rock, or eroding streambanks. Have respect for the force and power of these untamed places, and enjoy their beauty from points of safety.

BEST WATERFALLS LISTS

(Sorry, Yosemite. Your waterfalls were taken out of the running for all of the following lists because they would sweep too many categories.)

Best Short Backpack Trips to Waterfalls (2.5 to 8.0 miles):
Maple Falls (8.0 miles), *Marble Mountain Wilderness,* p. 40
Little Jamison Falls (3.0 miles), *Plumas National Forest,* p. 104
South Fork Kaweah River Falls (3.4 miles), *Sequoia National Park,* p. 257
Santa Paula Canyon Falls (6.0 miles), *Los Padres National Forest,* p. 366
Switzer Falls (2.5 miles), *Angeles National Forest,* p. 391

Best Long Backpack Trips to Waterfalls (10-plus miles):
Wilderness Falls (13.0 or 19.0 miles), *Siskiyou Wilderness,* p. 19
Grizzly Lake Falls (12.0 or 38.0 miles), *Trinity Alps Wilderness,* p. 47
Canyon Creek Falls (15.0 miles), *Trinity Alps Wilderness,* p. 52
Alamere Falls (10.5 miles), *Point Reyes National Seashore,* p. 291
Pine Falls (10.6 miles), *Ventana Wilderness,* p. 342

Best Easy Waterfall Walks—Southern California (0.5 to 3.5 miles):
Paradise Falls, *Wildwood Park,* p. 374
Sturtevant Falls, *Angeles National Forest,* p. 400
Monrovia Canyon Falls, *Monrovia Canyon Park,* p. 403
San Antonio Falls, *Angeles National Forest,* p. 407
Holy Jim Falls, *Cleveland National Forest,* p. 421

Best Easy Waterfall Walks—Northern California (0.5 to 3.5 miles):
McCloud Falls, *Shasta-Trinity National Forest,* p. 59
Burney Falls, *McArthur Burney Falls Memorial State Park,* p. 76
Frazier Falls, *Plumas National Forest,* p. 107
Grouse Falls, *Tahoe National Forest,* p. 140
Rainbow Falls, *Devils Postpile National Monument,* p. 217

Best Swimming Hole Waterfalls—Northern California:
Lower McCloud Falls, *Shasta-Trinity National Forest,* p. 59
Hatchet Creek Falls, *Shasta-Trinity National Forest,* p. 70
Indian Falls, *Plumas National Forest,* p. 91
Yuba River Falls, *South Yuba River State Park,* p. 119
Rainbow Pool Falls, *Stanislaus National Forest,* p. 169

Best Swimming Hole Waterfalls—Southern California:
Middle Fork Kaweah River Falls, *Sequoia National Park,* p. 255
Middle Fork Tule River Falls, *Sequoia National Forest,* p. 274
Santa Paula Canyon Falls, *Los Padres National Forest,* p. 366
Deep Creek Falls, *San Bernardino National Forest,* p. 412
Green Valley Falls, *Cuyamaca Rancho State Park,* p. 449

BEST WATERFALLS LISTS

Best Waterfalls in California State Parks:
Gold Bluffs Beach Falls, *Prairie Creek Redwoods State Park,* p. 22
Burney Falls, *McArthur Burney Falls Memorial State Park,* p. 76
Berry Creek Falls, Silver Falls, & Golden Falls Cascade, *Big Basin Redwoods State Park,* pp. 317, 320
McWay Falls, *Julia Pfeiffer Burns State Park,* p. 336
Limekiln Falls, *Limekiln State Park,* p. 340

Most Unusual Waterfalls:
Gold Bluffs Beach Falls, *Prairie Creek Redwoods State Park,* p. 22
Whitney Falls, *Mount Shasta Wilderness,* p. 55
Mossbrae Falls, *Dunsmuir,* p. 65
Darwin Falls, *Death Valley National Park,* p. 266
Borrego Palm Canyon Falls, *Anza-Borrego Desert State Park,* p. 443

Best Waterfalls at Family Campgrounds:
McCloud Falls, *Shasta-Trinity National Forest,* p. 59
Hidden Falls, *Mountain Home Demonstration State Forest,* p. 268
Rose Valley Falls, *Los Padres National Forest,* p. 364
Millard Falls, *Angeles National Forest,* p. 396
Dark Canyon Falls, *San Bernardino National Forest,* p. 429

Best Waterfalls to Visit by Bicycle:
Gold Bluffs Beach Falls, *Prairie Creek Redwoods State Park,* p. 22
Russian Gulch Falls, *Russian Gulch State Park,* p. 29
Feather Falls, *Plumas National Forest,* p. 100
Berry Creek Falls, *Big Basin Redwoods State Park,* p. 317
Los Peñasquitos Falls, *Los Peñasquitos Canyon Preserve,* p. 434

Best Waterfalls to Visit by Car:
Devil's Falls, *Auburn State Recreation Area,* p. 135
Leavitt Falls, *Humboldt-Toiyabe National Forest,* p. 162
Whiskey Falls, *Sierra National Forest,* p. 232
Grizzly Falls, *Sequoia National Forest,* p. 243
South Creek Falls, *Sequoia National Forest,* p. 280

Best Waterfalls to Visit by Wheelchair:
Rush Creek Falls, *South Yuba River Project,* p. 117
Bear River Falls, *PG & E Bear Valley Recreation Area,* p. 122
Roaring River Falls, *Kings Canyon National Park,* p. 245
McWay Falls, *Julia Pfeiffer Burns State Park,* p. 336
(plus Bridalveil Falls and Lower Yosemite Falls in Yosemite, of course)

Mendocino & North Coast

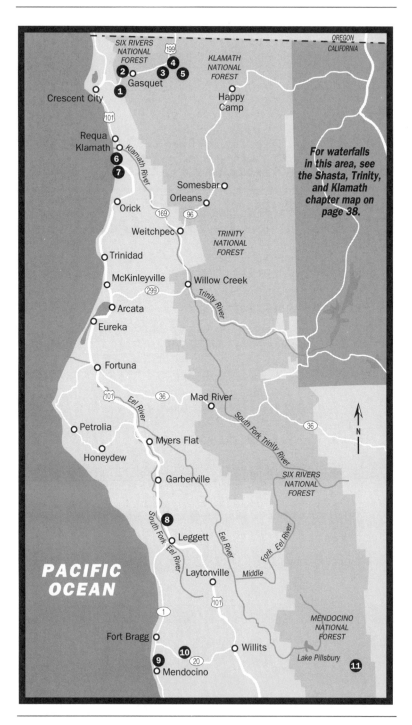

OREGON
CALIFORNIA

SIX RIVERS
NATIONAL
FOREST

199

KLAMATH
NATIONAL
FOREST

2
4
3
5
1
Gasquet

Crescent City

Happy
Camp

101

Requa
Klamath
6
7

Klamath River

Somesbar
Orleans

For waterfalls
in this area, see
the Shasta, Trinity,
and Klamath
chapter map on
page 38.

Orick

169
96

Weitchpec

TRINITY
NATIONAL
FOREST

Trinidad

McKinleyville
Willow Creek

299

Arcata
Trinity River

Eureka

Fortuna

101
Eel River
36
Mad River

South Fork Trinity River

Petrolia

36

N

Myers Flat

Honeydew

SIX RIVERS
NATIONAL
FOREST

Garberville

South Fork Eel River

8
Leggett

Eel River

Fork Eel River

Laytonville
Middle

101

PACIFIC
OCEAN

1

MENDOCINO
NATIONAL
FOREST

Fort Bragg

Lake Pillsbury
10
Willits
9
Mendocino
20
11

1. FERN FALLS

Jedediah Smith Redwoods State Park
Off U.S. 101 near Crescent City

Access & Difficulty: Hike-in 6.0 miles RT/Moderate
Elevation: Start at 250 feet; total gain 200 feet
Best Season: December to June

Fern Falls may not be the largest waterfall around, but it's one of the prettiest in the Redwood National and State Parks. It's hard to look big when you're surrounded on all sides by 300-foot-tall coastal redwood trees, with trunks large enough to build a room in.

The walk to 35-foot Fern Falls is filled with drop-dead gorgeous scenery along the Boy Scout Tree Trail—three continuous miles of old-growth redwood trees, giant sword ferns, and clover-like sorrel, with its deep green top sides and purple undersides. If you feel a little light-headed as you hike, it's probably because you're not used to such an abundance of plant life and all the oxygen it produces. Or maybe you're just feeling dizzy from spending so much time with your neck craned, gazing up toward the sky to see the tops of the big trees.

The Boy Scout Tree Trail is a gentle up-and-down route that never gains or loses more than 200 feet in elevation. Despite the minimal grade, the going is slow, because there's so much to see, photograph, and remark on. On our trip, we passed a hiker coming out of the forest who grinned at us and said, "Go back! We're outnumbered by the trees!" We knew exactly how he felt. It's downright humbling walking among these giants. At approximately two miles out you'll pass the largest one, on the right side of the trail. We had a hard time calling it

Fern Falls

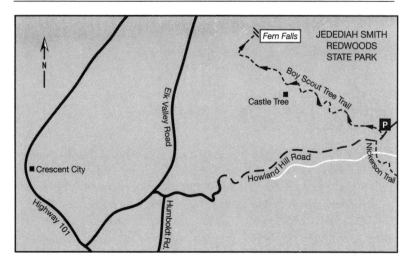

the Boy Scout, so we renamed it the Eagle Scout Tree.

The trail is simple to follow, and if you walk three miles to its end, you're rewarded by Fern Falls, a pretty 35-foot cascade on a tributary of Jordan Creek. The path ends at an overlook next to the waterfall, but if you wish, you can scramble a few feet down to its base. From either viewpoint, it's easy to admire the pretty S-curve the waterfall makes, rushing down the canyon wall, a twisting and turning rope of refreshing white set amid deep green ferns and redwoods.

Trip notes: There is no fee. For more information and a park map, contact Jedediah Smith Redwoods State Park, 1375 Elk Valley Road, Crescent City, CA 95531; (707) 464-6101.

Directions: From U.S. 101 at Crescent City, turn east on Elk Valley Road and drive 1.1 miles to Howland Hill Road on the right. Turn right and drive 3.5 miles to the Boy Scout Tree Trailhead on the left.

---

2. MYRTLE CREEK FALLS

Smith River National Recreation Area
Off Highway 199 near Gasquet

Access & Difficulty: Hike-in & Scramble 5.0 miles RT/Strenuous
Elevation: Start at 250 feet; total gain 400 feet
Best Season: December to June

The trip to Myrtle Creek Falls starts as a blissfully easy romp on an interpretive trail, but before long it turns into a treacherous, muddy scramble along the streambank, up and over rock slides, and against an advancing army of waist-high sword ferns. Depending on the season, you can slip in the mud on steep slopes, get scratched by thimbleberry bushes, or be soaked to the skin from heavy dew on the streamside plants. You might find yourself hoping you'll get eaten by a mountain lion; at least then you'll be saved from repeating the battle on your return trip.

Is it worth it, you ask? Maybe. If you know what you're doing, if your footing is sure when there's no trail to follow, if you know how to travel on steep, rough streamside routes—yes, Myrtle Creek Falls is worth it. It's a 60-foot waterfall on a roaring stream that feeds directly into the Middle Fork of the Smith River, and if you reach it, you're likely to have its beauty all to yourself.

Even if you're not willing to make the rough cross-country trip to the falls, the Myrtle Creek Trail is worth a gander for its first mile, where it's extremely well-maintained. The Gasquet ranger station hands out an interpretive brochure that goes along with the numbered posts on the trail, so you can learn all about the streamside flora and the area's gold mining history. For instance, can you guess the size of the largest gold nugget ever taken out of Myrtle Creek? Forty-seven ounces. That probably bought the miners a few dinners out.

The first mile of trail is built on an old mining ditch, high above the creek, so it's virtually flat. After signpost 15 and the end of the interpretive trail, the route continues but is quickly overgrown. In minutes you reach the first of several landslides, which you must navigate around.

And so it goes. There are three main slides to get past, plus numerous other obstacles, such as very wet, unstable soil and thick forests of ferns on steep slopes. (The good news is that because Myrtle Creek is fed by so many springs and feeder streams, you cross paths with many small, pretty cascades along the way. You could be content with these and turn around at any point.)

After an hour of slow off-trail travel, mostly high above the creek on a rough route that can be hard to discern, you'll come upon the first of several small cascades and falls on Myrtle Creek. From there, you've got another half-mile to cover, and if the creek is low, it's advisable to drop down to the creekbed to do it. If Myrtle Creek is running hard, as it was on our trip, you have no choice but to stay high, fighting for footholds amid the downed trees, tangled branches, and ubiquitous ferns. Are we having fun yet?

If all goes well, you should reach Myrtle Creek Falls in an hour and a half of scrambling, during which you will have covered only 1.5

miles from the end of the one-mile, maintained Myrtle Creek Trail. Don't say I didn't warn you.

By the way, there's one more hazard on the Myrtle Creek Trail. It's the carnivorous (actually insectivorous) pitcher plant, a distant cousin of the Venus fly trap plants we were fascinated by as kids. You'll see its two-foot-high stems with cobra-like heads growing along the trail, and although it won't bother you, make sure you keep your pet beetle on a short leash.

Trip notes: There is no fee. For a map of the Smith River National Recreation Area, send $4 to USDA-Forest Service, 1323 Club Drive, Vallejo, CA 94592. For more information, contact Smith River National Recreation Area and Six Rivers National Forest, P.O. Box 228, Gasquet, CA 95543; (707) 457-3131.

Directions: From Crescent City, drive north on U.S. 101 for four miles to the Highway 199 exit. Turn east on Highway 199 and drive 6.5 miles to the Myrtle Creek Trailhead, west of the Myrtle Creek bridge and the South Fork Road turnoff. Park on the south side of Highway 199, then cross the road to reach the trailhead.

---

3. HIGHWAY 199 FALLS

Smith River National Recreation Area
Off Highway 199 near Gasquet

Access & Difficulty: Drive-to/Easy
Elevation: 500 feet
Best Season: December to June

In the rainy season, so many waterfalls cascade alongside Highway 199 and the Smith River that it seems there are too many to count. I know; I tried counting several times, driving up and down the highway, and I couldn't keep track.

But if it's quality you want, not quantity, the tallest waterfalls along Highway 199 are in the proximity of Grassy Flat Campground. Across the river from the camp, an unnamed creek drops 80 feet along the steep slopes leading down to the Middle Fork Smith River. Then, three-quarters of a mile east of the camp on Highway 199, another 80-foot fall drops over a rockslide just off the highway, accessible by a gravel spur road.

The best way to see the fall across from Grassy Flat is to take the camp access road, then follow it past the camp, down to the river's edge. At the end of the road, you're directly across from the big fall, which often has a sibling waterfall running 50 yards distant from it. The two of them make quite a sight, racing down the hillside to join the Smith River. Of course, the Smith makes quite a sight on its own, running fast and green in winter and spring, dropping through rapids and into deep pools, and passing swiftly through granite gorges. It's the largest wild and undammed river still flowing in California.

You can get closer to this waterfall by driving a quarter-mile farther east on Highway 199, to the river access turnoff just past Grassy Flat Campground. Leave your car at the end of the access road, near the river, and scramble downstream a few hundred feet to the falls. If the weather is dry, this is easily accomplished, but if it's wet, scrambling over the jumbled base of a rock slide is slippery and difficult. Use your judgement.

Just down the road from the Grassy Flat Camp waterfall is another 80-foot cascade, spilling down a giant landslide and plainly visible from the highway. To reach it from Grassy Flat, drive east on Highway 199 for three-quarters of a mile. There's a gravel turnoff on the right, where you can pull off the highway, park, and walk to the base of the falls.

Trip notes: There is no fee. For a map of the Smith River National Recreation Area, send $4 to USDA-Forest Service, 1323 Club Drive, Vallejo, CA 94592. For more information, contact Smith River National Recreation Area and Six Rivers National Forest, P.O. Box 228, Gasquet, CA 95543; (707) 457-3131.

Directions: From Crescent City, drive north on U.S. 101 for four miles to the Highway 199 exit. Turn east on Highway 199 and drive 14 miles to Gasquet, then continue east for 4.5 miles more to the Grassy Flat Campground turnoff on the right. (The campground is often closed in winter, but you can still enter.)

4. MIDDLE FORK FALLS

Smith River National Recreation Area
Off Highway 199 near Gasquet

Access & Difficulty: Scramble 0.25 mile RT/Strenuous
Elevation: Start at 1,700 feet; total loss 150 feet
Best Season: December to June

We almost didn't bother to go see Middle Fork Falls, on the Middle Fork Smith River east of Gasquet and Patrick Creek. The ranger told us the waterfall was only 25 feet high, and because we

Middle Fork Falls, Smith River

knew it was a river fall, we expected a wide, rocky cascade and lots of white water, but not much drama. But when a rainy day cancelled our plans for a longer hike, we took the drive down Knopki Road off Highway 199 to see what Middle Fork Falls was all about.

The rain was lucky for us. Middle Fork Falls turns out to be a sensational drop of churning river over a 25-foot vertical cliff. Rather than pouring wide and evenly over its lip, the river has channeled a V-shape into the granite, funneling itself into a narrow stream. This makes the flow of water at the falls double or triple what it is elsewhere on the river. The Middle Fork Smith was running high on the day we visited, and the waterfall ran in two streams—one big drop on the left and an overflow drop on the right, creating a tremendous rush of water. The crashing fall has incredible impact, both on its viewers and where it strikes its wide pool below.

The unmarked route to the waterfall is not easy to find. Make sure you travel exactly 2.2 miles on Knopki Road, then start looking for the point where the Middle Fork Smith River separates from the road and heads south. If Knopki Road starts to follow Knopki Creek instead of the Smith River, you've gone past the trailhead. (A map of the Smith River National Recreation Area is immensely helpful.)

On our trip, the start of the route to the falls was marked with an odd, hand-lettered sign hanging high on a tree: "Hope is Eternal." It got our hopes up, and so did the noise of falling water, which was surprisingly loud at the road. One hundred feet of travel down a well-worn route over a rockslide brought us to a cluster of moss-covered oak trees. Some waterfall-lover had tied a strong rope to the largest oak, which we used to safely lower ourselves down to a rock outcrop with a wide-open view of the falls, on the far side of its giant pool. In wet weather, the outcrop is no place for the unsure-footed, since it has very little surface area and can be slippery.

Another rope leads down from the rock to the fall's pool, a perfect place for swimming on some fair summer day.

Trip notes: There is no fee. For a map of the Smith River National Recreation Area, send $4 to USDA-Forest Service, 1323 Club Drive, Vallejo, CA 94592. For more information, contact Smith River National Recreation Area and Six Rivers National Forest, P.O. Box 228, Gasquet, CA 95543; (707) 457-3131.

Directions: From Crescent City, drive north on U.S. 101 for four miles to the Highway 199 exit. Turn east on Highway 199 and drive 14 miles to Gasquet, then continue east for 15.5 more miles to the Knopki Road turnoff on the right. Turn right on Knopki Road/Forest Service Road 18N07 and drive 2.2 miles to the unmarked trailhead on the right. Park alongside the road, and look for a route leading from the south side of the road down to the river.

5. WILDERNESS FALLS

Siskiyou Wilderness
Off Highway 199 near Gasquet

Access & Difficulty: Backpack 13.0 miles RT/Moderate (Doe Flat)
or Backpack 19.0 miles RT/Moderate (Young's Valley)
Elevation: Start at 4,200 feet; total loss 1,200 feet (Doe Flat)
or Start at 5,200 feet; total loss 2,200 feet (Young's Valley)
Best Season: June to September

If you're planning to make the trek to Wilderness Falls, you've got some soul-searching to do. Two different trails can take you there, each with its individual challenges. You need to know the details of both itineraries, consider your options, then decide which path suits you best. Once that's accomplished, the hard work is over and the fun begins, because Wilderness Falls is the most spectacular cataract in the northwest corner of California.

The route from the Young's Valley Trailhead is the longest and most scenic route to Wilderness Falls. It requires a long, winding drive to reach the trailhead—at least an hour from Gasquet—then a 9.5-mile hike to the falls. If you've got the time and don't mind the mileage, this is the way to make the trip. The first two miles of trail are a closed road, but after that, you drop into the canyon of Clear Creek—a 600-foot elevation loss—and it's smooth sailing the rest of the way. The trail strolls pleasantly along the east side of the stream, mostly out in the sun, covering a gentle and gradual descent from the headwaters of Clear Creek at 4,600 feet to Wilderness Falls at 3,000 feet. The elevation loss is spread out over seven miles, so it makes for an easy climb on the return trip.

The alternative is to come in from the Doe Flat Trailhead at Siskiyou Pass, a shorter drive from Gasquet and a much shorter hike to the falls—only 6.5 miles one-way, with a 1,200-foot elevation loss. As with the Young's Valley Trail, here again you walk on a closed road for 1.5 miles before you reach the real trail, which is an old mining path along Doe Creek. You pass an old mine site on your way to Trout Camp at 3.5 miles, where the Doe Flat Trail ends and joins with the Clear Creek Trail out of Young's Valley. (There's also a turn-off here for the trail to Devil's Punchbowl, an area of stunning glacial beauty.) Then it's an easy three miles on the Clear Creek Trail to Wilderness Falls.

If the Doe Flat Trail seems like the obvious choice for the trip, be forewarned about the junction at Trout Camp where the trail ends and connects with the Clear Creek Trail. The problem? The Doe Flat Trail is on the west side of Clear Creek and the Clear Creek Trail is on the east side, and never the twain shall meet unless you ford the stream. Clear Creek is not a narrow, babbling brook. Especially early in the summer, when Clear Creek runs full with snowmelt and is freezing cold, the crossing can be difficult. You can't make the ford with your shoes off; your toes will go numb in no time, and the streambed is too slick. The only choice is to take off your socks and wear

Wilderness Falls

your boots on your naked feet, then grit it out till you get to the other side. Those warm, dry socks will feel heavenly when you put them back on. In late summer, some people walk up and down the stream near Trout Camp till they find a way to rock-hop across, but most hikers just give up and wade.

Consider your route options, make a choice, then one way or another get yourself to Wilderness Falls. What can you expect when get there? An excellent camp, for starters, just five minutes from the waterfall. It's located at a small clearing near the stream, where you can watch the stars all night. Then, just

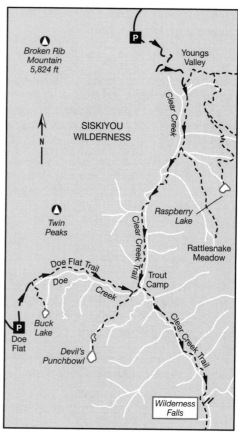

around a few boulders lies magnificent Wilderness Falls, where Clear Creek drops 50 feet in perfect freefall, then collides with a big rock and cascades downward. Although the Clear Creek Trail crosses the creek at a ford right above the falls, you need not do so to see the waterfall. There are two excellent overlook points on big boulders on the east side of the stream, just 50 feet from the falls. If you choose to make the ford, you can descend to the fall's spectacular 100-foot-wide pool, which is clear, deep, and white with foam from the continual pounding of water.

Keep in mind that because you've driven so far east on Highway 199 you've left the giant redwood forests and the cool, foggy coast far behind. That means they have "real" summer here, and because the forest is a mixed bag of Douglas firs, cedars, and Jeffrey pines, you're not protected by impenetrable shade all day long. It can be hot, especially when hiking back out and heading uphill on either of the trails. Make sure you have your water filter with you, and fill your canteen at every opportunity.

Trip notes: There is no fee. A free wilderness permit is required for overnight stays; they are available at the Gasquet Ranger Station, along with a free map of the Siskiyou Wilderness. For a map of the Smith River National Recreation Area, send $4 to USDA-Forest Service, 1323 Club Drive, Vallejo, CA 94592. For more information, contact Smith River National Recreation Area and Six Rivers National Forest, P.O. Box 228, Gasquet, CA 95543; (707) 457-3131.

Directions: For the Young's Valley Trailhead—From Crescent City, drive north on U.S. 101 for four miles to the Highway 199 exit. Turn east on Highway 199 and drive 14 miles to Gasquet, then continue east for 15.5 more miles to the Knopki Road turnoff on the right. Turn right on Knopki Road/Forest Service Road 18N07 and drive approximately 14 miles, passing Sanger Lake. The trailhead is at the end of the road.

For the Doe Flat Trailhead—Follow the directions above to Gasquet. From Gasquet, continue east on Highway 199 for 11 miles to the Little Jones Creek Road/Jawbone Road turnoff on the right, shortly past Patrick Creek Lodge. Turn right and drive for about 10 miles to the Bear Basin junction. Turn left and follow the road to Siskiyou Pass. The trailhead is at the end of the road.

6. GOLD BLUFFS BEACH FALLS
Prairie Creek Redwoods State Park
Off U.S. 101 near Orick

Access & Difficulty: Hike-in or Bike-in 3.0 miles RT/Easy
Elevation: Start at 90 feet; total gain 0 feet
Best Season: December to June

The only thing that keeps Fern Canyon, Gold Bluffs Beach, and the Coastal Trail's waterfalls from being completely overrun with tourists is the long, unpaved road to reach them. No trailers or RVs are allowed on gravely Davison Road, so that eliminates plenty of visitors right there. In addition, the road has different moods in different weather: Sometimes it's smoothly graded, almost like glass, and sometimes it's full of potholes, or has a foot-deep stream running across it. You just never know.

Well, if your vehicle can make the seven-mile drive from U.S. 101, you're in luck, because there are many hidden treasures at the end of Davison Road. Probably the most famous is Fern Canyon, a secluded, rocky grotto on Home Creek that is a veritable paradise of ferns growing on 50-foot-high canyon walls. (See the James Irvine Trail story that follows.) There's also an excellent chance of seeing magnificent Roosevelt elk, maybe even looking eye-to-eye with some of these resident deer-on-steroids. Plus there's Gold Bluffs Beach, a pristine, windswept stretch of sand along the Pacific, where you can beachcomb and walk for miles.

And last but certainly not least, there's the Coastal Trail, with three sweet waterfalls that drop alongside it. The trail traverses a flat route from the end of Davison Road to a backpacking camp 2.2 miles out, then it continues for another 2.2 miles along the coast before it climbs back out to the highway. If you just want to see its three falls along Gold Bluffs Beach, you need only walk (or ride your bike) 1.5 miles out from the parking lot.

The waterfalls are just slightly off the trail; you must listen for the gentle sound of splashing water, and keep looking to your right for spur trails leading into the trees. Each of these spurs is your ticket to one of three tall, narrow cataracts, all of them hidden in grottos carved from a canopy of spruce and alders.

Start your hike from the Fern Canyon parking lot by negotiating the sometimes tricky crossing of Home Creek. Coastal Trail starts due north of the lot, at a signpost on the far side of the creek. After the stream crossing, the rest of the trail is incredibly easy and level and it stays fairly dry even in the wettest weather. That's why bikes are allowed on this section of the Coastal Trail; the flat, windswept bluffs have soil tough enough to withstand their weight and speed.

Gold Dust Falls near Gold Bluffs Beach

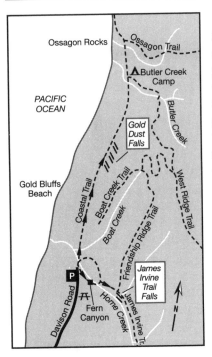

After a brief stint in the forest, the scenery opens up and you walk with the ocean on your left and tall vertical bluffs on your right. Be prepared to see big elk, who are usually grazing somewhere along the trail. In various trips here, I've always passed at least a dozen of them, usually big males with impressive racks. They tend to completely ignore hikers, but hikers rarely ignore them.

At 1.1 miles out, start listening for the sound of falling water and look for an unsigned spur trail penetrating the alder and spruce forest on your right. Follow the short spur and you'll find the first cascade, an 80-foot narrow freefall reminiscent of Hawaiian waterfalls—tall, slender, and delicate, and surrounded by a myriad of ferns. On one visit here, we spotted hundreds of three-inch-wide mushrooms growing on a log near the fall's base, forming a thick forest of fungus.

Walk a quarter-mile further, listen again for the sound of water, and watch again for a spur trail. You'll find yourself holding court with Gold Dust Falls, which is even taller and more mystical-looking than the first fall. (The park has put up a sign on Coastal Trail denoting the spur to Gold Dust Falls, but each time I've visited, the sign was laying on the ground or hidden in the bushes.) Gold Dust Falls has a wooden bench near its base for waterfall-watching, but it's often soaking wet and covered with moss.

Gold Dust is the only fall of the three that is named. It's dubbed for the short-lived 1850s gold rush along Gold Bluffs Beach, when five prospectors discovered gold dust in the sand and staked a claim. Thousands of others flocked to this beach and set up a tent city, but alas, extracting the gold turned out to be hard work that produced little profit. The mining boom ended almost as quickly as it began. (Too bad they weren't looking for waterfalls.)

The third waterfall is very close to Gold Dust Falls; another couple hundred feet on the Coastal Trail brings you to its spur trail. It, too, is a tall, narrow cataract, hidden in the deep shade of forest and ferns. Pay a visit, and then turn around and head back, or continue hiking on the Coastal Trail. Your options include an out and back trip of up to nine miles along the coast, or a seven-mile loop: You can turn right on the West Ridge Trail at 2.2 miles, then connect to the Friendship Ridge Trail, and follow it back to Fern Canyon and the parking area.

Trip notes: A $5 state park day-use fee is charged. A park map is available at the entrance kiosk for 50 cents. For more information, contact Prairie Creek Redwoods State Park, 1270011 Newton B. Drury Parkway, Orick, CA 95555; (707) 464-6101 or (707) 445-6547.

Directions: From Eureka, drive north on U.S. 101 for 41 miles to Orick. Continue north for 2.5 more miles to Davison Road, then turn left (west) and drive seven miles to the Fern Canyon Trailhead. No trailers or RVs are permitted on unpaved Davison Road.

7. JAMES IRVINE TRAIL FALLS

Prairie Creek Redwoods State Park
Off U.S. 101 near Orick

Access & Difficulty: Hike-in 2.0 miles RT/Easy
Elevation: Start at 90 feet; total gain 200 feet
Best Season: December to June

The wetter it is, the better it is. That's not the case with many hiking trails, but it's true if you're going to see the waterfalls in Fern Canyon and along the neighboring James Irvine Trail in Prairie Creek Redwoods State Park. It can rain cats and dogs all day long and you'll still have a fine time on your trip. That's convenient, because the area gets an average of 70 inches of rain a year.

Although the waterfalls benefit from the rain as much as anything else, they're really only a sideshow here. The falls in and around Fern Canyon are small and delicate, pretty to look at but unlikely to be the highlight of your trip. Instead, the foliage is the headliner, and because it's largely comprised of ferns, redwood trees, Sitka spruce, alders, and moss, the more it rains, the more these plants like it.

Start your trip at the trailhead at the end of Davison Road. If it's winter or spring, the first thing you need to do is survey the level of Home Creek, which crosses just to the north of the trailhead parking lot. In summer and early fall, the creek level drops, and park rangers put up little bridges and walkways in Fern Canyon, making travel easy. In winter and spring, the stream often floods the canyon, wiping out any semblance of a trail. Although much of the time you can wear good hiking boots and rockhop your way around, sometimes the stream level is too high even for that. Then, you have a choice: Put on your waterproof boots, and wade the half-mile to the back of the canyon, or skip the Fern Canyon section of the trip and proceed directly to the James Irvine Trail. The latter has two entry points, one at the back of Fern Canyon and one at the entrance to it. You'll still need to cross Home Creek to access it.

Let's assume you can travel the entire route on both trails. Start by heading to your right into the canyon, passing through a corridor of ferns. Keep walking up the streambed, observing as the canyon walls grow taller and squeeze tighter. Try to identify all the fern types—sword ferns, lady ferns, five-finger ferns, chain ferns, and bracken ferns. You're completely surrounded by greenery, rocks, and water. Stay alert for the rare Pacific giant salamander, as well as more common frogs, salamanders, and newts.

Near the back of Fern Canyon, be sure to enter the small side canyon that harbors a narrow, 12-foot waterfall. Then, pick up the well-signed James Irvine Trail on the left, and climb upward. You'll enter a lush mixed forest of Sitka spruce, redwoods, alders, ferns, and vines. Like in Fern Canyon, every inch is covered in green. You'll see some very large and old examples of "octopus" trees: Western hemlocks that have sprouted on the tops of redwood stumps, then grown

Walking into Fern Canyon

over and around them, clutching the stumps in their roots or "legs."

A half-mile after leaving the back of Fern Canyon (or one mile from the parking area, if you started hiking on the James Irvine Trail from there), you cross a bridge with two small benches where a 25-foot-tall, delicate waterfall drops into a remarkably narrow and deep canyon, eventually flowing to Home Creek and Fern Canyon. A sign denotes that the bridge and benches are dedicated to John Baldwin, and bears this lovely verse: "You shall walk where only the wind has walked before, and when all music is stilled, you shall hear the singing of the stream, and enter the living shelter of the forest."

You can turn around here and head back to the parking lot, either by following the James Irvine Trail the entire way or returning to Fern Canyon, but most likely you will want to walk further. The trail continues onward for 3.5 miles before it ends at the park visitor center. The entire distance makes a terrific out-and-back walk.

Trip notes: A $5 state park day-use fee is charged. A park map is available at the entrance kiosk for 50 cents. For more information, contact Prairie Creek Redwoods State Park, 1270011 Newton B. Drury Parkway, Orick, CA 95555; (707) 464-6101 or (707) 445-6547.

Directions: From Eureka, drive north on U.S. 101 for 41 miles to Orick. Continue north for 2.5 more miles to Davison Road, then turn left (west) and drive seven miles to the Fern Canyon Trailhead. No trailers or RVs are permitted on unpaved Davison Road.

---

8. DORA FALLS

Smithe Redwoods State Reserve
Off U.S. 101 near Leggett

Access & Difficulty: Hike-in 0.25 mile RT/Easy
Elevation: Start at 900 feet; total gain 20 feet
Best Season: December to May

The truth of the matter is: No one comes to Smithe Redwoods State Reserve just to see Dora Falls. They come because the tiny park is a good leg-stretcher, a place to pull off the highway among some big coastal redwoods, walk the dog, give the kids a snack, and take a look at the Eel River running by.

Only an elite few know that right across the highway from the big trees and the river is a hidden waterfall, accessible by a five-minute walk. Unfortunately, to visit it means crossing U.S. 101 on foot, which you must do with care. Then it's an easy 100-yard stroll

Dora Falls

behind the highway bridge guardrail and back into the canyon where Dora Falls drops, then pours under the highway and into the Eel River.

Poor Dora Falls has lost much of its original splendor. A huge landslide in 1978 filled in the lower portion of the falls, so its one-time 60-foot length is now only half that. The filled-in area at the fall's base is now overgrown with brush. It's easy to imagine what this canyon and waterfall looked like before the slide.

The grounds containing Smithe Redwoods State Reserve and Dora Falls were once the site of Lane's Redwood Flat, a popular 1920s resort with a museum, restaurant, and 18 cabins. Right next to the present-day parking lot is a wide redwood tree with a walk-through tunnel, which was once the entrance to the resort's restaurant. Lane's was destroyed in a 1930s fire, and eventually the state obtained the land and preserved it as a state reserve.

Dora Falls runs only after winter rains, so forget visiting it in summer or autumn. From December to May it can put on quite a show. That's also when the Eel River is most spectacular—high, green, and full of vigor. Of course, the redwoods in the park are a marvel in any season.

Trip notes: There is no fee. For more information, contact Richardson Grove State Park at (707) 247-3319, or Standish-Hickey State Recreation Area at (707) 925-6482.

Directions: From Willitts, drive north on U.S. 101 for 47 miles. Smithe Redwoods State Reserve is 2.4 miles north of Standish-Hickey State Recreation Area, on the west side of the road. Dora Falls is across the highway on the east side of the road.

9. RUSSIAN GULCH FALLS

Russian Gulch State Park
Off Highway 1 near Mendocino

Access & Difficulty: Hike-in 4.5 to 7.5 miles RT/Moderate
or Bike-in 3.0 miles & Hike-in 1.5 miles RT/Easy
Elevation: Start at 80 feet; total gain 200 feet
Best Season: December to June

One of the many great things about visiting Russian Gulch Falls is that you have so many options for making the trip. You can hike on luscious single-track through dense forest for a 6.5-mile out-and-back trek. You can increase or shorten that distance by taking different routes. You can even ride your bike on the flat, paved trail through the canyon, then lock it up at a bike rack and hike the remaining three-quarters of a mile to the falls.

No matter how you get there, visiting Russian Gulch Falls is a high-quality outdoors experience. It's an excellent place for introducing children to nature, or for convincing a reluctant friend or spouse that the outdoors is not just tough uphill ascents, mosquitos, and poison oak.

Make your way to the Fern Canyon Trailhead at Russian Gulch State Park's campground, then choose your route. The paved, 1.5-mile Fern Canyon Trail heads straight into the canyon, paralleling Russian Gulch, and it's the only choice for bike riders. Some hikers also prefer it, because it is the shortest route. The unpaved North Trail is for hikers only, and because it winds and meanders through the forest, it's one mile longer than the paved Fern Canyon Trail. Both trails end before the falls at a junction with the Waterfall Loop Trail. There, bikers must dismount and lock up their bikes, and all trail users continue on foot to the falls.

Russian Gulch Falls

But you still have choices. Because the waterfall is situated along a loop trail, you can take the left fork of the loop for the shortest trip to the falls—three-quarters of a mile—then simply turn around and head back. Or you can take the right fork of the loop and make a long 2.5-mile circle around to the falls and back to the junction.

Which route you take depends on your time and energy, because they're all equally good. Whereas the paved trail parallels the stream and is rife with vines, ferns, alders, and willows, the single-track North Trail has more ups and downs and travels through a mixed forest of larger trees—tanoaks, redwoods, and Douglas firs. It's not until both trails end and the Waterfall Loop begins that the path begins a more serious ascent. It's made easy by well-placed wooden stair-steps.

If you take the short end of the loop to Russian Gulch Falls, you'll climb gently most of the way, then make a short descent to the base of the falls. Russian Gulch Falls is 35 feet high, with an abundance of fallen redwood trees gathered in its hollow, separating the waterfall's flow into several streams. It's fascinating to look at it from different angles, observing how the water bobs and weaves its way around logs and branches before making its way to the waterfall's pool. Many of these fallen trees have been here so long that other plants have made a home on their trunks, creating a lush green frame for the falling water. Although the entire length of Fern Canyon is lavish with foliage, here at the waterfall the flora is most extravagant. It creates an exquisite scene.

Trip notes: A $5 day-use fee is charged by the state park. A free map is available at the entrance kiosk. For more information, contact

Russian Gulch State Park, P.O. Box 440, Mendocino, CA 95460; (707) 937-5804.

Directions: From Mendocino, drive two miles north on Highway 1 to the entrance for Russian Gulch State Park on the left. Turn left and then left again immediately to reach the entrance kiosk. After paying, drive through the kiosk and continue straight, crossing back under the highway, to the eastern side of the park. Drive through the campground to the parking area for Fern Canyon Trail. The trailhead is on the east side of the parking area. (If the campground is closed for the season, you must park near the recreation hall and walk in to the trailhead.)

10. CHAMBERLAIN FALLS

Jackson State Forest
Off Highway 20 near Fort Bragg

Access & Difficulty: Hike-in 0.5 mile RT/Easy
Elevation: Start at 2,400 feet; total loss 150 feet
Best Season: December to June

Although most people come to Mendocino to see its spectacular coast, there's another Mendocino that is less well known, yet equally beautiful. A drive inland on Highway 20 unveils the "other" Mendocino, a land of big conifers, roaring streams, and you guessed it—waterfalls.

A dozen miles from the windswept beaches, Mendocino's Jackson State Forest is comprised of thousands of acres of big trees, mostly redwoods and Douglas firs. Much of the land is used for logging, but plenty more is available for public recreation, including the trail to 50-foot Chamberlain Falls.

The route to the trailhead includes four miles of narrow dirt roads, with the possibility of logging trucks bearing down on you at any time, so drive with care. In good weather, passenger cars can handle the roads without a problem, but when the roads are wet, four-wheel-drive is more than a good idea.

After parking your car alongside the road at the trailhead, walk down the wooden steps that descend into the steep canyon, then continue downhill on the dirt trail. If the weather is wet when you visit, be wary both on the steps and on the trail, as the fallen oak leaves underfoot can be slippery.

The canyon is dense with plant life, including oaks, Douglas firs, redwoods, sword ferns, and sorrel. After 10 minutes of downhill walking, you'll catch sight of Chamberlain Falls and then walk right to its base. Its setting is stunningly simple—just a massive black cliff jutting out of the forest wall, forcing Chamberlain Creek to tumble over its bulk before cascading down-canyon. Look for white, three-leaved trilliums in early spring, growing amidst the ferns in the fall's grotto. In winter, the entire rock face is covered with rushing water; in summer, the stream is reduced to less than a foot wide. By July, the water is usually warm and tame enough that you can take a shower in the waterfall, or at least dip your head in.

There are many fallen logs on which you can sit and admire Chamberlain Falls, or you can continue hiking on the Chamberlain Creek Trail by crossing the waterfall's stream. Just around the canyon corner is a pristine stand of old-growth redwoods, a place where you can ponder your relatively short existence on the planet. From there, the trail begins to climb steadily out of the canyon, heading northward for one mile to its end.

Trip notes: There is no fee. A free trail map is available by writing to Jackson State Forest. For more information, contact Jackson State Forest, 802 North Main Street, Fort Bragg, CA 95437; (707) 964-5674.

Directions: From Fort Bragg, drive south on Highway 1 for one mile to the turnoff for Highway 20. Turn east on Highway 20 and drive 17 miles. Turn left on Road 200, an unsigned dirt road immediately past the Chamberlain Creek bridge. Drive one mile on Road 200 until it forks, then bear left and drive for 3.5 more miles. Look for a wooden railing on the left side of the road; this is the trailhead. Park in the dirt pullouts alongside the road.

11. STONY CREEK FALLS

Snow Mountain Wilderness
Off Interstate 5 near Willows

Access & Difficulty: Hike-in 5.0 miles RT/Moderate
or Backpack 13.0 miles RT/Moderate
Elevation: Start at 5,200 feet; total gain 700 feet (5.0-mile RT)
or Start at 5,200 feet; total gain 1,200 feet (13.0-mile RT)
Best Season: April to November

Snow Mountain Wilderness is a long way from everywhere. From Interstate 5, it's a 50-mile drive to the wilderness trailhead. From U.S. 101, it's 60 miles. Tucked into that never-never land west of the Central Valley and east of the Mendocino coast, Snow Mountain Wilderness is a place you must earn with a drive.

Its spectacular waterfall, on the other hand, is easy to reach. Located only 2.5 miles from West Crockett, the main Snow Mountain Wilderness trailhead, Stony Creek Falls can be seen in an easy afternoon of hiking. Or, if you want to make an overnight trip out of it, you can backpack the 13-mile Waterfall Loop Trail from West Crockett to Milk Ranch Meadows and back.

When I visited Stony Creek Falls, one thought kept running through my mind: Waterfalls are not supposed to be this good in November. Not in California, anyway. I had been to Yosemite the week before, and everything was bone dry. Feather Falls near

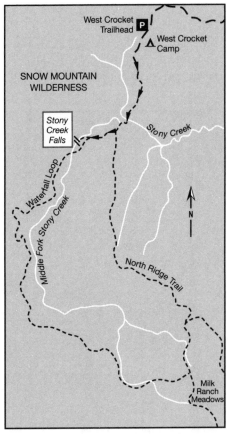

Oroville? It was a mere shadow of its former (spring) self. The coastal falls? Sadly lacking in H_2O. But Stony Creek Falls was running vigorously, as if it were the first of April. It turns out that the creek, like most of the streams in the Snow Mountain Wilderness, drains a huge, vegetation-filled area, so it stays full and wet year-round.

The countryside surrounding Stony Creek is as lush and lovely as the waterfall itself. Although you drive through endless farmlands, foothills, and oak woodlands to reach it, the Snow Mountain Wilderness is comprised of giant Douglas fir trees, Jeffrey pines, incense cedars, rushing creeks, steep hillsides, and quite often, plenty of snow. They've logged Mendocino National Forest very close to the wilderness boundary, but once your feet step inside that magic line, there's plenty of old growth, especially firs. The forest looks untouched, and largely, it is.

At the trailhead, a large sign marks the start of the Waterfall Trail. The path leads flat for a few hundred yards, then parallels a tiny stream as it descends to Middle Fork Stony Creek. Look for the variety of colors in the rocks at your feet, and drink in the aroma of firs and cedars. In autumn, vine maples and ferns turn yellow along

Stony Creek Falls

the creek, and willows turn rosy. In spring, the stream cultivates a multitude of wildflowers. This trail starts out good and stays good the whole way.

At 1.3 miles, you meet up with Middle Fork Stony Creek and must ford or rockhop, depending on the season. Once on the other side, prepare to switchback uphill, gaining back all the elevation you just lost, but in a shorter trail segment. At two miles, you top the ridge; the trail continues one-tenth mile to an unmarked fork, where you turn right. (The left fork is the return loop for backpackers making the Milk Ranch Meadows trip.) This was the only fork that was unsigned when I visited; the rest of the trail was surprisingly well-marked for a wilderness trail.

A quarter-mile from this junction, you'll reach another junction where a hairpin right turn leads to the waterfall, and heading left leads to Milk Ranch. Take the right spur, and after descending for a few hundred feet, you'll hear the roar of the falls. Keep walking until the spur trail ends, just 100 yards downstream of the fall, on a rise with a perfect view of the 50-foot plunge. Pull up a log and sit where you are to view it, or follow a rough route to your left along the canyon wall. In a few minutes, you'll drop to the foot of the waterfall, where a large pool awaits, plus very chilly air and water.

Stony Creek Falls is a perfect freefall drop over granite, set in the back of a forested canyon with steep walls on all sides. The fall spills over a mossy, rounded rock lip, then drops gracefully in one long plume to meet its pool and cascade downstream.

A few campsites are found on the canyon wall above the creek. If it was warm enough, I would camp here in a heartbeat. It's not a place you'll want to leave quickly.

Backpackers opting for the 13-mile loop must retrace their steps to the last junction, then head to the right for Milk Ranch. Once at the privately-owned meadows, they can choose to add on one or more shorter loop hikes to their trip. The return leg of the loop is on the steeper North Ridge Trail, but it's mostly downhill. Dayhikers simply head left at the junction and walk back to the trailhead, getting the opportunity to enjoy the forest all over again.

Trip notes: There is no fee. For a free map/brochure called "Foot and Horse Trails of Mendocino National Forest," write or phone Mendocino National Forest, 825 North Humboldt Avenue, Willows, CA 95988; (530) 934-3316. For a map of Mendocino National Forest, send $4 to USDA-Forest Service, 1323 Club Drive, Vallejo, CA 94592. For more information, contact Mendocino National Forest, Stonyford Ranger District, P.O. Box 160, Stonyford, CA 95979; (530) 963-3128.

Directions: From Willows, 70 miles north of Sacramento on Interstate 5, take Highway 162 west for 20 miles, then turn left and drive 1.3 miles through Elk Creek. Turn right on Road 308 and drive five miles. Bear right on Ivory Mill Road (Road 20N01), signed for the Snow Mountain Wilderness, and drive 9.8 miles. Turn left on Road M3 and drive 15.5 miles to the West Crockett trailhead sign (Road 18N66). Turn left and drive four-tenths mile to the trailhead parking area. High-clearance vehicles are recommended. (You can also access the trailhead via Road 18N02 out of Stonyford, but this is a much rougher dirt road.)

MORE WATERFALLS

in Mendocino & North Coast

•Usal Beach Waterfall, on the Lost Coast. Walk 4.5 miles round-trip along the beach from the end of the road near Usal Campground; requires low tide to reach. Access road is often closed in rainy season. For more information, phone Sinkyone Wilderness State Park at (707) 986-7711 or (707) 445-6547.

•Ukonom Falls, near Happy Camp. Requires a boat ride and a hike to reach, but it's gorgeous. For more information, phone Klamath National Forest, Orleans Ranger District, at (530) 627-3291.

Shasta, Trinity, & Klamath

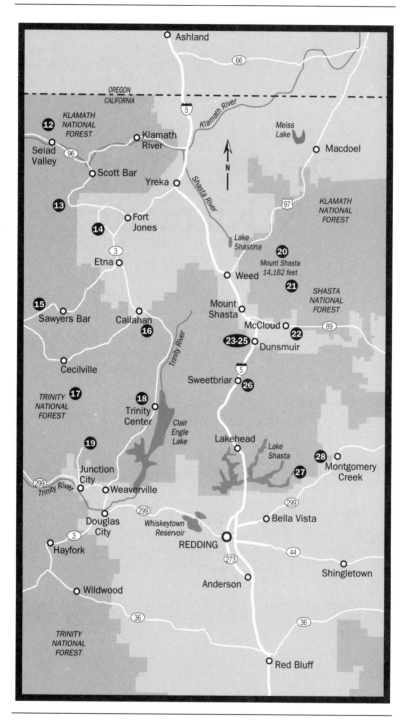

12. HORSETAIL FALLS

Klamath National Forest
Off Highway 96 near Seiad Valley

Access & Difficulty: Drive-to/Easy
Elevation: 5,500 feet
Best Season: April to July

You're so far north in California at Horsetail Falls that you're almost in Oregon. The fall is just below Cook and Green Pass, a mere five miles from the state border as the crow flies.

And waterfalls don't come much easier than this: You can drive right up to Horsetail, which drops on the East Fork of Seiad Creek, right next to the road. About 50 feet of the falls are visible above the road, on the east side, where the stream cuts down through a notch in the rock face. But Horsetail Falls also continues below the road in a long, white-water cascade, heading far downhill to Seiad Valley.

Listen carefully: You must visit this fall in springtime. Although Horsetail Falls still runs in late summer and fall, it isn't much to see. Be sure to call the Forest Service to check on road conditions before you head out in spring; although ordinary passenger cars can drive the dirt road some of the year, high-clearance vehicles may be necessary when it's wet.

Of course, once you drive up the long hill and take a few photos of the falls, you probably won't want to get back in your car immediately and drive home. The best option for a day-hike? Drive 1.7 miles north on Road 48N20 to Cook and Green Pass. Park there and walk up the gated road on the left, heading out on the Boundary National Recreation Trail. Look for the trail signed for Elk Lake on your right, about three miles out. It's another half-mile to the scenic lake, with great views along the way—both north into Oregon and south into California.

Trip notes: There is no fee. For a map of Klamath National Forest, send $4 to USDA-Forest Service Map Sales, 1323 Club Drive, Vallejo, CA 94592. For more information, contact Klamath National Forest, Happy Camp Ranger District, P.O. Box 377, Happy Camp, CA 96039; (530) 493-2243.

Directions: From Interstate 5 north of Yreka, drive west on Highway 96 for approximately 50 miles to Seiad Valley. Turn north on Seiad Creek Road and drive 10 miles to the falls on the right side of the road. At 3.8 miles, Seiad Creek Road becomes 48N20, a gravel road; be sure to take

---

the left fork to continue on 48N20. (Or, from Cook and Green Pass, drive south on 48N20 for 1.7 miles to the falls.)

13. MAPLE FALLS

Marble Mountain Wilderness
Off Highway 3 near Fort Jones

Access & Difficulty: Hike-in or Backpack 8.0 miles RT/Moderate
Elevation: Start at 2,400 feet; total gain 1,800 feet
Best Season: April to September, but good year-round

A trip to Maple Falls in the Marble Mountain Wilderness is a walk through history on the Kelsey National Recreation Trail, an 1850s supply route which once ran all the way from Fort Jones to Crescent City. It's a long, uphill walk through history, so make sure your boots are strapped on tight and your lunch is packed.

The trail starts to climb at the trailhead, and uphill is the status quo for... well, actually, all four miles to the waterfall. While you're hoofing it, think of the early travelers on this route who brought supplies to the U.S. Army military post at Fort Jones and settlers in Scott Valley, and carried gold and local commodities back to the coast at Crescent City. Hey, whatever your lunch weighs, it's gotta be lighter than gold.

Trailhead elevation is 2,400 feet, which means that the Kelsey Trail is open year-round to Maple Falls. (The upper part of the trail that accesses the Paradise Lake Basin can get snowed on, but that's another three miles past the waterfall.) Although Maple Falls is at its peak in the spring, I visited in September and found its flow was still full and lovely. An incentive for hiking here in autumn is that the trail's many maple trees, for which the falls are named, turn a brilliant gold in late September and October.

You've got 1,800 feet to gain in four miles, but the trail is well graded and the surroundings are inspiring. Kelsey Creek roars along below you, creating a ruckus even late in the year. Shade is the game plan for most of the trip, offered by oaks, maples, Douglas firs, and ponderosa pines. A dense army of low-elevation foliage surrounds your feet.

Hike upstream, and also up and above the stream, on the Kelsey Trail, which is cut into the steep canyon slopes. Most of the time you're at least 100 feet above the stream, but two miles out the trail drops down, and you'll see a couple of primitive campsites on Kelsey

Creek's bank. Another set of falls, about 25 feet high and tucked in behind a big boulder, drops below the camp. You can glimpse the waterfall from the trail just before you reach the camp. A short spur trail will take you closer.

As a matter of fact, you hear and occasionally behold dozens of water chutes, slides, and falls along most of the length of the Kelsey Trail. But because the trail is so high above the creek and the banks are so steep, most of these water drops are inaccessible. At any rate, none compare to Maple Falls, which dives 60 feet, mostly in freefall over cliff-like boulders, before cascad-

Maple Falls

ing and running level again. Still, Maple Falls can be a bit tricky to spot late in the summer, in low flow. The Kelsey Trail passes about 50 yards from it, and dense foliage obscures all except the top of the fall. Trust your ears to guide you. After four miles of fairly relentless uphill, you'll be searching anxiously for your destination.

Watch for these landmarks: At 2.6 miles, you'll pass a worn Marble Mountain Wilderness sign. Then, between miles 3.0 and 3.8, the trail crosses two good-size creeks, which run even in autumn. At 4.0 miles (about two hours of hiking time), you'll spy the falls across the canyon. Walk past them for a minute or so until you see a spur trail on your left. (The Kelsey Trail continues to climb, heading for Paradise Lake.) Take the spur, an excellent route that leads to the top of the falls, where a perfect makeshift campsite is located, complete with a crude table and fire grill. From the campsite, you can cross the creek by rockhopping (at low water), then scramble another 50 feet to get a good side view of the falls. As this is your first opportunity to see Maple Falls' full height, it may surprise you.

If you like rock scrambling, you can descend all the way to the base of the falls, where in summer and autumn there is a small rocky beach. Have a seat on a log and cast admiring glances at the wonderful watery scene before you.

Trip notes: There is no fee. For a map of the Marble Mountain Wilderness or Klamath National Forest, send $4 to USDA-Forest Service, 1323 Club Drive, Vallejo, CA 94592. For more information, contact Klamath National Forest, Scott River Ranger District, 11263 North Highway 3, Fort Jones, CA 96032; (530) 468-5351.

Directions: From Interstate 5 at Yreka, take the Highway 3 exit and drive west for 16.5 miles to Fort Jones. Turn right on Scott River Road and drive 16.8 miles to the Scott River Bridge. Cross the bridge and turn left immediately on to a dirt road. Drive three-tenths of a mile and bear right on another dirt road. (Don't continue to a second bridge which leads to some spawning ponds). Drive a quarter-mile further to the Kelsey Creek Trailhead.

14. SHACKLEFORD FALLS

Klamath National Forest
Off Highway 3 near Fort Jones

Access & Difficulty: Hike-in 0.5 mile RT/Easy
Elevation: Start at 2,400 feet; total gain 0 feet
Best Season: June to September

Shackleford Falls is one of those locals-only waterfalls, a rocky cataract and swimming hole that you'd never find unless somebody told you about it. Well, luckily somebody told me. Actually, they had to tell me twice, because the first time I drove off, got completely lost, and had to go back for better directions.

The waterfall is technically on private property within Klamath National Forest, so be on your best behavior here. It's owned by the Fruit Growers Supply Company, and although they allow people to use the area, they don't have to. It's a use-at-your-own-risk kind of deal.

Reaching the fall is an easy drive from Fort Jones (provided you have the right directions). After parking in the pullouts near the Shackleford Creek bridge, just walk up the dirt road next to the bridge, heading upstream. Stay to the left, as close to the creek as possible, and in just a few minutes, you're at a clearing just above the falls. People sometimes camp here.

The fall is about 15 feet tall, a rush of white water that flows so heavily even late in the year that it's difficult to make out the details of its shape. It drops over a large boulder and forms a pool for swimming—a great spot on a hot day.

Trip notes: There is no fee. For a map of Klamath National Forest, send $4 to USDA-Forest Service, 1323 Club Drive, Vallejo, CA 94592. For more information, contact Klamath National Forest, Scott River Ranger District, 11263 North Highway 3, Fort Jones, CA 96032; (530) 468-5351.

Directions: From Interstate 5 at Yreka, take the Highway 3 exit and drive west for 16.5 miles to Fort Jones. Turn right on Scott River Road and drive seven miles, then take the left fork, which is Quartz Valley Road. Drive 3.9 miles on Quartz Valley Road and turn right on 43N21, signed for the Shackleford Trailhead. Drive 1.2 miles on 43N21 until you cross the bridge over Shackleford Creek. Park near the bridge in any pullout, then walk up the dirt road on the far side of the bridge, heading upstream.

15. SUR CREE FALLS
Marble Mountain Wilderness
Off Highway 3 near Etna

Access & Difficulty: Hike-in 6.5 miles RT/Moderate
Elevation: Start at 2,000 feet; total gain 900 feet
Best Season: April to September, but good year-round

Sur Cree Falls may not be a star-quality waterfall, but one thing's pretty certain: If you've driven all the way out here to the Little North Fork Trailhead, you're not going to be bugged by a whole lot of other people. In fact, if your idea of a top-notch waterfall is one that you can have all to yourself, you should sign up for this trip immediately.

The Little North Fork Trail is where we managed to escape on the opening day of deer season in Trinity and Siskiyou counties. Our hiking trip to the Trinity Alps and Marble Mountain wildernesses was, shall we say, badly timed, because we had forgotten about the hunting opener. There were crowds at virtually every trailhead. Some were hunters, and others were hikers trying to get away from the hunters. But way out here at the Little North Fork, everything was peaceful and quiet. You could hear a bear drop a pin.

Off we went on the trail, which was signed for Specimen Gulch, English Peak, and Hancock Lake. In the first half-mile we reached an unmarked trail fork, but after much deliberation decided that this was one of those high-road/low-road trails, where you could take the route either way and end up at the same place. We took the high trail, although the low trail takes you closer to the rushing Little North Fork. If you've brought your fishing rod, take the lower trail.

The mostly level path follows a retired aqueduct ditch for a distance, crossing two creeks in the first mile. The trail tunnels through a mix of hardwoods, conifers, ferns, and vines. This is low-elevation hiking, which means you're surrounded by tons of foliage in all shapes and sizes. It also means plenty of shade, so the route is pleasant even on a warm summer day.

At 2.25 miles, the trail passes through a small burned area where the lower trail rejoins the upper trail. From there, the trail starts to climb. After the basic flatness of the first two miles, this comes as a bit of a surprise. We spotted a bear along this stretch, and as she ran off we warned her to look out for anybody wearing camouflage.

At 2.7 miles, a gravel road crosses the trail, leading down to Specimen Gulch. Cross the road, and continue straight ahead on the trail. It's about 20 minutes of hiking from Specimen Gulch to the falls, all uphill. The Little North Fork Trail crosses right in the middle of Sur Cree Falls, which empties into the Little North Fork, so it's impossible to miss. Unfortunately, most of the fall's drop is below the trail, with virtually no way to view it because the canyon is so steep. The total cascade is about 200 feet, but with only 30 feet above the trail and visible. Huge elephant ears, bigger than dinner plates, grow out of the nooks and crannies of the cascade. Rocks around the edges of the fall supply places where you can sit down, take off your pack, and soak your feet.

And guess what? Most likely, nobody else is going to show up. Sur Cree Falls is all yours.

Trip notes: There is no fee. For a map of the Marble Mountain Wilderness or Klamath National Forest, send $4 to USDA-Forest Service, 1323 Club Drive, Vallejo, CA 94592. For more information, contact Klamath National Forest, Scott River Ranger District, 11263 North Highway 3, Fort Jones, CA 96032; (530) 468-5351.

Directions: From Interstate 5 at Yreka, take the Highway 3 exit and drive west for 25 miles to Etna. At Etna, drive west on Etna-Sawyers Bar Road for 25 miles to Sawyers Bar. From Sawyers Bar, continue 4.2 miles west to Road 40N51 on the right. Drive a half-mile on 40N51 to the signed Little North Fork Trailhead.

16. EAST BOULDER LAKE FALLS

Marble Mountain Wilderness
Off Highway 3 near Callahan

Access & Difficulty: Hike-in 4.0 miles RT/Moderate
Elevation: Start at 5,800 feet; total gain 800 feet
Best Season: June to September

Pack up your family and put them in the car for the long drive to Callahan. Stop at the Callahan Emporium, pick up some picnic supplies (don't expect anything too gourmet), then head out to the East Boulder Lake Trailhead. You're about to take a day-hike that will make your spouse and kids think you are the greatest outdoor trip planner on earth.

You have to climb a bit, but the rewards are great. In fact, this is probably one of the greatest short hikes to an alpine lake in all of the Trinity Alps and Marble Mountain wildernesses. Using up only one hour of your allotted time on the planet, you will arrive aerobically fit and fully oxygenated at a scenic deep blue lake, with a pretty waterfall just below it.

East Boulder Lake Falls

The hike up to the lake has meadows mixed in with fir and pine groves, plus some great sections of knee-high fern fields. You follow East Boulder Creek for the whole route, but won't get close enough to see it until you're at its waterfall. The climb is fairly moderate, with a few level sections interspersed here and there. The only minus on this trail is the possible presence of bovines, because grazing is permitted here. We saw a dozen or so, but they ran away from us, their cow bells tinkling.

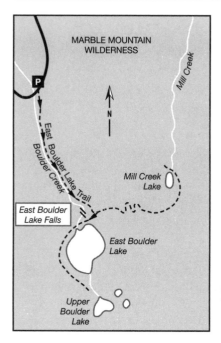

At 1.5 miles, you exit from the forest to a clearing and get a head-on view of the waterfall on East Boulder Creek. The fall is pretty and lacy in late summer and fall and a downright downpour in spring. It's a 50-foot freefall over volcanic black rock, very similar in appearance to Black Wolf Falls in Sequoia National Park or Sardine Falls in Toiyabe National Forest. Another 50-foot cascade continues below the freefall. Try to see East Boulder Falls in the morning, as it is north-facing and will be shaded by mid-afternoon.

The trail has its steepest pitch in the last half-mile from the waterfall to the lake, where you have to get up and over the fall. Fortunately, looking at the cascading water keeps you somewhat distracted from the work of your fast-pumping heart. Once you reach the waterfall's crest, it's only five minutes further on flat trail to the lake. You'll see evidence of a small avalanche above the falls—lots of uniformly downed trees. Some of them have been used to build a log walkway across the meadow. Follow it, then continue on the path alongside East Boulder Creek above the fall. When you top the ridge, check out the incredible view behind you, looking a few thousand feet down into Scott Valley.

Your first eyeful of the deep blue of the lake will knock your socks off. On a sunny day, East Boulder Lake is like a rare and expensive sapphire, shimmering within the walls of a rather barren cirque. Little grows around the lake's near side except sagebrush, manzanita, and the occasional pine. The far edge has a more substantial stand of pines. Even the lake bottom looks bare and sandy.

There are a few campsites around the lake, although it can be windy here without tree cover. A couple trails branch out from East Boulder Lake, the most popular being the route to Upper Boulder Lake in one mile.

Most people stop right here, however, content to gaze out over

32 acres of azure water and eat a sandwich, or wander around the circumference of the lake, marveling at the blueness of the blue.

Trip notes: There is no fee. For a map of the Marble Mountain Wilderness or Klamath National Forest, send $4 to USDA-Forest Service, 1323 Club Drive, Vallejo, CA 94592. For more information, contact Klamath National Forest, Scott River Ranger District, 11263 North Highway 3, Fort Jones, CA 96032; (530) 468-5351.

Directions: From Interstate 5 at Yreka, take the Highway 3 exit and drive southwest for 35 miles to Callahan. At Callahan, turn south on South Fork Road (next to the Callahan Emporium), which becomes 40N16. At one mile, bear right on 40N17. At 5.7 miles, take the left fork on to 39N10, which is signed for East Boulder Trail and "Dead End Road." It's two more miles to the trailhead. (Total 7.7 miles from Callahan.) Park alongside the road. High-clearance vehicles are recommended.

17. GRIZZLY LAKE FALLS

Trinity Alps Wilderness
Off Highway 3 near Cecilville

Access & Difficulty: Backpack 12.0 miles RT/Strenuous (China Creek)
  or Backpack 38.0 miles RT/Strenuous (Hobo Gulch)
Elevation: Start at 4,400 feet; total gain/loss 5,000 feet (China Creek)
  or Start at 4,800 feet; total gain/loss 4,500 feet (Hobo Gulch)
Best Season: July to September

At least once in your life, you should backpack to Grizzly Lake and its waterfall in the Trinity Alps Wilderness. Like climbing Half Dome in Yosemite or making the long trek to the top of Mount Whitney, this is an epic wilderness trip that you'll tell your grandchildren about.

If you have nearly a week's vacation time, you can take a long, 19-mile one-way backpack trip to the lake and its waterfall, traveling along beautiful Grizzly Creek on a moderate-grade trail. If you're short on time, you can make a grueling six-mile one-way trip to Grizzly, but the route is such a butt-kicker that you should plan on at least two days for the round-trip. Some people go out and back in a day, but that leaves little time and energy for enjoying the waterfall and the lake.

Alas, despite the fact that the long route is far more enjoyable, most people opt for the short route. Even with its extreme changes in elevation, the six-mile trail from China Creek has become incredibly popular, sometimes even getting crowded on summer weekends. It seems that most people are willing to pay the price to get to Grizzly Lake and Grizzly Falls as quickly as possible.

If you decide to join that club, start your trip at the China Creek Trailhead near Cecilville. Be forewarned of the facts: The trail gains 1,500 feet in the first mile. Then, unbelievably, it drops 1,000 feet in the second mile. Are we having fun yet? The next three miles are the "easy" ones; their total gain is only 1,500 feet. The final, brutal mile rises nearly 1,000 feet.

What's good about the trail from China Creek? I'm thinking, I'm thinking. Let's see, the first mile is shaded and thick with fir trees. In the second mile you start to get some good views of the peaks and canyon ahead. At 2.5 miles, when you reach the junction with Grizzly Creek Trail, you can rejoice because much of the worst is over. Bear left on the Grizzly Creek Trail, passing several campsites along the way. You'll begin to feel extremely jealous of hikers coming from

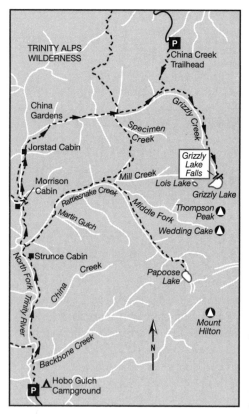

the other trailhead on the Grizzly Creek Trail, because even though they've been hiking longer, they haven't suffered like you have.

At 1.5 miles from the junction of the two trails, you get your first look at stunning Thompson Peak, elevation 9,002 feet. Your destination is located below the snow-field-lined mountain, the most impressive peak in Switzerland, I mean the Trinity Alps. You'll see what I mean.

Next you pass Grizzly Meadows, laden with corn lilies in early summer. Then comes a series of unbelievable mountain vistas, with every color and reflection of granite, sky, snow, sunlight, and rock you can imagine. As you draw nearer, Grizzly Falls completes the scene, a vista that's as epic as any in Yosemite Valley. Grizzly is an 80-foot, near-perfect freefall, tumbling off the perpendicular cliff that supports Grizzly Lake. The waterfall is formed as the lake's outlet creek drops over a square lip of stacked granite blocks, then hits a less vertical surface and cascades hundreds of feet farther.

The Grizzly Lake Trail officially ends after a series of stone steps that ascend a boulder field. From there to the lake you're basically on your own, scrambling up the often-vertical route. Since this is such a popular destination, the route is extremely well-marked, and you're likely to see other people using it, but do not expect a real trail. Your hands will need to assist your feet in keeping you connected to the bare rock. If you have any doubts about your ability to make the final ascent to the lake, just park yourself in Grizzly Meadows and drink in the unbelievable view. One could hardly call this second-best.

If you decide to trek the final mile, your reward is a close-up look at one of the largest alpine lakes in the Trinity Alps. Grizzly has 42 surface acres and is 170 feet deep. Situated at the base of Thompson Peak, it mirrors the peak's pure white snowfields and the hardy groves of firs and pines below them. Needless to say, it's gorgeous.

If you can possibly spare the time to take the long route to Grizzly Lake and Falls, I highly recommend it. Not only is the trail grade far more sensible, but fishing prospects are excellent along the entire route. The trail starts at Hobo Gulch (access is from Highway 299 near Weaverville), then heads north about five miles along the North Fork Trinity River to Rattlesnake Camp, a large flat where the trail junctions with the Rattlesnake Creek Trail.

Ford Rattlesnake Creek and keep hiking northward. Get this: The first 10 miles of trail have only a 1,200-foot elevation gain. It's mixed conifers almost all the way. From Rattlesnake Camp, hike another three miles, passing Morrison Cabin and various mining relics, to Pfeiffer Flat and another mining cabin. A half-mile further, the North Fork Trinity is joined by Grizzly Creek. The trail to Grizzly Lake follows Grizzly Creek eastward from this point on, meeting up with the China Creek Trail at 14.5 miles from the trailhead. The rest of the trip is the same as on the shorter route, but you should be much better rested and prepared for the final climb to Grizzly Lake.

Trip notes: There is no fee. For a map of the Trinity Alps Wilderness, send $4 to USDA-Forest Service, 1323 Club Drive, Vallejo, CA 94592. For more information, contact Shasta-Trinity National Forest, Big Bar

Ranger District, Star Route 1, Box 10, Big Bar, CA 96010; (530) 623-6106. Or contact Klamath National Forest, Scott River Ranger District, 11263 North Highway 3, Fort Jones, CA 96032; (530) 468-5351.

Directions: To the Hobo Gulch Trailhead—From Redding, drive west on Highway 299 for approximately 50 miles to Weaverville. Continue west on Highway 299 for 14 miles past Weaverville to Helena. Turn north on East Fork Road and drive four miles, then turn left on Hobo Gulch Road and drive 13 miles to the Hobo Gulch Trailhead and Campground.

To the China Creek Trailhead—From Interstate 5 at Yreka, take the Highway 3 exit and drive southwest for 35 miles to Callahan. At Callahan, turn west on Callahan/Cecilville Road 93, and drive 27 miles to Road 37N24. (If you reach Cecilville, you've gone two miles too far.) Turn south and drive 3.8 miles to the intersection with Road 37N07 for China Creek Trailhead. Take Road 37N07, and drive six miles to the trailhead (the route is well-signed). Park alongside the road.

18. SWIFT CREEK FALLS

Trinity Alps Wilderness
Off Highway 3 near Trinity Center

Access & Difficulty: Hike-in & Scramble 2.5 miles RT/Moderate
Elevation: Start at 4,000 feet; total loss 200 feet
Best Season: June to September

A short walk in the Trinity Alps takes you to a dramatic rocky gorge with four waterfalls, but the stream keeps its watery treasures well-hidden from the average passerby. The walk alone won't give you the rewards you seek; it's only with a short but steep off-trail scramble that you get a good look at the falls.

First, be forewarned that the trailhead parking lot can be loaded with horse trailers, and the first section of trail is somewhat beaten down by the continual weight of hooves. Other destinations from this trailhead are popular with horse packers and hunters in the fall.

Swift Creek Falls are only one mile in on the Swift Creek Trail, a few hundred yards before a trail junction for the Granite Lake Trail. The hike to the general location of the falls is easy, but you're unlikely to be satisfied with the trail's long-distance, peek-a-boo view of them. The hard part is finding the best place to scramble down for a closer look, because the canyon slope is dauntingly steep.

The falls are encased in a 200-yard-long rock gorge, which you see only fleetingly from the trail. The location of the gorge and falls is given away by the continual roar of water. Although you can glimpse falling white water from one point on the trail, this is not the best place to try to scramble downslope; it's too steep and slick with fallen leaves. Instead, backtrack a few hundred feet to where the slope is gentler, then make your way down to the stream. You'll wind up looking upstream at the falls, which is the best view of them. If you don't want to descend all the way to the streambed, look for some rock outcrops about halfway down the canyon wall, where the waterfall views are also good. Be wary of slippery leaf litter, though.

Swift Creek Falls

Four main falls drop in this 200-yard-long area, plunging as white-water chutes over and through the smoothed granite. All of them are between 20 and 35 feet in height. If you look carefully, you'll see that many small trout swim in their rocky pools.

If scrambling isn't your bag, and you prefer to hike on a "real" trail, continue past the falls to the junction of Swift Creek Trail and Granite Lake Trail. The left fork stays along Swift Creek for another two-tenths of a mile, then crosses a picturesque footbridge on its way to Granite Lake in five miles. (Once you pass this junction, you're free of pack animals sharing the trail.) Granite Lake makes a great day-hike or backpacking destination, but be prepared to climb.

Trip notes: There is no fee. For a map of the Trinity Alps Wilderness, send $4 to USDA-Forest Service, 1323 Club Drive, Vallejo, CA 94592. For more information, contact Shasta-Trinity National Forest, Weaverville Ranger District, P.O. Box 1190, Weaverville, CA 96093; (530) 623-2121.

Directions: From Redding, drive west on Highway 299 for approximately 50 miles to Weaverville. At Weaverville, turn north on Highway 3 and drive 28 miles to Trinity Center. Turn west on Swift Creek Road and drive 6.8 miles to the trailhead.

19. CANYON CREEK FALLS

Trinity Alps Wilderness
Off Highway 299 near Weaverville

Access & Difficulty: Hike-in or Backpack 8.0 to 15.0 miles RT/Moderate
Elevation: Start at 3,100 feet; total gain 2,500 feet (15.0-mile RT)
Best Season: June to September

The Canyon Creek Trail is the "glamour" trail of the Trinity Alps Wilderness, the route that everybody takes if they can only hike one trail in the area. Like the glamour trails at Tuolumne Meadows in Yosemite or Desolation Wilderness by Lake Tahoe, the Canyon Creek Trail earns its reputation for two main reasons: 1—It has drop-dead gorgeous scenery, including waterfalls, lakes and old-growth forest; and 2—It has tons of people hiking it, even on weekdays and even post-season.

But don't be scared off; make the trip anyway, and take your pick between a day-hike of eight miles round-trip to Lower Canyon Creek Falls, a longer day-hike of 11 miles round-trip to Middle Canyon Creek Falls, or an easy overnight backpacking trip to Upper Canyon Creek Falls, camping near the spectacular Canyon Creek Lakes.

It's an easy trip, because the trail climbs only moderately and is mostly shaded for the first few miles. As the route gradually becomes more exposed, hikers are rewarded with increasingly better views of surrounding peaks and ridges. Even most beginning backpackers can hike the 7.5 miles in to the lakes on the first day.

The 13-mile-long paved road to the trailhead, and the giant-sized parking lot at its end, give you an idea of how well-loved and well-used Canyon Creek is. From the trailhead sign, hike to your left on the Canyon Creek Trail. In about 10 minutes of walking you cross Bear Creek, not Canyon Creek, but then the trail winds around to meet Canyon Creek, and parallels it continually from there. The trail gets better and better the further upstream you go, with the scent of Douglas firs and incense cedars intoxicating you along the way. Two miles in, there's a campsite on the creek at a tiny waterfall. Three miles in, a short but steep spur trail on your left is signed for The Sinks, a boulders-and-pools section of Canyon Creek near a large rockslide. More campsites are located along the creek there.

At four miles, you reach a clearing across from a 20-foot waterfall, with still more campsites. This fall is pretty in its own right, tumbling over a granite ledge into a perfectly rounded aquamarine pool, but don't finish your trip here: This is not Lower Canyon Creek Falls, although some people call it that. Actually it is best described as the upper cascade of Lower Canyon Creek Falls, because if you scramble downstream for a tenth of a mile, you'll find a much larger fall below it, the true Lower Canyon Creek Falls. Apparently the trail used to be routed right alongside the 100-foot lower fall, but now it bypasses it and reaches only its upper cascade. But why quibble? Either fall is a great day-hike destination, both possessing marvelous turquoise pools for swimming on summer days.

From this four-mile point onward, the trail runs very close to the creek and has a more level grade. Pass a meadow on your left as the path continues for another mile. At 5.5 miles, while under the magic spell of an old-growth Douglas fir forest, listen for the roar of Middle Canyon Creek Falls, just off the trail to your left. A short cutoff trail will take you to the base of the 150-foot-tall cascade, a series of 25- to 40-foot drops over granite. This is probably the most beautiful of all the

Middle Canyon Creek Falls

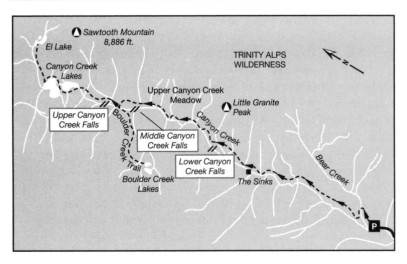

falls on Canyon Creek, and ironically, it's the one that most hikers miss. (They're probably expecting the trail to be routed right next to the fall.) If you reach the trail intersection for Boulder Creek Lakes, you have missed the cutoff trail.

While day-hikers will probably choose to make Middle Canyon Creek Falls their destination and then head back for an 11-mile round-trip, backpackers should either start looking for a campsite or push onward to the upper falls and the lakes. There are dozens of established campsites along Canyon Creek, so despite the popularity of the trail, there should be plenty of room for everybody to find a private spot for the night. (Remember: No camping in the fragile meadow areas near Canyon Creek. Also, camping is limited at the lakes, and may eventually be forbidden to protect their fragile shores, so you're better off choosing a spot below them.)

From Middle Canyon Creek Falls, it's only a mile to 50-foot Upper Canyon Creek Falls. This fall is smaller than both the lower and middle falls, and it has a vastly different shape—more of a classic river fall at the top, but then smooth and sloping at the bottom, like a water slide. Because it is set right alongside the trail, this is the waterfall that everybody sees, and the campsites near it are coveted.

Less than a mile of trail, a few switchbacks, and several thousand tons of granite separate Upper Canyon Creek Falls from Lower Canyon Creek Lake. You're so close, you might as well continue. Follow the trail up and above the falls and then to the west side of the deep-blue lake, to check out the views of Sawtooth Mountain, elevation 8,880 feet, to the east. Should you wish to press on, rock cairns lead the way to Upper Canyon Creek Lake, where there are a few campsites and even better vistas. You'll be rewarded for the climb with long looks at towering granite crags, ages-old snowfields on the slopes of Thompson Peak, tumbling streams of snowmelt, and stands of red fir and Jeffrey pine encircling the lake. Wow? Yes, wow.

Trip notes: There is no fee. For a map of the Trinity Alps Wilderness, send $4 to USDA-Forest Service, 1323 Club Drive, Vallejo, CA 94592. For more information, contact Shasta-Trinity National Forest, Weaverville Ranger District, P.O. Box 1190, Weaverville, CA 96093; (530) 623-2121.

Directions: From Redding, drive west on Highway 299 for approximately 50 miles to Weaverville. Continue west on Highway 299 for 8.1 miles past Weaverville to Junction City and Canyon Creek Road. Turn right on Canyon Creek Road and drive 13 miles to the trailhead. (It's paved all the way.)

20. WHITNEY FALLS

Mount Shasta Wilderness
Off Interstate 5 near Weed

Access & Difficulty: Hike-in 3.5 miles RT/Easy
Elevation: Start at 5,500 feet; total gain 800 feet
Best Season: May to July

You like drama? You came to the right place. You like to see water in your waterfalls? You better come early in the year, because Whitney Falls usually disappears by the Fourth of July.

But even when Whitney Creek is dry, this hike and its destination are still first-rate. That's because Whitney Falls is set in an incredible canyon on the back side of Mount Shasta, accessible by one of the few trails that enter Shasta's northern wilderness.

You get an idea of what's ahead right at the trailhead sign. While you fill out your self-serve day-hiking permit, check out the views of Mount Shasta and smaller Shastina on its right flank. Snowy Whitney Glacier sits between them, the source of the flow for Whitney Falls.

Head right and cross the often-dry Bolam Creek, then follow a wide trail for about a mile along Bolam Creek canyon. It's a bit desert-like out here, with only a few pines and lots of brush and manzanita, but the route gets more forested as you walk. The trail veers away from the creek twice, and the second time provides sweeping views of the Shasta Valley, plus a peek at Lake Shastina. It's so

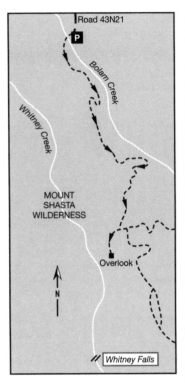

Road 43N21
Bolam Creek
Whitney Creek
MOUNT
SHASTA
WILDERNESS
Overlook
N
Whitney Falls

quiet up here, you can hear a train 15 miles away.

One and a half miles from the trailhead, look carefully for an unsigned path that veers right, off the main trail. This is the Whitney Falls Trail; the trail continuation to the left leads another 1.5 miles to a summit climbing route. (If you have the time and inclination, you can follow this trail for a look at pretty Coquette Falls, which, like Whitney, is often dry.)

Turn right on the Whitney Falls Trail, following it for a quarter-mile through pines and firs to an incredible overlook and picnic site. Did I say incredible? Yes. You are standing on the rim of Whitney Creek's canyon, staring up at the peaks of Shasta and Shastina, Whitney Glacier, and if you time it right, Whitney Falls. The fall drops 200 dramatic feet over a jagged rock face, then hits boulders and continues to cascade down-canyon. Unlike at the viewing spot for Mud Creek Falls on the southeast side of Mount Shasta, here you are less than a quarter-mile from the fall. Everything—even the peak of Mount Shasta—seems within an arm's reach across the great chasm.

A few words on timing: Probably the best period to see Whitney Falls is when there is still a bit of snow on the trail, usually in early May. But when the trail has snow patches, the Whitney Falls turnoff can be very difficult to discern. Be on the lookout for it.

If you miss the early season, you can also see the waterfall run just after a spring or summer storm. And don't worry if there's no water in Whitney Creek when you cross it on Highway 97; there can still be water in the fall, far upstream.

Trip notes: There is no fee. Day-hikers must fill out a self-serve wilderness permit at the trailhead. For a map of Shasta-Trinity National Forest, send $4 to USDA-Forest Service, 1323 Club Drive, Vallejo, CA 94592. A more detailed map of the Mount Shasta Wilderness is available from Tom Harrison Cartography at (415) 456-7940. For more information, contact Shasta-Trinity National Forest, Mount Shasta Ranger District, 204 West Alma, Mount Shasta, CA 96067; (530) 926-4511.

Directions: From Interstate 5 at Weed, take the Highway 97 exit and drive north through Weed for three-quarters of a mile. Turn north on Highway 97 and drive eight miles, then turn right on unsigned Forest Service Road 43N21. (If you reach Road A12, you've gone a quarter-mile too far.) Continue four miles to the Bolam Creek Trailhead at the end of the road. A high-clearance vehicle is necessary.

21. MUD CREEK FALLS

Mount Shasta Wilderness
Off Highway 89 near McCloud

Access & Difficulty: Hike-in 2.0 miles RT/Easy
Elevation: Start at 6,400 feet; total gain 600 feet
Best Season: June to September

Some waterfalls are found in settings so grand and dramatic that they dwarf the fall itself, even though its size and flow may be tremendous. Such is the story with Mud Creek Falls, a geologic wonder that pours hundreds of feet from Mud Creek Glacier down the side of 14,162-foot Mount Shasta. When you're dealing with a background that tall, it tends to minimize things.

You know you're in for an unusual trip right from the Clear Creek trailhead sign. While you're filling out your free day-hiker's permit to enter the Mount Shasta Wilderness, be sure to read the sign. In addition to the usual cautionary statements about carrying plenty of water and letting someone know where you're going, the sign bears an interesting quote from Carlos Castaneda: "All paths leads to nowhere. You might as well choose a path with a heart." It goes on to warn that people who go into the Mount Shasta Wilderness unprepared can get lost, die, or just plain "go crazy." Hmm. Well, you're only heading out for about an hour's walk, so you should be all right.

Mud Creek Falls

The Clear Creek Trail is a steady uphill walk through Shasta red firs, just steep enough to make you feel like you're getting aerobic exercise. It's a bit odd

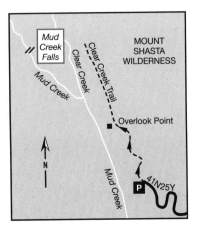

knowing that you're so close to magnificent Mount Shasta, but not seeing anything but trees, trees, trees. Have patience. First you must climb high enough to get over a ridge, one mile distant from the trailhead. Once there, you reach a clearing, and with an off-trail walk of 30 feet, your view opens wide: You look directly at the southeast side of Mount Shasta and down and across 1,000-foot-deep Mud Creek Canyon, with Mud Creek Falls billowing down its long crevice.

Your view also includes Konwakiton and Mud Creek Glaciers, the Thumb Rock climbing route to Shasta's peak, distinctive Thumb Rock itself at 12,923 feet, and the edge of the Shasta ski bowl, far above the falls. A giant rockslide has left an untidy pile of talus across the canyon, which makes you think twice about sitting too close to the edge for long.

Although you're about a mile from Mud Creek Falls, its roar is carried across the canyon, a steady stream of sound. If you bring binoculars with you, you can get a better look at the waterfall and see that it drops over an intricate rock cliff. Of course, the close-up view is just an extra blessing, because the long view is so extraordinary.

The trail continues for another mile or so uphill, mostly through trees, then peters out. This clearing is by far the best destination on the route. In addition to the world-class view, the ground is sprinkled with clumps of mountain pride and Indian paintbrush.

If you drive Highway 89 east of McCloud and happen to notice where the highway crosses Mud Creek (there's a small sign), you'll see that the stream is, indeed, mud-colored. From the Clear Creek Trail, it's harder to see Mud Creek's color, because there is so much snow surrounding the creek from the permanent snowfields and glaciers. (Often the white snow looks like white water.) The creek's brown tint is glacial change in action: The east side of Mount Shasta is being slowly carried away in Mud Creek. Not only water is flowing though the creek, but also rock and debris from the remaining glaciers chewing up the mountain. At this rate, Mount Shasta will virtually disappear in about five million years. What a pity.

Trip notes: There is no fee. Day-hikers must fill out a self-serve wilderness permit at the trailhead. For a map of Shasta-Trinity National Forest, send $4 to USDA-Forest Service, 1323 Club Drive, Vallejo, CA 94592. A more detailed map of the Mount Shasta Wilderness is available from Tom Harrison Cartography at (415) 456-7940. For more information, contact Shasta-Trinity National Forest, Mount Shasta Ranger District, 204 West Alma, Mount Shasta, CA 96067; (530) 926-4511.

Directions: From Redding, drive 65 miles north on Interstate 5. Take the Highway 89/McCloud/Reno exit and drive east on Highway 89. Pass the town of McCloud in nine miles, then continue three miles further east to Pilgrim Creek Road (Road 13). Turn left and drive five miles, then turn left on Road 41N15 and follow it for another five miles. Continue straight on 41N61, then bear left on 41N25Y and follow it 2.8 miles to the signed trailhead for the Clear Creek Trail. The last few junctions are well-signed. A high-clearance vehicle is recommended.

22. McCLOUD FALLS

Shasta-Trinity National Forest
Off Highway 89 near McCloud

Access & Difficulty: Hike-in 3.5 miles RT/Easy
Elevation: Start at 3,050 feet; total gain 600 feet
Best Season: April to August

The McCloud River has three falls within two river miles of each other, each with its own distinct personality. Lower Falls is a busy family swimming hole, complete with a metal ladder to assist jumpers and divers as they exit the chilly water. Middle Falls is one of the most spectacular river falls in Northern California—wide, powerful, and commanding—and lures photographers and the hardiest of swimmers. Upper Falls is exotic-looking, a narrow funnel of water that drops into a circular turquoise pool, but it's difficult to view. One hiking trail links all of the McCloud Falls, so you can visit them all in about an hour.

Start hiking at Lower Falls, located just below Fowlers Camp. Lower Falls is the smallest of the McCloud Falls, a 12-foot plunge into a giant pool. In the spring, it's a popular put-in spot for kayakers heading down the McCloud River. In summer, it's crowded with people who want to jump in and cool off. Usually there's someone trying to catch a fish or two amid all the chaos.

Check out the action at Lower Falls, then walk the half-mile paved trail along the river that leads through Fowlers Camp. On the east side of the camp, near the restrooms, you'll find the start of the trail to Middle Falls, signed only with a wildlife-viewing marker. Take the flat, Douglas fir-lined route along the McCloud River, and in 20 minutes you'll find yourself face-to-face with Middle McCloud Falls. Tall, wide, and regal-looking, Middle McCloud Falls drops 50 feet over a cliff and then forms a deep pool at its base before continuing downstream.

Bold teenagers sometimes jump off the basalt cliffs on the left side of the fall, diving into the chilly waters. Plenty of boulders downstream make good perches for watching the scene. Elephant ears grow in and around the falls, and water ouzels somehow manage to build

Middle McCloud Falls

their homes behind the fall's tremendous flow of water.

As is common with river waterfalls, Middle McCloud is at least twice as wide as it is tall, adding breadth to its grandeur. The resulting flow is lavish, especially in spring. It's as if the fall is making a statement, something like: "There may be other falls on this river, but I am the king."

Pay homage and then get ready for an easy ascent to Upper Falls. A series of long, well-graded switchbacks take you gently up to the top of Middle Falls where there is a classic

Upper McCloud Falls

photo opportunity, a view of the fall's brink and the creek above it. The trail then levels out and continues upriver, clinging to the edge of the canyon wall. Views of the coursing stream below capture and hold your attention.

Keep your eyes peeled for the first sight of Upper Falls. This waterfall is more secretive than the two downriver; rarely do you get a look at its entire length. At a few scattered points along the trail, you can see five tiers of Upper Falls, but only in fleeting glimpses. When you reach an exposed outcrop of basalt boulders across from the fall, you can see only the two lowest tiers, where they plunge into a rocky bowl. They're gorgeous, with circular pools colored a remarkable shade of aquamarine. Although the trail continues around to the top of the fall, the best place for viewing is here, on the rock outcrop.

You'd think three waterfalls would be about all the excitement you could take on one trail, but a further surprise awaits you on your return trip: an extraordinary view of Mount Shasta, which was hiding behind your back on the way in. It appears to be so close, you could reach out and touch it.

Trip notes: There is no fee. For a map of Shasta-Trinity National Forest, send $4 to USDA-Forest Service, 1323 Club Drive, Vallejo, CA 94592. For more information, contact Shasta-Trinity National Forest, McCloud Ranger District, P.O. Box 1620, McCloud, CA 96057; (530) 964-2184.

Directions: From Redding, drive 65 miles north on Interstate 5. Take the Highway 89/McCloud/Reno exit and drive east on Highway 89. Pass the town of McCloud in nine miles, then continue 4.5 miles further east to a small Forest Service sign for "River Access." Turn right and follow the signs to the McCloud River Picnic Area and Lower McCloud Falls. (Bear right at the road forks, driving past Fowlers Camp.) Park in the day-use parking area.

23. BURSTARSE FALLS

Castle Crags Wilderness
Off Interstate 5 near Dunsmuir

Access & Difficulty: Hike-in & Scramble 5.0 miles RT/Strenuous
Elevation: Start at 2,300 feet; total gain 900 feet
Best Season: April to June

There may be some whining on the first mile of trail to Burstarse Falls. Worse than that, if you don't time your trip for the wet season, there will surely be some whining when you reach Burstarse Falls and find it dry.

So listen up: Visit Burstarse as soon as the snow has melted off the trails in the Castle Crags Wilderness, when the creeks are running full and the temperatures on the steep hillsides are still cool and comfortable. We're talking mid-June at the latest; April and May are preferred.

Once you've got your calendar set, be prepared for a short but steep climb from the parking lot on the strangely named Dog Trail. Why Dog Trail? We never found out. Maybe because you're panting like a tired puppy by the time the Dog Trail reaches a junction with the Pacific Crest Trail, where your climbing is largely finished. It's only six-tenths of a mile from the parking lot to the PCT intersection, but it's a steep grade on loose rocks and exposed to the sun all day long. (I muttered many expletives when I hiked it on a hot June afternoon.)

When you reach the PCT, turn left, breathe a sigh of relief, and cruise along on the shady route that laterals the mountainside. You're accompanied by manzanita, some oaks and conifers, and about a million lizards scurrying along the trail. Some interesting views of the tops of Castle Crags come into view as you round bends in the trail. The crags are hauntingly beautiful granite spires, 200-million-year-old pieces of rock that rise as high as 6,544 feet. The best view of them comes shortly after your first crossing of Burstarse Creek.

Look for small wooden signs posted on trees as you cross Popcorn Spring, then Burstarse Creek, and Ugly Creek. Don't expect to see the falls at your first crossing of Burstarse Creek; they're higher up on the stream. Don't expect Ugly Creek to be ugly, either; it's a cascading, clear-water stream in a bed of granite lined with ferns and Indian rhubarb.

Start paying close attention after you cross Ugly Creek. You should follow the trail for only one-tenth of a mile further, to the next switchback where the trail curves around to your left and continues uphill. Don't take that switchback; instead, head straight, cutting off the trail. If the fall is running, you'll hear it loud and clear, although you can't see it from here, just the cascades below it.

Descend off-trail about 50 feet to Burstarse Creek, taking careful measures on the steep hillside. Many rocks are unstable, and the oak leaves can be deadly slippery. Look for a fairly well-defined route made by others who've been here; roughly you will head downhill to the creek and then upstream along it. If the water is too high and you can't walk up the creekbed, follow the rough route along the far side of the creek, safely above water level. Don't try to head uphill immediately from where you've cut off the PCT; this route is treacherous.

Fifty yards upstream, Burstarse Falls plunges 50 feet off a rock ledge. Its lower reaches are a series of little pools and cascades. Stay for a while, enjoy the scenery, and then carefully scramble your way back to the PCT.

Trip notes: There is no fee. For a map of Shasta-Trinity National Forest, send $4 to USDA-Forest Service, 1323 Club Drive, Vallejo, CA 94592. For more information, contact Shasta-Trinity National Forest, Mount Shasta Ranger District, 204 West Alma, Mount Shasta, CA 96067; (530) 926-4511.

Directions: From Redding, drive 50 miles north on Interstate 5 and take the Castle Crags/Castella exit, which is four miles south of Dunsmuir. Turn west and follow Castle Creek Road for 3.2 miles. Turn right into the unsigned parking area. The trail is on your left as you drive in, although it's hard to see from the parking lot.

24. HEDGE CREEK FALLS

City of Dunsmuir
Off Interstate 5 in Dunsmuir

Access & Difficulty: Hike-in 0.25 mile RT/Easy
Elevation: Start at 2,300 feet; total loss 100 feet
Best Season: April to July

Imagine you're hightailing it up Interstate 5 with the kids, on your way to visit Grandma in Portland. They're going berserk from being locked in the car for hours, and you're about to lose it if you see any more concrete, guard rails, or fast-food chains. But then you reach the town of Dunsmuir, 57 miles north of Redding, and you remember a freeway antidote: Hedge Creek Falls.

Get off the freeway and head to Dunsmuir Avenue. Park in the small lot, do a few warm-up stretches in the tiny park where the waterfall trail begins, and then hike down the path. Blink and you'll miss it—not the waterfall but the walk to it, because you'll reach the falls in about five minutes of downhill cruising.

Hedge Creek Falls drops 30 feet over a sheer granite slab into a shallow pool and a pretty babbling stream. The cliff that forms the fall is so sheer that it makes the water chute appear much grander than it really is. A large indentation in the bottom of the cliff, near where the fall hits the pool, creates a small cave. When the water flow is somewhat diminished in summer, you can sneak behind the falls and pretend you are a water ouzel, that funny bird that makes its home behind waterfalls.

Hedge Creek Falls

Prolong your visit to this paradise just off the freeway by settling in on the bench by the falls. Consider the history of this pastoral spot: It is said to have been a secret hideout of the notorious 1850s stagecoach robber, Black Bart. In this century, it was saved from the bull-dozers when Interstate 5 was built through Dunsmuir. Local citizens rallied to move the freeway a few yards to the east, just far enough to preserve Hedge Creek Falls.

More benches are positioned up and down the trail, which may come in handy on the return climb. When you hike back uphill, be sure to turn around a few times for parting glances at the falling water. At a few points, about 20 to 30 feet from the drop, you can peer through the lush canopy of leaves and see another waterfall directly above this one, set back in the canyon about 50 feet.

Trip notes: There is no fee. For more information, contact the Dunsmuir Chamber of Commerce, P.O. Box 17, Dunsmuir, CA 96025; (530) 235-2177 or the city of Dunsmuir at (530) 235-4822.

Directions: From Redding, drive 57 miles north on Interstate 5 to Dunsmuir and take the Dunsmuir Avenue/Siskiyou Avenue exit. Turn left at the stop sign and cross under the freeway, then turn right (north) on Dunsmuir Avenue, travel about 20 yards, and turn left into the small parking area.

25. MOSSBRAE FALLS
City of Dunsmuir
Off Interstate 5 in Dunsmuir

Access & Difficulty: Hike-in 3.0 miles RT/Easy
Elevation: Start at 2,300 feet; total gain 0 feet
Best Season: May to August

Getting to Mossbrae Falls requires the most unusual walk of all the waterfalls in this book. It's a weird trek, maybe even a little spooky, but don't let that keep you away. Mossbrae is also one of the most unique of the 200 falls in this book, and witnessing its singular beauty is definitely worth the trip.

The only way to access the waterfall is to walk 1.5 miles along the railroad tracks upstream from Shasta Retreat in Dunsmuir. There's no room for a foot trail alongside the Sacramento River, so every-body—anglers, swimmers, dog-walkers, and waterfall enthusiasts alike—walks along the tracks. That means about 40 minutes of level hiking on the gravel railroad bed, during which it's helpful to pray that a train doesn't happen by. It's not that a train would be danger-ous—it isn't, as long as you stay off the tracks—it's just that you don't want to be near one when it's moving. They're loud and powerful, and their colossal noise can ruin the peaceful solitude of your walk.

We managed to walk back and forth to Mossbrae without encountering a train, but even so, walking on a gravel railroad bed is not quite as pleasant as strolling on a pine-needle-covered path in the woods. Just bear with it, and get yourself as quickly as possible to the falls' cutoff trail, located just before you reach a steel railroad trestle. A dirt path leads 30 yards down to Mossbrae Falls, which pours into the wide

Mossbrae Falls

Sacramento River. (You can see and hear the falls from the railroad trail, so you can't miss it.)

You've never seen a waterfall quite like Mossbrae. It's only about 50 feet tall at its highest point, but it's about 150 feet wide, creating an entire wall of delicate spray pouring out of the moss-covered canyon wall and into the river. It looks more like a water sculpture than a waterfall, with over 100 separate rivulets and thousands of tiny holes shooting water out of the cliff. Yes, that's *out* of the cliff, rather than over the top of it, like at most waterfalls. The fall's source is natural springs, so the water flows from underground, making it freezing cold, even in summer. The many cascading streams of the waterfall create a truly gorgeous effect, something like an assembly of lawn sprinklers, all spraying in unison. Mossbrae Falls looks and feels like hundreds of waterfalls, not just one.

It's not just the water that creates the beauty. Mossbrae Falls is completely surrounded and gracefully framed by elephant ears, maidenhair ferns, and bracken ferns. Dense mosses grow underneath the spring water flow, making Mossbrae one of the few waterfalls in California that has been rightfully named. The fall is so photogenic that it has appeared in magazines, travel brochures, and even on the cover of the local phone book. Every photographer in the area has hundreds of pictures of Mossbrae—its charm is irresistible.

Earlier in this century, passenger trains would stop at the falls so travelers could get out and admire them. Today, your best bet for admiring Mossbrae Falls is to pick a spot on the little rocky beach along the river. When the flow is low enough, you can rockhop halfway out into the stream and stand just a few feet from the falls. Of course, most people who do this bring along a fishing rod, because the Upper Sacramento is an angler's paradise. It all depends on where your interest lies.

A warning: The first tenth of a mile of the railroad trail is the worst, because it has the least room between the tracks and the steep river canyon. The railroad bed gravel can make for tricky footing, so keep a hand-hold on small children. After five minutes of walking, the trail widens and is safer.

Trip notes: There is no fee. For more information, contact the Dunsmuir Chamber of Commerce, P.O. Box 17, Dunsmuir, CA 96025; (530) 235-2177 or the city of Dunsmuir at (530) 235-4822.

Directions: From Redding, drive 57 miles north on Interstate 5 to Dunsmuir and take the Dunsmuir Avenue/Siskiyou Avenue exit. Turn left and cross under the freeway, then turn left again (south) and head into the town of Dunsmuir. In six-tenths of a mile, make a sharp right turn on to Scarlett Way (drive under the arch that is signed "Shasta Retreat.") Bear right at the fork and cross the bridge over the Sacramento River, then cross the railroad tracks and park on the far side, alongside the tracks. (Total distance on Scarlett Way is one-quarter mile.) Start walking upstream (to your right as you drive in) along the tracks.

26. SWEETBRIAR FALLS

Sacramento River/Sweetbriar Creek
Off Interstate 5 near Dunsmuir

Access & Difficulty: Hike-in 0.25 mile RT/Easy
Elevation: Start at 2,300 feet; total gain 0 feet
Best Season: February to June

The truth is, nobody comes to Sweetbriar Falls just to see the waterfall. It's only about 20 feet tall, and the trek to reach it is little

Sweetbriar Falls

more than 100 yards, so it doesn't exactly make for a great outdoor adventure. The falls probably wouldn't even have made it into this book if it weren't for two significant nearby features: mighty Mount Shasta and the Sacramento River. At Sweetbriar Falls, you get great views of the former and access to the latter.

Still, Sweetbriar Falls is sweet. Its only failing is that a road was built right above it, so a metal guard rail above its lip mars your view somewhat. It's a pint-sized cataract, best seen as early in the spring as possible. Because the elevation here is only 2,300 feet, snow is rarely an obstacle to visiting.

To reach the falls, leave your car on the west side of the railroad tracks in the community of Sweetbriar. Cross the tracks and walk up Sweetbriar Road toward the Sacramento River, passing several cozy-looking cabins. As you cross the river bridge, look upstream for a perfectly framed view of Mount Shasta. You get a head-on look at the huge, snowy volcano, glistening white even in summer, one of the greatest sights in all of Northern California.

At the far side of the bridge, walk 50 feet to your right (downstream) on the trail along the river. This puts you smack in front of small Sweetbriar Falls. A wooden footbridge crosses the creek near the fall's base, giving you the option to continue your hike along the river. On a warm day, you can combine a visit to Sweetbriar Falls with a few hours of fishing or swimming in the Sacramento River.

Trip notes: There is no fee. For more information and a brochure on area waterfalls, contact Redding Convention and Visitors Bureau, 777 Auditorium Drive, Redding, CA 96001; (530) 225-4100. Or phone the Shasta Cascade Wonderland Association, 1699 Highway 273, Anderson, CA 96007; (800) 474-2782.

Directions: From Redding, drive 49 miles north on Interstate 5 to eight miles south of Dunsmuir and two miles south of Castle Crags State Park. Take the Sweetbriar exit, drive east for a half-mile, and park alongside the train tracks (just before crossing them, on their west side).

27. POTEM FALLS

Shasta-Trinity National Forest
Off Highway 299 near Redding

Access & Difficulty: Hike-in 0.5 mile RT/Easy
Elevation: Start at 1,800 feet; total loss 50 feet
Best Season: April to August, but good year-round

When you're in the waterfall-watching business, every now and then a beautiful fall gets handed to you on a silver platter, and you can't believe your good luck. Potem Falls, on the Pit River Arm of Lake Shasta, is such a place. It's a pristine and beautiful waterfall, with a perfect swimming hole, that you can reach with little effort.

It takes a long but simple drive, plus a short and easy hike, to reach Potem Falls. Located 30-plus miles east of Redding, the waterfall never gets visited by anyone who just happens to be passing by. Those who show up are mostly locals who consider the place a secret swimming hole, or lovers looking for a spot to hold hands and gaze at something inspiring.

Once you make the drive on paved and dirt roads to the unmarked parking pullout above the fall, you have only a ten-minute walk ahead of you. Potem Falls drops into the Pit River arm of Lake

Potem Falls

Shasta, but this spot doesn't look anything like the overcrowded reservoir you see while driving Interstate 5, or from the deck of a rented houseboat.

A well-built trail leads from the dirt road and parking pullout, descending to the stream canyon in four switchbacks, straight to the waterfall's pool. Along the way you'll have to stop to ooh and ahh, because the view of the falls from a distance is just as stunning as from up close.

Potem Falls is 70 feet high, plunging in a single compact stream over a rock cliff, surrounded by thick and leafy oak trees. It's a perfect freefall, like a miniature Yosemite Falls, but beautifully framed by a plethora of foliage. An ideal swimming pool lies at its base—circular, wide, and reasonably warm—with a gravel beach large enough to lay a towel or two at its edge. For those who prefer picnicking or hand-holding to swimming, there are plenty of big rocks to sit on and admire the scene, as well as a bench situated near the foot of the falls.

Trip notes: There is no fee. For a map of Shasta-Trinity National Forest, send $4 to USDA-Forest Service, 1323 Club Drive, Vallejo, CA 94592. For more information, contact Shasta-Trinity National Forest, Shasta Lake Ranger District, 14225 Holiday Road, Redding, CA 96003; (530) 275-1587.

Directions: From Redding, take Highway 299 East and drive 29 miles. Turn left on Fenders Ferry Road and drive nine miles (the pavement ends at 3.5 miles and the road turns to dirt). Look for a large unmarked parking pullout on the left side of the road. You can hear the falls from the road. High-clearance vehicles are recommended.

28. HATCHET CREEK FALLS
Shasta-Trinity National Forest
Off Highway 299 near Redding

Access & Difficulty: Hike-in 0.5 mile RT/Easy
Elevation: Start at 1,800 feet; total gain 50 feet
Best Season: Year-round

Sure, Hatchet Creek Falls is pretty. But people who make the long drive east of Redding to Hatchet Creek aren't usually visiting for the scenery; they're looking for a place to swim. Hatchet Creek Falls has a deep, clear pool at its base that must be considered one of the finest swimming holes in the Redding and Shasta area.

Getting to the waterfall is simple. After the pleasant drive out of

Redding, you park in a pullout by the highway bridge over Hatchet Creek, jump out of your car, and follow the obvious path upstream. In about 150 yards, you'll have to cut down the steep bank to the creek, then wade across and rockhop your way up to the fall's base.

Hatchet Creek Falls

When we visited in August, this was fairly easy, but it could be much more difficult soon after the rainy season. Hatchet Creek's current is strong and its rocks are slippery. Use caution and good judgment if the water is high.

The waterfall is 25 feet high and its flow is almost 20 feet wide, even in late summer. A large fir tree trunk has toppled over its lip and bisects the cataract. The canyon surrounding Hatchet Creek burned in a wildfire in 1996, leaving many downed fir trees, but it is now completely green again with new growth.

Hatchet Creek Falls features a spectacular pool at its base that is at least 40 yards wide and round. Although the pool is shallow around its edges and lined with smooth, rounded rocks, it's surprisingly deep in the center near the falls (over my head). If you swim, you'll find it's hard to get close to where the waterfall hits the pool because its current is so forceful. Also, the temperature drops several degrees in the deeper areas. The pool is continually refreshed by the falls's constant rushing flow, creating beautifully clear water. On a warm day, you'll have to drag yourself out of the swimming hole and back out to your car.

Trip notes: There is no fee. For a map of Shasta-Trinity National Forest, send $4 to USDA-Forest Service, 1323 Club Drive, Vallejo, CA 94592. For more information, contact Shasta-Trinity National Forest, Shasta Lake Ranger District, 14225 Holiday Road, Redding, CA 96003; (530) 275-1587.

Directions: From Redding, take Highway 299 East and drive 35 miles. Turn left on Big Bend Road and drive eight-tenths of a mile to the bridge over Hatchet Creek. Park in the dirt parking area just before the bridge on the right side of the road. An unsigned trail begins from this parking area; hike upstream.

MORE WATERFALLS

in Shasta, Trinity, & Klamath

•Brandy Creek Falls, Whiskeytown National Recreation Area. Small falls and swimming holes are located near Brandy Creek Campground. For more information, phone Whiskeytown at (530) 242-3400 or (530) 246-1225.

•Kickapoo Falls, Trinity Alps Wilderness. Backpack trip along North Fork Coffee Creek. For more information, phone Klamath National Forest, Scott River Ranger District, at (530) 468-5351.

Plumas, Lassen, & Modoc

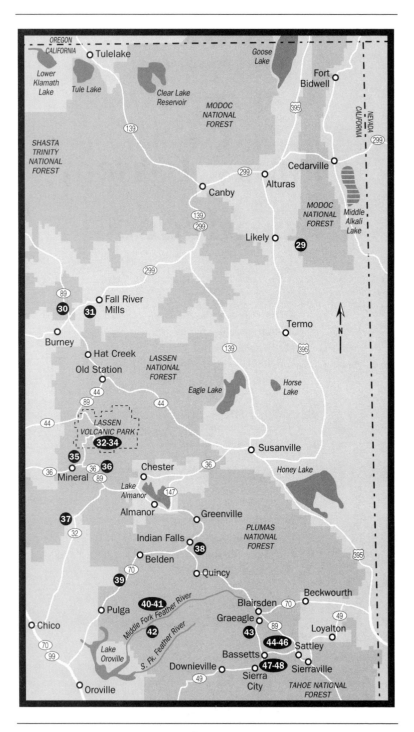

29. MILL CREEK FALLS

Modoc National Forest
Off U.S. 395 near Likely

Access & Difficulty: Hike-in 0.5 mile RT/Easy
Elevation: Start at 5,700 feet; total gain 50 feet
Best Season: May to September

Most people need a pretty good reason to travel all the way out here to Modoc County in the remote northeastern corner of California. Here's a good reason: Mill Creek Falls in the Warner Mountains.

You can leave your hiking boots in your tent for this trip. Mill Creek Falls are a mere quarter-mile from the Forest Service campground that bears the same name. To see the waterfall, take the trail out of camp and bear left at the fork. The right fork goes to Clear Lake and then deep into the South Warner Wilderness, a rugged land that ranges from sagebrush and grasslands to high alpine lakes and peaks. The wilderness, which Mill Creek Falls sits just inside the border of, is well known for having snowstorms in every month of the year. Like I said, it's a rugged land.

In just a few minutes of walking through a forest of white firs, you're at an overlook area for the 100-foot falls, watching Mill Creek make a vertical plummet over a narrow sandstone cliff. A railing keeps eager waterfall enthusiasts from falling into the creek.

You're only about 200 feet from the falls at the overlook, an ideal spot for taking pictures. Don't try to go any closer by scrambling off-trail, especially in spring and early summer when the creek level is high, because many slippery rocks line the edge of Mill Creek Falls.

Later in the summer, you can swim in Mill Creek, although not right by the falls—the current is too strong. Head downstream, between the falls and the camp, to any of numerous swimming holes. It's usually not hard to find a secluded pool to call your own.

While you're out moseying around, be sure to take the quarter-mile hike to Clear Lake, elevation 5,900 feet. From the campground, just continue past the waterfall fork and bear right, following the clearly marked signs. Clear Lake is a decent-sized lake with big fish, both brown and rainbow trout. The catch is so dependably good, people even come here in the winter to ice-fish. A trail follows along the right side of the lake.

Trip notes: There is no fee. For a map of Modoc National Forest or the South Warner Wilderness, send $4 to USDA-Forest Service, 1323 Club

Drive, Vallejo, CA 94592. For more information, contact Modoc National Forest, Warner Mountain Ranger District, P.O. Box 220, Cedarville, CA 96104; (530) 279-6116.

Directions: From Alturas, drive south on U.S. 395 for 18 miles to Likely. Turn east on Jess Valley Road (County Road 64) and drive nine miles. When the road forks, bear left on Forest Service Road 5 and drive 2.5 miles, then turn right on Forest Service Road 40N46 and continue two miles to the campground and trailhead.

---

30. BURNEY FALLS

McArthur Burney Falls Memorial State Park
Off Highway 89 near Burney

Access & Difficulty: Hike-in 1.0 to 4.0 miles RT/Easy
Elevation: Start at 3,100 feet; total gain 150 feet
Best Season: Year-round

It's a fact that Burney Falls is more of a tourist attraction than a mountain sanctuary. It's true that they made the falls too easy to see—just pay your five bucks and drive right up to the overlook. But when you visit the towering 129-foot waterfall at McArthur Burney Falls Memorial State Park, you understand why it's worth the trip even just to sightsee.

Watching 100 million gallons of water pour over a cliff, rain or shine, snowmelt or no snowmelt, is an experience you don't forget. President Theodore Roosevelt, a devout nature-lover, went so far as to call Burney Falls the eighth wonder of the world.

The good news is that you have options for viewing Burney Falls. There's the drive-up-and-peer-over-the-railing routine, two different one-mile loop trips, or longer hikes along Burney Creek. The most peaceful waterfall watching route is via the Headwaters Trail, which starts from the parking area to the left of the entrance kiosk (not the main lot on the right). You walk upstream, heading away from the falls. With this approach, you get a pretty hike through the forest with much less company than on the main Falls Trail, and you save your waterfall visit for last.

Headwaters Trail's woodland is filled with ponderosa pines, big Douglas firs, and white and black oaks. A half mile out, you reach a long footbridge over Burney Creek and an intersection with the Pacific Crest Trail. Cross the bridge and follow the PCT downstream, now heading in the direction of Burney Falls. In another half mile, exit the PCT and turn right on Falls Trail. A few switchbacks lead you downhill to a sign for the Burney Falls overlook and a small clearing, where your view of the huge waterfall is framed by trees. This perspective is different from most photographs you've seen of the falls; they're usually taken from the overlook on the east side of the creek.

Burney Falls' height at 129 feet doesn't tell the whole story of its splendor. Many waterfalls in this book are far taller, yet few have the grandeur to match Burney Falls. It is unique because it flows at basically the same rate all year, making it one of the few waterfalls in California that you can visit in every month of the calendar. That's because the water from Burney Creek comes from underground springs and stored snowmelt in the basalt rock layers that make up the falls. If you look closely, you can see that much of the fall's flow actually pours out of the face of the cliff, rather than over the top of its lip. Due to its underground source, the fall's water temperature, even on warm summer days, is a chilly 42 degrees Fahrenheit.

Burney Falls

To make a loop back to the parking area, backtrack up Falls Trail for a few hundred yards, then turn left on another footbridge that will take you back to your car in one-tenth of a mile. Or you can continue past the overlook, heading further downstream on Falls Trail, to yet another footbridge that returns you via the most popular route in the park. This is the Falls Trail Loop proper, a one-mile trail that begins and ends by the eastern falls overlook

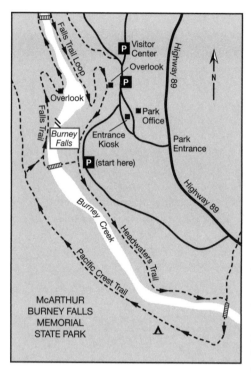

and crosses two different footbridges over Burney Creek. The best feature of this trail is that it's routed near the base of the falls, where you can admire its huge sapphire pool and be doused with spray and mist. The bad news is that the path is paved and crowds are a problem, especially on summer weekends. Some visitors don't follow the whole loop; they just walk from the main overlook to the base of the falls and back.

You're likely to see fly fishermen working the waters in the deep, cold pool of Burney Falls, or further upstream along the Headwaters Trail. Burney Creek is a well-loved trout stream, although novices don't fare well here.

If you want to hike farther, you can make a terrific loop by heading out on the Falls Trail from the main overlook, continuing straight on the Burney Creek Trail rather than crossing the creek, then looping back on the Rim Trail for a three-mile loop. Or combine this loop with the loop on the Headwaters Trail and Pacific Crest Trail for a 4.5-mile hike.

Trip notes: There is a $5 entrance fee at McArthur Burney Falls Memorial State Park. Park maps are available for $1 at the entrance station. For more information, contact McArthur Burney Falls Memorial State Park, 24898 Highway 89, Burney, CA 96013; (530) 335-2777 or (530) 538-2200.

Directions: From Interstate 5 at Redding, turn east on Highway 299 and drive 50 miles to Burney. At Burney, continue five miles east on Highway 299 to its intersection with Highway 89. Turn left and drive north on Highway 89 for 5.5 miles to the park entrance. Park at the main lot and follow the signs to the overlook and Falls Trail, or park at the lot to the left of the entrance kiosk and begin hiking on the Headwaters Trail.

31. PIT RIVER FALLS

American Land Conservancy
Off Highway 299 near Fall River Mills

Access & Difficulty: Drive-to/Easy
    or Scramble 2.5 miles RT/Moderate
Elevation: Start at 3,300 feet; total loss 400 feet
Best Season: April to September

Pit River Falls is one of those easy way or hard way falls. You can take the easy way, which is to simply drive up to the overlook, preferably with a pair of binoculars and a picnic; or you can take the hard way, which is to make a steep off-trail descent through scratchy brush to the bottom of the deeply cut canyon where the falls spill. It's your choice.

The overlook is a bit of a disappointment, partly because you are too distant from the waterfall and mostly because people party here at night and leave trash laying around. In the daytime, you'll probably have the place to yourself, and it's a good spot to get a view of the impressively steep Pit River canyon. It's deep and surrounded by basalt cliffs and boulders, which tells you something about this area's geology—it was formed by volcanic activity.

Pit River Falls

If you decide to make the scramble to the falls, take note of how steep the canyon is, because if you go down, you've gotta come back up. You'll see two rough routes that lead from the overlook, but neither of these are good trails. Instead, drive down the road another half-mile, toward Fall River Mills, to a parking area on the right side of the road. Follow the dirt road, which leads toward the river. When you reach the canyon rim, put on your pants and long-sleeve shirt and take any of the rough routes down. After you touch bottom, head downstream on an old dirt road, which leads to a broken-down metal bridge just below Pit River Falls. Stay off the bridge; instead, clamber down below it to the waterfall's base. You'll be surprised at the fall's height and velocity, which can't be discerned from the drive-to overlook. The falls drop 40 feet over a basalt cliff and are similar in size and appearance to Middle McCloud Falls on the nearby McCloud River. (See page 59.)

If you like, you can swim downstream of the falls where the current is milder. Enjoy the Pit River, then get mentally prepared for the breathtaking, brushy scramble back uphill.

Trip notes: There is no fee. For more information, contact the Fall River Mills Museum, (530) 336-5110. This land currently belongs to the American Land Conservancy but will soon fall under Bureau of Land Management, Alturas Resource District jurisdiction. For more information, phone (530) 233-4666.

Directions: From Redding, take Highway 299 east for 58 miles to the junction of highways 299 and 89. Continue east on Highway 299 for 10 more miles to one mile west of Fall River Mills. Watch for the blue "Vista Point" sign and then turn into the parking area on the right side of the road.

32. WEST FORK HAT CREEK FALLS

Lassen Volcanic National Park
Off Highway 89 near Manzanita Lake

Access & Difficulty: Hike-in 2.8 miles RT/Easy
Elevation: Start at 6,300 feet; total gain 600 feet
Best Season: June to September

Let's call a spade a spade right here and say that the waterfall on Hat Creek by Paradise Meadows in Lassen Park is really only a cascade, and not even a big one at that. But the rangers told us to go see it anyway because there were secret rewards to be found on the hike to Paradise Meadows, rewards that would make a 20-foot cascade seem like an excellent excuse for a hike.

Those rangers know their stuff. There are actually two good-size cascades in the last quarter-mile of trail to Paradise Meadows, and both are great spots for a picnic or for shooting a few pictures. But the route wowed us in other ways as well. First, it's only a 1.4-mile walk to Paradise Meadows, but it's uphill the whole way until the last tenth of a mile, and at this 6,300-foot elevation, our hearts were pumping aerobically in no time. Second, the area's wildflowers are tremendous. In July, there was truly a heart-stopping display of color along the trail and stream. Third, there's Paradise Meadows itself, a large green expanse that's the size of a couple of football fields, strewn with lavender wandering daisies. We wandered, too, among the daisies, and resisted the temptation to roll around in them, fearing we might squash too many.

Of the two Hat Creek cascades, the upper one is the most impressive, especially if you cut down off the trail and sit close to its base. It has more of a freefall to its flow, and makes a startling show of white against the green of the grasses surrounding it.

Few people stop at the falls, though, because it's only 10 more minutes of walking to reach Paradise Meadows. When they reach it, hikers tend to stand respectfully at its edge, staring out at the wonder of Paradise, afraid to tread on even one precious blade of grass. It's that pristine-looking.

Along the trail, we counted more than a dozen kinds of wildflowers, even in midsummer when most places in California have lost their bloom. We saw both blue and yellow lupine, shooting stars, corn lilies, columbine, daisies, gentian, and wallflowers. So much color, so little time.

If you want more hiking, you can continue beyond the meadow to Terrace and Shadow Lakes, another two miles further. And if you need one more reason to make the trip to Hat Creek's cascades and Paradise Meadows, the trail's abundant views of glistening, snow-capped Mount Lassen should do it.

Trip notes: There is a $10 entrance fee at Lassen Volcanic National Park, good for seven days. Park maps are available for free at the entrance stations. A more detailed map is available for a fee from the park's Loomis Museum. For more information, contact Lassen Volcanic National Park, P.O. Box 100, Mineral, CA 96063; (530) 595-4444.

Directions: From Interstate 5 at Redding, turn east on Highway 44 and drive 46 miles to the park's northern entrance. Continue southeast on Highway 89 for 10 miles to the Paradise Meadows trailhead on the right (south) side of the road. Park near the sign for Hat Lake.

33. KINGS CREEK FALLS

Lassen Volcanic National Park
Off Highway 89 near Summit Lake

Access & Difficulty: Hike-in 2.4 miles RT/Easy
Elevation: Start at 7,200 feet; total loss 700 feet
Best Season: June to September

For a moment, I was confused. Was I walking on the granite stair-steps of the Mist Trail in Yosemite National Park, on my way downstream to Vernal Fall? Impossible. Of course not. Here I was in Lassen Volcanic National Park, following the rocky stairway to Kings Creek Falls.

But the two trails share so many similarities, it seems like the two national parks hired the same trail-makers. Parts of the granite walkway to Kings Creek Falls are just as scenic, and just as treacherous, as the world-famous Mist Trail in Yosemite. The only difference is that about one-tenth the number of people walk the Kings Creek Trail. In some ways, that makes it superior.

The waterfall is only an 8 but the trail is a 10. The route follows Kings Creek all the way, is frequently shaded by big fir trees, and descends from the parking lot for 1.1 miles to the falls, with a nice level section in the middle along Lower Meadow. The meadow is dark green and teeming with ebullient corn lilies in summer. It makes a perfect place to rest on the uphill hike back.

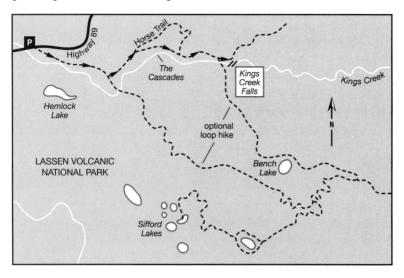

Beyond the meadow, you have two options, just like on the Mist Trail in Yosemite: the Foot Trail or the Horse Trail. The Horse Trail is more level and less treacherous, but it's nowhere near as scenic because it moves away from Kings Creek. Take the Foot Trail, which leads steeply downhill on stairsteps cut into the rock just inches from The Cascades on Kings Creek. Before you begin your descent, be sure to look ahead of you at the incredible valley vista far off in the distance. You can see for miles.

Kings Creek Falls

Once you're on the rock stairsteps, you must keep your eyes on your feet and their careful placement because you are stepping only a few feet from the continual rushing cascade of white water. This is difficult, however, since The Cascades are so mesmerizing, serving as an opening act for the waterfall to follow. (Some people mistake The Cascades for Kings Creek Falls, and they unknowingly turn around before they reach the real thing. Keep going until you come to a fenced overlook, where you're witness to a vertical drop.)

Kings Creek Falls are about 50 feet high, split by a rock outcrop into two main cascades, which make a steep and narrow drop into the canyon. The fence surrounding the waterfall keeps people out of trouble on the unstable slopes. A picnic lunch at the overlook and a turnaround there makes a lovely 2.4-mile round-trip. If you wish to hike farther, you can make a five-mile loop by crossing the footbridge just 100 yards before the falls and following the trail to Bench Lake and beyond. Be sure to take the spur off the loop to the Sifford Lakes.

Trip notes: There is a $10 entrance fee at Lassen Volcanic National Park, good for seven days. Park maps are available for free at the entrance stations. A more detailed map is available for a fee from the park's Loomis Museum. For more information, contact Lassen Volcanic National Park, P.O. Box 100, Mineral, CA 96063; (530) 595-4444.

Directions: From Interstate 5 at Red Bluff, turn east on Highway 36 and drive 47 miles. Turn north on Highway 89 and drive 4.5 miles to the park's southwest entrance. Continue 12 miles to the parking area and the trailhead on the right, near milepost 32. Park along the road.

Or, from Interstate 5 at Redding, turn east on Highway 44 and drive 46 miles to the park's northern entrance. Continue southeast on Highway 89 for 17 miles to the trailhead on the left side of the road at milepost 32. Park in the pullouts on either side of the road.

34. MILL CREEK FALLS

Lassen Volcanic National Park
Off Highway 89 near Mineral

Access & Difficulty: Hike-in 4.0 miles RT/Moderate
Elevation: Start at 6,700 feet; total loss/gain 300 feet
Best Season: June to September

The woman at the entrance gate told us Mill Creek Falls was the highest waterfall in Lassen Volcanic National Park, but she forgot to mention that it's also the prettiest, despite some serious contenders.

The fall has an excellent hiking trail leading to it, only four miles round-trip and with a constant up-and-down undulation, so you're never sure if you're losing elevation or gaining it. The trailhead is on the south side of Lassen Park, near Lassen Chalet and Southwest Campground. A brief stint on pavement takes you through the campground, but after you pass the tents and picnic tables things start to look a whole lot better.

"Better" begins at a log bridge over West Sulphur Creek, just beyond the campground. Acres and acres of mule's ears grow on the

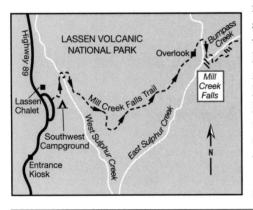

far side of the bridge, and a postcard-perfect view of Mount Lassen lies straight ahead. A memorable vista awaits here, encompassing the lush, emerald green valley that lies between Sulphur Creek and the old, snowy volcano.

The trail laterals across hillsides and over

feeder streams for two miles. Most of the time you walk under a canopy of red firs, white firs, and pines, many of them covered with bright green staghorn moss, but occasionally the trail leads to small open meadows rife with corn lilies and grassy wildflowers.

After a while, you begin to wonder where you're going and if you'll ever get there, as the trail heads steadily eastward through the trees. But then comes the magic moment when you hear the sound of water plummeting—and in moments you are standing at an overlook, peering across the canyon at Mill Creek Falls.

A 75-foot plunging freefall, Mill Creek makes a solid impression. It's not only big, it's also quite graceful. Two creeks join together at its lip, then spill as one through a very deep and narrow canyon. Sulphur Creek contributes to Mill Creek Falls' greatness; it's the pairing and funneling of the two streams that results in the tremendous water flow. The outcome is a classic double waterfall; the upper section drops about 25 feet, then collects in a bowl and gathers force to drop again, this time about 50 feet, in one long chute of water. Perhaps what is most spectacular about the waterfall is the rock face over which it pours— it's a rather knobby-looking cliff with multiple layers of moss and algae growing on it, in colors ranging from rust and orange to deep green. Huge old-growth fir trees grow on top of the cliff, adding to the majesty.

Mill Creek Falls

It's nearly impossible to access the bottom of the fall because the canyon walls are a near-vertical, 100-foot drop. The waterfall view is best from this overlook, but you can continue on the trail another quarter-mile to the fall's brink.

Trip notes: There is a $10 entrance fee at Lassen Volcanic National Park, good for seven days. Park maps are available for free at the entrance stations. A more detailed map is available for a fee from the park's Loomis Museum. For more information, contact Lassen Volcanic National Park, P.O. Box 100, Mineral, CA 96063; (530) 595-4444.

Directions: From Interstate 5 at Red Bluff, turn east on Highway 36 and drive 47 miles. Turn north on Highway 89 and drive 4.5 miles to the park's southern entrance. Continue 100 yards to the parking area and trailhead on the right side of the road, near the restroom by Southwest Campground. Begin walking on the paved trail by the restroom, heading through the camp to its north side.

35. BLUFF FALLS

Lassen National Forest
Off Highway 89 near Mineral

Access & Difficulty: Hike-in 0.25 mile RT/Easy
Elevation: Start at 6,500 feet; total gain 40 feet
Best Season: June to September

Bluff Falls may not be worth a special trip all the way out to this remote corner of northern California, but if you happen to be in Lassen Volcanic National Park and it's crawling with tourists, you might just want to stop by. You can probably get yourself your own private waterfall.

The 50-foot cataract is just outside of the park's southern border, visible from the road if you're looking carefully. Getting close to it is no mystery—just follow the rough route from the closest parking pullout (across the road), which winds around to near the base of the fall. You'll have to walk over quite a few boulders, not all of which were made by nature. Bits of concrete, cables, and other evidence of mining activity remain here; Bluff Falls was once the site of a quarry. Even the waterfall's cliff has been excavated. When you see it, it's clear how Bluff Falls got its name.

It's critical to see this fall in the morning, and as soon after snow-melt or rainfall as possible. By late afternoon, the sun goes behind the bluff of Bluff Falls, putting the waterfall in shadow.

Trip notes: There is no fee. For a map of Lassen National Forest, send $4 to USDA-Forest Service, 1323 Club Drive, Vallejo, CA 94592. For more information, contact Lassen National Forest, Almanor Ranger Station, P.O. Box 767, Chester, CA 96020; (530) 258-2141.

Directions: From Interstate 5 at Red Bluff, turn east on Highway 36 and drive 47 miles. Turn north on Highway 89 and drive 3.5 miles. The waterfall is visible on the left (west) side of the road. If you're coming from Lassen Volcanic National Park, Bluff Falls is 1.5 miles south of the park's southern entrance.

36. CANYON CREEK FALLS

Lassen National Forest
Off Highway 89 near Mineral

Access & Difficulty: Hike-in or Backpack 11.6 miles RT/Strenuous
Elevation: Start at 4,900 feet; total gain 2,000 feet
Best Season: June to September

If you want to see Canyon Creek Falls, you must be willing to sign up for a long day hike or backpacking trip. Is it worth it? Yes. Just pack along a good lunch and prepare to make a day of it, or load up your backpack for a longer trip beyond the falls.

The path to the waterfall is the Spencer Meadow National Recreation Trail, which begins just outside of Childs Meadows, only a few miles from the southern entrance to Lassen Volcanic National Park. While the national park may be crowded on summer weekends, things are sure to be quieter out here in the neighboring national forest. From the trailhead, the trail begins a long climb up a ridge. The good news is that it is shaded by pine and fir trees all the way; the bad news is that both the forest and the ascent seem relentless. At the trail's one and only fork, bear left. At 2.4 miles you break out of the trees to some fine views of wide, green Childs Meadows. The continuing ascent provides you with even wider vistas, now looking northwest to Brokeoff Mountain, Mount Diller, and Mount Lassen.

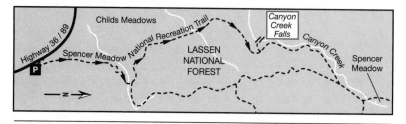

Canyon Creek Falls at low flow in autumn

Your final views before you head back into dense forest are down into the valley of Canyon Creek. From your perch on the trail you are high above it.

At 4.0 miles the trail levels out along a ridge-line, curving in and out of small ravines. You'll cross several of these, including a sizeable one lined with large boulders, in the last mile before the falls. Don't be alarmed if the small streams are dry. Canyon Creek has a dependable year-round flow.

Finding the fall isn't easy, however, because it doesn't drop right along the trail. Use your ears to guide you to the sound of rushing water. Watch carefully for an informal spur heading left at approximately 5.8 miles from the trailhead. It's only a 75-yard walk to the edge of the narrow stream canyon, then a steep descent down to the creek below the falls. If Canyon Creek's water level is low enough, you can pick your way up and around boulders to reach the base of the waterfall, which drops 50 feet over a steep rock-lined cliff.

Note that if you choose to backpack the Spencer Meadow Trail, you can continue another 1.3 miles to Spencer Meadow, spend the night, then make a loop back to the trailhead.

Trip notes: There is no fee. For a map of Lassen National Forest, send $4 to USDA-Forest Service, 1323 Club Drive, Vallejo, CA 94592. For more information, contact Lassen National Forest, Almanor Ranger Station, P.O. Box 767, Chester, CA 96020; (530) 258-2141.

Directions: From Interstate 5 at Red Bluff, turn east on Highway 36 and drive 47 miles. At the junction of highways 36 and 89, continue east on Highway 36 for another five miles, or three-tenths of a mile past Childs Meadows Resort. The signed trailhead and parking lot are on the north side of Highway 36.

37. DEER CREEK FALLS

Lassen National Forest
Off Highway 32 near Chester

Access & Difficulty: Hike-in 3.5 miles RT/Easy
Elevation: Start at 3,300 feet; total gain 300 feet
Best Season: April to August

When most people come to Deer Creek in Lassen National Forest, they have only one thing in mind: trout fishing. While we think angling is a fine pursuit, we came with a different goal: to cast a discerning eye on Deer Creek Falls and its sibling, Lower Deer Creek Falls, and determine if they were worthy of this book.

They didn't disappoint us. Not only were both waterfalls pretty white-water cataracts that were running full even in late July, the lower fall provided us with a 3.5-mile hike through a forest canopy and some of the quickest skinny-dipping we've ever done. Deer Creek is frigid, even late in the season.

From the parking area, the trail is routed downstream along the river through dense firs, pines, and live oaks. Lower Deer Creek Falls is 1.7 miles from the trailhead. I'd like to say it was a nice walk, but the truth is that the gnats were driving us crazy. If you have the bad luck to visit during the few weeks of gnat season, you have to wear sunglasses to keep them out of your eyes or keep fanning yourself continually. Otherwise, they relentlessly hover around your face.

The trail is mostly flat and pleasantly shaded till the last quarter-mile before the falls; then the route climbs a bit and is

Lower Deer Creek Falls

more exposed. The good news is that the gnats leave you alone when you are in the sun—a blessed reprieve.

Two left spur trails cut off from the Deer Creek Trail to go down to the falls. When you descend to the creek, you see that a fish ladder has been built around the main waterfall, consisting of a series of four stair-stepped concrete dams with notches cut into them, creating one-foot-high falls that the fish can easily jump over, and a tunnel in the rock for them to swim through. If you take the second of the two spur trails, it leads you right to the fish ladder. Your view of the falls is partially blocked by the huge boulder housing the fish tunnel, but you can sit on a small rocky beach and watch the 15-foot cascade, hoping that a fish will come by and climb the ladder. (The first spur trail gives you a view of the entire height of the fall and its powerful, churning white water.)

If you like to fish, don't forget your tackle box on this trip. Deer Creek is stocked with rainbow and brook trout almost every week near the two upstream campgrounds, Potato Patch and Alder Creek. Plenty of those fish make it downstream. However, don't get any ideas about fishing near the fish ladder, because it is clearly posted as a big no-no within 250 yards.

Now that you've seen Lower Deer Creek Falls, you should take the shorter trip to the upper falls as well. They're four miles upstream, so you can't get there from here. Walk back to the trailhead parking area, then drive northeast on Highway 32 to 1.5 miles east of Potato Patch Campground, where there are some springs on the side of the road and a parking pullout. Park there and look for an unmarked route that leads from the road down to the waterfall. It's steep, but only about 100 yards long. You'll find that Upper Deer Creek Falls is about the same size as the lower one, and it provides more swimming and fishing holes nearby.

Trip notes: There is no fee. For a map of Lassen National Forest, send $4 to USDA-Forest Service, 1323 Club Drive, Vallejo, CA 94592. For more information, contact Lassen National Forest, Almanor Ranger Station, P.O. Box 767, Chester, CA 96020; (530) 258-2141.

Directions: From the intersection of highways 32 and 99 in Chico, drive 40.2 miles northeast on Highway 32. Cross the Deer Creek bridge and park in a dirt pullout on the right. Cross the road to reach the trailhead on the northeast side of the bridge. Or, coming from the east, drive 14 miles west of Chester on Highway 36. Turn south on Highway 32 and drive 14 miles to the Deer Creek bridge and trailhead. (The trailhead is also 1.5 miles southwest of Potato Patch Campground on Highway 32.)

38. INDIAN FALLS

Plumas National Forest
Off Highway 70 near Quincy

Access & Difficulty: Hike-in 0.5 mile RT/Easy
Elevation: Start at 3,500 feet; total loss 50 feet
Best Season: April to August

The farther northeast from Oroville you travel, the better the Feather River canyon gets. Highway 70, which parallels it for 60 miles, gives you an up-close look at the river's sculptured rock formations, granite cascades, and thickly forested banks, all the way to the road's intersection with Highway 89. And what do you see when you get there? A waterfall, of course.

That's Indian Falls on Indian Creek, a major offshoot of the North Fork Feather River, with a backyard swimming hole and a waterfall that is well-loved by locals and visitors alike. The fall is in a beautiful rock gorge setting, not far off the road, and it's accessible by an easy walk through the trees.

On summer afternoons, it's no sweat to find the trailhead, because cars are always parked there. The trail is nicely maintained by the volunteer group Friends of Indian Falls, who are clearly a fine group of human beings. In five minutes of walking, you'll reach a picnic table and wooden fence, and from there you can continue

Indian Falls

hiking to your right to reach a calm swimming beach across from the falls. Or, you can scramble downhill to your left and come out on jagged rocks closer to the falls, the best place for taking photographs or just watching the action. You'll probably find several families and groups swimming, picnicking, and playing at the falls.

Strong swimmers play in the spray at the base of Indian Falls, while small children and dogs seem to prefer the calmer beach area. If you want to swim, you should enter the water at the beach, then paddle 50 yards upstream to the falls. Although Indian Falls is only about 20 feet tall, it runs with a forceful flow even in late summer. Many people wear lifejackets here; it's recommended because the current is strong.

Trip notes: There is no fee. For a map of Plumas National Forest, send $4 to USDA-Forest Service, 1323 Club Drive, Vallejo, CA 94592. For more information, contact Plumas National Forest, Quincy Ranger District, 39696 State Highway 70, Quincy, CA 95971; (530) 283-0555.

Directions: From Quincy, drive approximately 10 miles north on Highway 70/89 to the right turnoff for Highway 89 North to Greenville and Lake Almanor. Drive three miles north on Highway 89, watching for Indian Falls Road. Drive two-tenths of a mile further north on Highway 89, past the Indian Falls Road turnoff, to a dirt road on the right (east). Park along the side of the dirt road, then walk down it for one-tenth of a mile. Look for the single-track trail on the left. (If you are coming from Oroville, drive northeast on Highway 70 for 65 miles to the Highway 89 turnoff.)

39. CHAMBERS CREEK FALLS

Plumas National Forest
Off Highway 70 near Quincy

Access & Difficulty: Hike-in 4.0 miles RT/Strenuous
Elevation: Start at 2,000 feet; total gain 1,800 feet
Best Season: April to June

Do you like to listen to the sound of yourself panting hard on a hot summer day? If so, here's your trail.

The Chambers Creek Trail leads four miles uphill from Highway 70 and the North Fork Feather River Canyon to Chambers Peak, elevation 5,800 feet. Halfway there, it crosses Chambers Creek at a set of picture-perfect waterfalls and an historic 1932 Conservation Corps footbridge. If you enjoy hard work, you'll hike the two miles and 1,800-foot elevation gain to the falls. If you're somewhat masochistic, you'll do it at high noon on a hot July day. If you're totally out of your mind, you'll go all the way to the peak, for a 4,000-foot elevation gain and the feeling that you can survive anything.

Take your pick. Just remember that this trail is almost entirely out in the sun, especially for the first two miles, so you must have plenty of water with you. You can filter more water at Chambers Creek Falls, but from the trailhead to the falls, there's not a drop to be found. Oh yeah, and if you're having a particularly bad day, expect the gnats to show up.

Begin by hiking 100 yards on an old dirt road, then turn off the road on to a single-track trail on the right. Cross a creek and parallel Highway 70, ignoring all trail spurs and heading upward, ever upward. Here's what you have to look forward to: Half a dozen brutal, exposed, sunny, manzanita-lined switchbacks, which take more than 30 minutes to assault. Whenever you hit a tiny patch of shade, stop and watch the sweat drip off your nose. Say a few choice words. Look down at the road far, far below you and feel jealous of people in their air-conditioned cars.

Finally, after almost an hour of hiking, there's a change in the action—a left bend in the trail which leads you up and along the edge of the Chambers Creek canyon. It's blissfully shady here, and soon you will be able to hear the creek, although it's too far down below for you to be able to see it. The forest gets thicker and more interesting, with dogwoods and more varied conifers. The sound of water spurs you on, and voila! Shortly you round a curve and come out to Chambers Creek Falls and the quaint wooden footbridge that crosses it. The bridge is painted a bright aquamarine, which seems a little strange way up here in the middle of nowhere, but you'll be so happy to see the water that you won't worry about aesthetics.

The fall cascades about 250 feet, and one of the nicest drops and pools is right below the bridge. The granite that forms this drop makes it slippery and inaccessible, so scramble upstream for about 50 yards above the bridge, climbing over boulders to another pretty cascade. Pick a spot hidden from the trail, throw off your clothes, and go wading. You deserve it.

You can't scramble any further upstream, because you're blocked by the cliff of this waterfall. You have two choices: continue hiking beyond the bridge, heading further uphill toward Chambers Peak for more ascent and greater views, or turn around and head back down, this time with enough oxygen to enjoy the vistas of the valley, the river below, and its forested canyon. And if you're in a hurry, don't fret: While it took me 70 minutes to climb up to the falls, it took me only 40 minutes to return.

Trip notes: There is no fee. For a map of Plumas National Forest, send $4 to USDA-Forest Service, 1323 Club Drive, Vallejo, CA 94592. For more information, contact Plumas National Forest, Quincy Ranger District, 39696 State Highway 70, Quincy, CA 95971; (530) 283-0555.

Directions: From Oroville, drive northeast on Highway 70 for 42.5 miles to the Chambers Creek Trailhead, which is on the north side of Highway 70, across from a school and a closed campground. There is a dirt parking pullout by the trailhead sign. (Coming from the east at Quincy, it's 40 miles northwest on Highway 70.)

40. SEVEN FALLS (South Branch Falls)
Plumas National Forest
Off Highway 70 near Oroville

Access & Difficulty: Scramble 1.0 mile RT/Strenuous
Elevation: Start at 2,300 feet; total loss 1,500 feet
Best Season: April to August

Let's say straight off that there are two ways to make the trek to spectacular Seven Falls in Feather Falls Scenic Area near Lake Oroville. One is to fire up your high-clearance, four-wheel-drive vehicle, tie down anything that might fly loose, then make the slow, jolting, rock-strewn drive to the unmarked, inconspicuous trailhead off Milsap Bar Road—all the while praying that you find it.

The other way is to take your regular old car, pack up some food and maybe your passport and toothbrush for the long journey ahead, and drive 20 long miles to reach Seven Falls via the back route around Feather Falls, requiring only 2.5 miles of bumpy dirt-road travel—all the while still praying that you can find the darn trailhead.

Then again, there's still one more way: You can call up Dee Randolph at DeeTours in Oroville, have him pick you up at your hotel or house, and whisk you to Seven Falls in his air-conditioned tour van. After leading you down to the completely awesome set of thundering waterfalls on the South Branch of the Middle Fork Feather River, he'll serve you a gourmet lunch. The only thing Randolph doesn't do is hike back up the canyon for you. Too bad.

Randolph's guiding will cost you a few bucks, and making the trek on your own will cost you driving time and energy, but Seven

One of Seven Falls (front and side view)

Falls is worth any price. The falls are a series of freefalls—some as tall as 100 feet high—set in a hidden, pristine canyon that's hard to reach by car and by foot. But they are so spectacular that the Forest Service is considering building an overlook platform with an official trail to reach it, and possibly even paving the road to make the area more accessible. Since Seven Falls are so close to popular Feather Falls (see story on page 100), it just seems logical to open them up for greater recreational use.

Not everybody is in favor of this idea, of course, so while it's being debated, Seven Falls remain a secluded, special place that only those willing to labor can visit. That's what keeps guide Randolph in business. For starters, the long, rocky drive and the unmarked trailhead scare off many potential visitors. (On my first trip here, I made the entire 20-mile journey from Feather Falls and then couldn't find the trail, despite having decent directions from the Forest Service and being able to hear the falls from the road. When I went back a month later, with even more specific directions, I realized I had walked right past the "trailhead" without ever recognizing it.) The steep descent on a rough route, not a real trail, keeps away plenty of other folks. It's slippery, it drops 1,500 feet in a half-mile, and if you think going down is tricky, wait till you have to come back up. It's not for the faint of heart.

But the falls . . . Ahhh the falls. Once called Pompy's Falls, for a Maidu shaman who used to worship above the falls at Pompy's Point, Seven Falls are actually seven-plus falls. It depends on who you talk to, but many folks claim that Seven Falls is really nine or eleven falls. You can explore as many or as few of them as you like, but remember, this is not hiking, it's more like rock scrambling or climbing.

The rough route from Milsap Bar Road brings you right along-side three of the main drops of Seven Falls. Each one is between 50 and 100 feet high; they're showering white-water walls that run wide and forceful even as late as August. In springtime, they can be down-right frightening in their power.

If you're planning a trip to Seven Falls, consider taking advantage of Randolph's guide service. He can ensure that you get to your desti-nation, and he's also extremely knowledgeable about local geology, flora, and fauna. If you decide to make the trip on your own, remem-ber that this is a very challenging route for those who enjoy driving dirt roads in high-clearance vehicles, careful route finding, and steep descents on a barely visible route—not a well-built trail.

Trip notes: There is no fee. For a map of Plumas National Forest, send $4 to USDA-Forest Service, 1323 Club Drive, Vallejo, CA 94592. For more information, contact Plumas National Forest, Feather River Ranger District, 875 Mitchell Avenue, Oroville, CA 95965; (530) 534-6500 or (530) 675-1146. Or phone Dee Randolph at DeeTours in Berry Creek; (888) DAY-HIKE or (530) 589-2750.

Directions: There are two possible routes. The first is routed around Feather Falls and is mostly paved, although the final 2.5-mile dirt section can sometimes be rough enough to require a high-clearance vehicle: From Highway 70 in Oroville, take the Oroville Dam Boulevard exit (Highway 162) east and drive for 1.6 miles to Olive Highway/ Highway 162. Turn right and drive for 6.5 miles on Highway 162. Turn right on Forbestown Road and drive for six miles. Turn left on Lumpkin Road and drive for 10.8 miles to the left turnoff for Feather Falls. Reset your odometer here and continue on Lumpkin Road, past the Feather Falls turnoff. At 1.2 miles past the Feather Falls turnoff, take the right fork on to Forest Service Road 27. At 7.9 miles, stay straight at the junction; this puts you on Road 94. At 14.5 miles, reach a major fork and turn right. At 16.2 miles, bear left. At 19.0 miles, take the left fork off pavement and on to dirt. At 19.4 miles, take the left fork on to Road 22N62, Milsap Bar Road. At 21.7 miles, you'll see a good-size clearing on the left before the dirt road curves to the right. Park here and walk back down the road (in the direction you came) for about one-third mile to a spot that has small pullout space on both sides of the road. Listen for the falls, which you will not be able to see because of the deep, forested canyon, and look for an unmarked route by the small pullouts that leads down-canyon in the direction of the roaring falls. A fallen log obscures the start of the route. Good luck!

The second route is through Brush Creek on an extremely rough four-wheel-drive route via Milsap Bar Camp. Follow the directions as above, but drive 25 miles on Highway 162 to the Brush Creek Ranger Station. Turn right (south) on the eastern end of Bald Rock Road and drive a half-mile to Forest Service Road 22N62, Milsap Bar Road. Turn left and drive 7.4 miles to the campground. The road gets progressively more rocky. Continue for 4.6 miles past the campground on Milsap Bar Road to the unmarked route to Seven Falls. Look for the dirt clearing and pullouts along the road, as in the above directions, to guide you.

41. CURTAIN FALLS
Plumas National Forest
Off Highway 70 near Oroville

Access & Difficulty: Hike-in & Scramble 5.0 miles RT/Strenuous
Elevation: Start at 2,800 feet; total loss 2,000 feet
Best Season: May to August

If you've hiked the well-maintained national recreation trail to Feather Falls, scrambled your way down steep slopes to Seven Falls, and still haven't had your fill of waterfalls in the Feather Falls Scenic Area, well... you have one more trip to take. And unless you're an ace kayaker willing to make the run down the Middle Fork of the Feather River, you have a long hike and an interesting river trek ahead of you.

The first time I tried to reach Curtain Falls, I was told by the Forest Service that the best way to get there was to rent a boat, motor it up the Middle Fork Feather river arm as far as possible, then tie it up and hike along the riverbank to the falls. What they didn't tell me is that the bank is steep granite—sometimes vertical granite—and that hiking it is treacherous and nearly impossible.

After that attempt, I got in touch with Dee Randolph, who runs DeeTours in the Feather Falls Scenic Area. Randolph said he never heard of anyone getting to Curtain Falls that way, and added that the 40-foot fall is best seen by kayaking in high water. But Randolph takes groups on foot to Curtain Falls every summer. He does it by leading them on a two-mile hike on the Dome Trail, descending 2,000 feet to the river canyon over two-plus miles. It's a steep trek.

It's also a scenic trek, skirting under 3,200-foot Bald Rock Dome. From the trailhead, you begin walking on an old skid trail that barrels down the ridge. In about 200 yards it leads to the actual start of the Dome Trail, which cuts off to your left. Then you simply follow the main trail, with no junctions or intersections to bother with, for two miles downhill. Views of both the river canyon below and the granite of Bald Rock Dome above are spectacular the whole way. In the spring, buckeye trees are in full bloom; their sweet scent wafts along the path with you.

The second mile of the Dome Trail is for those who are unafraid of heights. The Forest Service blasted the trail out of the canyon's granite wall, then installed railings to keep people from falling off the edge. In one section, where blasting was impossible, the trail makers built a steep, 75-foot-tall staircase and bolted it into the rock to bridge the trail.

Where the Dome Trail ends at the river's edge, you're still a half-mile downstream from Curtain Falls. Some people try to walk from here, but the granite walls are sheer, and footing is dicey. Accidents are reported every year. Instead, it's better to wade or swim, but the river current is strong even in late season. Randolph gets his tour clients across the river by supplying each of them with an inner tube, hooking the tubes to a rope, and letting the current carry them safely across. On the far side, a rough route leads upcanyon, via some rock

Curtain Falls

scrambling and inner-tubing down granite waterslides. It's great fun, but you must be prepared to get wet.

A half-mile of this partly-by-land, partly-by-water trekking brings you to the pool in front of Curtain Falls. At 40 feet high and at least 100 feet wide, Curtain is a formidable river fall. Top-notch kayakers make the run over its lip in springtime, but they're the brave and the few. It's not for everybody. Curtain's pool is almost as impressive as the fall itself, with a depth of at least 50 feet and an intense aquamarine hue. Some people have tried scuba-diving in the crystalline pool, but alas, no secret treasures have been found.

Randolph believes the waterfall is called Curtain Falls because its cliff is divided by a rock tongue. During heavy rain, when the river level rises, the tongue disappears and the curtains of water seem to close. Then when the rain stops and the river level drops, the tongue re-emerges and divides Curtain Falls' flow, giving the appearance of curtains opening.

A dynamited staircase on the fall's right side, probably left from ambitious miners in the late 1800s, runs up and over Curtain Falls. Ledges above the falls make perfect jumping platforms. While the sun is high, you can hang out and swim here in your own private paradise. Just be sure to save some energy for the return trip. It's easy to forget that after scrambling back downstream to the end of the Dome Trail, you have a two-mile hike and a 2,000-foot elevation gain ahead of you. Most important of all: Save some water for this part of the hike. It's completely exposed, and can be hot and dry in the afternoon.

Trip notes: There is no fee. For a map of Plumas National Forest, send $4 to USDA-Forest Service, 1323 Club Drive, Vallejo, CA 94592. For more information, contact Plumas National Forest, Feather River Ranger District, 875 Mitchell Avenue, Oroville, CA 95965; (530) 534-6500 or (530) 675-1146. Or phone Dee Randolph at DeeTours in Berry Creek; (888) DAY-HIKE or (530) 589-2750.

Directions: From Highway 70 in Oroville, take the Oroville Dam Boulevard exit (Highway 162) east and drive for 1.6 miles to Olive Highway/Highway 162. Turn right and drive for 17 miles on Highway 162 to Bald Rock Road on the right. (This is the western end of Bald Rock Road.) Turn right and drive five miles, then turn left on Zink Road. Drive three more miles until you reach a four-way intersection; continue straight across on Forest Service Road 21N51Y. Drive three miles to a fork in the road; take the left spur. In a few hundred feet, take the left spur to the Dome Trail trailhead.

42. FEATHER FALLS

Plumas National Forest
Off Highway 70 near Oroville

Access & Difficulty: Hike-in or Bike-in 7.4 to 9.8 miles RT/Moderate
Elevation: Start at 2,400 feet; total gain 1,000 feet
Best Season: April to October, but good year-round

Let's get the tricky part out of the way first. What river does Feather Falls fall on? Feather Falls falls on the Fall River, near Fall River's confluence with the Middle Fork of the Feather River. Despite its name, it doesn't fall on the Feather River.

It's easy to see why it's hard to get this right. So, all together now: Feather Falls falls on the Fall River.

Of course, few people concern themselves with river nomenclature while they're hiking the Feather Falls National Recreation Trail, because they're too busy having the time of their lives. Feather Falls is one of the most famous waterfalls in California outside of Yosemite, and that's because it has status: It's the sixth highest freefalling waterfall in the continental U.S. and the fourth highest in California. Its flow drops 640 feet, then continues for another half-mile till it joins the Middle Fork Feather River, which is dammed as Lake Oroville in these parts. (Dammed or damned, depending on how you look at it.)

The waterfall is so spectacular, it has a whole recreation area named after it—the 15,000-acre Feather Falls Scenic Area in Plumas National Forest. The land includes part of the Middle Fork Feather River canyon and three of the river's tributaries: Fall River, Little North Fork, and South Branch. Within its reaches are three other record-class waterfalls: Seven or South Branch Falls, Curtain Falls, and Brush Creek Falls. But Feather Falls outdoes them all.

A few options exist for hiking to the fall, all of them good. The trail is a loop: One side is short and steep; the other side is longer and more flat. After your first quarter-mile of walking, you reach a fork and it's decision time: Do you want to get to the falls faster but with a tougher climb, or slower and more gradually? The two routes join again a quarter-mile before the falls, so you have to ask yourself a similar question on the return trip.

My suggestion is to take the short way up (the left fork) and return on the longer trail. That makes a 9.8-mile round-trip, which combined with a couple hours of waterfall-watching, swimming, and picnicking with someone you love, makes about the most perfect day

I can imagine. If you need to shave a little time off, you can take the short route out and back, for a 7.4-mile round-trip.

You can visit any time; the Feather Falls Trail is accessible in all seasons. Although the waterfall and wildflowers are most dramatic in spring, the autumn colors make October an excellent time to visit.

Feather Falls

Summertime can be hot, but if you start early in the morning, you can beat the 95-degree afternoon heat and be rewarded with swimming holes above the fall. In late winter, a wondrous event happens every year near Frey Creek, about 1.7 miles from the trailhead: Ladybugs who have hibernated near the creek from November to January will suddenly wake up and take flight. Thousands of them can fill the air in a single day as they prepare to travel back to the Central Valley to feed. In the process, they alight on the arms and legs of passing hikers. It's an amazing and delightful scene to experience.

Although Feather Falls is in the northern Sierra Nevada foothills and the elevation is low, its trail is surprisingly shaded and lush. A great feature of this 2,400-foot elevation is the incredible speciation of plant life. Along the trail you pass 17 species of trees, including ponderosa pine, incense cedar, Douglas fir, black oak, canyon oak, madrone, bigleaf maple, white alder, bay, dogwood, and digger pine. They're joined by 20 kinds of shrubs, 11 types of vines, and 10 different ferns. If wildflowers are your bag, visit in March or April, when more than 180 species have been identified. These include purple shooting stars, scarlet Indian pinks, star tulips, Indian paintbrush, starflowers, western bleeding hearts, violets, wild ginger, bush monkeyflower, wild roses, and red clarkia.

Because it's a designated National Recreation Trail, the Feather Falls route is incredibly well-maintained, with posted trail markers every half-mile, letting you know exactly where you are. Bikes are allowed on the trail with a 10-mile-per-hour speed limit, but the route is far more popular with hikers. (If you're on a bike, you should take the easier side of the loop in both directions.)

Start walking from the parking lot trailhead and reach the start of the loop in an easy quarter-mile. Take the left fork (the short way), and drop elevation for the first two miles, crossing a bridge over Frey Creek. Be sure to look for ladybugs. Then parallel the creek, and come out to a stunning view of the Middle Fork Feather canyon and Bald Rock Dome. The granite dome rises 2,000 feet above the river canyon. It's a sacred meditation place for Maidu Native Americans.

After the dome vista, the trail starts to climb, and it continues to do so steadily between the two- and three-mile markers. Just after three miles, you reach a wooden bench and the junction where the two legs of the loop connect. They become one for the final half-mile ascent to the falls overlook. A couple of easy switchbacks bring you to a fenced viewpoint above the Middle Fork Feather; after a few more minutes of walking, you're at the left turnoff for the falls overlook.

Walk to the overlook before continuing uphill to the top of the falls. The trail is an elaborate series of short walkways that lead to the top of a granite outcrop jutting out into the middle of the canyon. There you get a straight-on view of Feather Falls and the Fall River canyon that is guaranteed to take your breath away.

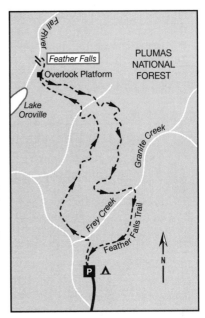

Feather is a horsetail-shaped fall. The first 100 feet are slightly slanted, somewhat like a cascade, then the whole thing dumps into freefall for 500 magnificent feet. Because the overlook platform situates you at nearly the same height as the top of the fall, you get an exciting vista of its entire length. Downstream from the fall, you can see the confluence of the Fall River with the Middle Fork Feather River, where boaters sometimes cruise up from Lake Oroville to get a look at Feather Falls.

When you're ready for a different view, head back to the main trail and continue toward the fall. A quarter-mile of walking puts you above Feather's crest, where several routes lead to terrific pools for swimming. Make sure you choose one that is back far enough so that you can't get swept into the current. The water is cold, but it feels incredibly refreshing after the climb.

If you choose the longer but easier trail for your return trip, be prepared for a smoothed-out grade, more like a serpentine. The trailmakers added a few curves and lengthened the route, making it suitable for mountain bikers and hikers with bad knees. Hiking the entire loop with the steep side up and the easy side down makes for a perfect 9.8-mile day-hike, with plenty of extra time for photography, skinny-dipping, berry-picking, picnicking, or just standing around at the overlook and grinning a lot.

Trip notes: There is no fee. For a map of Plumas National Forest, send $4 to USDA-Forest Service, 1323 Club Drive, Vallejo, CA 94592. For more information, contact Plumas National Forest, Feather River Ranger District, 875 Mitchell Avenue, Oroville, CA 95965; (530) 534-6500 or (530) 675-1146.

Directions: From Highway 70 in Oroville, take the Oroville Dam Boulevard exit (Highway 162) east and drive for 1.6 miles to Olive Highway/Highway 162. Turn right and drive for 6.5 miles on Highway 162. Turn right on Forbestown Road and drive for six miles. Turn left on Lumpkin Road and drive for 10.8 miles. Turn left at the sign for the Feather Falls Trail and drive 1.6 miles to the trailhead.

---

43. LITTLE JAMISON FALLS

Plumas National Forest/Plumas-Eureka State Park
Off Highway 89 near Graeagle

Access & Difficulty: Hike-in or Backpack 3.0 miles RT/Easy
Elevation: Start at 5,200 feet; total gain 500 feet
Best Season: May to July

Sometimes when you go looking for one thing, you wind up finding something even better. That's how it was for us at Plumas-Eureka State Park, when we set off on the Grass Lake Trail in search of lakes with trout. While we didn't catch any fish, we did find Little Jamison Falls, a freefalling cataract that in early season has the size and flow of a river fall.

The trail begins in the state park, then leaves the boundary line and enters Plumas National Forest. For that reason, you don't have to pay a day-use fee to hike here. That's one bonus, and when you get to the trailhead, you'll find more. Like the fact that the trail begins at the old Jamison gold mine, and some of its buildings are still standing in decent repair. You get an interesting glimpse into California mining history right at the trailhead: The mine was in operation from 1887 to 1919, producing gold for the Sierra Buttes Mining Company.

Bear left at the buildings, head uphill on the steep and rocky path, and follow Little Jamison Creek for the entire route. Pass a left fork for Smith Lake (a steep trail but worth the trip another time), then continue straight through a canopy of firs and pines till you leave the state park boundary. Ironically, as soon as you pass a sign noting that you are now in national forest, you enter an area of logged trees. Bummer.

Just an eighth of a mile further, you hear the sound of roaring water. Look for an unsigned trail spur on your right, which takes you to Little Jamison Creek's edge and 40-foot-high Little Jamison Falls. It's a surprisingly wide, dramatic drop, especially early in the year.

Since you've climbed up here, you might as well continue on for another five minutes to Grass Lake, elevation 5,842 feet, a scenic alpine lake surrounded by Jeffrey pine, lodgepole pine, and red fir. It has a few excellent campsites and many good picnic spots. Hike around to the west side of the lake for a stunning view of the water backed by surrounding craggy peaks. The trail also extends another one to two miles to Rock Lake, Jamison Lake, and Wades Lake, all excellent destinations for fishing, camping, and swimming.

Trip notes: There is no fee. A state park trail map is available at the park museum and office for $1. (The state park office is a half-mile past the trailhead access road on County Road A-14.) For a map of Plumas National Forest, send $4 to USDA-Forest Service, 1323 Club Drive, Vallejo, CA 94592. For more information, contact Plumas-Eureka State Park, 310 Johnsville Road, Blairsden, CA 96103; (530) 836-2380 or (530) 525-7232.

Directions: From Truckee, head north on Highway 89 for about 50 miles to Graeagle. At Graeagle, drive west on County Road A-14 for 4.5 miles to the Jamison Mine/Grass Lake access road on the left. Turn left and drive one mile, past Camp Lisa, to the trailhead parking area. The trailhead is on the far side of the lot, signed for Grass, Smith, Rock, Wades, and Jamison lakes.

44. HALSEY FALLS

Plumas National Forest
Off Highway 89 near Graeagle

Access & Difficulty: Hike-in 2.0 miles RT/Easy
Elevation: Start at 6,400 feet; total gain 100 feet
Best Season: May to July

Staying at Gray Eagle Lodge is my idea of the perfect vacation. The lodge has cozy cabins, a good restaurant, and access to all the hiking and fishing that anybody could want. But whether you stay there or just use the excellent trailhead a quarter-mile from the lodge, your first trip should be to pretty little Halsey Falls.

Find the Halsey Falls trail marker on the left side of the trailhead parking lot, and start walking upstream, following Gray Eagle Creek for your entire route. Shady conifer forest alternates with open areas and views of surrounding ridgelines along the way. One small climb takes you to the top of a low ridge directly behind Gray Eagle Lodge, but the rest of the hike is flat. You'll cross two small feeder streams, which empty into Gray Eagle Creek.

Halsey Falls

Although the trail markers can be a little confusing along this trail, sometimes greatly exaggerating the mileage, just follow the creek and you'll be fine. As you near one mile, your ears guide you to the sound of rushing water and the fall.

The roar of water grows louder and the air cooler as you come nearer. Standing close to 20-foot Halsey Falls, you can feel the breeze from its billowy cascade. If you want to cool off from your hike, climb on the rocks and fallen trees until you're underneath the spray.

The Gray Eagle trailhead offers many other hiking options, and you'll want to try them all. Although the trip to Halsey Falls is the easiest hike, a separate trail leads to Smith Lake in one steep mile, and the Halsey Falls trail continues to Long Lake and Grassy Lake, each about one mile beyond the falls.

Trip notes: There is no fee. For a map of Plumas National Forest, send $4 to USDA-Forest Service, 1323 Club Drive, Vallejo, CA 94592. For more information, contact Plumas National Forest, Beckwourth Ranger District, P.O. Box 7, Blairsden, CA 96103; (530) 836-2575.

Directions: From Truckee, drive north on Highway 89 for about 50 miles to Forest Service Road 24—Gold Lake Highway—and turn left. (Forest Service Road 24 is 1.3 miles south of Graeagle on Highway 89.) Drive five miles south on Road 24 to the sign for Gray Eagle Lodge. Turn right and drive three-tenths of a mile to the trailhead for Smith Lake and Halsey Falls, which is two-tenths of a mile before the lodge. The Halsey Falls Trail starts on the left side of the parking lot.

45. FRAZIER FALLS

**Plumas National Forest
Off Highway 89 near Graeagle**

Access & Difficulty: Hike-in 1.0 mile RT/Easy
Elevation: Start at 6,200 feet; total gain 50 feet
Best Season: May to July

Sure, Frazier Falls is one of the most famous landmarks in all of the Lakes Basin area. True, it gets visited by hundreds of people a day on peak weekends. I know I'm supposed to be jaded about celebrated waterfalls like this one, but Frazier Falls still gives me a thrill every time I see it. It's just that good.

Frazier is a 176-foot freefall with a total height of 248 feet if you include its lower cascade. (I estimated 250 feet, but someone far more anal retentive than I must have measured it.) The fall is big, but more importantly, it's dramatic; it has style. Its creek is incredibly flat and mild both above and below the falls. Frazier Creek is just a medium-sized stream channeling around and through granite. Then all of a sudden, its flow hits a big cliff and *whoosh!*—over it goes, creating a tremendous freefall.

The crest of Frazier Falls

Frazier Falls is similar in shape but not as large as Feather Falls in southern Plumas. (See the story on page 100.) In springtime, millions of gallons of water hurtle over the fall's granite lip, producing a convincing display of the power of melting snow. But by the Fourth of July, Frazier Falls may appear almost tame.

The walk to the fall's observation point is as delightful as the fall itself. It's an easy one-mile round-trip, which explains why it's so popular. Families love this walk. The trail is almost completely flat, and even restless toddlers are momentarily impressed by the sight of the giant waterfall.

From the parking lot, head east on the well-marked trail, surrounded by shiny, polished granite, ponderosa and Jeffrey pines, and pretty bunches of lupine and Indian paintbrush. Cross a footbridge over Frazier Creek, and gaze downstream. You'll notice the water seems to disappear over the edge—you can't hear it yet, but you're on top of the waterfall.

Loop around to Frazier Falls' overlook, a fenced-in platform across the creek canyon and 200 yards from the fall. The overlook has the best possible view of the fall's entire length. Check out the visitors' sign-in register to see how many people made the trek to Frazier that day, or write in a few comments yourself. When we visited in May, an earlier visitor had simply scribbled, "Holy snowmelt."

Trip notes: There is no fee. For a map of Plumas National Forest, send $4 to USDA-Forest Service, 1323 Club Drive, Vallejo, CA 94592. For more information, contact Plumas National Forest, Beckwourth Ranger District, P.O. Box 7, Blairsden, CA 96103; (530) 836-2575.

Directions: From Truckee, drive north on Highway 89 for about 50 miles to Forest Service Road 24—Gold Lake Highway—and turn left. (Forest Service Road 24 is 1.3 miles south of Graeagle on Highway 89.) Drive 8.4 miles south on Road 24 and turn left at the sign for Frazier Falls (on Old Gold Lake Road, directly across Road 24 from Gold Lake). Drive 1.5 miles north on the dirt road to the trailhead parking lot.

46. FERN FALLS
Plumas National Forest
Off Highway 89 near Graeagle

Access & Difficulty: Hike-in 0.25 mile RT/Easy
Elevation: Start at 6,200 feet; total gain 0 feet
Best Season: May to July

In an area as waterfall-laden as Plumas National Forest, Fern Falls isn't exactly an award-winner. On the other hand, if Fern Falls was in some other place in the state, it might be the centerpiece of its own park.

It's all relative. If you want splash and melodrama in Plumas, visit Feather Falls or Frazier Falls (see pages 100 and 107). If you want a quiet, watery place to have a picnic, with little chance of anybody else showing up, a trip to Fern Falls might suit you fine.

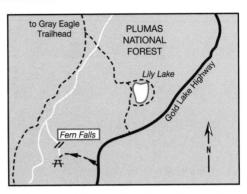

Take the drive down Gold Lake Highway and decide for yourself. The waterfall is marked by a sign noting "Fern Falls Picnic Area and Vista Trail," which is a bit of an exaggeration. The picnic area consists of merely two picnic tables, one near the road and one above the falls. But hey, who needs a picnic table to have a picnic? And the Vista Trail is not much of a trail, more like a footpath a few hundred feet long. But never mind.

Vista Trail takes you through big conifers, across a footbridge, and up to a granite knoll where you can view Fern Falls. From there, you can wander around on the rock slabs to get closer to the water. Fern Falls drops 15 feet over big boulders on the outlet creek from Grassy Lake, one mile upstream. From the waterfall, the bustling creek tumbles downstream till it joins with larger Gray Eagle Creek, which in turn flows downstream all the way to Graeagle and the Middle Fork of the Feather River. That gives you something to think about while you watch the cascading water.

If you're in the mood for a little more walking, you can get in your car and drive a half mile up the road to the Lily Lake Trailhead. A short jaunt of about 10 minutes will bring you to the edge of the lily-pad-covered lake. A path circles the lake, connecting with a trail from the Gray Eagle Trailhead, from which you can hike to Halsey Falls (see pages 105-106). You might as well make a day of it.

Trip notes: There is no fee. For a map of Plumas National Forest, send $4 to USDA-Forest Service, 1323 Club Drive, Vallejo, CA 94592. For more information, contact Plumas National Forest, Beckwourth Ranger District, P.O. Box 7, Blairsden, CA 96103; (530) 836-2575.

Directions: From Truckee, drive north on Highway 89 for about 50 miles to Forest Service Road 24—Gold Lake Highway—and turn left. (Forest Service Road 24 is 1.3 miles south of Graeagle on Highway 89.) Drive six miles south on Road 24 to a pullout marked "Fern Falls Picnic Area and Vista Trail."

47. LOVE'S FALLS

Tahoe National Forest
Off Highway 49 near Sierra City

Access & Difficulty: Hike-in 0.5 mile RT/Easy
  or Hike-in 4.5 miles RT/Moderate
Elevation: Start at 4,400 feet; total gain 600 feet (4.5-mile RT)
Best Season: May to August

You have a choice. Do you wanna take the easy way or the not-so-easy way to Love's Falls? Both routes are good, and the destination is terrific, so you can't miss however you go. The easy way requires only a 10-minute walk on a nearly level trail. The not-so-easy way is a two-mile up-and-down route that will wake up your cardiovascular system. Both routes lead to a great waterfall vista with terrific fishing and picnicking spots. It's your call.

For the easy way, look for the Pacific Crest Trail (PCT) signs on Highway 49, just east of Sierra City. (There are small markers on both sides of the highway, where the trail crosses.) Start walking on the PCT as it parallels Highway 49, heading southeast. In a few

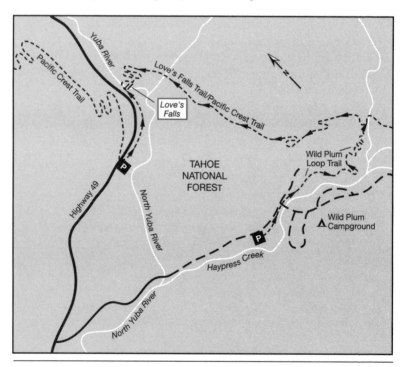

Love's Falls

minutes of easy walking, you're at the PCT bridge over the North Yuba River, perched right on top of the best cascade of Love's Falls.

Love's is a typical river waterfall, wide and full of white water, but its biggest drop is only about 20 feet high. It's surrounded by huge boulders and a narrow gorge cut through volcanic rock, which forms deep pools. While you're still on the bridge, be sure to look up-canyon as well as downstream at the falls. The river gorge makes the water appear gold and green from all the minerals in the rock, a gloriously colorful sight.

You can scramble down to the fall from the far side of the bridge and choose a spot near its pool for fishing or picnicking, but you have to get there early in the day. Since Love's Falls is so close to the road, the small beach area under the bridge usually gets spoken for quickly.

For the longer, more aerobic route to Love's Falls, start at the Wild Plum Campground. If you're not camping there, you must park at the trailhead parking lot a quarter-mile before the camp, then follow the access trail toward the camp. Begin hiking at the trailhead on the west side of the Haypress Creek bridge, which is signed as "Haypress Trail, Pacific Crest Trail, Wild Plum Loop." Off you go through a mixed forest of cedars, firs, and hardwoods. Walk along a flat section of trail paralleling Haypress Creek for about a half-mile, then start switchbacking up a ridge. When you reach the top, check out the stellar view of the back side of the Sierra Buttes. If you're lucky, they'll still be crowned with snow.

Meet up with the PCT, also signed for Love's Falls, and turn left. One-and-a-half miles of well-graded trail, with some downhill switchbacks at its end, leads you to the bridge over the falls.

Trip notes: There is no fee. For a map of Tahoe National Forest, send $4 to USDA-Forest Service, 1323 Club Drive, Vallejo, CA 94592. For more information, contact Tahoe National Forest, Downieville Ranger District, 15924 Highway 49, Camptonville, CA 95922; (530) 288-3231.

Directions: From Truckee, drive north on Highway 89 for about 30 miles to Highway 49 at Sattley. Drive west on Highway 49 for 15 miles toward Sierra City. For the shorter hike, watch for the Pacific Crest Trail signs along Highway 49, exactly one-half mile east of Nevada Drive in Sierra City. Park along the road in any of the nearby pullouts. For the longer hike, drive to the trailhead at Wild Plum Campground in Sierra City (see directions for Great Eastern Ravine Falls in the following story).

48. GREAT EASTERN RAVINE FALLS

Tahoe National Forest
Off Highway 49 near Sierra City

Access & Difficulty: Hike-in 6.0 miles RT/Moderate
Elevation: Start at 4,400 feet; total gain 1,500 feet
Best Season: May to July

Great Eastern Ravine is a waterfall to see if you like to hike. Hike uphill, that is. The trail that takes you there doesn't fool around—it just climbs nonstop from Wild Plum Campground for three miles, then levels out just before the fall. Luckily, the trail is good, the scenery is beautiful, and the sound of Haypress Creek accompanies you the whole way.

You can reach the fall in about an hour and a half of climbing.

Start by finding the Haypress Creek trailhead in Wild Plum Camp; there are two, but the best one for this hike is on the east side of the camp. It climbs more gradually at the start. Walk into Wild Plum, crossing a road bridge over Haypress Creek. Then walk to your left, through the upper campground loop, until you reach a forked dirt road. Take the upper road which leads uphill and out of camp. Watch carefully for a left turnoff onto single-track in a half-mile. (There's a trail sign posted high on a tree, but it's easy to miss.) Follow the single-track through forest for a half-mile, crossing a footbridge over Haypress Creek. (Parts of this route are signed as the Pacific Crest Trail and Wild Plum Loop.) Check out the incredible view of the back of the Sierra Buttes.

Shortly after the bridge, take the right fork, which is signed as the Haypress Creek Trail. There are no more junctions after this point. Just climb, first through a rocky, open area, then a mixed conifer forest, then on an old logging road through some private property. The fragrant scent of white- and blue-flowered ceanothus bushes envelopes you in early season. Haypress Creek Trail has some very sunny, open areas, so bring plenty of water with you. You're too high above the creek to be able to access it for water.

The route veers right on a dirt road, then eventually leaves the private property and re-enters National Forest land, becoming single-track again. Haypress Creek Trail's only drawback is that it's routed on logging roads too much of the time. When the trail becomes single-track again, life suddenly seems better.

The route finally goes flat at 2.8 miles, just before you reach the fall. The cascade on Great Eastern Ravine is easy to spot, because your trail crosses right over it. It's 20 feet tall and narrow, a tumbling stream of white. A big flat rock a few yards in front is the perfect place to sit and have a snack.

An award-winner? No, but you've got one near-certain guarantee: If you've climbed all the way up here, you're probably going to have the waterfall all to yourself.

Trip notes: There is no fee. For a map of Tahoe National Forest, send $4 to USDA-Forest Service, 1323 Club Drive, Vallejo, CA 94592. For more information, contact Tahoe National Forest, Downieville Ranger District, 15924 Highway 49, Camptonville, CA 95922; (530) 288-3231.

Directions: From Truckee, drive north on Highway 89 for about 30 miles to Highway 49 at Sattley. Drive west on Highway 49 for 15 miles toward Sierra City. Turn left on Wild Plum Road, one mile east of Sierra City. Drive 1.2 miles on Wild Plum Road to the trailhead parking area, one-quarter mile before Wild Plum Campground. Begin hiking at the trail marker on the left side of the lot. This access trail leads you to the camp in a quarter-mile.

MORE WATERFALLS

in Plumas, Lassen, & Modoc

•The Cascades, on the Feather River near Keddie. A half-mile hike from Highway 70. For more information, phone Plumas National Forest, Greenville Ranger District, at (530) 284-7126.

Tahoe &
Gold Country

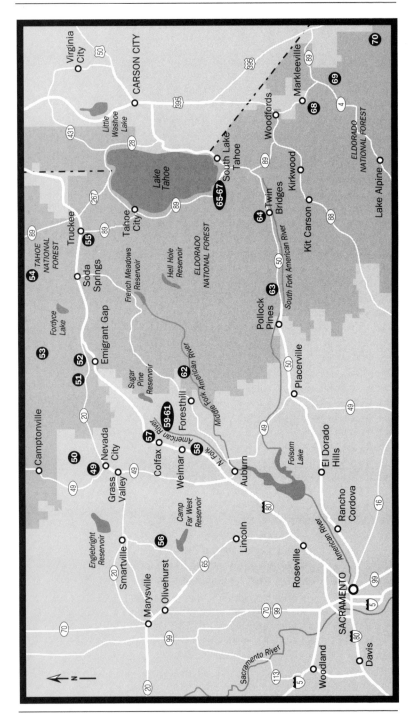

49. RUSH CREEK FALLS

South Yuba River State Park
Off Highway 49 near Nevada City

Access & Difficulty: Hike-in or Wheelchair 2.0 miles RT/Easy
Elevation: Start at 2,600 feet; total gain 0 feet
Best Season: April to July

The problem with most wheelchair-accessible trails is simple: They're paved. Although this may seem necessary, and even beneficial, trail users often say that paving the ground takes away from the experience of being in the outdoors. In fact, most people come to the outdoors to get away from artificial materials like pavement.

So for wheelchair-users, the South Yuba Independence Trail is a stroke of genius and a blessing. It's the first identified wheelchair wilderness trail in the United States, and it leads a total of six miles on hard-packed dirt and over wooden flumes along the Yuba River canyon. We came to see it because of the promise of a waterfall, but what kept us hiking further was how splendid the route is.

Everything about this trail has been done right. A nonprofit group called Sequoya Challenge looks after the trail, in partnership with California State Parks. It was originally built in 1859, not as a hiking trail but as a canal to carry water from the South Yuba River to a hydraulic mining site in Smartville, 25 miles downstream. Consisting of rock-lined ditches with adjacent paths for ditch tenders, plus wooden flumes (bridges) allowing passage over creeks, the canal followed a nearly level contour along the steep hillsides above the South Yuba.

Since 1970, the abandoned water canal has been undergoing a transformation, with the old flumes being upgraded and rebuilt, and new sections of trail being opened up for all-access hiking. In many places, two trails run parallel, one for wheelchairs and one for hiking legs. Outhouses built for wheelchair users are positioned along the trail, as well as accessible platforms for picnicking and fishing on Rush Creek.

At the trailhead, you have a choice of hiking east or west. (The trail does not loop; if you want to walk the whole route, you must go out-and-back in both directions.) To see the waterfall, head to the right (west). In the first 100 yards from the parking area, you must duck your head and pass through a tunnel under Highway 49. Rush Creek Falls is exactly one mile from here. Along the way, you walk

One of Rush Creek's cascades

through a densely wooded area and pass a roofed platform with a scenic overlook of the South Yuba River canyon.

Shortly you leave the forest and come out to an amazing cliff-hanging flume, its wooden boards making a horseshoe-shaped turn around the back of a canyon. Above and below it, Rush Creek Falls flows over polished granite. The waterfall has many tiers. The best place to see its lower cascades is from the eastern edge of the flume, before you reach the creek itself. The flume forms a bridge just above the tallest drop of the falls, a double tier that's 50 feet tall.

This area is known as the Rush Creek Ramp at Flume 28, where volunteers built an intricate wooden ramp that circles down from the flume to the edge of Rush Creek, above the main drop of the fall. Several smaller cascades tumble upstream of the ramp, near a picnicking and fishing platform that's in place in summer months.

If you choose to continue beyond the falls, you can go another mile to Jones Bar Road, but then you must turn around and hike back, making a four-mile round-trip. You can also hike the eastern section of trail from the parking area, a five-mile round-trip that includes more flumes, views of the river and foothills, and springtime wildflowers.

Trip notes: There is no fee. For more information and a map/brochure, contact South Yuba River State Park, Bridgeport Ranger Station; (530) 432-2546 or (530) 273-3884.

Directions: From Interstate 80 at Auburn, drive north on Highway 49 for

27 miles to Nevada City. Continue on Highway 49 for eight miles past Nevada City to the trailhead parking area along the highway (just before the South Yuba River bridge). Park at the large paved pullout—it's well-signed but comes up fast.

50. YUBA RIVER FALLS

South Yuba River State Park
Off Highway 49 near Nevada City

Access & Difficulty: Hike-in 1.2 miles RT/Moderate
Elevation: Start at 2,600 feet; total gain 200 feet
Best Season: May to September

The Yuba River is one of the most beautiful rivers in Northern California. It's set in a steep, rugged canyon filled with oaks, bays, and gray pines. Water-polished rock creates pool after pool of liquid emerald water interrupted by flowing cascades. The remarkable color of the water is what sticks in your mind long after you've left the riverbanks; it's an alluring, gem-like green you can see clear through.

Fly fisherman comb these river pools for trout and gold prospectors ply the waters for their prize. But the river may be best loved by swimmers, who seek out its deep stretches and smooth granite banks for long days in the sun. If you happen to enjoy a good waterfall with your swimming hole, you're in luck.

The adventure begins at Edwards Crossing, where North Bloomfield Road out of Nevada City crosses the South Yuba River. This stretch of land is managed by South Yuba River State Park, so signs are posted for gold diggers stating "Pans and Hands" only. No mechanized dredging is allowed, which keeps the river pure.

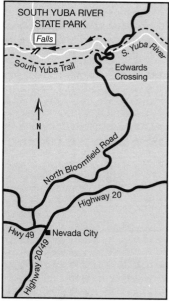

Park at the wide pullouts on the south side of the bridge, then walk across the bridge to the north side and take the trail to the left, leading west. Follow the path along the river's north side, heading upriver. The footpath is a little rough in places and it has some steep dropoffs. Watch your footing

Yuba River Falls

and you'll be fine. The worst problem is not the rough trail but rather the spectacular color of the Yuba River, which makes it impossible to keep your eyes on the path.

In a little more than a half mile, a major stream cascades down across the trail and into the river. The trail leads upstream (away from the river) to a suitable place where you can cross the stream by rockhopping. As soon as you land on the other side, leave the trail and cut down to the river.

Somewhat hidden by the cliff-like riverbank, the stream forms a 20-foot free-falling waterfall that plunges into the Yuba River. Imagine the coldest shower you've ever taken. Even on the hottest summer day, that's what this waterfall feels like. Most visitors wade into its pool, dunk their heads under the cascading flow, then yell like hell when they feel how cold the water is.

Right alongside the waterfall is a deep, clear, 40-yard-long pool in the Yuba River, where medium-sized trout and water-loving bathers while away their afternoons. Bring a picnic and your towel. One thing to consider: On our trip, we found that this pool's bathers were evenly divided between those wearing bathing suits and those wearing birthday suits. Just a warning, in case you have strong opinions about such things.

Trip notes: There is no fee. For more information and a map/brochure, contact South Yuba River State Park, Bridgeport Ranger Station; (530) 432-2546 or (530) 273-3884.

Directions: From Highway 20 in Nevada City, take the Highway 49 exit. Drive three-tenths of a mile and turn right on North Bloomfield Road. Drive a half-mile and turn right again, staying on North Bloomfield Road. Drive seven miles to Edwards Crossing, the bridge crossing the Yuba River. Take the footpath on the northwest side, leading west.

51. SCOTCHMAN CREEK FALLS

Tahoe National Forest
Off Highway 20 near Washington

Access & Difficulty: Scramble 1.0 mile RT/Moderate
Elevation: Start at 2,700 feet; total gain 50 feet
Best Season: May to August

A trip to the town of Washington on the Fourth of July is like stepping on to a movie set or walking backward in time to the America of the thirties or forties. The white clapboard buildings look scrubbed clean. Flags are flying high. On a hot summer day, everybody is either at the general store buying ice cream or floating around on inner tubes in the Yuba River.

It figures that a place this good would have a waterfall.

To see it, take a drive through the town of Washington, then continue beyond it to the Keleher Picnic Area on the South Yuba. A short walk from the parking lot takes you past the picnic tables and down to the river's edge, which is set in a beautiful canyon with a colorful array of rocks and water. Most visitors are too concerned with trout fishing, gold panning, swimming, and keeping cool to be scrambling around looking for waterfalls, but if that's what you came for, there's plenty of time for the other activities later.

To find the waterfall, you've got to head to your left (upstream) and cross the river. The only way to do it is to swim or wade. Old shoes are highly recommended. If you wear old tennis shoes instead of hiking boots, you can alternate hiking and rock scrambling with swimming and wading. Going barefoot is not a good idea, because the rocks along the river's edge are quite jagged.

Cross the river as soon as possible after leaving the picnic area, because the land on the east side of Keleher is private property. The owner spends countless hours chasing people off his land, particularly the fine cliffs at the river's edge. Local kids have learned that those cliffs make excellent jumping-off points for cannonball splashes into a 20-foot-deep pool. That splashing sound probably drives the land-owner crazy all summer long.

Swim, wade, or scramble over rocks on the south shore for about a half-mile to the spot where Scotchman Creek feeds into the river. Back in this rocky canyon, tucked out of sight, are the falls. Now your old shoes will really come in handy; you must climb up the granite streambed, which is often slippery. Ten minutes of scrambling will bring you to a series of cascades molded into the rock, and to a multitude of places to sit and watch the crystal water splash and fall. Some people swim in the pools above the falls, but the water here is much colder than in the Yuba. This canyon gets very little sunlight.

When you're ready, it's a short scramble back to the river. And now that you've seen the waterfall, there's still plenty of time to paddle around in the swimming hole, study the small trout in the clear water, or park yourself in an inner tube with an ice cream bar.

Trip notes: There is no fee. For a map of Tahoe National Forest, send $4 to USDA-Forest Service, 1323 Club Drive, Vallejo, CA 94592. For more information, contact Tahoe National Forest, Nevada City Ranger District, 631 Coyote Street, Nevada City, CA 95959; (530) 265-4531.

Directions: From Auburn, drive east on Interstate 80 for 40 miles to the Highway 20 exit. Drive northwest on Highway 20 for 13.5 miles to the turnoff for Washington Road on the right (shortly past Skillman Group Camp). Turn north on Washington Road and drive 6.5 miles, passing through the town of Washington, then crossing the bridge over the Yuba River. Almost immediately, take the right fork on to Maybert Road. Drive three-quarters of a mile and turn right at the Keleher Picnic Area.

52. BEAR RIVER FALLS

PG & E Bear Valley Recreation Area
Off Highway 20 near Interstate 80

Access & Difficulty: Hike-in or Wheelchair 1.0 mile RT/Easy
Elevation: Start at 4,500 feet; total gain 20 feet
Best Season: April to July

The Pacific Gas and Electric Company has done a good deed in the form of the PG & E Sierra Discovery Trail at Bear Valley, where everyone, regardless of hiking ability, can take a pleasant loop trip that culminates at Bear River's waterfall.

Although the fall is only rated a 6, mostly due to its small size, the trail is a 10. The surface is pavement and gravel with some boardwalk sections, all of which are suitable for wheelchairs and baby strollers. The one-mile loop packs in a lot of information about Bear Valley's ecosystems, wildlife, geology, and cultural history. It offers far more than a typical "this is a sugar pine; this is a Jeffrey pine" interpretive trail, although you will learn to identify some trees here—various pines as well as willows, white alders, and incense cedars.

The walk begins at the parking lot, where there is an information kiosk that explaining the geology of the Sierra Nevada and the life of the Maidu Indians who lived here before white settlers arrived. From the kiosk, you bear left, following a boardwalk over a meadow that is green with corn lilies in the spring. At the bridge crossing over the Bear River, visitors eager to reach the waterfall immediately can head left, and those with more patience can head right and loop around to it. You might as well walk the whole loop—it's short, pretty, and educational.

Bear River Falls

The falls are only 12 feet high, but about 15 feet wide, and completely surrounded by big-leaf maples and alders. The river drops in a solid block of water, and if you stay and watch for a few minutes, you're sure to see a water ouzel flitting in and out of the fall. A plaque at the overlook describes the life of the water ouzel or dipper, the only American songbird that can swim below the surface of the water. They make their nests on rocky ledges behind waterfalls.

The wildflowers along this trail are best in June and July, but the waterfall is best even earlier. If you can, time your trip for just after the snow has melted in Bear Valley.

Trip notes: There is no fee. For more information, contact PG&E Recreation Areas at (916) 386-5164. Or visit their website at www.pge.com/customer_services/other/rec_areas/

Directions: From Auburn, drive east on Interstate 80 for 40 miles to the Highway 20 exit. Drive west on Highway 20 for 4.3 miles to Bowman Lake Road. Turn right and drive six-tenths of a mile to the Sierra Discovery Trail parking lot on the left side of the road.

53. BOWMAN LAKE FALLS
(Canyon Creek Falls, Sawmill Falls)
Tahoe National Forest
Off Highway 20 near Interstate 80

Access & Difficulty: Hike-in 0.8 mile RT/Moderate
Elevation: Start at 5,700 feet; total gain 500 feet
Best Season: June to October

Everybody has their own name for the waterfall that drops into Bowman Lake. Although the waterfall falls on Canyon Creek, almost nobody calls it Canyon Creek Falls. Instead, it's usually called Bowman Lake Falls, or sometimes Sawmill Falls after nearby Sawmill Lake. Canyon Creek is Sawmill Lake's outlet stream and Bowman Lake's inlet stream.

Call it what you like, this is a spectacular 80-foot cascade that carves its way down a granite cliff. Although it forms some gorgeous, clear pools, the water is bitter cold for swimming, even in late summer and autumn.

You first glimpse the falls as you drive the dirt road that runs alongside huge, deep blue Bowman Lake, a popular reservoir for camping and fishing. The dirt road starts out smooth but gets rougher as you go, although passenger cars can frequently make the trip in good weather. As you drive along Bowman's shoreline, look to the lake's eastern end to spot the cascade tumbling down the granite slope. (You won't see it until you're about two-thirds of the way along the lakeshore.) At the far end of the lake, park your car near the sandy wash where the lake peters out and a feeder stream pours in. (This area is often used for camping or as a put-in spot for car-top boats.)

Don't try to follow the lakeshore to reach the falls; although this seems logical, it's actually longer and more difficult. (The waterfall is set back about 200 yards from the lakeshore. After the main cascade, the stream runs fairly level for the last 200 yards to the lake.) Instead, walk across the wash, rockhopping across one of the lake's inlet streams, Jackson Creek. Then make a beeline due south through the forest, passing a primitive campsite and heading up and over a small ridge. You should be able to discern a primitive use trail to keep you on track. If not, just keep heading for the sound of the falls. You'll cross an area with heavy deadfall and reach a small, 15 by 15 foot meadow. Before you know it, you'll come out about 100 feet below the main cascade. The entire walk should take only about 15 minutes from the wash where you left your car.

Hike upstream to get closer to the fall. You can follow the granite slabs along the streambed or take the use trail higher up on the slope. If you do the latter, you'll have to fight your way through some pretty scratchy manzanita. From any standpoint, your main view is of the last 50 feet of the cascade; another 30 feet of white water is obscured above it. More aggressive

Bowman Lake Falls

climbing will take you to the upper cascade, but be sure to exercise caution on the slick granite. Downstream are many smaller cascades and good swimming holes where the water is more placid.

Trip notes: There is no fee. For a map of Tahoe National Forest, send $4 to USDA-Forest Service, 1323 Club Drive, Vallejo, CA 94592. For more information, contact Tahoe National Forest, Nevada City Ranger District, 631 Coyote Street, Nevada City, CA 95959; (530) 265-4531.

Directions: From Auburn, drive east on Interstate 80 for 40 miles to the Highway 20 exit. Drive west on Highway 20 for 4.3 miles to Bowman Lake Road. Turn right and drive 15 miles to the western edge of Bowman Lake (the road turns to dirt after the first 10 miles and may require a high-clearance vehicle). Continue driving along the edge of the lake to its eastern end; you'll see the falls flowing down into the lake. Park just off the road in the sandy wash area at the east end of the reservoir. (People launch kayaks and car-top boats in this area.) Walk across the rocky wash, heading south, to access the falls.

54. WEBBER FALLS

Tahoe National Forest
Off Highway 89 near Sierraville

Access & Difficulty: Scramble 0.25 mile RT/Easy
Elevation: 6,800 feet
Best Season: May to September

A thousand thank-yous to the Louisiana Pacific Lumber Company for allowing day-use on their private property at Webber Falls. Their rules are clearly posted at the informal dirt parking lot: No camping and no fires. Fair enough. But swimming and jumping in the waterfall pool are okay, and on any summer weekend, you're bound to see plenty of people doing just that.

Webber Falls is a beautiful double waterfall with two big drops and a deep pool in between. The top fall is 25 feet tall and 35 feet wide; the second drop is more dramatic—about 80 feet tall and 25 feet wide. While the top fall and its big pool can be easily seen from the edge of the creek, a few feet from the parking area, it takes some careful footing along steep canyon walls to get a good look at the bigger, lower fall. It can be done from both sides of the creek, although the ground is very unstable. Use good judgement.

The top of Webber Falls

Most folks just walk the few yards downhill from the parking area to the near side of the big pool. Some folks rockhop over the top of the waterfall and make their way to the far side, where the best rocks for diving are; others just jump in and swim around on the near side. On the Saturday we visited, there were about 30 people, mostly kids of various ages, taking turns diving into the big pool in between the upper and lower fall. And everybody we saw, every single person, was smiling. Thanks again, Louisiana Pacific.

Trip notes: There is no fee. For a map of Tahoe National Forest, send $4 to USDA-Forest Service, 1323 Club Drive, Vallejo, CA 94592. For more information, contact Tahoe National Forest, Sierraville Ranger District, P.O. Box 95, Sierraville, CA 96126; (530) 994-3401.

Directions: From Truckee, drive north on Highway 89 for 14 miles, then turn west on Road 07, signed for Independence Lake and Webber Lake, and drive 6.6 miles. Watch for the Lake of the Woods turnoff on the right, then turn left just beyond it on an unsigned dirt road. Turn left again on another unsigned dirt road, drive about 50 feet, then turn right into the dirt parking area. (You will travel about 200 yards off Road 07.)

55. HEATH FALLS

Tahoe National Forest
Off Interstate 80 near Soda Springs

Access & Difficulty: Hike-in 10.0 miles RT/Strenuous
Elevation: Start at 6,600 feet; total loss 1,700 feet
Best Season: May to July

A hike to Heath Falls is like going on a vacation on your credit card. You can have all the fun you want, but when you return home, you gotta pay up.

That's because the trip to the Heath Falls Overlook is downhill nearly all the way, dropping 1,700 feet over the course of five miles, through scenery that is so stunning you'll snap pictures, grin wide smiles at your hiking companions, and sing happy hiking songs as you go. Five miles never seemed so easy. But alas, eventually it's time for the return trip, a long and steady climb which lasts two to three long hours.

The trail begins at the dam between the two Cascade Lakes, the first of many lakes you'll pass on this trip. See that imposing chunk of rock straight ahead that juts out high above everything else around it? That's 7,704-foot Devil's Peak, and you'll head straight toward it, then lateral around its left (east) side. You'll be seeing a lot of it in the first two miles.

Walk across the dam and spillway, then pick up the trail through the lodgepole pine forest, heading to your right at a sign for the North Fork American River. (The left fork drops down to Long Lake, a nice side trip.) You'll ascend slightly for the first mile, as you leave the trees and enter into polished granite country, all the while getting better and better views of Devil's Peak.

The first two miles of trail can be characterized in three words: lakes, granite, vistas. Not only do you pass the Cascade Lakes and shortly thereafter, Long Lake on your left, but half a dozen more lakes follow. They're small and unnamed, so you can name them anything you like. Granite surrounds you; this land is classic glacial moraine, where glaciers moved through and left mounds of rock in their wake. Watch for trail cairns to keep you on the right path. Few trees can grow in this territory, so the views are wide-reaching, not just of nearby Devil's Peak but also of far-off peaks to the north and east.

When you reach the southeast flank of Devil's Peak at 2.2 miles, you're in for a terrain change: Suddenly you move into a thickly forested area, parallel a small creek, and then head into a sweet glen of aspens, ferns, vine maples, and corn lilies mixed in among the giant conifers. You may see some evidence of logging here; much of this

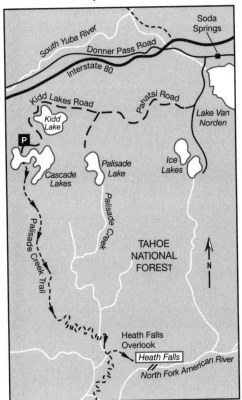

land is private property that belongs to a lumber company. Luckily, they haven't cut much.

The downhill steepens and the trail begins some gentle switchbacks, dropping toward the American River Canyon. You're so deep in forest—mostly cedars, firs, and pines—that you cannot see the canyon unless you go off-trail and climb onto high rocks. Even then, you can't see all the way down to the river. You're still too far off.

At 4.25 miles, after a long downhill stint through the woods, you reach the Palisade Creek Bridge. Cross it, and in about 300 yards, there's a trail junction for the Heath Falls Overlook Trail heading east. Don't miss the fork; it's not always signed. Now it's only a half-mile further (still downhill) to the overlook of Heath Falls on the North Fork American. Although the entire trail makes for excellent hiking any time it's snow-free, Heath Falls is only impressive in late spring and early summer, before the river level drops. The overlook is quite a distance from the fall, which is sheltered deep in the canyon, but you can still hear and see it thundering over rock cliffs and into big pools.

After soaking in the scenery for as long as you wish, have a snack and drink some water to prepare yourself for the long uphill return trip. Unfortunately, you can't camp here and put off the return till tomorrow. The overlook is on the boundary line between Forest Service land and private property, and camping is not allowed. The land surrounding the waterfall is also private property, so exploring any closer than the overlook is *verboten*. There's nothing left to do but head uphill and pay that credit card bill.

Trip notes: There is no fee. For a map of Tahoe National Forest, send $4 to USDA-Forest Service, 1323 Club Drive, Vallejo, CA 94592. For more information, contact Tahoe National Forest, Truckee Ranger District, 10342 Highway 89 North, Truckee, CA 96161; (530) 587-3558.

Directions: From Auburn, drive east on Interstate 80 for 55 miles to Soda Springs. Take the Soda Springs/Norden exit and follow Old Highway 40 east for eight-tenths of a mile to Soda Springs Road. Turn south (right) and drive for another eight-tenths of a mile to Pahatsi Road. Turn right. Pahatsi Road turns to dirt in two-tenths mile, and its name changes to Kidd Lakes Road. At 1.5 miles, reach a fork and continue straight for 2.5 more miles, passing Kidd Lake on your left, and the Royal Gorge Devil's Lookout Warming Hut on your right. (Take the left fork after the warming hut; it's a half-mile further.) The trailhead is on the north side of Cascade Lakes, signed as Palisade Creek Trail.

56. DRY CREEK FALLS
Spenceville Wildlife Area
Off Highway 20 near Marysville

Access & Difficulty: Hike-in or Bike-in 5.0 miles RT/Easy
Elevation: Start at 400 feet; total gain 100 feet
Best Season: November to May

From the first autumn rain till midsummer, Dry Creek is anything but dry. Because the creek is located in the middle of arid oak-and-grassland country in the Central Valley, it's surprising that

Dry Creek Falls

Dry Creek keeps a steady flow of water year-round. An even greater surprise is that although the terrain it traverses is mostly flat, the creek possesses a steep and narrow rock gorge which forms two sizable waterfalls.

Access to Dry Creek Falls is through Spenceville Wildlife Area, a place that is seldom visited by hikers but frequently visited by hunters and equestrians. Leashed dogs are allowed in the refuge, and horses and bikes are allowed on the fire roads. A small campground is located near the end of Spenceville Road, shortly before the start of the trail to the falls.

Don't be put off by Dry Creek Falls' trailhead, which is a blocked-off, nearly worn-out bridge at the end of Spenceville Road. At one time, you could drive across this bridge over Dry Creek, but those days are long gone. When you walk across it, watch out for gaping holes that have been burned in some of the planks.

Turn right on the dirt road immediately following the bridge and hike eastward. Dry Creek is on your right, gurgling over rounded rocks. The route is wide, flat, and easy, winding through open grasslands and stands of white, valley, and canyon oaks. When the white oaks' leaves drop in winter, you see that their branches are completely shrouded with lime-colored lichens. The creek has more dense foliage; willows and alders line its banks.

Keep on the lookout for wild turkeys. We saw a large flock of them, as well as a couple of handsome ring-necked pheasants, scurrying across the trail.

Stay on this main road, ignoring any side trails, for just shy of a mile, then bear right and hike south on another dirt road. (The left fork is gated off; the right fork is wide open.) The trail begins to descend slightly, and at 2.5 miles from the trailhead, you'll notice a large flat clearing on your right, alongside Dry Creek. Shortly after this clearing, side trails branch off from the main trail, and if you follow any of them you wind up alongside the creek and downstream of Dry Creek's rocky gorge. The first waterfall is about 30 feet tall, pouring through a notch in the rounded rock. It's somewhat difficult to get a full-length view of it. If you scramble around, you can find some good picnicking spots on the rocky, serpentine outcrops above the creek.

A more impressive fall awaits about 100 yards upstream, this one dropping 60 feet into an immense pool. It freefalls, then hits a slanted ledge, then freefalls again, creating an interesting angular shape. The trail side of the cliff is barricaded with a 50-yard-long chain-link fence, so you can view the fall without plummeting over the edge. A sign warns against diving off the cliffs, but it's hard to believe that anyone would try it. It's a long, scary drop to the pool.

At the upper fall, the dirt road you were following joins the side trails along the creek, so you can simply backtrack on the road for your homeward trip. At one time, this road continued along Dry Creek, but it eroded away long ago, and now stops at the waterfall overlook.

Trip notes: There is no fee. Free maps of Spenceville Wildlife Area are available at information signposts in the refuge. For more information, contact Spenceville Wildlife Area, c/o Oroville Wildlife Area, California Department of Fish and Game, (530) 538-2236.

Directions: From Marysville, drive east on either Highway 20 or Hammonton-Smartville Road for approximately 15 miles to Smartville, then turn right (south) on Smartville Road. Drive 4.5 miles to Waldo Road and bear left on to the gravel road. Follow Waldo Road for 2.1 miles to Spenceville Road, then turn left and drive two miles to the end of the road at a blocked-off bridge. Park by the bridge and hike across.

57. STEVENS CREEK FALLS

BLM Folsom Resource Area
Off Interstate 80 near Colfax

Access & Difficulty: Hike-in 3.0 miles RT/Easy
Elevation: Start at 2,500 feet; total loss 600 feet
Best Season: April to July

The little gold country town of Colfax is the secret land of waterfalls. It's only a couple of exits off Interstate 80, and the town doesn't look like much from the road, but if you take any of Colfax's side roads or trails down into the American River canyon, you'll be on your way to a waterfall.

The Stevens Creek Trail, which leads 4.5 miles one-way to the North Fork of the American River, passes by one of my favorite Colfax falls. To reach it, you need only hike 1.5 miles down the trail to where it crosses Stevens Creek. If you have the time and inclination, however, you should explore further, and follow the trail all the way to the North Fork, where there are terrific swimming holes.

Keep in mind that the trail is downhill all the way. If you're only going as far as the waterfall, you'll have a 600-foot gain on your return to the trailhead, spread out over 1.5 miles. It will get you puffing. If you hike all the way to the river, you'll have a 1,200-foot gain on the return, spread out over 4.5 miles, which will really get you puffing. Still, it's great fun. Just be sure to bring plenty of water with you, and hike the trail as early in the year as possible, before it gets too hot.

The Stevens Creek Trail requires a small leap of faith, however. When you get out of your car at the trailhead, you're inundated with highway noise from nearby I-80. The sound follows you for the first

Stevens Creek Falls

few minutes of trail, and it doesn't exactly make for a wilderness experience. But keep moving, because the trail quickly drops below the highway, and the sound of rushing 18-wheelers is soon replaced by the twittering of birds and rustling of leaves.

Unquestionably the best time to hike here is the spring, not only because that's when the waterfall is at its best, but also because that's when the wildflowers in the Sierra foothills are the most abundant. On the Stevens Creek Trail in spring, you'll see dogwoods and redbuds busting out all over, and colorful clouds of baby blue eyes, shooting stars, and lupine at your feet.

The trail has a few junctions, which you must watch for. A half-mile in, you leave the forest single-track and turn left on an open dirt road. A few minutes later, you come to an intersection of four dirt roads where you turn right. Finally, you reach another road intersection, but continue straight, then pick up the single-track on the left. The trail is well-signed the entire way, but the vegetation is so lush that it sometimes obscures the signs. In addition to all the vines and wildflowers, the trail is lined with a thick forest of oaks, pines, and firs, as well as many buckeye trees growing along the creek.

The trail reaches the waterfall about 1.5 miles out and crosses right over the middle of it. In high water, tiptoeing across the slippery granite slab can be interesting. One cascade spills below the trail, and a larger one drops about 25 yards upstream, accessible by a short spur. Because it's hidden from the trail by thick vines and branches, it's a good place for a quick dip. At the very least, take off your hiking boots and soak your feet. There's nothing quite like the cool, refreshing feeling of it.

Trip notes: There is no fee. For more information and a map/brochure, contact the Bureau of Land Management, Folsom Resource Area, 63 Natoma Street, Folsom, CA 95630; (916) 985-4474.

Directions: From Sacramento, drive east on Interstate 80 for 45 miles to Colfax. Take the Colfax/Grass Valley exit, turn left at the stop sign, and drive east on the frontage road (North Canyon Way) for seven-tenths of a mile to the trailhead parking area.

58. CODFISH CREEK FALLS
Auburn State Recreation Area
Off Interstate 80 near Weimar

Access & Difficulty: Hike-in 3.0 miles RT/Easy
Elevation: Start at 1,500 feet; total gain 50 feet
Best Season: April to September

It's unlikely that you'll see any codfish swimming in Codfish Creek, but you will have a chance at some private time by a pretty waterfall along the North Fork of the American River.

Nobody could tell me where this creek got its name, but everyone said I had to see its waterfall in springtime. So off we went on a fair Saturday in May, following Ponderosa Way from the little town of Weimar down to the American River canyon. Just before the river bridge, we parked along the road and started hiking on the unmarked trail on the north side of the river. (The Tahoe National Forest map shows the trail starting further uphill on Ponderosa Way, but the only trail we found was right at the river bridge.)

The route is surprisingly well-maintained, compared to many other river trails on this stretch of the American. We hiked to the west, paralleling the river for about a mile, watching occasional fortune-hunters looking for gold in the river and sun-lovers floating on their backs in the blue-green pools.

At 1.2 miles, the trail turns right and leads upstream along Codfish Creek, heading away from the river. We passed a hand-painted plaque naming the Codfish Creek Trail, with a dedication to a certain someone "and all others who love nature." It was put there by a group of wonderful people called PARC, for Protect the American River Canyon. (If you want to join their group, help them maintain trails, go on their guided hikes along the river, or be on their mailing list, write to them at P.O. Box 9312, Auburn, CA 95604.)

Although the trail along the river was very sunny, Codfish's canyon is shaded by big manzanitas and deciduous trees. After just a few minutes of walking under the forest canopy, your ears decipher the sound of falling water. The trail brings you to the smack-middle of the waterfall, which is a big cascade totaling at least 100 feet.

The fall's lower reaches are cascades, while the top is more vertical and dramatic. We climbed up the side of the fall and lay around on the rocks, which are a colorful black and gray with rust-colored highlights. A few clumps of Indian rhubarb grow with great enthusiasm by the water's edge.

A nice feature of Codfish Falls is that it doesn't take any creek crossings to reach it, so you can visit the fall even in late winter and early spring, as long as Ponderosa Way is open. The drive itself is a fun adventure on the narrow canyon road. It's not paved, but it's still manageable in a passenger car as long as the road's not too muddy.

Trip notes: There is no fee. For a map of Tahoe National Forest, which includes Auburn State Recreation Area lands, send $4 to USDA-Forest Service, 1323 Club Drive, Vallejo, CA 94592. For more information, contact Auburn State Recreation Area, 501 Eldorado Street, Auburn, CA 95603; (530) 885-4527.

Directions: From Sacramento, drive east on Interstate 80 for 40 miles to Weimar. Take the Weimar/Cross Road exit, then turn south on Ponderosa Way. In three miles, Ponderosa Way turns to dirt. In 2.5 additional miles, you reach a bridge over the American River (total 5.5 miles on Ponderosa Way). Don't cross the bridge, but park along the road near it. Begin hiking on the trail on the north side of the bridge, heading west (downstream).

59. DEVIL'S FALLS

Auburn State Recreation Area
Off Interstate 80 near Colfax

Access & Difficulty: Drive-to/Easy
Elevation: 1,500 feet
Best Season: April to July

It seems almost unfair that a waterfall this pretty is set right along the road. Most of the year, it doesn't even take four-wheel-drive to reach it. But visiting Devil's Falls by car can be the start of a day of adventure on the American River, with its emerald green pools, big fish, gold-panning prospects, and numerous camping and hiking possibilities.

Reach Devil's Falls by driving on Yankee Jim's Road, either from Colfax or from Foresthill. Whichever route you take, you must descend all the way to the bottom of the river canyon, a drop of about 1,200 feet. The road leads 3.8 miles from Colfax and 5.1 miles from Foresthill to the river, and although it's not paved, it's well-graded dirt the whole way. It traverses a narrow series of hairpin turns, the kind where you hope that nobody is

Devil's Falls

coming in the opposite direction. The falls are located at one of those hairpins on the Foresthill side of the American River, just a half-mile south of the picturesque suspension bridge on Yankee Jim's Road.

When 75-foot Devil's Falls is running full, it divides into six or seven big chutes, then runs underneath Yankee Jim's Road and continues to drop till it joins Shirttail Creek, which empties into the American River. Considering the size of Devil's Falls, it's surprising that its creek is not a tributary to the American River, but only a tributary to a tributary.

Signs posted near the fall state "No parking 10 P.M. to 6 A.M." lest you should want to camp right here by the road. Auburn State Recreation Area has designated this area as Shirttail Picnic Area, for day-use only. On spring and summer weekends, the road from the old suspension bridge to the falls can be lined with parked cars, as this stretch of river is popular for both fishing and swimming. Local teenagers sometimes hang a long rope from the suspension bridge, then take turns swinging on it and jumping in to the river. The scene looks like something right out of *Huckleberry Finn*.

Trip notes: There is no fee. For a map of Tahoe National Forest, which includes Auburn State Recreation Area lands, send $4 to USDA-Forest Service, 1323 Club Drive, Vallejo, CA 94592. For more information, contact Auburn State Recreation Area, 501 Eldorado Street, Auburn, CA 95603; (530) 885-4527.

Directions: From Sacramento, drive east on Interstate 80 for 45 miles to Colfax. Take the Colfax/Grass Valley exit, turn right at the stop sign, then drive west on the frontage road (North Canyon Way) for 1.2 miles to Yankee Jim's Road. Turn left (south) on Yankee Jim's Road. The road turns to dirt; drive 3.7 miles to the bridge over the North Fork American River, then continue a half-mile further to Devil's Falls on the right.

60. INDIAN CREEK FALLS

Auburn State Recreation Area
Off Interstate 80 near Colfax

Access & Difficulty: Hike-in 3.0 miles RT/Moderate
Elevation: Start at 1,500 feet; total gain 50 feet
Best Season: Late May to early July

It took three trips till we finally got to see Indian Creek Falls. The hike starts off with a creek crossing, and you've got to time it right to get across. In early May it was too high. In early June it was still too high. On the Fourth of July, we finally made it, but not by rockhopping. We just took off our shoes and waded in.

You have to be lucky to time it right. Only a couple of weeks exist in the small window of time when Shirttail Creek is low enough to cross and Indian Creek is high enough to have a good waterfall. If you come too early, you can't access the trail. If you come too late, there's no pretty cascade at the end of the walk. In most years, June or early July is just about right.

From the parking pullouts at the south side

Indian Creek Falls

of the bridge, take the stair-steps down from the road to the river canyon, then walk to your right, upstream along the river. You'll only go a few feet before you'll have to size up Shirttail Creek and decide whether or not you can cross without getting wet.

Once you're past Shirttail, the rest is easy. Follow the miner's trail that runs east along the south side of the river, a basically flat route that is in various states of repair and disrepair. Watch out for some steep dropoffs. A few spur trails lead down to the river, giving you the option of cooling off on a hot day, but stay on the high road if you want to head straight for the falls.

Since there are no trail signs, count creek crossings to mark your distance traveled. You've already crossed Shirttail, and in a quarter-mile you'll cross a tiny unnamed stream—that makes two. The third and fourth streams are just over a mile out and close together, and they have a decent flow in spring. The fifth creek at 1.5 miles is your ticket—Indian Creek. Even though the falls aren't visible from the trail, it's easy to recognize the creek because just before it, the trail goes through a large landslide of rounded rocks that flow right into the river. Pick your way across the rocks and find the stream, which is sometimes marked by neatly placed rock cairns on top of the haphazard rock piles.

Then start scrambling upstream, heading away from the river. The easiest and quickest way to manage the scramble is to wear shoes that you can get wet. That way you can spend your time both in and out of the water, picking the most efficient route as you go. (There is also a high trail that goes above the landslide, for those who don't want to wade in the creek, but this seems needlessly treacherous. The stream scrambling is safer and more fun, as long as the water is low enough to make it possible.)

Fifteen minutes of this soggy but enjoyable travel brings you to Indian Creek Falls, which are really two waterfalls, one right above the other. Their combined height is about 30 feet. The creek is very densely shaded, mostly by oaks, which provides a nice contrast to the exposed slopes along the river trail. Be sure to stick your head under the falls to cool off, or spend a few moments looking for gold flecks in the stream.

Trip notes: There is no fee. For a map of Tahoe National Forest, which includes Auburn State Recreation Area lands, send $4 to USDA-Forest Service, 1323 Club Drive, Vallejo, CA 94592. For more information, contact Auburn State Recreation Area, 501 Eldorado Street, Auburn, CA 95603; (530) 885-4527.

Directions: From Sacramento, drive east on Interstate 80 for 45 miles to Colfax. Take the Colfax/Grass Valley exit, turn right at the stop sign, then drive west on the frontage road (North Canyon Way) for 1.2 miles to Yankee Jim's Road. Turn left (south) on Yankee Jim's Road. The road turns to dirt; drive 3.7 miles to the bridge over the North Fork American River, then cross it and park on the south side of the bridge.

---

61. CHAMBERLAIN FALLS
Auburn State Recreation Area
Off Interstate 80 near Colfax

Access & Difficulty: Hike-in & Scramble 3.0 miles RT/Strenuous
Elevation: Start at 1,500 feet; total gain 200 feet
Best Season: April to July

Trail? What trail? If it's a trail you're after, don't try the hike to Chamberlain Falls. Once upon a time there was a trail, but a series of slides in the 1980s almost completely wiped it out. A route? Sure, there's a route. But it disappears in places, has plenty of death-defying dropoffs, and will leave you wondering why the heck you didn't just swim downstream to the falls instead.

The trip to Chamberlain Falls isn't for everybody. You've got to be prepared for some pretty treacherous hiking along the steep North Fork American River Canyon, where a misplaced foot or a loose rock means a near-certain fall. Plus, there is only a small window of time when the fall runs and is accessible.

There's deception in the fact that the trip starts out so easy. From the day-use parking area at Mineral Bar Campground, a dirt trail leads steeply down to the river, then quite easily downstream for a half-mile. Auburn State Recreation Area keeps this part of the trail trimmed and maintained for people staying at the campground. You pass some old, rusted mining equipment as you hike through thick vines and foliage growing at the river's edge. Things look promising.

The trail leaves the river and heads uphill, along the steep oak- and bay-shaded canyon slopes. For another third of a mile, the trail gets progressively harder to follow but is still manageable. Views of the exquisite, turquoise-green pools below spur you onward. The river water is unbelievably clear; the rocky canyon appears jewel-like. In the spring, the grassy slopes are sprinkled with wildflowers. River rafters and kayakers zip down the river. Life seems good.

But suddenly the route becomes dicey, if you can still find it. By the way, where is the route? It's nearly impossible to tell. Leaf litter makes the slopes treacherously slippery, and coupled with your near-perpendicular position to the river, it seems germane to start bargaining with some deity—any deity. Turning around looks just as dangerous as continuing onward, so take your pick.

Just creep along. Be careful. Take your time. At nearly 1.5 miles from the trailhead, the route drops down to the river. Kiss the shoreline in gratitude, then scramble over the rocks for another 100 yards downstream to where Chamberlain Creek forms a pretty 30-foot cascade over boulders as it drops into the American River. It's what's known as a "constriction" waterfall, where a big boulder chokes a stream canyon and in high water forms a fall.

Chamberlain runs full until July in most years, and by then the creek has warmed up enough for swimming in its upper pools. The waterfall is most spectacular in April and May, however, and the same is true for the river canyon, when the wildflowers and the river boaters are out in full force.

Trip notes: There is no fee. For a map of Tahoe National Forest, which includes Auburn State Recreation Area lands, send $4 to USDA-Forest Service, 1323 Club Drive, Vallejo, CA 94592. For more information, contact Auburn State Recreation Area, 501 Eldorado Street, Auburn, CA 95603; (530) 885-4527.

Directions: From Sacramento, drive east on Interstate 80 for 45 miles to Colfax. Take the Colfax/Grass Valley exit, turn right at the stop sign, and drive west on the frontage road (North Canyon Way) for three-tenths of a mile to Iowa Hill Road. Turn left (south) on Iowa Hill Road. In three miles, cross the bridge over the North Fork American River to Mineral Bar Campground. Park just beyond the bridge in the dirt parking lot on the right (day-use only, across the road from the camp host). Begin walking southwest (downstream) along the river.

---

62. GROUSE FALLS
Tahoe National Forest
Off Interstate 80 near Foresthill

Access & Difficulty: Hike-in 1.0 mile RT/Easy
Elevation: Start at 5,400 feet; total loss 100 feet
Best Season: March to July

Are you willing to drive 25 miles out of your way just to see a waterfall? No? Okay, what if the waterfall is several hundred feet high, so tall that even the Forest Service doesn't know exactly how tall it is? What if you get a spectacular short and easy walk through a forest of big trees in the process? What if your destination is a wooden deck

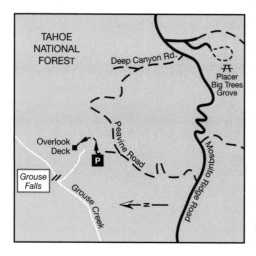

overlooking the falls, with a canyon vista that is so spectacular you'll want to pitch a tent on the spot and spend the rest of your days here?

The drive is worth it. The hike is worth it. Grouse Falls is definitely worth it.

To get there, first you must get to the town of Foresthill. Stop at the grocery store and pack a picnic, because you'll be gone for several hours. Then head east on Mosquito Ridge Road through a rocky, rugged canyon. Before you drop down too far, watch for a glimpse of the snowy peaks of the Sierra, which you can see from the ridge near the start of the road. The route is paved and winding, and curves its way through big trees and steep hillsides, with good views all the way.

After 19 miles, turn left on Peavine Road, a well-graded gravel road, drive 5.5 miles, then turn left again for a short half-mile on dirt. Finally

Grouse Falls

you're at the trailhead. Passenger cars can easily handle the trip.

The trail leads downhill, deep into the woods, and at first it's hard to get a bead on where you're heading. You're surrounded by dense conifers, and huge pine cones litter the trail. In 15 minutes you hear the sound of roaring water, then you suddenly come out to a beautiful wooden deck with a wide-open view of the canyon. On your right is Grouse Falls, one of the finest waterfalls in Northern California, especially at peak flow.

Grouse Creek drains into the North Fork of the Middle Fork American River, and it earns its "10" rating for sheer grandeur alone. Early in the year, the fall doesn't stream, cascade, or drop, but rather it hurtles itself down the mountainside. Grouse Falls is a half-mile away from your perch on the overlook, yet it's so large, it's majestic even from a distance. Two main cascades tumble down the forested slope; the one on the right is larger. It has a visible drop of about 250 feet, then it disappears into the trees and reappears 100 feet below. Be sure to visit this fall soon after snowmelt to get the full effect.

The scene is made even more impressive because the waterfall's canyon is steep, thickly forested, and completely uninhabited. There isn't a glimpse of a building, road, or trail anywhere.

Luckily the overlook has a bench, because you won't want to leave too quickly. If nobody else is around, which is often the case, you might want to spread out a picnic. If you plan to photograph the falls, midday is the best time to visit, when the sun is directly overhead. The rest of the time, the waterfall is shaded by the canyon walls.

Oh, and one more reminder. Mosquito Ridge gets its name from . . . You guessed it. Pack along the bug spray.

Trip notes: There is no fee. For more information and a map/brochure on the Foresthill Divide, contact Tahoe National Forest, Foresthill Ranger District, 22830 Foresthill Road, Foresthill, CA 95631; (530) 367-2224.

Directions: From Interstate 80 at Auburn, take the Foresthill/Auburn Ravine Road exit, then drive 16 miles east to Foresthill. In Foresthill, turn right (east) on Mosquito Ridge Road, across from the Foresthill post office. Drive 19 miles to Peavine Road (Road 33). Turn left on Peavine Road and drive 5.5 miles to the Grouse Falls turnoff on the left. Turn left and drive a half-mile to the trailhead.

---

63. BRIDAL VEIL FALLS

Eldorado National Forest
Off Highway 50 near Placerville

Access & Difficulty: Drive-to/Easy
Elevation: 3,500 feet
Best Season: April to June

Not to be confused with *the* Bridalveil Falls in Yosemite National Park, Highway 50's Bridal Veil Falls is spelled as two words, not one, and it bears little resemblance to the more famous cataract. The name's derivation is a mystery, but seeing the fall is not, because you drive right by it on Highway 50 heading from Placerville to South Lake Tahoe.

In the spring, Bridal Veil Falls is a winner, even as you fly by at 60 miles per hour. If you want to stop for a closer look, there are pullouts on both sides of the highway by the falls. Also, the waterfall is less than a half-mile west (and across the road) from Bridal Veil Picnic Area, which was once a campground but is now a day-use area that offers great swimming holes along the South Fork of the American River.

Bridal Veil Falls drops 80 feet over a big sheet of gray rock, and it's partially obscured by some tall maple trees growing in front. By late summer you can drive right by without even noticing it, but in springtime, you can't miss its brilliant white stream.

The best way to view Bridal Veil is from across the road, rather than at the foot of the fall, because only from that distance can you see its full height. Your best bet: Park at the picnic area, take a short walk west along the highway to the waterfall (don't bother crossing the highway), then walk back to the picnic area and claim your spot along the turquoise waters of the American River.

Trip notes: There is a $3 day-use fee to park at Bridal Veil Picnic Area. To view the falls from the parking pullouts along the road, there is no fee. For a map of Eldorado National Forest, send $4 to USDA-Forest Service, 1323 Club Drive, Vallejo, CA 94592. For more information, contact Eldorado National Forest, 3070 Camino Heights Drive, Camino, CA 95709; (530) 644-6048.

Directions: From Placerville, drive 19 miles east on Highway 50. Look for the waterfall on the right side of the road, 5.5 miles east of the town of Pollock Pines. There are parking pullouts on both sides of the road, or you can park at Bridal Veil Picnic Area on the north side of the road, east of the fall.

64. HORSETAIL FALLS

Eldorado National Forest
Off Highway 50 near South Lake Tahoe

Access & Difficulty: Hike-in 2.0 miles RT/Easy
Elevation: Start at 6,100 feet; total gain 200 feet
Best Season: April to September

You'll know why they call it Horsetail Falls the minute you see it, while cruising west on Highway 50. Straight and narrow at the top and fanning out to a wide inverted V at the bottom, Horsetail Falls swishes hundreds of feet down Pyramid Creek's glacier-carved canyon. Its powerful stream is reinforced by four different lakes: Toem, Ropi, Pitt, and Avalanche.

Don't be put off by the crammed parking lot at Twin Bridges, the trailhead for the falls. Many of the cars belong to backpackers who are far off in the Desolation Wilderness on multi-day trips, and many more belong to people just milling around the trailhead, picnicking and admiring the falls from afar.

Beginning on the west side of the highway bridge, pick up the trail heading north, toward the falls. Hike through the dense cedar and pine forest, which smells like Grandma's cedar chest in the attic, only fresher and better. You leave most of your trail companions behind in the first quarter-mile, as people drop off the route and choose their spots along Pyramid Creek. The trail continues into an exposed, rocky area—the glaciers paid a visit here—moving farther away from the creek and the cool shade of the forest.

About a half-mile in, you have a choice: continue straight toward Horsetail Falls and the Desolation Wilderness boundary, or veer off and follow the 1.5-mile Pyramid Creek Loop Trail. The latter is a new trail that was built in 1999 specifically with day-users in mind. This well-marked trail offers terrific long-distance views of Horsetail Falls and is routed past a beautiful stretch of Pyramid Creek called The Cascades. If you haven't obtained a wilderness permit and just

Horsetail Falls

want a nice day-hike with a waterfall vista and access to swimming holes, this is your ticket.

If you choose to continue on the Horsetail Falls Trail, in a short distance you may notice a bizarre phenomenon: arrows painted on the granite slabs pointing out the direction of the trail. It's devastating but true: some ingrate vandalized this area in September 1995, spray-painting hundreds of green arrows on pristine granite. Apparently the culprit thought the trail was too difficult to follow and painted the arrows as some kind of a "service" to other hikers. (Go figure.) Eldorado National Forest rangers and various volunteer groups have made efforts to remove the graffiti, but there is so much that it will take years to get rid of it all.

Recreation managers in the Pacific Ranger District say that the Horsetail Falls Trail has long been a source of controversy. Although the trail up to the wilderness boundary is fairly well-defined, after the boundary line it is really just a route, not a trail. Many people try to walk to the foot of Horsetail Falls, traveling past the wilderness boundary, but they often get lost or hurt on the crude path. A slip near the waterfall or along the edges of fast-moving Pyramid Creek means near-certain death. Every year there are fatalities and injuries.

Despite the ruckus, Horsetail Falls is still a favorite hike around South Lake Tahoe. An estimated 15,000 people visit this trailhead and hike at least a portion of the trail each summer.

Stay below the wilderness line and you're certain to stay out of trouble, although you'll have to be satisfied with long-distance views of Horsetail Falls. You can take any route you like over the granite slabs. Some people stay close to the creek, while others follow a more direct path over rock, in between occasional twisted junipers or sturdy Jeffrey pines. Take time to examine the brightly colored lichens that coat many of the granite boulders.

When you reach the boundary sign, you may only continue further if you have filled out a self-serve permit at the trailhead. If so, you can walk right to the base of the big fall, but remember, this is a route, not a trail. Be extremely careful near the edge of the creek.

For most people, turning back at the boundary sign is no great compromise. The return trip offers views of Lover's Leap and surrounding peaks to the south, far across the highway. On your walk back, be sure to turn around every now and then for a parting look at Horsetail Falls.

Trip notes: There is no fee. A wilderness permit is necessary if you are going to travel beyond the wilderness boundary. For a map of Eldorado

National Forest, send $4 to USDA-Forest Service Map Sales, 1323 Club Drive, Vallejo, CA 94592. For more information, contact Eldorado National Forest, 3070 Camino Heights Drive, Camino, CA 95709; (530) 644-6048.

Directions: From South Lake Tahoe, drive south on Highway 89 to Highway 50. Drive west on Highway 50 for about 15 miles to Twin Bridges, where there is a huge pullout on the north side of the highway just before the bridge. (The pullout is a half-mile west of the turnoff for Camp Sacramento.) Park in the pullout, then walk across the highway bridge about 500 feet to the well-marked trailhead.

65. EAGLE FALLS

Lake Tahoe Basin Management Unit
Off Highway 89 near South Lake Tahoe

Access & Difficulty: Hike-in 0.5 mile RT/Easy
  or Hike-in 2.0 miles RT/Easy
Elevation: Start at 6,600 feet; total gain 50 feet (0.5-mile RT)
  or Start at 6,600 feet; total loss 400 feet (2.0-mile RT)
Best Season: April to July

There's the Eagle Falls you see from the short trail at Eagle Falls Picnic Area, and then there's the other Eagle Falls just downstream and across Highway 89. While you're in the neighborhood, you might as well go see both Eagle Falls. Let's face it, it's one of the rare things at Lake Tahoe that you can do without a bank loan.

Start with the upstream Eagle Falls, the one that you reach via a quarter-mile trail from the Eagle Falls Picnic Area. Unfortunately, they've made this into a "designer" trail, by cutting the natural granite into flagstone-like stairsteps and building a wooden bridge with metal railings to escort you over the top of the falls. The route has been flattened by so many hikers' feet that even the sandy parts are packed smooth and hard.

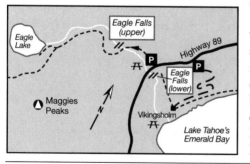

It's a beautiful walk, nonetheless. It's also extremely popular, not just with people coming to see the falls, but also with those continuing into the Desolation Wilderness. For the most peaceful experience, visit as early in the morning as possible, like before 9 A.M.

The upstream Eagle Falls is only 50 feet tall, pouring directly underneath the hiker's bridge. In springtime, right after heavy snowmelt, the bridge can be an exciting place to stand. By fall, the flow of water is merely tame, making the falls overlook a pretty spot, but without much drama.

If you decide to hike beyond Eagle Falls, you'll enter a vastly different land. The trail heads uphill and becomes very rocky, losing its "designer" quality almost immediately. You need a permit to enter the Desolation Wilderness, even for day-hiking. Get one at the trailhead. The trail leads to Eagle Lake in one mile and to Velma Lakes in four, with spectacular views of exposed granite and dramatic, glaciated landscapes. Welcome to the Sierra high country.

If you don't continue onward, the short walk back to the parking lot from Eagle Falls has its own drama—a terrific view of Lake Tahoe that was behind your back on the way in.

Now that you've seen the upper Eagle Falls, head for the lower fall. From the Eagle Falls Picnic Area parking lot, carefully cross Highway 89 on foot (be very wary of drivers watching the lake instead of the road), then peer down over the top of the falls.

Hikers' bridge over Upper Eagle Falls, late summer

The lower fall is visible from the highway; it's a can't-miss-it traffic-stopper during spring snowmelt. During May and June, drivers constantly slam on their brakes, pull off the road, then risk their lives by dashing across the highway to get a closer look at the falls. Many people scramble down the side of Eagle Falls from the road, but this isn't recommended unless it's very late in the season, the fall's flow is low, and the surrounding granite is completely dry. There have been more than a few accidents here.

Instead, see the lower fall from the bottom up, by walking or driving a half-mile north on Highway 89 to the Emerald Bay Overlook parking lot on the lake side of the road. From there, hike down the steep one-mile dirt road to Vikingsholm, the fancy replica of a Viking castle that once belonged to an heiress and is now a state park. From Memorial Day to Labor Day you can pay a fee and tour the castle, but I'd skip it and go straight to the waterfall instead. The Eagle Falls trail begins directly across from Vikingsholm, and a quarter-mile walk takes you to the base of it. This is probably my favorite view of Eagle Falls, a roaring cascade that in springtime is a true testament to the power and force of snowmelt.

Trip notes: There is no fee. For a map of the Lake Tahoe Basin, send $4 to USDA-Forest Service, 1323 Club Drive, Vallejo, CA 94592. For more information, contact Lake Tahoe Basin Management Unit, 870 Emerald Bay Road, South Lake Tahoe, CA 96150; (530) 573-2600.

Directions: From South Lake Tahoe, drive northwest on Highway 89 for 8.5 miles to the Eagle Falls Picnic Area and Trailhead. Turn left into the parking area, or park in the pullout just beyond the picnic area on the west side of Highway 89. To hike to Vikingsholm and view only the lower fall, park in the Emerald Bay Overlook and parking area, a quarter-mile north of the Eagle Falls Picnic Area.

---

66. CASCADE FALLS

Lake Tahoe Basin Management Unit
Off Highway 89 near South Lake Tahoe

Access & Difficulty: Hike-in 2.0 miles RT/Easy
Elevation: Start at 6,800 feet; total gain 100 feet
Best Season: April to July

The hike to Cascade Falls is far and away the best easy hike at Lake Tahoe. It's short and flat enough for almost anybody to make the trip, including young children. It has enough spectacular scenery to keep even the biggest whiners-in-the-outdoors from complaining. And the trail leads you right to the side of a stunning 200-foot cascade that drops into the southwest end of Cascade Lake. What more could you ask for?

Cascade Falls has only one drawback—you have to see it early in the year. By September, the 100-yard-wide tower of water has become a thin, willowy stream, which greatly diminishes its dramatic effect. Plan your trip for sometime between the start of snowmelt and July, but no later.

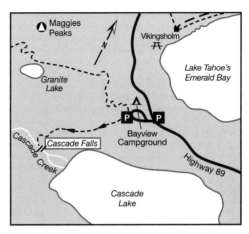

From the trailhead parking lot at Bayview Campground, hike to your left on the well-signed trail. The route is pretty every step of the way. It meanders in and out of pine forest and open sunshine, alternately providing shade and views. After a mere five minutes of walking, you're rewarded with a tremendous vista of Cascade Lake, elevation 6,464 feet. The lake looks so large you may think it's part of Lake Tahoe, but with your bird's-eye view you can see how it's separated from Tahoe by a thin strip of forest and highway.

Moments later, the rumbling of the falls greets you as you break out of the forest and are given a clear view of the tumbling water. From here onward, the trail is out in the open on exposed granite. Watch your footing on the rocks, and keep a firm handhold on small children.

The closer you get to the falls, the more the trail disintegrates, but numerous rock cairns show you the way. How far you go is up to you, and should be determined by your comfort level with route-finding. The best views of Cascade Falls are actually farther back on the trail; once you are alongside it, you can't see its entire 200-foot length. But upstream of the falls' lip are some lovely emerald green pools, as well as large shelves of granite where you can sit and picnic.

Cascade Falls was once called White Cloud Falls, and when you near it, you can understand why. In the wind, it billows and scatters so much over its base of granite stair-steps that it creates a cloud of spray. Wildflowers enjoy all the water, and the blue lupines and pink mountain pride present a superb springtime show, clinging to crevices in the rock.

Trip notes: There is no fee. For a map of the Lake Tahoe Basin, send $4 to USDA-Forest Service, 1323 Club Drive, Vallejo, CA 94592. For more information, contact Lake Tahoe Basin Management Unit, 870 Emerald Bay Road, South Lake Tahoe, CA 96150; (530) 573-2600.

Directions: From South Lake Tahoe, drive northwest on Highway 89 for 7.5 miles to the Bayview Campground and Trailhead. Turn left and drive to the far end of the campground to the trailhead parking area. If it's full, you can park across Highway 89 in the Inspiration Point parking lot.

67. GLEN ALPINE CREEK FALLS

Lake Tahoe Basin Management Unit
Off Highway 89 near Fallen Leaf Lake

Access & Difficulty: Hike-in 1.0 mile RT/Easy
    or Drive-to/Easy
Elevation: Start at 6,560 feet; total gain 50 feet
Best Season: May to August

Glen Alpine Creek is abundant with waterfalls, affording hikers, bikers, and drivers the chance to "have it their way."

The biggest and most accessible fall on Glen Alpine Creek is on Road 1216, a left fork off Fallen Leaf Lake Road, on the way to the Desolation Wilderness trailhead. In the spring, many people make the drive down impossibly narrow Fallen Leaf Lake Road to see the fall. Bike riders, too, enjoy the route. Because the road is so narrow, cars have no choice but to go slow, which gives bikers a chance to ride in relative safety.

The falls are located right along the road, less than two-tenths of a mile after the point where Fallen Leaf Lake Road forks and a sign points to the left for Lily Lake, Glen Alpine Falls, and the Desolation Wilderness Trailhead. The road deteriorates substantially at the fork, but you can park your car there and walk a few hundred yards to the falls, or drive a little further and pull off right by the falls. There are several dirt pullouts, but they fill up on spring weekends. Just be sure that wherever you park, you aren't on private property or blocking someone's driveway.

Glen Alpine Falls is a 100-foot cascade that spills over jagged rocks of all shapes and sizes. It's an incredible sight in spring, when the water seems to be shooting out in every direction as it hits a multitude of ledges and outcrops. The best viewing is from the foundation of an old stone house, directly in front of the fall. Although this cabin is long gone, there are several others still standing nearby. They're on 99-year leases with the Forest Service, leftover from the days when the government was trying to encourage recreational activity here. That means that a lucky few have weekend cabins surrounded by a waterfall, junipers, firs, and big pines, as well as Fallen Leaf Lake itself.

If you want to do a little hiking and see another waterfall on Glen Alpine Creek, drive past the first fall and continue a half-mile to the Desolation Wilderness trailhead. Fill out a self-serve permit at the kiosk, then begin walking on the gated dirt road. Reach the fall in a mere half-mile, hiking on a very rocky road past more leased cabins. The trail comes within 50 yards of the cascade, but you can scramble a little closer, making your way carefully through the scrub oaks that line the creek. This Glen Alpine Falls has two main cascades, one on top of the other, for a combined height of 70 feet.

If you like, you can continue hiking into the wilderness. Just this half-mile of trail gives you a good idea of why the Desolation Wilderness is so popular; it's a land of bare granite peaks and lush streamside vegetation. Unfortunately, the area has overuse problems; you're bound to encounter plenty of other trail users. The best remedy is to hike during the week or in the off-season. If you continue on, the trail leads to Grass Lake, 1.7 miles further, and Susie Lake, 3.5 miles further, passing yet another waterfall along the way.

If it's too crowded at Glen Alpine but you'd like to hike some more, drive back down Fallen Leaf Lake Road for four miles to the Fallen Leaf Lake Trailhead, eight-tenths of a mile from Highway 89 (just retrace your route). The short, mostly level trail leads

Glen Alpine Creek Falls

along the lake's edge and then across its dam, with excellent views of Glen Alpine canyon and Mount Tallac. In the fall, this is one of the best spots near Tahoe to admire the quaking aspens turning gold.

Trip notes: Hikers must fill out a self-serve permit at the wilderness trailhead. There is no fee. For a map of the Lake Tahoe Basin, send $4 to USDA-Forest Service, 1323 Club Drive, Vallejo, CA 94592. For more information, contact Lake Tahoe Basin Management Unit, 870 Emerald Bay Road, South Lake Tahoe, CA 96150; (530) 573-2600.

Directions: From South Lake Tahoe, drive northwest on Highway 89 for 2.9 miles to Fallen Leaf Lake Road. Turn left and drive 4.8 miles, first through a logged area and then through a stretch of lakeside homes on a very narrow road. Take the left fork on to Road 1216, signed for Lily Lake, Glen Alpine Falls, and the Desolation Wilderness Trailhead. You'll reach the trailhead in seven-tenths of a mile. Begin hiking on the gated dirt road to the right of the trailhead sign.

68. HOT SPRINGS CREEK WATERFALL
Grover Hot Springs State Park
Off Highway 89 near Markleeville

Access & Difficulty: Hike-in 3.0 miles RT/Easy
Elevation: Start at 5,900 feet; total gain 200 feet
Best Season: April to July

Grover Hot Springs State Park in Markleeville is located only a half-hour from the urban bustle of South Lake Tahoe, but it feels like a different world. Markleeville is a small town—a real small town. Although it's fairly well-known as a weekend meeting place for motorcyclists cruising the area's back roads, it's better known for its neighboring state park and mineral-water bathing pools. What is less known, however, is that a short trail from the state park campground leads to a spring and early-summer waterfall, an easy walk of only 1.5 miles one-way.

Even if you're not camping, it's worth the $5 admission fee to take a walk to the waterfall, then laze around at the park's bathing pools for the rest of the day. If you come during the week, especially before or after summer vacation from school, you can even get a little peace and quiet.

The trail begins on a dirt and gravel service road just beyond the campground, signed as Trail 1006. Hike to your left on the road, then take the left fork off the road and on to single-track. If you encounter

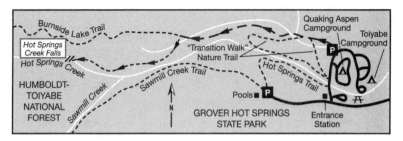

any mountain bikers in your first few minutes of walking, have no fear; they'll be veering off shortly on their way to Charity Valley in Humboldt-Toiyabe National Forest. That fork comes up in just over a half-mile; you'll bear left for the waterfall.

Your route parallels Hot Springs Creek, although you aren't near enough to pay it much attention. You will notice the huge sugar pines all around you, which create a shower of needles in the wind, plus green meadows filled with sagebrush surrounded by hillsides bearing oddly shaped rock outcrops.

When the trail reaches a jumbled, boulder-filled area, there's no place to go but up and over. This is the first point where your trail is anything but flat. A good footpath leads over the boulders; find it and take it. Ignore any spur trails that go down to the creek and the wide trail you may spot on the opposite side; these will send you up the wrong fork of the canyon.

Pick up the trail again on the far side of the boulders; now the waterfall is only five to ten minutes away. Keep the creek on your left, and hike up Hot Springs Canyon as it narrows to the waterfall. The fall is about 50 feet tall, dropping over a tower of rocks, with plenty of pools below it for swimming and admiring the small trout who live there. In spring, Hot Springs Creek's waterfall runs quite full, loud, and fast, calling lots of attention to itself, but by late summer you have to look and listen carefully for it.

The official trail ends near the base of the waterfall, but various routes take you to the top, where there is a makeshift camp (this is now Humboldt-Toiyabe National Forest land, beyond the state park boundary, so camping is allowed). Hot Springs Creek is surrounded by pine, cedar, juniper, cottonwood, and willow trees, as well as elderberry bushes; it's a lush environment compared to the sandy pine forest at the start of the trail.

When you've finished your visit to the falls, you can hike back to the park and walk the pleasant interpretive trail that leads around the meadow, or just spend the rest of day at the hot springs. A bonus at

Grover is that unlike many hot springs, these have very little sulphur, meaning you don't have to hold your nose from the smell. The park has two concrete pools, which are fed from six different springs and regulated to about 103 degrees Fahrenheit.

Natural hot springs and a waterfall in the same park? Wow, it just doesn't get any better than this.

Trip notes: A $5 day-use fee is charged by Grover Hot Springs State Park. A park map is available for $1 at the entrance station. For more information, contact Grover Hot Springs State Park, P.O. Box 188, Markleeville, CA 96120; (530) 694-2248.

Directions: From Meyers at the junction of Highway 50 and Highway 89, drive south on Highway 89 for 24 miles to Markleeville. At Markleeville, turn right (west) on Hot Springs Road and drive 3.5 miles to the state park entrance. Drive through the entrance kiosk, then take the left fork past the campground to the signed trailhead, a gated dirt road.

69. WOLF CREEK FALLS

Carson-Iceberg Wilderness
Off Highway 4 near Markleeville

Access & Difficulty: Hike-in or Backpack 10.0 miles RT/Moderate
Elevation: Start at 6,500 feet; total gain 800 feet
Best Season: June to October

It may take 10 miles of walking (round-trip) to see Wolf Creek Falls, but they're darn easy miles, with an almost negligible elevation gain. The 50-foot waterfall is worth the long miles, not only for a chance to sit alongside its sparkling whitewater plunge, but also to admire the rugged volcanic landscape that surrounds it.

Wolf Creek runs dependably even into early autumn, but the best time to see the waterfall is unquestionably soon after snowmelt, which means sometime in June or July. Then the fall will completely flood the steep, rugged volcanic chasm it cuts through. Later in the year, Wolf Creek Falls dwindles to a narrower, more stream-like cataract, although it's still worth a gander.

The first four miles of Wolf Creek Trail are practically level, with just a gentle, steady uphill grade. The route, an old jeep road, is almost completely shaded by Jeffrey pines and white firs. The only downer is that late in the summer, the trail is often dusty and carved up from horses' hooves. The soft volcanic soil can be as sandy as an ocean beach in places, making walking more difficult than you'd expect. Pine needles cover much of the path.

The trail parallels Wolf Creek the entire way, never very close to it but always within earshot. You'll cross a few feeder streams; one or two may require you to remove your shoes in the early season. At 4.3 miles from the trailhead, you reach your first junction, where Bull Canyon Trail forks to the right to Bull Lake. Stay left on Wolf Creek Trail. Finally the trail nears the creek. Right after this junction you'll face a short, steep uphill that leads over and around a rock outcrop. At the top of the rise, you get your first expan-

Wolf Creek Falls at low flow in autumn

sive views of the day. The ridge on your right has two huge volcanic outcrops poking up into the sky. They stand like two castles on the hill, or giant sentries guarding this canyon.

Now you're clearly in volcanic country. Sagebrush is everywhere and the only trees left are a few hardy junipers. Scattered rock outcrops are covered with colorful lichens. The landscape looks barren but beautiful. From the high point, the trail starts to descend. You'll pass through a cattle fence and Wolf Creek Falls is only 50 yards farther, where Wolf Creek suddenly narrows and steepens and the stream drops over volcanic rock. Early in the summer, your ears will lead you to the falls. By autumn, you'll need to look carefully on your left for its sheltered chasm.

Wolf Creek Falls makes three drops. The middle one is the tallest, about 40 feet. Several smaller cascades frame it above and below. If you wish to leave the trail and scramble down to the edge of the creek, be careful—the volcanic rock is very crumbly and loose. Anywhere near the falls is a fine place to sit and enjoy the scenery.

Trip notes: There is no fee. For a map of Humboldt-Toiyabe National Forest (Carson District), send $4 to USDA-Forest Service, 1323 Club Drive, Vallejo, CA 94592. For more information, contact Humboldt-Toiyabe National Forest, Carson Ranger District, 1536 South Carson Street, Carson City, NV 89701; (775) 882-2766.

Directions: From Meyers at the junction of Highway 50 and Highway 89, drive south on Highway 89 for 24 miles to Markleeville. Continue south on Highway 89 for four miles past Markleeville, then bear right (south) on Highway 4. Drive 2.5 miles on Highway 4, then turn south on Wolf Creek Road. Drive 4.9 miles to the trailhead. The road turns to dirt, but it is well graded and suitable for most cars. The trail (a closed, gated road) begins on the right about 100 yards before the campground at Wolf Creek Road's end.

70. LLEWELLYN FALLS

Carson-Iceberg Wilderness
Off U.S. 395 near Walker

Access & Difficulty: Hike-in or Backpack 13.0 miles RT/Strenuous
Elevation: Start at 8,100 feet; total gain 1,000 feet
Best Season: June to September

Llewellyn Falls is not an extraordinary waterfall by Sierra standards. But it's a good waterfall, and conveniently located so it's in the exact middle of a 13-mile loop trip in the Carson-Iceberg Wilderness. That's reason enough to take this long day-hike or easy backpacking trip through some beautiful scenery in the northern Sierra. Although the mileage is long, the route has only moderate ups and downs, making the trip less strenuous than you'd expect. The only downer is that grazing is still permitted in this part of the wilderness, so you may have to put up with some bovine companions along the trail.

Start your trip at the Corral Valley Trailhead near the small town of Walker on U.S. 395 (a great place to stock up on supplies). The loop can be hiked in either direction. I've described it by taking the western (right) leg first, but since the elevation change is so minimal, it really doesn't matter. From the trailhead, head southwest along the Driveway Trail, ignoring the right fork to Antelope Valley Pack Station. You'll climb steadily through fir and pine forest, soon breaking out to a more exposed landscape with spectacular views of surrounding valleys. At less than one mile out the climb is over and you soon reach the start of the loop; I took the right fork, remaining on Driveway Trail. Immediately you pass the trail's historical highlight, an "ari mutillak" or rock pile that resembles a chimney, which was built by Basque sheepherders in the 1920s. At seven feet high, it looks something like a giant trail cairn. The rock piles served no purpose; building them simply helped to pass the time for the bored shepherds.

The trail proceeds on a generally downward trend all the way to Llewellyn Falls, passing by granite outcrops, green meadows, and forest. A ford of Silver King Creek at three miles out will require you to remove your boots; the water can

be quite deep and fast, so exercise caution. On the far side you join Silver King Trail heading south (bear left at the fork). Many campsites are found here along the stream. A second ford of trout-filled Silver King Creek closely follows the first. (Anglers, don't forget your tackle for this first leg of the trip.)

At just over six miles from the trailhead, you'll reach Commissioners Camp in Lower Fish Valley, a large camping area for packers. If you haven't seen any cows on your hike yet, this is where you'll find them. From the camp, continue another half mile to reach Llewellyn Falls. The 25-foot cascade is just off the trail by 100 yards (a sign may be in place to direct you; if not, use your ears). The waterfall curves around fractured granite bedrock in a boisterous, enthusiastic drop.

After enjoying the falls, you could return the way you came. But since this is the halfway point on the loop, you might as well continue on the other leg and see some more scenery. The trail continues south to another packer's camp and a junction with Snodgass Canyon/Fish Valley Trail. Head northeast (left) here to make your return. Note that fishing is not permitted on this leg of the loop; upstream of Llewellyn Falls the creeks are off-limits to protect a rare species of native Paiute trout. The second leg's landscape is more of the same lovely ilk as the first—views of close-up granite boulders, distant ridges and valleys, green meadows, and groves of quaking aspens near the streams. Take your time and soak in as much of the scenery as you can before returning to the start of the loop. From there, continue straight to head back to your car at Corral Valley in one mile.

Trip notes: There is no fee. For a map of Humboldt-Toiyabe National Forest (Carson District), send $4 to USDA-Forest Service, 1323 Club Drive, Vallejo, CA 94592. For more information, contact Humboldt-Toiyabe National Forest, Carson Ranger District, 1536 South Carson Street, Carson City, NV 89701; (775) 882-2766.

Directions: From Walker on U.S. 395, drive two miles north on U.S. 395 to the Mill Canyon Road turnoff. (Mill Canyon Road is 7.5 miles south of the junction of U.S. 395 and Highway 89.) Turn west on Mill Canyon Road, then in a quarter-mile take the right fork. Continue six miles to a junction at Rodriguez Flat. Turn left and drive a half-mile to the Corral Valley Trailhead. (This last stretch is very rocky and may require a high-clearance vehicle.)

Yosemite & Eastern Sierra

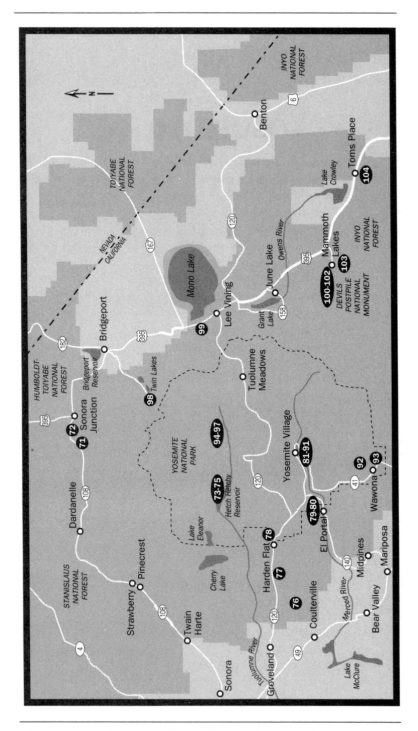

71. SARDINE FALLS

Humboldt-Toiyabe National Forest
Off Highway 108 near Sonora Pass

Access & Difficulty: Hike-in 2.5 miles RT/Easy
Elevation: Start at 8,800 feet; total gain 300 feet
Best Season: June to September

You have to do some route-finding to reach Sardine Falls, but you can leave your compass at home. The falls are easily visible from the highway, and it's a one-mile beeline walk through a high alpine meadow to reach them.

You might have to get your feet wet, though. Any route you take has to cross Sardine Creek, and early in the year, it's easiest just to take off your shoes and wade right in.

Leave your car in one of the gravel pullouts along Sardine Meadow, 2.5 miles east of Sonora Pass Summit on Highway 108. Because there is no real trail, it's easiest to start walking on one of the overgrown jeep routes, most of which are marked with the Forest Service's "No Motorized Vehicles" symbol. The shortest route is an old jeep trail on the northwest side of the meadow that is clearly signed "Route Closed" (to off-road vehicles, that is, not to hikers). If you look straight across the meadow from that sign, you can see the largest cascade of Sardine Falls. From there, it's obvious where to

On top of Sardine Falls

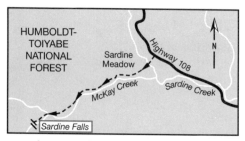

go—just head across the meadow and upstream.

Cross Sardine Creek, which parallels Highway 108, then start walking up the right side of larger McKay Creek, making a more-or-less straight route for Sardine Falls. A dirt path leads the way, lined with yellow Sierra daisies, vibrant blue lupine, monkeyflower, purple wandering daisies, mariposa lilies, and mule's ears. Dozens of small butterflies join in the scene.

Climb uphill over a rise, then cross a feeder stream coming in from the right. At one mile, you first hear and then see Sardine Falls. It drops boisterously over a rocky cliff of about 75 feet, with a few lodgepole pines framing the picture. There are many good viewpoints and picnic areas. Don't forget the sardine sandwiches.

Trip notes: There is no fee. For a map of Toiyabe National Forest, send $4 to USDA-Forest Service, 1323 Club Drive, Vallejo, CA 94592. For more information, contact Toiyabe National Forest, Bridgeport Ranger District, HCR 1 Box 1000, Bridgeport, CA 93517; (760) 932-7070.

Directions: From the junction of U.S. 395 and Highway 108, drive 12.5 miles west on Highway 108. (You will be 2.5 miles east of Sonora Pass Summit.) Park along the road in the gravel pullouts, near the overgrown jeep roads on the northwest side of the meadow.

72. LEAVITT FALLS

Humboldt-Toiyabe National Forest
Off Highway 108 near Sonora Pass

Access & Difficulty: Drive-to/Easy
Elevation: 7,000 feet
Best Season: June to September

Highway 108, the Sonora Road, has some of the most stunning drive-to scenery in the entire Sierra Nevada, and Leavitt Falls exemplifies it. You can't hike to the falls, because it's trapped in the back of a box canyon, but there's a great drive-to overlook that affords a stellar view.

To reach the Leavitt Falls Vista, drive 1.7 miles west of Leavitt Meadows Campground on Highway 108. The turnoff is well signed and there is ample parking. A short walk leads you to a railed wooden overlook, which faces south; peering over its right side, you see across the canyon to Leavitt Falls. The fall cascades several hundred feet on Leavitt Creek, a tributary to the West Walker River. It plunges through a shadowy chasm, over and in between chiseled, rectangular boulders. Surrounded by majestic firs and junipers, Leavitt is a classic double waterfall with an upper drop, then a series of pools, followed by another, longer drop.

Leavitt Falls

The Leavitt Falls Vista also provides a sweeping view of the West Walker Valley, hundreds of feet below, where the West Walker snakes its way through Leavitt Meadow and Leavitt Creek rushes to join it. Beyond the meadow are far-off views into the desert and mountains of Nevada to the east, and the snowy Sierra to the west.

The only possible downer at Leavitt Falls Vista is the wind, which can howl across Leavitt Meadow and nearly blow you off the overlook. The view can't be beaten, but if you want to stay a while to enjoy it, come dressed for a gale.

Trip notes: There is no fee. For a map of Toiyabe National Forest, send $4 to USDA-Forest Service, 1323 Club Drive, Vallejo, CA 94592. For more information, contact Toiyabe National Forest, Bridgeport Ranger District, HCR 1 Box 1000, Bridgeport, CA 93517; (760) 932-7070.

Directions: From the junction of U.S. 395 and Highway 108, drive 8.7 miles west on Highway 108 to the signed falls vista on the left (south) side of the road. (You will be 6.3 miles east of Sonora Pass Summit and 1.7 miles west of Leavitt Meadows Campground.)

73-75. TUEEULALA, WAPAMA, & RANCHERIA FALLS

Yosemite National Park
Off Highway 120 at Hetch Hetchy

Access & Difficulty: Hike-in 4.8 miles RT/Easy (Tueeulala & Wapama)
or Hike-in or Backpack 13.0 miles RT/Moderate (Rancheria)
Elevation: Start at 3,800 feet; total gain 300 feet to Tueeulala & Wapama
or Start at 3,800 feet; total gain 1,500 feet to Rancheria
Best Season: March to June

When people see pictures of what Hetch Hetchy Valley looked like before it was dammed and flooded in 1914 to provide water for San Francisco, they're always struck by how much it resembles today's Yosemite Valley (minus the parking lots, pavement, and tour buses, of course). Photos show the stark, pristine granite of Kolana Rock and Hetch Hetchy Dome jutting upward from the valley floor, waterfalls dropping thousands of feet from hanging valleys like rivers falling from the sky, and lush, flower-filled meadows lining the edge of the meandering Tuolumne River.

You gotta wonder, what in the hell were those politicians thinking? Maybe something like: Hey, two Yosemites is one too many. Let's flood one, and keep the other for the tourists.

But here's the great irony: Despite man's best efforts to destroy it, Hetch Hetchy remains beautiful. Of course it's not as spectacular as its former self, and never can be again. But when you hike along the shoreline of Hetch Hetchy Reservoir, and observe the higher sections of granite and waterfalls that still tower imposingly above the 400-foot-deep water line, you get the sense that Nature has ceased crying over Hetch Hetchy. Instead, she has done what she does best—heal, beautify, and make the most of what is.

And waterfall-lovers still find plenty to treasure at Hetch Hetchy. For the best display, the key is to visit early in the year, no later than June. By July, Tueeulala Falls is almost always dry, and Wapama and Rancheria falls are less showy. Also, Hetch Hetchy Reservoir is at a low elevation—3,800 feet—so it's imperative to hike here before the summer gets too hot. The elevation is the same as Yosemite Valley, but Hetch Hetchy is usually about 10 to 15 degrees warmer. If you have to make your trip later in the summer, be sure to get an early morning start, and bring plenty of water or a water purifier with you.

The perk is that Hetch Hetchy is one of the few places in Yosemite that is accessible for day-hiking nearly year-round. The sun-baked north shore of the eight-mile-long reservoir can be warm even in the middle of winter, especially when you're climbing uphill on exposed granite. Occasionally the trail may be closed in spring when Wapama Falls is at flood and high water and heavy spray completely cover the trail. Call the park to check on conditions before you make the trip.

Wapama Falls

From the parking lot by O'Shaughnessy Dam, start your walk by crossing over the dam, then enter the long tunnel on the dam's far side and walk through. Exit into a leafy oak and bay forest, and listen to the water lapping along the deep reservoir's shore. After the first mile of trail, you'll reach a junction and head right, continuing along Hetch Hetchy Reservoir's edge for the entire length of your trip.

You'll notice a surprising amount of plant and tree life around you. At this elevation, just about anything can grow. Springtime gives rise to a good wildflower display, including Indian paintbrush, mariposa lilies, purple brodiaea, and blue penstemon, in addition to the omnipresent bear clover and plenty of poison oak.

Tueeulala is the first waterfall you reach at 1.5 miles out. It's tall, wispy, and becomes increasingly frail as the season wears on. If you arrive in July, it may have already disappeared, and you will wonder why they built all those trail bridges over a pile of dry rocks. The fall drops about 1,000 feet before it hits the lake's edge, so it must have been about 1,400 feet tall before the great flood.

The star waterfall of the trip is Wapama, which you reach at 2.4

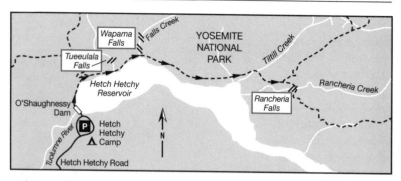

miles out. Wapama Falls on Falls Creek has such a wide, forceful flow that you can see it quite easily from O'Shaughnessy Dam and Hetch Hetchy Road even in midsummer. But the only place you can see the very top of the fall is from right below it, standing on one of its western bridges. In spring, you can't stand there for long without getting soaked. Bring your rain gear if it's a cool day.

Many folks simply hike to Wapama and back for an easy dayhike that's just shy of five miles long. The trail is remarkably level, and it is shaded by oaks, bays, and pines all the way up to Wapama Falls. Like at Tueeulala, you cross over Wapama's flow on a series of sturdy wood and steel bridges. Make sure you walk to the far end of them to see every possible perspective on the big fall.

If you decide to stop for a rest or a picnic anywhere along the trail, keep in mind that the rules are strict at Hetch Hetchy: no swimming, no boating, no water contact, but fishing is okay. One ranger told us it was okay to wade into the creeks to cool off, and we saw several hikers doing this. But since the creeks empty into the reservoir, the logic seems rather strange.

For those continuing to Rancheria Falls, the bad news is that the trail now starts to climb and is less shaded than before. The good news is that it's well-graded, with lots of gentle switchbacks. You walk on granite and you cast admiring glances at granite—Kolana Rock rises grandly from Hetch Hetchy's southern shore. From the bridges at Wapama Falls, it's four more miles and a 1,200-foot elevation gain to Rancheria Falls.

Because the trail rises, your wide-angle views of the reservoir improve. The water is so deep and so dramatically edged by granite, sand, and pines that sections of it are reminiscent of Lake Tahoe. Its depth creates a similar rich sapphire color. In the afternoon, the sunlight does some incredible twinkling on the reservoir's surface.

You reach Rancheria Creek about 5.7 miles out. Look for an

unmarked fork a quarter-mile after you first see the creek, at a notice-able clearing along the right side of the trail. This spur trail passes a backpackers' camp that is currently being restored, then it leads to a section of stream 100 yards below 30-foot Rancheria Falls.

Here at creekside, under the shade of Jeffrey pines and black oaks, is a choice spot for waterfall-viewing, a picnic, and a rest. But watch out for bears—a small one tried to steal our lunch when we turned our backs for 30 seconds to look at the falls. If you're back-packing, use a bear-proof food canister or hang your food high. The bears at Hetch Hetchy are some of the biggest thieves in Yosemite.

For another look at Rancheria Falls, continue on the main trail for a half-mile beyond the spur trail. At a trail junction, continue straight for Pleasant Valley. One-tenth mile further is a bridge above Rancheria Creek, where in high water you can glimpse the down-stream falls.

Trip notes: There is a $20 entrance fee at Yosemite National Park, good for seven days. A free wilderness permit is required for overnight stays. They are available on a first-come, first-served basis at the wilderness kiosk near your chosen trailhead, or in advance by mail or phone; call (209) 372-0740. Park maps are available for free at the entrance stations. A more detailed map is available for a fee from Tom Harrison Cartography, (415) 456-7940. For more information, contact Yosemite National Park Public Information Office, P.O. Box 577, Yosemite National Park, CA 95389; (209) 372-0200.

Directions: From Groveland, drive east on Highway 120 for 22.5 miles to the Evergreen Road turnoff signed for Hetch Hetchy Reservoir (one mile west of the Big Oak Flat entrance to Yosemite). Follow Evergreen Road north to Camp Mather, then bear right and continue on Hetch Hetchy Road for a total of 16 miles to the dam and trailhead.

76. DIANA FALLS

Stanislaus National Forest
Off Highway 120 near Yosemite

Access & Difficulty: Hike-in 1.0 mile RT/Easy
Elevation: Start at 3,100 feet; total loss 50 feet
Best Season: April to October

You could think of it as a neighborhood backyard swimming hole, except there's no neighborhood anywhere nearby. Diana Falls is set in Stanislaus National Forest, not far from the towns of Groveland

Diana Falls

and Coulterville and within an hour's drive of Yosemite National Park. But it's not on the road to any of those places, so you won't come across it by accident. It's an out-of-the-way, 20-foot-tall waterfall on Bean Creek, near its confluence with the North Fork Merced River.

From the trailhead, hike along the west side of the river, following an old dirt road for a half mile. Here the Merced River is a small, tame stream, with bunches of elephant ears growing along its banks. The dirt road gets narrower as you walk, eventually becoming singletrack. At a fork in the trail, bear right. You'll leave the river and hike along the Bean Creek canyon. In just a few minutes, or about 150 yards, you'll reach the brink of Diana Falls. Several spurs descend the slope to its base.

Although the small, pretty waterfall looks tame enough, exercise extreme caution on the slick granite surrounding it. I had the worst accident of my entire hiking career right here—a long and unhappy story. Still, Diana Falls and its canyon are lovely, its swimming holes are first-rate, and you could easily spend a fun-filled afternoon here.

Trip notes: There is no fee. For more information, contact Stanislaus National Forest, Groveland Ranger District, 24545 Highway 120, Groveland, CA 95321; (209) 962-7825.

Directions: From Groveland, drive east on Highway 120 for seven miles to Smith Station Road (also signed as County Road J132 to Coulterville). Drive 5.7 miles, then make a sharp left turn on Greeley Hills Road. Drive 4.2 miles to the trailhead, just before a one-lane bridge. The trailhead (a gated dirt road at a "Road Closed" sign) is on the right and a large parking pullout is on the left. (Or, from Coulterville at the junction of highways 132 and 49, go east on Coulterville Road (County Road J132) for 8.5 miles, then bear right on Greeley Hills Road for 4.2 miles.)

77. RAINBOW POOL FALLS

Stanislaus National Forest
Off Highway 120 near Yosemite

Access & Difficulty: Hike-in 0.25 mile RT/Easy
Elevation: Start at 3,100 feet; total loss 50 feet
Best Season: April to October

Yosemite National Park is so spectacular that it often over-shadows many equally beautiful areas just outside the park borders. Visitors are often so busy trying to take in all of Yosemite that they miss other special places that are just minutes away.

Rainbow Pool Falls is such a place. It's a combination 20-foot waterfall and swimming hole, located on Highway 120 in Stanislaus National Forest, just 10 miles from the Big Oak Flat entrance to Yosemite and directly on the route to Cherry Lake and Hetch Hetchy.

Rainbow Pool Falls

It's the perfect place to take your kids swimming for the afternoon when Yosemite Valley is too hot and crowded, or to go waterfall-watching and people-watching any time.

The entrance to Rainbow Pool is marked with a somewhat nondescript Forest Service sign, so be sure to watch for it at the highway bridge over the South Fork of the Tuolumne River. From the parking lot, a paved path leads a few hundred feet down to the fall's giant pool, one of the finest swimming holes I've ever seen at the base of a waterfall.

Rainbow Pool Falls is a river fall, so although it's not tall, it's wide and powerful with a full, rushing flow year-round. At its base is a perfectly round rock basin, bigger than most backyard swimming pools, with a small beach area. This is where people bring their lawn chairs to watch bold swimmers dive, jump, slide, and wade around the falls and in the pool.

Teenagers seem particularly drawn to the waterfall's rock cliffs, about 20 feet high, which they use as a jumping-off place. Younger kids and more cautious adults prefer to slide down the granite chute next to the main body of the waterfall. Many people do this in their bathing suits, but the timid (or wise) wear denim to protect their backsides.

Besides the pretty waterfall and the natural diving board and slide, another great bonus here for swimmers is that the water is warm. You don't have to jump in and jump back out again immediately, and there is enough circumference to the pool to swim around a bit without fear of getting hit by other divers. It's good fun.

It's also popular. If you want privacy, try swimming in the smaller pools above the falls. A trail leads upstream along the right side of the river, and you can walk as far as you like until a particular basin strikes your fancy. (Look for the trail at the closed bridge just above the waterfall, at the far edge of the parking lot.)

One caveat: Be sure to time your visit between 8 A.M. and 6 P.M., because the Forest Service locks the gates after hours to prevent people from getting rowdy at the falls in the evening. Rainbow Pool Falls is meant for good clean fun and rangers plan to keep it that way.

Trip notes: There is no fee. For more information, contact Stanislaus National Forest, Groveland Ranger District, 24545 Highway 120, Groveland, CA 95321; (209) 962-7825.

Directions: From Groveland, drive east on Highway 120 for 13 miles (toward Yosemite National Park). The Rainbow Pool turnoff is on the right, at the highway bridge over the South Fork of the Tuolumne River, just before the road to Cherry Lake/Sweetwater Camp on the left.

78. CARLON FALLS

Stanislaus National Forest
Off Highway 120 near Yosemite

Access & Difficulty: Hike-in 4.5 miles RT/Easy
Elevation: Start at 4,500 feet; total gain 150 feet
Best Season: Year-round

In the minds of most park visitors, the words "Yosemite" and "waterfalls" go together like peanut butter and jelly. Except in fall. That's when people show up in Yosemite Valley, look at all the dark, dried-up water stains on the granite walls, and have to squint real hard and visualize.

If you prefer your autumn waterfalls to be real and not imagined, autumn is a perfect time to make the trip to Carlon Falls, on the South Fork Tuolumne River in the northwest section of Yosemite. The trip begins on Stanislaus National Forest land, then enters the Yosemite Wilderness, so a bonus is that you can visit Carlon Falls any time you want, without having to deal with the crowds and the day-use fees in Yosemite.

It's an easy hike, suitable for everyone. The key is to make sure you walk on the north side of the river and not on the south side, where the picnic area is located. The north side has an excellent trail with an easy grade. The south side has an unmaintained

Carlon Falls

fisherman's route, which is fun to take if you don't mind scrambling through branches, climbing over rocks, and doing the limbo under fallen trees.

Make it easy on yourself and hike on the river's north side, heading upstream. You'll pass a Yosemite Wilderness sign a few hundred yards in, then walk by the foundation of an old house. The trail stays close to the creek for the first mile, then moves away from it as it climbs gently in its second mile.

It's just over two miles to Carlon Falls, which means you'll be there in about an hour. The 35-foot fall drops over a granite ledge in a wide stream, with more flow than you might expect from the size of the river. (It's additionally fueled by a feeder creek just upstream from the falls.) About 100 yards downstream of the main fall, there's a long, lacelike cascade, with water streaming over and around potholes in the granite.

This area is open for hiking almost year-round because it receives little snow. In spring, the river and falls run with incredible velocity and power. In summer, the air temperature is warm for hiking, but there are plenty of swimming holes for cooling off, including a wide one at the waterfall's base. In autumn—my favorite season here—the dogwoods and black oaks turn gold and red, the bear clover is aromatic in the crisp air, and miraculously, the waterfall still flows.

An incredible amount of plant speciation surrounds the river and waterfall, a result of the low elevation. In addition to the hardwoods, there are plenty of cedars and pines, many of them covered with thick moss, and tons of ferns and reeds growing near the water. The Indian rhubarb clumped around the falls is some of the largest I've seen anywhere, and together with the ferns, it turns a dazzling yellow color in October.

Trip notes: There is no fee. For more information, contact Stanislaus National Forest, Groveland Ranger District, 24545 Highway 120, Groveland, CA 95321; (209) 962-7825.

Directions: From Groveland, drive east on Highway 120 for 22.5 miles to the Evergreen Road turnoff signed for Hetch Hetchy Reservoir (one mile west of the Big Oak Flat entrance to Yosemite). Follow Evergreen Road north for one mile to the far side of the bridge, just past Carlon Day-Use Area. Park on the right at the closed-off road on the north side of the bridge. (There is room for about five cars.) Begin hiking on the closed road, heading upstream. The road turns to single-track in about 100 yards.

79. FORESTA FALLS

Yosemite National Park
Off Big Oak Flat Road in Foresta

Access & Difficulty: Hike-in & Scramble 0.5 mile RT/Easy
Elevation: Start at 4,000 feet; total loss 100 feet
Best Season: March to July

If you're looking for an easy walk with a pretty waterfall, maybe a little solitude to go along with it, a drive to the small town of Foresta can fulfill your desire.

Foresta's not much of a town, just a group of private cabins tucked inside the border of Yosemite National Park. The little community is unknown to most park visitors because it's situated down in a valley below Big Oak Flat Road, hidden from sight to people driving by. Most of the cabins are rented to park employees.

Most people know the Big Oak Flat Road area as the fire-scarred stretch you drive through on your way from Yosemite Valley to Tioga Road. In 1990, a lightning fire ignited here. Fueled by fierce winds, it started a firestorm that burned a total of 17,000 acres, including the little town of Foresta. The fire raged out of control for weeks.

Foresta Falls

But, as usually happens after a wildfire, Mother Nature got busy. Although there are many burned and blackened trees still standing, making thousands of acres look like a ghost forest, the undergrowth has come back in full force. Homeowners in Foresta have rebuilt their cabins and the area is quickly returning to its old state.

Foresta Falls on Crane Creek sits on the perimeter of the burned area, just outside a cluster of cabins. When you hike around the falls, you can clearly see the patchwork of burned and untouched vegetation. One tree is green and thriving; its neighbor is blackened. The effect can be kind of eerie, yet hauntingly beautiful.

To see the falls, you don't have to walk far. Park where the pavement stops on Foresta Road, then walk a quarter-mile on the dirt road, past a "closed road" sign, till you're next to the falls. If you want to see the falls close-up, you'll have to make a path through some brush. It's a good idea to wear long pants and a long-sleeved shirt. Even though it's only about 50 yards to creekside, poison oak is thriving in the fire's aftermath. (Poison oak and bracken ferns are usually the first plants to regenerate in a burned area.)

The waterfall is a long series of drops over granite, with cascades that continue for several hundred feet. In summer, Foresta Falls has little water, but in spring it can be a glorious deluge. Indian rhubarb grows in large clumps in the stream, poking out of the granite creekbed from the smallest of cracks.

We didn't explore too far, as we became particularly captivated with one nice drop near the top of Foresta Falls. When we visited in late summer, the cascade had a flat pool below it that was only a couple of inches deep, with a tiny island of granite in the middle. In the late afternoon light, it looked more like a mirror than a waterfall pool. We sat alongside it to chew on some turkey jerky and ponder the power of the falls and the fire.

Trip notes: There is a $20 entrance fee at Yosemite National Park, good for seven days. Park maps are available for free at the entrance stations. A more detailed map is available for a fee from Tom Harrison Cartography, (415) 456-7940. For more information, contact Yosemite National Park Public Information Office, P.O. Box 577, Yosemite National Park, CA 95389; (209) 372-0200.

Directions: From Merced, drive 75 miles northeast on Highway 140 to Yosemite National Park. Follow the signs toward Yosemite Valley, entering through the Arch Rock entrance station. Continue 4.5 miles to the left turnoff for Tioga Road/Highway 120, looping back out of the valley on Big Oak Flat Road. In 3.4 miles, turn left on the unsigned Foresta Road. (It comes up six-tenths of a mile after exiting the third tunnel on Big Oak Flat Road.) Follow Foresta Road for 2.5 miles to the falls, just beyond a group of cabins. (Stay to the left at the fork.) Park where the pavement ends, and walk on the dirt road for a quarter-mile, past a sign that says "Road closed; unmaintained road only for emergencies."

80. LITTLE NELLIE FALLS

Stanislaus National Forest/Yosemite National Park
Off Big Oak Flat Road near Foresta

Access & Difficulty: Hike-in or Backpack 5.5 miles RT/Moderate
or Drive-to (4WD required)/Moderate
Elevation: Start at 4,000 feet; total gain 600 feet
Best Season: April to October

Little Nellie Falls on Little Crane Creek can be a drive-to waterfall or a hike-to waterfall, but I've done it both ways and I highly recommend the latter. If you begin your trip in the small community of Foresta in Yosemite National Park, you can hike less than three miles one-way to the waterfall, out of the park boundary and into Stanislaus National Forest. The route is a rough four-wheel-drive road that is rarely used. It's best taken on foot anyway, because it climbs above Foresta and Big Meadow to a rise just high enough for a view into the smack-dab-center of Yosemite Valley. There you are, 15 miles from Half Dome, and it looks close enough and imposing enough that you could reach out and touch it.

Little Nellie Falls

If you like, you can shave a little mileage off your route by driving your vehicle part of the distance. I recommend leaving your car just outside of Foresta, near either Big Meadow or Foresta Falls (see the previous story), and hiking the entire route. Along the way, keep looking over your right shoulder for the incredible view of Yosemite Valley.

It's a good climb to the top of the rise, heading northward with about a 500-foot gain, but then the trail levels out as you veer west. You leave the fire-scarred area around Foresta and enter into thick conifer and hardwood forest on the border of Stanislaus National Forest.

About a half-mile from the fall, you pass through a metal gate that you must close behind you. Then the road drops down to where Little Crane Creek crosses it. Little Nellie Falls is just above the road, in plain sight, a pretty drop of about 30 feet over a rock ledge, nestled in Indian rhubarb. There's a terrific campsite just across the road, next to Little Crane Creek, with a great view of the fall. You can spend the night here, if you like, with the sound of the water lulling you to sleep, but most people just hike in for the day, then make the easy trip back downhill to Big Meadow and Foresta.

If you happen to be in the northwest corner of Yosemite, near the Big Oak Flat entrance station, you can drive to Little Nellie Falls without entering Yosemite National Park. It's a long drive and four-wheel-drive is highly recommended. Here's how you do it: From Highway 120, turn south on to the eastern end of Harden Flat Road, 1.5 miles west of the Big Oak Flat entrance. In less than a half-mile, bear left on Forest Service Road 2S30, which is also signed as Road 20 in places, and head for Five Corners. Follow 2S30 for 8.5 miles along Crocker Ridge, through a burned area, until you reach Five Corners. Turn left on 1S12, a dirt road, heading for Trumbull Peak. Stay on 1S12 for 15 miles, following the road signs for Moss Canyon and then Little Nellie Falls.

Check out the incredible views into Yosemite Valley at approximately 13 miles on 1S12. At 15 miles, reach a hairpin left turn; take it and continue for three-tenths of a mile to Little Nellie Falls. (If you miss the hairpin turn and continue straight, the road dead-ends.)

Whether you drive or hike to the falls, a map of Stanislaus National Forest is highly recommended. A vast web of forest roads and spurs surrounds Little Nellie Falls.

Trip notes: To access the falls from Foresta, you must pay a $20 entrance fee at Yosemite National Park, good for seven days. The hike begins in Yosemite National Park but enters Stanislaus National Forest, so a Stanislaus National Forest map is recommended. For more information, contact Stanislaus National Forest, Groveland Ranger District, 24545 Highway 120, Groveland, CA 95321; (209) 962-7825.

Directions: From Merced, drive 75 miles northeast on Highway 140 to Yosemite National Park. Follow the signs toward Yosemite Valley, entering through the Arch Rock entrance station. Continue 4.5 miles to the left turnoff for Tioga Road/Highway 120, looping back out of the valley on Big Oak Flat Road. In 3.4 miles, turn left on the unsigned

Foresta Road (it comes up six-tenths of a mile after exiting the third tunnel on Big Oak Flat Road). Follow Foresta Road for 1.8 miles to a fork, where you should bear right and skirt along the edge of Big Meadow. Park off the road, being careful to stay off private property, and continue hiking up the dirt road, heading north and then west. (Most of the year, you can also drive this route, but four-wheel-drive is required.)

81-82. THE CASCADES & WILDCAT FALLS

Yosemite National Park
Off Highways 120/140 in Yosemite Valley

Access & Difficulty: Drive-to/Easy
   or Hike-in 0.5 mile RT/Easy
Elevation: Start at 3,900 feet; total gain 0 feet
Best Season: March to June

Of all the scenic places in California, only in Yosemite Valley can you have so many waterfall experiences so easily, and in such close proximity to one another.

Take Wildcat Falls and The Cascades, for example. To enter Yosemite National Park from the west, you make the narrow, winding drive along the Merced River on Highway 140. Then you pay your national park entrance fee and pick up a free map at the Arch Rock station. You drive less than three miles further and—wham! your head is turned by an incredibly tall and narrow spill of white water down the canyon wall on your left. Before you even have the chance to hit the brakes, your eyes are riveted to a wide, plunging cataract just a tenth of a mile later. This time you're prepared, and you make a quick turn into the parking lot to investigate.

Welcome to Yosemite. Wildcat Falls and The Cascades in spring serve as the valley's welcoming committee on Highway 140—a sure sign that you're here, you've made the long trip, and now the fun is about to begin. Many first-time visitors to the park are so excited by the sight of these falls, especially The Cascades, that they think they are looking at Yosemite Falls. Almost every spring you hear someone at The Cascades' parking lot asking to have their picture taken in front of "Yosemite Falls." Well, these falls are certainly good, but they're just a warm-up.

The two waterfalls are only a tenth of a mile apart, but they're vastly different in appearance and character. Wildcat Falls is by far the lesser known, mostly because it doesn't have a parking lot right in front of it. Some people drive by and don't even see it. The Cascades is impossible to miss, especially in springtime, but the waterfall is not signed in any way, so people rarely learn its name.

You can see both falls in the same visit, parking at either of the two lots near them and then walking a short route in between. You can park at Cascades Picnic Area on the south side of the road, which is actually closer to Wildcat Falls, or you can park at the parking lot by mile marker M1 on the north side of the road, which is where The Cascades falls.

The Cascades are easy to view. An overlook area by the M1 parking lot offers the best perspective, even though it's about 200 yards away from the base of the falls and off to the side. Many people get out of their cars, take a few pictures, and go sit somewhere close to the stream to inhale the sweet air of Yosemite. There are plenty of

The Cascades

huge boulders for kids to climb on and for adults to claim as a picnic spot. Each rock has a slightly different view of the falls.

From here, you can take a 10-minute walk to the west, paralleling the road on the north side, to see Wildcat Falls. Wildcat is more hidden by trees than The Cascades, so it's easier to see by foot than by car. From the M1 parking lot, you'll see a good use trail leading west that stays safely off the road. If you're parked in the Cascades Picnic Area lot, just cross the road and pick up the route on the other side, still heading west.

Wildcat is a tall, narrow freefall, very different in shape from The Cascades. You can walk right to its base, but I like to stand back about 50 feet, next to a large Jeffrey pine, where the cataract's great height is visible.

Surprisingly, both waterfalls continue to flow in autumn, when most waterfalls in Yosemite Valley are dry. They're not their lavish springtime selves, of course, but they run. Wildcat Falls is formed on little Wildcat Creek, which has a relatively small watershed but a lot of vegetation, whereas The Cascades are formed by two streams, Cascade Creek and Tamarack Creek. The two streams join several hundred feet above you, just below Big Oak Flat Road. Cascade Creek forms waterfalls all the way up and above Big Oak Flat Road, although none is as pretty as The Cascades.

To view Cascade Creek's higher falls on Big Oak Flat Road, take the left turnoff for Highway 120/Tioga Road 1.7 miles east of the M1 parking lot, then drive 1.9 miles, through two tunnels, to the parking pullouts on both sides of the bridge over Cascade Creek. You can walk on the bridge to look at the fall.

Many people stop to admire Cascade Creek's upper falls on Big Oak Flat Road without realizing that further downstream, where Cascade Creek joins with its next-door neighbor, Tamarack Creek, the real falls begin. People often visit both sets of falls on Cascade Creek—those on Big Oak Flat Road and Highway 140—without realizing they are formed by the same creek.

For a look at the full 500-foot height of The Cascades, you must drive east on Big Oak Flat Road, coming from the Big Oak Flat park entrance or from Tioga Road into the valley. A half-mile west of the bridge over Cascade Creek, there's a long pullout on the south side of the road, offering an incredible sweeping view of the entire height of The Cascades, with Yosemite Valley as a backdrop.

Trip notes: There is a $20 entrance fee at Yosemite National Park, good for seven days. Park maps are available for free at the entrance stations. A more detailed map is available for a fee from Tom Harrison Cartography, (415) 456-7940. For more information, contact Yosemite National Park Public Information Office, P.O. Box 577, Yosemite National Park, CA 95389; (209) 372-0200.

Directions: From Merced, drive 75 miles northeast on Highway 140 to Yosemite National Park. Follow the signs toward Yosemite Valley, entering through the Arch Rock entrance station. Set your odometer at Arch Rock, and drive 2.8 miles east, into the valley. Park at either the Cascades picnic area/parking lot on the right side of the road, or the parking lot by the M1 road marker on the left side of the road. (The parking lot by the M1 road marker is one-tenth mile further east.)

83. STAIRCASE FALLS

Yosemite National Park
Off Highways 120/140 in Yosemite Valley

Access & Difficulty: Drive-to/Easy
Elevation: 3,200 feet
Best Season: March to July

Staircase Falls delivers exactly what its name promises—a waterfall that drops in a perfect series of stair-stepped right angles. Instead of seeing the "staircase" from the front, you see it from the side, and are treated to an unusual view of a tidy chain of linked L-shapes descending gracefully down the cliff behind Curry Village.

People who vacation in the village in springtime tend to think of Staircase Falls as their own private waterfall, but you can see it without staying at the hotel or camping in the tent cabins. The best vista is not in Curry Village at all, but in the large meadow just north of the village, called Stoneman Meadow on some maps.

Staircase is one of Yosemite Valley's ephemeral falls—the kind you have to act fast to see. By late July, it will have vanished. The fall is very narrow compared to many others in the valley, but it wins the Most Unusual Shape award, hands-down. Binoculars are a good idea, although you can see the outline of the falls without them.

From your viewpoint in the meadow, you also have a fine lookout on Half Dome, North Dome, Washington Column, and Glacier Point. If you time it just right, you may be able to spot Royal Arch Cascade on the opposite canyon wall, flowing downhill just to the left of the Royal Arches. (The Arches are easily distinguishable on the north canyon wall by their archlike shape.)

Trip notes: There is a $20 entrance fee at Yosemite National Park, good for seven days. Park maps are available for free at the entrance stations. A more detailed map is available for a fee from Tom Harrison Cartography, (415) 456-7940. For more information, contact Yosemite National Park Public Information Office, P.O. Box 577, Yosemite National Park, CA 95389; (209) 372-0200.

Directions: From Merced, drive 75 miles northeast on Highway 140 to Yosemite National Park. Follow the signs toward Yosemite Valley, entering through the Arch Rock entrance station. Continue on El Portal Road, which becomes Southside Drive, for 11.6 miles to the Curry Village day-use parking area. Don't turn right into Curry Village; instead, continue straight to the pullouts on the north side of the big meadow. Park and look at the south canyon wall, behind Curry Village.

84. RIBBON FALL

Yosemite National Park
Off Highways 120/140 in Yosemite Valley

Access & Difficulty: Hike-in or Wheelchair 0.5 mile/Easy
   Drive-to/Easy
Elevation: Start at 3,980 feet; total gain 50 feet
Best Season: March to June

When all the waterfalls are flowing in Yosemite Valley, usually in that brief March-to-June period of snowmelt and spring rain, you may notice a curious pattern: At several places in the park, if you stand facing one waterfall, another waterfall can be found directly at your back.

For instance, Yosemite Falls plunges off the canyon's north wall, while across from it, Sentinel Fall dives off the south wall. Staircase Falls stairsteps down the canyon's south wall, while across from it, Royal Arch Cascade tumbles down the north wall. Bridalveil Fall hurtles off the canyon's south wall, while across from it, Ribbon Fall leaps off the north wall.

I call this pattern the "pairing" of Valley waterfalls. There's no logical or even geological explanation for it, and the phenomenon doesn't last long. Many of these falls dry up before summer arrives.

One of the best spots to see the pairing effect is at the Bridalveil Fall overlook (a short walk from the Bridalveil parking area). If you stare up at Bridalveil, then do an about-face and turn your back on it, you're looking directly at 1,612-foot Ribbon Fall, a tall, delicate, silver thread of a waterfall. It seems impossibly long and narrow, just like its name. Many people see Ribbon from the Bridalveil overlook and mistake it for Yosemite Falls, probably because of its position on the north wall of the canyon, but Ribbon's yearly life span is far shorter than Yosemite's, and its flow is much weaker.

Although Ribbon Fall doesn't have the splashy, showy presence of other Valley falls, it holds the illustrious title of being the highest free-leaping waterfall in Yosemite. The operative word is free-leaping, because unlike most falls, Ribbon has no points where its stream contacts the granite wall behind it, forming a cascade. Instead, its fall remains unbroken. (Yosemite Falls, in contrast, free-leaps 1,430 feet, then cascades 675 feet, then free-leaps another 320 feet.)

Ribbon Fall also has the distinction of having El Capitan for its neighbor. If you park your car in the parking pullouts on either side of Southside Drive near Cathedral Rocks (look for road marker V14, a half-mile east of the Highway 41/Bridalveil Fall turnoff), you get an incredible vista of El Capitan (7,042 feet) with Ribbon Fall on its left. And of course, if you simply turn around, you can see Ribbon's pair, Bridalveil Fall, dashing off the south canyon wall. Be sure to get a photo of Ribbon Fall arm-in-arm with El Capitan, because next to that huge piece of granite, Ribbon looks even more spectacular.

But remember, you've got to make your trip early. By midsummer each year, Ribbon Fall disappears.

Trip notes: There is a $20 entrance fee at Yosemite National Park, good for seven days. Park maps are available for free at the entrance stations. A more detailed map is available for a fee from Tom Harrison Cartography, (415) 456-7940. For more information, contact Yosemite National Park Public Information Office, P.O. Box 577, Yosemite National Park, CA 95389; (209) 372-0200.

Directions: To see Ribbon Falls from the Bridalveil overlook, follow the driving directions for Bridalveil Fall on page 198. Another good viewing point is near road marker V14 on Southside Drive, 6.6 miles east of the Arch Rock entrance (a half-mile east of the Highway 41/Bridalveil Fall turnoff).

85. SILVER STRAND FALLS

Yosemite National Park
Off Highway 41 near Yosemite Valley

Access & Difficulty: Hike-in 7.6 miles RT/Strenuous
  or Hike-in 13.0 miles RT/Moderate
Elevation: Start at 4,400 feet; total gain 2,200 feet (7.6-mile RT)
  or Start at 7,000 feet; total loss 400 feet (13.0-mile RT)
Best Season: April to June

The funny thing about Yosemite waterfalls is that there are so many of them, you can get a little jaded. Even some cartographers have gotten blasé about Yosemite waterfalls—so much so that they don't bother drawing them in on maps, unless the falls happen to be world-famous, such as Yosemite Falls or Bridalveil. Many other excellent park waterfalls suffer from neglect, because everybody is off visiting the celebrated ones.

Take Silver Strand Falls, on the south canyon rim. Silver Strand would be worthy of its own park in any other part of California, but here in Yosemite, you can't even find it on the park map. It's a pity, because hiking to Silver Strand Falls is a stellar trip, complete with thick forest, a huge waterfall, and unparalleled scenic vistas.

Silver Strand is perched between Inspiration Point and Stanford Point, closer to the latter, a quarter-mile off the Pohono Trail. There's a long way and a short way to get there, and most people choose to hike the short way, starting from the Wawona Tunnel trailhead. Heading steadily uphill the whole way, the trail reaches stunning Inspiration Point at 1.3 miles, followed by Stanford Point at 3.8 miles. Stanford Point is accessible via a short spur trail to the left, which extends to the valley's rim, and from there, you can observe the waterfall's 1,170-foot drop, formed where Meadow Brook takes a dive off Yosemite's south canyon wall.

The Wawona trailhead itself is a destination for many park visitors, because the views from here are as good as anywhere in the park, with the possible exception of Glacier Point. The parking lot has stellar vistas of Bridalveil Fall, Half Dome, El Capitan, and the entire valley. Park on either side of the road just east of the Wawona Tunnel; then find the trailhead on the south side.

Three facts should be understood when planning your trip: First, the Pohono Trail does not go directly to Silver Strand Falls; in fact, no trail does. The only way to see it is to hike to Stanford Point, then look to the west. The fall is only a quarter-mile away, over your left shoulder as you face Yosemite Valley. The view from the point is remarkable, taking in Silver Strand Falls, Bridalveil Fall, Ribbon Falls, and the valley floor 3,000 feet below you.

Second, the waterfall's duration is short—it flows only in spring. By July, Meadow Brook (Silver Strand's stream) dries up completely. And finally, there are no bridges on this part of the Pohono Trail. Hiking from the Wawona Tunnel, you must cross Meadow Brook to reach Stanford Point, and this can be a challenge. When Silver Strand is at its strongest flow, conditions will be either very wet or very snowy along the Pohono Trail, especially at the stream crossing. When we hiked it, snow still covered the ground and a snow bridge carried us across. You must check with rangers about springtime trail conditions before you head out.

It's a grunt of a climb to get to Stanford Point from the Wawona Tunnel trailhead, with a gain of 2,200 feet. This explains why some people opt for the longer-but-more-level route, which starts at the McGurk Meadow trailhead on Glacier Point Road. From there, you head out on the McGurk Meadow Trail for 2.2 miles, then turn left on the Pohono Trail. Hike four miles, then take the right cutoff for

Stanford Point. In addition to an easy grade, this longer route has some incredible scenic offerings, including pristine McGurk Meadow (1.2 miles in) and three vista points: Dewey (5.2 miles in), Crocker (5.8 miles in), and Stanford (6.5 miles in). Perched at 7,300 feet in elevation, these three points have unique perspectives on just about everything in the valley. Bring plenty of film.

Trip notes: There is a $20 entrance fee at Yosemite National Park, good for seven days. Park maps are available for free at the entrance stations. A more detailed map is available for a fee from Tom Harrison Cartography, (415) 456-7940. For more information, contact Yosemite National Park Public Information Office, P.O. Box 577, Yosemite National Park, CA 95389; (209) 372-0200.

Directions: Wawona Tunnel Trailhead—From Merced, drive 75 miles northeast on Highway 140 to Yosemite National Park. Follow the signs toward Yosemite Valley, entering through the Arch Rock entrance station. Continue on El Portal Road, which becomes Southside Drive, for 6.3 miles, then turn right at the fork for Highway 41/Wawona/Fresno. Continue 1.5 miles to the parking lots on either side of the road just before you enter the Wawona Tunnel. The trailhead is at the parking lot on the left (south) side of the road.

McGurk Meadow Trailhead—Follow the directions as above, but continue through the Wawona Tunnel and beyond for another eight miles to Glacier Point Road. Turn left on Glacier Point Road, and drive 7.5 miles to the McGurk Meadow Trailhead on the left. Park in the pullout about 75 yards further up the road.

---

86. SENTINEL FALL

Yosemite National Park
Off Highways 120/140 in Yosemite Valley

Access & Difficulty: Hike-in 4.0 miles RT/Moderate
   or Drive-to/Easy
Elevation: Start at 7,214 feet; total gain 500 feet
Best Season: March to June

In the list of the 10 Highest Freefalling Waterfalls in the World, waterfalls in Yosemite Valley claim two spots—number 5 and number 8. Yosemite Falls on the north valley wall is rated as a freefall of 2,425 feet, and Sentinel Fall on the south valley wall is rated as a freefall of 2,000 feet. (These two are only beaten by Angel Falls in Venezuela at 3,212 feet, Tugela Falls in South Africa at 3,110 feet, and a few hard-to-spell Norwegian waterfalls in the 2,500-foot range.)

Well, just about anybody who has ever been to the Sierra Nevada has seen Yosemite Falls. But in an unofficial poll I took one spring day in Yosemite Valley, few people had even heard of Sentinel Fall, even though they were all standing within easy view of it.

You can see it by car or you can see it by foot. We first found it while driving on Northside Drive, heading west out of the valley. When we pulled into a small parking area between the Three Brothers and El Capitan and walked a few yards down to the Merced River's edge, we spotted an incredibly long, thin waterfall leaping and sliding down the right side of Sentinel Rock, far across the canyon.

Of course, if you are going to view Sentinel Fall from this far away, you'll need to bring your binoculars. Or do what we did, which was to loop back around the valley to get a better look from Southside Drive, near the Four Mile Trail trailhead. Pullouts are located on both sides of the road, and if you aren't too distracted by the views to the north of Yosemite Falls, you'll be able to spot Sentinel Fall to the south. To make it easy, first locate Sentinel Rock, then look for the fall pouring down to the right. Sentinel Fall is set back slightly from Sentinel Rock, and it has three main free-leaping sections connected by brief cascades.

So if Sentinel Fall is the eighth largest waterfall in the world, why doesn't it get more attention? Sentinel Fall, like dozens of other waterfalls in Yosemite, is an ephemeral waterfall, which means it doesn't run year-round. In fact, if you don't get to Yosemite in springtime, you have to wait a whole year for another chance to see Sentinel Fall. Although Yosemite Falls is also an ephemeral fall, its creek is full enough and drains a large enough watershed so that it runs a few months longer than Sentinel, and with a more spectacular show.

If you prefer to see Sentinel Fall close-up, drive to Glacier Point Road and lace up your hiking boots. In addition to having the chance to see the fall from its brink, you also get to take a classic Yosemite high-country hike that is short enough and easy enough for families to enjoy. The trip is a great four-mile loop from the Sentinel Dome and Taft Point trailhead, and if you add an extra mile to it, you can visit Taft Point, with its spectacular rock fissures and view of the valley floor 3,000 feet below.

It's best to start the loop by heading left, toward Taft Point. After a half-mile, take the right fork to go directly to Sentinel Fall (the trail is signed for Sentinel Dome and Glacier Point), or take the left fork for a half-mile side-trip to Taft Point, then return to the junction. If you head directly to Sentinel Fall, you'll walk through dense Jeffrey pine forest for a mile and then meet up with Sentinel Creek. There's no bridge, so if the creek is flooding, cross it with great care.

Take the spur trail on the far side of the creek that runs for 50 yards to the canyon rim, where you can peer over the edge (very carefully) at Sentinel's big drop. In springtime, the sight of the powerful plunge can make your toes curl. Check out the interesting view of the back side of Sentinel Rock, which is just ahead of you.

From Sentinel Creek, the trail climbs for a mile, reaching some spectacular overlooks of Yosemite Valley and Yosemite Falls, then reaches a junction where you head right for Sentinel Dome, a half-mile away. Climb some more to reach its base, where you can decide whether or not to take another side-trip off your loop—ascending to the top of the dome for spectacular views to the north and east. If you've got any energy left, go for it. It only takes about 10 minutes to reach the top, and it makes you feel like a real mountaineer.

At the base of the dome, pick up the paved trail that curves around to its south side, then head back to the dirt single-track path for the final leg of your loop. It's just one mile back to the trailhead.

Trip notes: There is a $20 entrance fee at Yosemite National Park, good for seven days. Park maps are available for free at the entrance stations. A more detailed map is available for a fee from Tom Harrison Cartography, (415) 456-7940. For more information, contact Yosemite National Park Public Information Office, P.O. Box 577, Yosemite National Park, CA 95389; (209) 372-0200.

Directions: From Merced, drive 75 miles northeast on Highway 140 to Yosemite National Park. Follow the signs toward Yosemite Valley, entering through the Arch Rock entrance station. Continue on El Portal Road, which becomes Southside Drive, for 6.3 miles, then turn right at the fork for Highway 41/Wawona/Fresno. Continue for 9.2 miles, then turn left on Glacier Point Road and drive 13.2 miles to the Taft Point/Sentinel Dome trailhead parking lot, on the left side of the road.)

87. ILLILOUETTE FALL

Yosemite National Park
Off Highway 41 near Glacier Point

Access & Difficulty: Hike-in 4.0 miles RT/Moderate
or Hike-in 8.5 miles one-way via shuttle/Moderate
Elevation: Start at 7,214 feet; total loss 1,200 feet (4.0-mile RT)
or Start at 7,214 feet; total loss 3,200 feet (8.5-mile one-way trip)
Best Season: May to October; road closed in winter

There are two good ways to make the trip to Illilouette Fall: You can take an easy and unbelievably scenic out-and-back hike from Glacier Point, or a longer one-way journey from Glacier Point all the way to the valley floor, passing Illilouette, Vernal, and Nevada falls on your way.

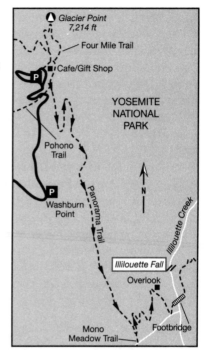

Both trips offer mindboggling scenery—the kind that gets imprinted on your brain so that you can't forget it—on the well-named Panorama Trail from Glacier Point. The trail offers bird's-eye views of Vernal and Nevada falls, Half Dome, and plenty more of the valley's stunning geological features.

Both trips are moderate day-hikes. But the out-and-back to Illilouette from Glacier Point takes only about two hours as you cover four miles, downhill on the way to the falls and uphill on the way back. The one-way hike from Glacier Point to the valley floor is 8.5 miles, downhill almost all the way with some steep descents as you stairstep alongside Vernal and Nevada falls. It takes about five hours. In addition, you need to ride the Yosemite Hiker's Bus back to Glacier Point to retrieve your car, or arrange a car shuttle or pickup from a friend in the valley. (There is a fee for the Hiker's Bus. Phone 209/372-1240 for rates, pickup times, and locations.) Adding in the transportation arrangements, the 8.5-mile hike usually expands into a full day.

Which trip you take to Illilouette is really a decision based on time and logistics more than anything else. Either way, you start at Glacier Point, elevation 7,214 feet, the trailhead with what is probably the grandest view in the West, encompassing Half Dome, Basket Dome, North Dome, Liberty Cap, and Vernal and Nevada falls. When you leave your car and begin hiking on the Panorama Trail, you get the same vista as from Glacier Point, but you get more of it. Your view changes with every footstep; a different angle on the scene is offered with each passing moment.

A trail sign tells you that Illilouette Fall is two miles away, but you quickly forget about the destination as the journey provides eyefuls upon eyefuls of grandeur.

The Panorama Trail slowly switchbacks downhill, curving through a fire-scarred area. Shrub-type growth proliferates, typical after a fire, including ceanothus, bear clover, and young dogwoods. Deer adore the newly grown foliage found on the slopes. On each of my trips here, I've had a few does or a buck for companions along the trail.

After a series of downhill switchbacks, Panorama Trail junctions with a trail leading to Mono Meadow, but you continue left for Illilouette. In a few minutes you'll reach an overlook directly across from the fall, and you may be surprised to see that you've approached it from a sideways angle, rather than from behind or in front. That's because Illilouette doesn't pour from the back of a canyon, rather it rushes over its side wall, where the creek drops 370 feet over a granite lip. The canyon is pencil-thin with vertical rock walls, so the only vantage point is from the side. It's a spectacular sight.

Illilouette Fall

Illilouette must be one of the greatest place names in all of Yosemite. It sounds French, but it's not; it's actually a bastardized English translation of a Yosemite Indian word, which was originally something like "Tooloolaweack." To the Indians, the word was the name for the place where they gathered to hunt for deer.

After you've rested a while and enjoyed the view, follow the trail as it descends and then crosses a bridge over Illilouette Creek, just above the falls. Posted signs warn people not to swim here, because the bridge is only about 50 yards above the drop. Don't try it in a barrel, either.

Those opting for the shorter hike should turn around at the Illilouette bridge, preparing themselves for the 1,200-foot climb back to Glacier Point. Hikers continuing all the way to the valley floor will find that the trail now switchbacks uphill for the first time, leading to the high southeast canyon wall. From there, you can see all the way across Yosemite Valley to Upper Yosemite Fall, and after a few more minutes of walking, you can see all the way to Lower Yosemite Fall as well. Your perspective on the falls is an unusual one: From most vantage points, Upper and Lower Yosemite Falls appear to be right on top of each other, but from here, you can clearly see how far apart they are. The middle cascades, which separate them, are long and nearly horizontal.

Keep walking; more waterfalls await. In a little more than an hour from the Illilouette Fall bridge, you reach a cutoff trail for 594-foot Nevada Fall, now only two-tenths of a mile away.

The trail takes you to a bridge just above the big drop, where the Merced River gathers steam to form the fall's tremendous flow. You can cross the bridge to an overlook area on the fall's north side, although you can't see very much when you're at its brink. If you lean over the piped railing (hold on tightly), you can look deep into the swirling mist at the bottom of the fall, which appears like a giant block of dry ice, clouded and mysterious.

From here, you have two choices for your descent: You can take the John Muir Trail (on the south side of the falls) or the Mist Trail (on the north). The Mist Trail is more well-known, and perhaps more dramatic, but both trails offer great views. If your knees or ankles are bothering you from the five-plus miles of downhill hiking you've already done, give yourself a break and take the John Muir Trail, which is less steep. You can always cut over to the Mist Trail at Clark Point, just before Vernal Fall, so you get a taste of both routes.

The John Muir Trail offers a tremendous full-length view of Nevada Fall as its route leads along a rocky cliff edge. Keep looking back at the fall as you walk away from it. (If you take the Mist Trail, you'll be so busy watching your step as you descend on the slippery, rocky staircase—and watching out for other hikers ascending—that you probably won't be admiring the scenery much.) Watch for the cutoff on your right for the Mist Trail, which will take you to 317-foot Vernal Fall. Even if you choose to take the John Muir Trail all

Nevada Falls from the John Muir Trail

the way down to the valley, at least take the cutoff trail a half-mile back and forth to the top of Vernal Fall. (The John Muir Trail does not go to Vernal.)

Vernal Fall, like Nevada, has a railed overlook area at the fall's lip, but again this on-top perspective is not your best view. From the top of Vernal Fall, you can return to the John Muir Trail (adding an extra mile to your trip, but with less of a steep downhill grade) or take the Mist Trail's stunning staircase descent. If you want to see the best views of Vernal Fall, continue down-canyon on the Mist Trail. This is the time to don your rain gear, especially in spring, when the waterfall's spray can be a downpour.

The most famous vista of Vernal Fall is further downstream at the Vernal Fall footbridge, only seven-tenths of a mile from Happy Isles. After taking a few pictures here, it's an easy stroll back to the trail's end. Be sure to check out the last-minute, bonus view of Illilouette Falls in the last half-mile of trail after you cross the Vernal Fall footbridge. This time you see it from the bottom looking up.

At Happy Isles, ride the free Yosemite Valley shuttle bus to your shuttle car parked in the valley or to the pickup point for the Yosemite Hiker's Bus.

(For more information about the Mist Trail, John Muir Trail, and Vernal and Nevada falls, see the Vernal and Nevada falls story that follows.)

Trip notes: There is a $20 entrance fee at Yosemite National Park, good for seven days. Park maps are available for free at the entrance stations.

A more detailed map is available for a fee from Tom Harrison Cartography, (415) 456-7940. For more information, contact Yosemite National Park Public Information Office, P.O. Box 577, Yosemite National Park, CA 95389; (209) 372-0200.

Directions: From Merced, drive 75 miles northeast on Highway 140 to Yosemite National Park. Follow the signs toward Yosemite Valley, entering through the Arch Rock entrance station. Continue on El Portal Road, which becomes Southside Drive, for 6.3 miles, then turn right at the fork for Highway 41/Wawona/Fresno. Continue for 9.2 miles, then turn left on Glacier Point Road, and drive 16 miles to Glacier Point at the end of the road. Park in any of the parking lots, then walk to the point. The trailhead is on the right side of Glacier Point.

88-89. VERNAL & NEVADA FALLS
Yosemite National Park
Off Highways 120/140 in Yosemite Valley

Access & Difficulty: Hike-in 1.4 miles RT/Easy (Vernal Fall bridge)
　　　or Hike-in 2.4 miles RT/Moderate (top of Vernal Fall)
　　　or Hike-in 6.5 miles RT/Strenuous (top of Nevada Fall)
Elevation: Start at 4,020 feet; total gain 400 feet to Vernal Fall bridge, 1,050 feet to top of Vernal Fall, 2,000 feet to top of Nevada Fall
Best Season: March to July

Vernal and Nevada falls are best described with a long line of superlatives punctuated by commas: awesome, majestic, breathtaking, magnificent, and so on. Or maybe they are best described not with words at all, but by the millions of photographs, famous and not-so-famous, that have been taken of them over the years.

All the same disclaimers apply with Vernal and Nevada falls as with other celebrated sights in Yosemite Valley: 1) Come ready for hordes of people. 2) Bring rain gear if you don't like getting wet. 3) Start as early in the morning as possible to avoid the crowds. 4) Prepare to be awed.

First, a little geology lesson. Whereas Yosemite Fall and Bridalveil Fall are classic examples of waterfalls that drop over a "hanging valley"—an upper canyon perched high above a valley after glaciers eroded away the lower portion—Vernal and Nevada falls merely drop over soft or fractured rock masses that glacial ice has eroded into huge "stairsteps." These rocky "stairs" on the eastern end of Yosemite Valley are called the Giant Stairway, with Vernal Fall being the lower step and Nevada Fall the upper step.

Some aficionados would argue that a hanging valley waterfall is more dramatic than a stairstep waterfall. Hanging valley falls have a sensational jumping-off-the-edge-of-the-world appearance. They are usually described as leaping off their cliffs in some heroic fashion. But a stairstep waterfall can be just as theatrical, and Vernal and Nevada falls are cascading proof.

Happy Isles is your trailhead, unless you opt for a one-way shuttle hike from Glacier Point to Vernal and Nevada falls (see the Illilouette Fall story on pages 186 to 190). Many people will recall Happy Isles as the site of the incredible rockslide of the summer of 1996, when a huge chunk of Glacier Point broke off and dropped 3,000 feet to the valley floor, devastating the area and killing one bystander. Today you must look hard to see evidence of the slide, since the granite rubble quickly becomes a normal-looking part of the ever-changing glacial landscape.

Walk three-quarters of a mile on the paved, uphill-but-easy trail to the Vernal Fall bridge. There you get your best view of the beautiful 317-foot fall, a voluminous block of water that forms

The brink of Vernal Fall

where the Merced River drops over vertically jointed rock. At peak flow, the fall can be as much as 80 feet wide.

Many people shoot off a roll of film and turn around here, but if you don't mind some stair-climbing, you should continue to the fall's lip, a half-mile further up the trail. This infamous route is called the Mist Trail, and it's as good as all the guidebooks say. Just make sure your knees are in good shape before you attempt it; the trail climbs up a steep granite stair-case, which curves tightly around the waterfall's right side. Sections of the trail are completely covered by the fall's billowing mist and spray. Raincoats are often a necessity in spring, especially if the day is not particularly warm.

(One note: If you are traveling the Mist Trail with kids, keep a hand-hold on them. The wet, rocky stairs, combined with the hundreds of people coming at you from ahead and behind, can be hazardous.)

If you can look up from the sight of your feet clinging to the granite stairs, you'll notice a tremendous amount of moss and deep green foliage growing alongside the fall. This lush vegetation thrives even on granite because of Vernal Fall's nonstop misting action. When you reach the top of the fall and the overlook, you'll find that you're in barren, exposed granite country again. It's stark, dramatic, and awe-inspiring.

From the top of Vernal Fall, you have a choice: Turn back or continue onward another two miles to the top of Nevada Fall. If you opt to head uphill, you can take one of two routes: The Mist Trail or the John Muir Trail. The latter is far less steep but slightly less dramatic. My choice would be to continue upward on the Mist Trail, then take the John Muir Trail back downhill, so you can sample both trails. (Besides, steep uphills are good for your heart; steep downhills are bad for your knees.)

The brink of Nevada Fall

Tighten your boot laces, and climb, climb, climb up the Mist Trail, finally ascending the left flank of Nevada Fall. The ascent is hard work, but your heart will pound more from the stunning waterfall view than from the cardiovascular workout. Continually fed by upstream snowfields and glaciers, Nevada Fall

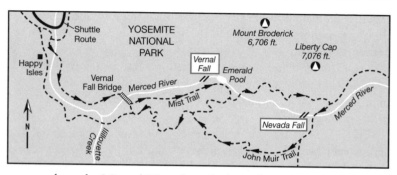

occurs where the Merced River funnels through a narrow, rocky chute. Named for the Spanish word for snow-covered, Nevada drops 594 feet like a liquid avalanche—a seemingly endless cataract of white, churning water. Whereas Vernal Fall is a square, block-type waterfall, Nevada has a more unusual shape, something like a horse-tail or an inverted V. Ansel Adams took what is probably the most famous photograph of Nevada Fall in 1947, on a day when a rainbow was draped gracefully across its white plunge.

You'll notice that from the fall's summit and overlook area, you have less of a vista than you had on your climb up. Looking down at the fall, it is difficult to see its full grandeur. Not to worry; you get more views on the way back downhill.

Take the John Muir Trail back for variety and a lesser grade. Watch for tremendous vistas of Nevada Fall framed by Liberty Cap and Half Dome as you lateral away from the fall along a rocky cliff edge. (Keep looking over your shoulder, or stop and turn around.) At one point, you get a picture-perfect view of both Nevada and Vernal falls simultaneously; there's a small hiker's pullout along the trail here. It's a great spot for picture-taking or just admiring the scene.

If all the steep downhill hiking is giving your joints and muscles a hard time, you can walk the entire route back to the valley floor on the John Muir Trail, although it adds an extra mile to your trip. If you'd prefer to see Vernal Fall again and hike at least a portion of the Mist Trail again, you can transfer over at Clark Point, just above Vernal Fall.

Trip notes: There is a $20 entrance fee at Yosemite National Park, good for seven days. Park maps are available for free at the entrance stations. A more detailed map is available for a fee from Tom Harrison Cartography, (415) 456-7940. For more information, contact Yosemite National Park Public Information Office, P.O. Box 577, Yosemite National Park, CA 95389; (209) 372-0200.

Directions: From Merced, drive 75 miles northeast on Highway 140 to Yosemite National Park. Follow the signs toward Yosemite Valley, entering through the Arch Rock entrance station. Continue on El Portal Road, which becomes Southside Drive, for 11.6 miles to the day-use parking lot at Curry Village. Then ride the free Yosemite Valley shuttle bus to Happy Isles, stop #16. In winter, when the shuttle does not run, you must hike from the day-use parking lot in Curry Village, adding another two miles to your round-trip.

90. BRIDALVEIL FALL

Yosemite National Park
Off Highway 41 in Yosemite Valley

Access & Difficulty: Hike-in or Wheelchair 0.5 mile RT/Easy
Elevation: Start at 3,980 feet; total gain 50 feet
Best Season: April through July

There's a story about a guy who visits Yosemite National Park for the first time and says to a park ranger, "I only have one day to spend in Yosemite. What should I do with my time?" And the park ranger says, "If I only had one day to spend in Yosemite, I'd just sit down and have myself a good cry."

Well, if you've only got one day in Yosemite, stop your cryin' and make a beeline for Bridalveil Fall, which drops 620 feet over the south wall of Yosemite's valley in a spectacular display of spray and mist. In spring, the water can flow with such force that seasoned waterfall-goers know to wear rain gear when visiting the fall's overlook. Otherwise, you just get wet.

Probably the best thing about Bridalveil, besides its incredible beauty, is its reliability. Whereas other falls in Yosemite Valley can dry up completely by late summer, Bridalveil Fall has a dependable flow year-round. That's because Bridalveil Creek drains a large area, including a lush upper valley with plenty of vegetation and deep, rich soil, which acts as a sponge, releasing water slowly and steadily. Many other Yosemite falls are situated at the base of stark granite terrain, where snow melts all at once off the rocks. When the snow is done melting, the waterfall display ends. Not so with Bridalveil, which in most months is a continually replenished, swaying plume of white water pounding over the canyon's rock wall.

It's less than a quarter-mile walk to the fall's overlook on a paved trail that is suitable for wheelchairs and baby strollers. Follow the trail from the parking lot, then take the right cutoff that is signed "Vista

Bridalveil Fall from the overlook

Point." The path also continues straight to Southside Drive for folks who choose to walk to the falls from other points in the valley.

The name "Bridalveil" is fairly recent, given by the editor of the Mariposa newspaper in the 1850s. The fall was called "Pohono" by the Yosemite Indians, and some translations suggest that Pohono meant "evil wind" or "puffing wind." I don't know about the evil part, but "puffing wind" seems accurate. When the fall's flow is heaviest, you can feel the wind it creates long before you see the water. The trees within a quarter-mile of Bridalveil suffer from wind-pruning, the result of constant exposure to the downdrafts and spray of the fall. They look as if they've been tended by a mad gardener, who pruned only one side of each tree. The sound of the waterfall in spring and early summer is often as loud and staccato as gunshots, with the water dropping in great sheets and then billowing out in layers of mist.

As with the other famous sights of Yosemite Valley, a good trick is to visit Bridalveil Fall between 6 and 7 A.M., when nobody is around but the morning light is perfect. From the Bridalveil Fall overlook, you also get a great view of Ribbon Fall on the opposite canyon wall—just do an about-face, turning your back to Bridalveil. Check your calendar first, though, because Ribbon Fall usually disappears by July, while Bridalveil keeps right on flowing.

Like its taller neighbors Upper and Lower Yosemite Falls, Bridalveil Fall can often be seen swaying or scattering in strong wind. When the breeze really kicks up, Bridalveil Fall can even blow sideways. This effect is best seen from a slight distance, such as from the Bridalveil Fall parking lot. On a windy day you can photograph dozens of pictures of the fall in just a few minutes, each revealing a different shape and character of the plunging water. From the fall's vista point, you're too close to see Bridalveil's full length, but from the western side of the parking lot, the entire waterfall is framed perfectly for photos.

Another good viewpoint is along Northside Drive as you drive west out of the valley, at a parking pullout near Bridalveil Meadow, just before you reach the turnoff for Highway 41. But my absolute favorite long-distance view is from the Wawona Tunnel parking lot on Highway 41. From here, all of Yosemite Valley is in view, including El Capitan, Half Dome, Sentinel Rock, and Cathedral Rocks, with sweet Bridalveil Fall flowing into the edge of the frame. It gives you the feeling that perhaps you are entering the Garden of Eden.

Your perspective from the tunnel is such that without prior knowledge, you cannot guess at the enormity of Yosemite's canyon walls and the gigantic proportions of all that is within them. When John Muir first saw Bridalveil Fall from a spot near here, he guessed it was a 50-foot waterfall, and he said he would like to camp at its base to see the pretty ferns that might grow there.

Bridalveil Fall from Southside Drive

When Mr. Muir finally made the trip to Bridalveil, he found that his 50-foot cascade was actually a 620-foot white-water plunge of amazing force and power. As he learned about the vegetation above the fall and how it feeds and moderates the flow of water, Muir pushed for legislation that would expand the park's boundaries to protect Bridalveil's entire watershed, not just the fall alone. Eventually, this was accomplished, and visitors to Bridalveil Fall have Muir and others to thank for the fact that Bridalveil Creek remains undammed, pristine, and awesome in its perpetual flow.

Trip notes: There is a $20 entrance fee at Yosemite National Park, good for seven days. Park maps are available for free at the entrance stations. A more detailed map is available for a fee from Tom Harrison Cartography, (415) 456-7940. For more information, contact Yosemite National Park Public Information Office, P.O. Box 577, Yosemite National Park, CA 95389; (209) 372-0200.

Directions: From Merced, drive 75 miles northeast on Highway 140 to Yosemite National Park. Follow the signs toward Yosemite Valley, entering through the Arch Rock entrance station. Continue on El Portal Road, which becomes Southside Drive, for 6.3 miles, then turn right at the fork for Highway 41/Wawona/Fresno. Turn left almost immediately into the Bridalveil Fall parking lot. The trail begins at the far end of the parking lot. (If you are driving into the park from the southern entrance near Wawona, watch for the Bridalveil Fall turnoff on your right as you drive into the valley on Highway 41.)

91. UPPER & LOWER YOSEMITE FALLS
Yosemite National Park
Off Highways 120/140 in Yosemite Valley

Access & Difficulty: Hike-in or Wheelchair 0.5 mile RT/Easy (Lower)
    or Hike-in 7.2 miles RT/Strenuous (Upper)
Elevation: Start at 3,990 feet; total gain 50 feet to Lower Fall
    or Start at 3,990 feet; total gain 2,700 feet to Upper Fall
Best Season: December through July

Probably the most stunning sight from a walking path in Yosemite Valley is the straight-line view of Upper and Lower Yosemite Falls piggybacked one on top of the other, which awes visitors as they walk up the paved route from the Lower Yosemite Fall parking lot to the base of the lower falls. John Muir said, "Yosemite Fall comes to us as an endless revelation," and he wasn't exaggerating.

At a combined height of 2,425 feet—almost a half-mile—Yosemite Falls is ranked as the fifth highest freefalling waterfall in the world and the highest in North America. It is also probably the most visited and most famous waterfall in the world. Upper Yosemite Fall alone is a whopping 1,430 feet of plunging water. It leaps off the canyon rim, reaches a less-vertical chunk of rock and cascades for

675 feet, then hits a ledge and forms Lower Yosemite Fall, which plunges for another 320 feet.

Upper Yosemite Falls scattering in the wind

There are several good ways to view Yosemite Falls, but however you do it, make sure you include in your itinerary the quarter-mile path from the Lower Yosemite Fall parking lot to the bridge below the falls. It's the classic short walk that everyone takes when they come to Yosemite. If you've avoided it because of the crowds, take it anyway. The viewing area for the lower fall is huge, sporting several benches and a wide footbridge across Yosemite Creek, inviting you to stay a while. If the falls are at full flood, you'll need to bring your rain gear if you want to hang around. In the spring, while standing at the viewing area, you can get soaked by mist so heavy it falls like rain.

The entire area around the lower fall is a massive parade of people almost any time the fall is running. Because the path is paved, wheelchairs and baby strollers can make the trip, although bikes are not allowed. The route is almost flat, with a slight uphill grade as you near the fall. If you don't like sharing your waterfalls with the masses, take this walk between 6 and 7 in the morning, when almost nobody is around. There is nothing like getting a rare moment of solitude in front of Yosemite Falls—you'll feel like you've been blessed.

Another great time to view the lower fall is on full moon nights in April and May, when lucky visitors get the chance to see pale-colored "moon-bows" dancing in the waterfall's spray. It's the most

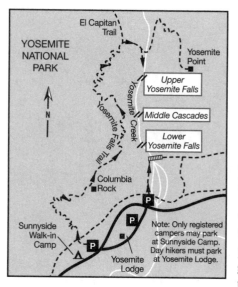

YOSEMITE NATIONAL PARK

El Capitan Trail

Yosemite Point

N

Yosemite Falls Trail

Yosemite Creek

Upper Yosemite Falls

Middle Cascades

Lower Yosemite Falls

Columbia Rock

Sunnyside Walk-in Camp

P

P

P

Yosemite Lodge

Note: Only registered campers may park at Sunnyside Camp. Day hikers must park at Yosemite Lodge.

romantic sight in Yosemite Valley. And speaking of romantic, check out Yosemite Falls in winter, when a giant ice cone forms at the base of the upper fall. Composed of frozen spray and fallen chunks of ice, the ice cone can sometimes grow to a height of 300 feet.

Inevitably, many who visit the lower fall and feel the thrill of its tumultuous presence get a hankering to get close to the upper fall, too. You can do this, but the trick is, you can't get there from here. To hike to Upper Yosemite Fall, you must start from a separate trailhead across from Yosemite Lodge on Northside Drive, adjacent to Sunnyside Campground.

Be forewarned that the hike to the upper fall is not for everybody. It's a grunt of a trip, climbing 2,700 feet over 3.6 miles one-way, with more than 100 switchbacks. Then on your return, you must jar your knees and ankles for another 3.6 miles heading downhill. It's one heck of a workout, but then again, it offers one heck of a view, and if you're in good shape, you shouldn't miss it.

In order to keep too many other trail users from trying your patience, start hiking as early in the morning as possible, and pick a weekday, preferably not during peak vacation season. (Summer is too hot on this trail, anyway.) Pack along plenty of water and some trail food. If you don't need it yourself, you can share it with someone else on the trail.

The route begins to climb immediately. At 1.2 miles and 1,000 feet up, you reach Columbia Rock (5,031 feet), an extraordinary viewpoint that looks out over the valley floor and east toward Half Dome. Many people tire of the climb and are satisfied with the view here, but if you push on, you near Upper Yosemite Fall at 1.4 miles, after a brief downhill stretch. From several points along the trail, you get a front seat perspective on the towering plume of water. You're eye to eye with the waterfall, close enough to feel its tremendous energy.

More ascent lies ahead, as the trail switchbacks above the trees and into a rocky area that is the recipient of frequent slides. In 1980, a rockfall covered about a mile of the trail here. The moral is: don't stand still for long. But keep drinking water. This section of trail is completely exposed and can be very warm, especially because your legs are pushing through a steady climb. Luckily, the view keeps getting more and more expansive. It will distract you from the hard work.

At 3.4 miles, you've completed your ascent, and the trail levels out and heads east, reaching a trail junction. Head

Nearing the top of Yosemite Fall

right toward Yosemite Point, then take the short right spur trail signed as "Overlook," which leads downhill on a treacherous set of granite stairsteps to near the edge of roaring Yosemite Creek—literally on top of Upper Yosemite Fall. Check out the stunning view of the valley from this incredible vantage point, but stay safely behind the metal railing.

Still haven't had enough? Go back to the main trail and continue another three-quarters of a mile, crossing a bridge above the falls, to Yosemite Point (6,936 feet). There you get an even better view of the south rim of the canyon, as well as Half Dome and North Dome, and a look at the top of Lost Arrow Spire, a single shaft of granite jutting into the sky.

For waterfall lovers who are less fond of heights and the climb they require, a great feature of Upper Yosemite Fall is that it is so clearly visible from various points in the valley. My vote for the best "no climbing" way to view Upper Yosemite Fall is on a bike on the bike path. From the saddle of a bike, you can see various views of the falls on the looping section of the paved path that runs west of Yosemite Village. If you're on foot, that's a lot of pavement-walking, but on a bike, it's perfect. Plus, there are bike racks positioned near the foot trail to the base of Lower Yosemite Fall, so you can lock up your bike and walk the short path to the falls.

Even people who don't want to get out of their cars can get a dozen good chances to view the falls. The best roadside falls vista is along Southside Drive, as you head east into the valley. Smart park planners built pullouts along the road because they understood that so many drivers would have no choice but to stop and rubberneck. It's practically a requirement to take a photo from your car window or through your sunroof along this stretch. The pullouts provide a perfectly framed shot of Upper Yosemite Fall with a verdant meadow in the foreground. Check out the view from near road marker V19. If you drive to the farthest end of the parking pullout (near the Yosemite Chapel), you get a vista of Upper Yosemite Fall that also includes a glimpse of Lower Yosemite Fall.

If there is any downer to Yosemite Fall, it's that it doesn't flow year-round. Plenty of first-time visitors show up in August or September, or any time during serious drought years, and wonder why the park rangers turned off the waterfall. Yosemite Falls drains a watershed that is composed of smooth, bare granite and little vegetation. Runoff from snowmelt and rainfall is rapid—the all-or-nothing effect of water on a hard, impenetrable surface. Once the rain and snow have drained, the waterfall show is over for the year. For the fullest flow of water, visit between March and the Fourth of July.

Trip notes: There is a $20 entrance fee at Yosemite National Park, good for seven days. Park maps are available for free at the entrance stations. A more detailed map is available for a fee from Tom Harrison Cartography, (415) 456-7940. For more information, contact Yosemite National Park Public Information Office, P.O. Box 577, Yosemite National Park, CA 95389; (209) 372-0200.

Directions: From Merced, drive 75 miles northeast on Highway 140 to Yosemite National Park. Follow the signs toward Yosemite Valley, entering through the Arch Rock entrance station. Continue on El Portal Road, which becomes Southside Drive, for 10.5 miles. Just beyond the Yosemite Chapel, bear left at the fork and head toward the village and visitor center, then turn left and drive west on Northside Drive for three-quarters of a mile to the Lower Yosemite Fall parking lot on your right. (If you are riding the free Yosemite Valley shuttle bus, take stop #7.)

For the Upper Yosemite Fall trailhead—Follow the directions as above, but turn left into the Yosemite Lodge parking lot (across from the Lower

Yosemite Fall parking lot on Northside Drive). Park there and walk to the Upper Fall trailhead, which is across the road and a quarter-mile to the west, between the parking lot for Sunnyside Walk-In Campground and the camp itself. You may not park in the Sunnyside lot unless you are camping there. (If you are riding the free Yosemite Valley shuttle bus, take stop #8.)

92. ALDER CREEK FALLS

Yosemite National Park
Off Highway 41 near Wawona

Access & Difficulty: Hike-in or Backpack 8.2 miles RT/Moderate
Elevation: Start at 4,800 feet; total gain 1,000 feet
Best Season: April to July

Yosemite National Park is home to some of the world's most famous waterfalls. But after you've tromped around and made your obligatory visit to Bridalveil, Vernal, Nevada, and Yosemite Falls, you may want to seek out a waterfall that few people know about and even fewer visit.

Alder Creek Falls is your ticket. It's a waterfall you can call your own for a while, but you have to work a little to earn it. For starters, you have to find the unmarked trailhead along Wawona Road—no small feat. (Follow the directions exactly.) Then you have to hike straight uphill into the Yosemite Wilderness, with nary a switchback, for just shy of a mile. After that, things start to get easier.

Catch your breath after your one-mile ascent, then make a left turn at the signed trail junction, which indicates that Alder Creek is 3.2 miles away (the trail on the right goes to Wawona in 2.9 miles). Your route continues to climb through dense ponderosa pines and incense cedars, although the grade is now a bit tamer.

After a total of three miles of climbing through the forest—just trees, trees, and more trees—the trail suddenly levels out and goes completely flat. You're now walking on an old railroad grade, and if you look carefully, you'll occasionally see wooden railroad ties still embedded in the dirt. It was on this section of trail that we surprised a big black bear lumbering along in front of us, making his morning rounds. He turned around and looked at us with a shocked expression on his face, then darted off into the woods.

You may be as surprised as he was when suddenly you hear pounding water through the silence of the trees. In a few moments

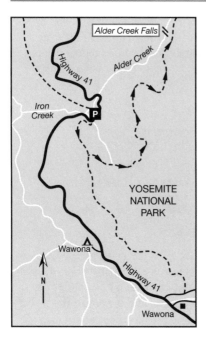

your view opens up to Alder Creek and its 250-foot fall, pouring grandly over a granite lip. The railroad grade laterals alongside it, heading upstream, taking you near the brink of the falls. The best view of the entire drop is right along the trail, about 100 yards before the falls. (Stay on the trail; there is no way to get any closer by scrambling off-trail because the waterfall's canyon is too steep.)

Beyond the fall, the trail continues along Alder Creek, paralleling it for 3.5 miles all the way to Deer Camp and Empire Meadow. If you're backpacking, Deer Camp is the best place to spend the night. We walked just a quarter-mile beyond the falls, where there is a tiny feeder stream that inspires some great wildflowers, including mariposa lilies, iris, blue lupine, and purple vetch, and an interesting rock formation with trees growing on top. Any number of places make good stopping points along the creek, where you can drop your packs and pull out your lunch.

Trip notes: There is a $20 entrance fee at Yosemite National Park, good for seven days. A free wilderness permit is required for overnight stays. They are available on a first-come, first-served basis at the wilderness kiosk near your chosen trailhead, or in advance by mail or phone; call (209) 372-0740. Park maps are available for free at the entrance stations. A more detailed map is available for a fee from Tom Harrison Cartography, (415) 456-7940. For more information, contact Yosemite National Park Public Information Office, P.O. Box 577, Yosemite National Park, CA 95389; (209) 372-0200.

Directions: The easiest way to find this unmarked trailhead is to travel north from Wawona. Follow the directions for Chilnualna Falls on page 207, but from the turnoff for Chilnualna Falls Road, drive north on Highway 41 for 4.2 miles. (You can also set your odometer at Wawona Campground; the trailhead is 3.4 miles north of the camp.) The trailhead is at a hairpin turn on the east side of Highway 41. (There is another trailhead for the Alder Creek Trail on the west side of the road, about one mile north, but don't take this trail.) There is no marker except for a Yosemite Wilderness sign, which you can't see from the road. There is parking for about eight cars in the large dirt pullout on the west side of the road.

93. CHILNUALNA FALLS

Yosemite National Park
Off Highway 41 near Wawona

Access & Difficulty: Hike-in or Backpack 8.0 miles RT/Strenuous
Elevation: Start at 4,200 feet; total gain 2,400 feet
Best Season: March to July

Most people don't expect much from the southern section of Yosemite National Park. Sure, everyone visits the Mariposa Grove to see the big Sequoias, but other than that, the area doesn't take up too much of the average visitor's itinerary. But while everyone else is in the valley, or at Glacier Point or Tuolumne Meadows, you can sneak off to the southern part of the park, take a rigorous hike, and be rewarded with a terrific waterfall: Chilnualna Falls near Wawona, one of my favorite falls in Yosemite.

Remember, however, that you'll begin hiking at low elevation—4,200 feet—and you'll gain 2,400 feet over four miles to reach the falls. It's a steady, nonstop climb through only partial shade. If you don't like to hike up, don't sign up. If you relish a good climb, bring plenty of water for your two-hour aerobics session, plus the long downhill return.

The trail's big surprise is that you don't really have to walk four miles to see falls. From the Chilnualna Falls parking lot, hike about 10 minutes uphill and already you're at a tremendous cascade on

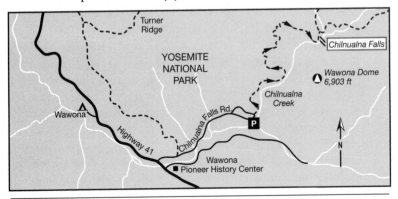

Chilnualna Falls

Chilnualna Creek, where the stream rushes furiously over room-sized boulders. It looks like someone took Stonehenge apart, piled up all the rocks, then started a downpour over them. Plenty of large, flat rocks abound where you can sit and watch the spectacle. It's beautiful and very loud in spring and early summer.

When you're ready to continue, say farewell to the creek, because you won't see it again for a few miles. Heading up the trail, you'll reach a Yosemite Wilderness sign and begin to switchback your way up, up, and up through manzanita, mountain misery, and bear clover. In spring, the aroma of all this flowering brush is intoxicating—it's easy to see why bears and deer munch it down.

After nearly an hour of climbing (about two miles), you come to a large granite overlook with a terrific view of the tree-filled canyon below and Wawona Dome (6,897 feet) across from you. Stop here to stretch your hamstrings, eat a snack, and make comments like, "Geez, these falls better be good."

They are, and you're halfway there. The nearby roar of Chilnualna Creek assures you that you're doing the right thing. A half-mile past your rocky perch, start looking for glimpses of Chilnualna Falls on the far back wall of the canyon, way up high. What you can see is only a small section of the fall, and as you switchback uphill your view of it will change, to include more and more length. It provides an incentive to spur you on.

At three miles, you reach a small stream crossing the trail, which makes a lovely miniature stairstepped waterfall just above the trail.

Since you've gained so much elevation, the forest is now dense with shady pines and incense cedars. Finally, you come to what seems like the canyon rim, and start to lateral toward the fall. From here it looks like a giant freefalling plume of water. Your trail turns to granite, and it is pleasingly flat after so much uphill.

Now for the bad news: You never get to see that big freefalling plume close up, because the trail brings you on top of it, not in front of it. But the good news is that the freefall is just the lower part of Chilnualna Falls, a series of cascades totalling hundreds of feet, and you can climb some more to get to the upper tiers.

Walk on granite, over rocky stairsteps, on a ledge at the edge of the world, until you reach a cascade above the long freefall. Pause to admire it, then keep climbing. In another half-mile, you'll reach a trail sign where the trail leads off to Turner Meadows, Grouse Lake, and Chilnualna Lakes. On your right is another huge Chilnualna cascade, our favorite of the trip—a series of six rounded granite pools connected by a continually descending flow of water. Leave the trail and walk 100 yards to your right to reach the waterfall's edge. Here, on the bare outcrop of granite surrounding the waterfall, is the perfect place to open up your pack and have lunch.

Trip notes: There is a $20 entrance fee at Yosemite National Park, good for seven days. A free wilderness permit is required for overnight stays. They are available on a first-come, first-served basis at the wilderness kiosk near your chosen trailhead, or in advance by mail or phone; call (209) 372-0740. Park maps are available for free at the entrance stations. A more detailed map is available for a fee from Tom Harrison Cartography, (415) 456-7940. For more information, contact Yosemite National Park Public Information Office, P.O. Box 577, Yosemite National Park, CA 95389; (209) 372-0200.

Directions: From Merced, drive 75 miles northeast on Highway 140 to Yosemite National Park. Follow the signs toward Yosemite Valley, entering through the Arch Rock entrance station. Continue on El Portal Road, which becomes Southside Drive, for 6.3 miles, then turn right at the fork for Highway 41/Wawona/Fresno. Drive south on Highway 41 for 25 miles to Wawona, then turn left on Chilnualna Falls Road. Drive 1.7 miles east and park in the lot on the right side of the road. Walk back to Chilnualna Falls Road and pick up the single-track trail across the pavement.

Alternatively, from the Wawona/southern entrance to Yosemite National Park on Highway 41, drive north on Highway 41 for 7.5 miles to Wawona. Turn right on Chilnualna Falls Road and follow the directions as above.

94-97. TUOLUMNE, CALIFORNIA, LeCONTE, & WATERWHEEL FALLS

Yosemite National Park
Off Highway 120 near Tuolumne Meadows

Access & Difficulty: Hike-in or Backpack 9.0 miles RT/Easy (Tuolumne Falls) or Hike-in or Backpack 16.0 miles RT/Strenuous (Waterwheel Falls)
Elevation: Start at 8,600 feet; total loss 400 feet to Tuolumne Falls or Start at 8,600 feet; total loss 1,900 feet to Waterwheel Falls
Best Season: June through October

I call this hike the Epic Waterfall Trip. If you hike the entire route, you'll see so many waterfalls and so much water that you'll have enough memories to get you through a 10-year drought.

Before you start, it's important to know what you're in for. There's a great deal of discrepancy between various maps and park trail signs as to the actual mileage of this route, but the blisters on my big toes say that the round-trip from the Lembert Dome parking lot all the way to Waterwheel Falls is a whopping 16 miles. You can do the trail as a long day-hike if you're in good condition, or you can get a camping permit and have a great two- or three-day backpacking trip. Or, you can hike only a portion of the route, making a short day-trip to Tuolumne Falls (nine miles round-trip and nearly flat). California and LeConte Falls are midway in between Tuolumne and Waterwheel, and these also make good day-hike destinations.

In choosing your route, keep in mind one fact: Although there is a mere 400-foot elevation difference between the trailhead and Tuolumne Falls, followed by only a 1,500-foot elevation difference between Tuolumne Falls and Waterwheel Falls, it's downhill on the way out and uphill on the way back. As a day-hike, 16 miles can get pretty long when you're going uphill on the return. You need plenty of food, water, and energy for the trip home.

If you choose to make the Epic Waterfall Trip an overnight

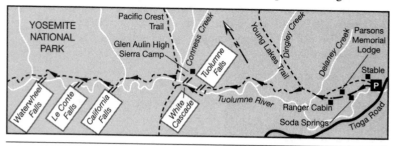

Top of Tuolumne Falls (left) and a cascade of California Falls (right)

excursion, you'll need to get a wilderness permit, then hike in five miles to the backpacker's camp, which is a half-mile beyond Glen Aulin High Sierra Camp and Tuolumne Falls. Most people spend the night, then wait till the next day to hike three more miles down to Waterwheel Falls. After enjoying the day there, they return to camp, get a good night's sleep, and hike five miles homeward on the third day. It's a perfect entry-level backpacking trip, the kind of vacation that turns people into lifelong outdoors enthusiasts.

If you must make the trip as a day-hike, follow a few tips: First, be in good hiking shape, accustomed to walking at least 10 miles a day. Start early in the morning, say by 7 or 8 A.M. Hike the full one-way distance out to Waterwheel Falls with only short breaks, covering the eight miles in about four hours. (The best place for a snack and a stretching break is at the bridge below Tuolumne Falls.) Have lunch and relax at Waterwheel. Then, since you've got some uphill climbing on the way back and you're already somewhat fatigued, take the route home slowly and in sections. Stop and swim in the placid sections of the river. Stop and eat in all the shady spots. Climb a granite staircase and stop to drink some water. Take a nap along the river somewhere. You can do the whole trip, all 16 miles, between 8 A.M. and 6 P.M., hiking for a total of about eight hours and fooling around for the other two.

The Waterwheel trip is only doable as a day-hike because the trail has a relatively small elevation gain. Hiking to Half Dome is about the same trail distance, but far more exhausting because of the elevation gain and loss. The key to your trip: Drink a ton of water—you're at a very high elevation from the trailhead onward. Bring your canteen and be sure to filter water out of the river; it can be a heavy load if you try to carry enough bottled water for the entire trip.

Start your trip at the trailhead parking area for Dog Lake, Lembert Dome, and Soda Springs. Begin hiking on the gated dirt road that is signed "Soda Springs 0.5 mile," walking until you near Parson's Lodge and see the trail sign for the Glen Aulin Trail. The sign says it's 4.7 miles to Glen Aulin High Sierra Camp (located at the base of Tuolumne Falls) and 5.2 miles to Glen Aulin backpackers' camp (where you'll spend the night if you have a wilderness permit).

The first couple miles of trail are quite flat, only faintly downhill, but the downhill increases as you near Glen Aulin and waterfall country. The scenery is spectacular all the way; after leaving the forest in the first mile, the trail gets closer to the Tuolumne River and moves from trees to granite. The result is wide-open views of Cathedral and Unicorn peaks and Fairview Dome to the south. The trail meanders through a mix of meadows, granite, and woodland, where deer and other wildlife abound. On our trip, we saw what has to be the cutest of all High Sierra mammals—baby marmots, playing hide-and-seek with us from behind rocks, while Mom

White Cascade (Glen Aulin Falls)

Side view of two "waterwheels" at Waterwheel Falls

Marmot watched a bit more cautiously from a distance.

When the trail reaches its first footbridge over the Tuolumne River, a sign states that Glen Aulin is now only 1.7 miles away. In fifteen minutes of walking, you reach the top section of Tuolumne Falls, a stunning 100-foot drop, but that's merely a preview of good things to come. Now you begin a steep downhill to the base of the falls and another bridge, which takes you across the river again to Glen Aulin High Sierra Camp. (If you want to stay here or at any High Sierra Camp, you must make reservations a year in advance through the High Sierra Camp lottery system. However, if you just want a terrific hot meal, you can show up any time and see if they have room for you.)

When you cross the river bridge to the Glen Aulin side, be sure to descend to the small, pebbly beach at the river's edge, where there's a great spot for viewing and taking pictures of the lower drop of Tuolumne Falls. From the bridge itself, your view is slightly obstructed by trees, but from this beach, you have a clear shot. Some people call this waterfall Glen Aulin Falls or White Cascade, but most consider it to be a section of Tuolumne Falls.

The second bridge to your right heads to the High Sierra Camp, but continue straight, then take the left fork which continues downstream along the river. As you climb up on granite, turn around for a parting look at some of the upper cascades of Tuolumne Falls.

Day-hikers looking for a nine-mile round-trip should call it a day here, have a picnic near the river, and then head back up the granite alongside Tuolumne Falls. A turnaround here will make your trip four to five hours long, and although the homeward route climbs, the worst of it is in the first half-mile—getting up and around Tuolumne Falls. After that, the grade is fairly tame.

Those continuing on will find that the path drops down to a level section in a beautiful meadow, where backpackers make their camps near the river. If you're spending the night, pick out your spot. Here the lupine grows waist high, the river is placid, and ferns and aspens make their home. You may never want to leave, but if you want to see more falls, you'll have to move on. Waterwheel, the final fall on this stretch, is only three miles away, and cascading California and LeConte falls can be enjoyed along the way.

Another section of granite leads you to another flat, flower-filled meadow, a place where the river is so quiet that it's hard to believe it could produce any more falls. But then a roaring sound comes from up ahead, and you pass by boisterous California Falls, just off the trail by a few hundred feet. A side trail on your left leads to a huge block-shaped waterfall with some great swimming holes near its base.

Note that while the stretch of river between Glen Aulin High Sierra Camp and California Falls is extremely flat, the stretch downstream from California Falls is almost nonstop cascades and falls, separated only by brief quiet pools. Because of the continual series of cascades and the fact that the river is sometimes obscured by the forest, it can be tricky for first-time visitors to identify California and LeConte falls' exact locations—where one ends and the other begins. If you're not certain, just take all the short spur trails that fork from the main trail, each of which brings you to either a stunning vista of the falls or a perfect swimming/fishing hole. You can't miss.

Officially, LeConte Falls shows up about a half-mile after California Falls, following a large, placid, green pool. At the edge of the pool it seems that the world drops off and disappears, but you're just at the top of LeConte Falls' main cascade.

The trail, which was a fairly even grade up to California Falls, now drops steeply downhill on rock for just shy of eternity. As you descend, watch for a trail sign for Pate Valley and Tuolumne Meadows, and near it, another spur trail on your left. This one takes you to your final destination, Waterwheel Falls, often billed as Yosemite's most unusual waterfall. Shortly you'll discern why; the side trail brings you to the center of the giant Waterwheel cascade, where you are directly across from some of the lower "waterwheels." These are sections of churning water that dip into deep holes in the granite, then shoot out with such velocity that they seem to double back on themselves, appearing to circle around like waterwheels. As soon as you see them, you understand the fall's moniker. Six different waterwheels spin in the middle section, and a few more circle up above. Find a spot on the granite alongside them, pull out your camera, and linger a while.

Trip notes: There is a $20 entrance fee at Yosemite National Park, good for seven days. A free wilderness permit is required for overnight stays. They are available on a first-come, first-served basis at the wilderness kiosk near your chosen trailhead, or in advance by mail or phone; call (209) 372-0740. Park maps are available for free at the entrance stations. A more detailed map is available for a fee from Tom Harrison Cartography, (415) 456-7940. For more information, contact Yosemite National Park Public Information Office, P.O. Box 577, Yosemite National Park, CA 95389; (209) 372-0200.

Directions: From Merced, drive 75 miles northeast on Highway 140 to Yosemite National Park. Follow the signs toward Yosemite Valley, entering through the Arch Rock entrance station. Continue 4.5 miles to the left turnoff for Tioga Road/Highway 120, looping back out of the valley. In another 9.5 miles, turn right on Highway 120 and drive 40 miles to the parking lot for Dog Lake/Lembert Dome/Soda Springs on the left. Park as far to the west of Lembert Dome as possible, and start hiking at the gated dirt road that is signed "Soda Springs 0.5 mile."

98. HORSE CREEK FALLS

Inyo National Forest/Hoover Wilderness
Off U.S. 395 near Bridgeport

Access & Difficulty: Hike-in 4.0 miles RT/Moderate
Elevation: Start at 7,100 feet; total gain 950 feet
Best Season: June to September

They say the Horse Creek Trail is one of the busiest trails in the Hoover Wilderness, but they may be counting just the first half-mile. On our first trip, we hiked in only to the lowest cascade along Horse Creek, a mere half-mile from Twin Lakes and its huge campground, and we passed several dozen people along the way, mostly families with children. Feeling discouraged, we left the area and found some-place quieter to hike. But on our next trip, we hiked two miles on the Horse Creek Trail, passing several cascades along the way, and we saw almost no one after the initial stretch.

The hardest part of the trip is finding the trailhead. The friendly attendant at the campground entrance kiosk usually gives out directions, but if no one is available, here's what you do: Walk past the entrance kiosk, and take the left fork through the campground. Look for a dirt road on your left; follow it and cross a footbridge. Hike to your right on the far side of the bridge, passing some tent campers on the hillside. Cross the creek again, and reach a wilderness information sign. From there, hike to your right, switchbacking uphill.

The trail stays roughly parallel to Horse Creek, as it winds back and forth and uphill into the Hoover Wilderness. The views are great from the get-go, both of Twin Lakes below you and the spectacular Sawtooth Ridge all around you. After ten minutes of walking past the wilderness sign, you're right alongside the first rushing cascade on Horse Creek, and the whitewater continues above and below you for as far as you can see.

Keep hiking uphill through more switchbacks. These can be extremely hot and dry in summer, so bring plenty of water with you. In about an hour of nearly relentless climbing, you'll reach the best falls on Horse Creek, where the stream drops over a low hanging valley. The trail continues beyond the waterfall to a small lake and a startlingly beautiful meadow. It's wise to come prepared with a picnic.

Trip notes: There is no fee. For a map of Toiyabe National Forest, send $4 to USDA-Forest Service, 1323 Club Drive, Vallejo, CA 94592. For more information, contact Toiyabe National Forest, Bridgeport Ranger District, HCR 1 Box 1000, Bridgeport, CA 93517; (760) 932-7070.

Directions: From U.S. 395 at Bridgeport, drive west on Twin Lakes Road for 13.2 miles. Park near the far end of the lake, just before the campground entrance kiosk, then walk into the campground.

99. LUNDY CANYON FALLS

Inyo National Forest
Off U.S. 395 near Lee Vining

Access & Difficulty: Hike-in 4.5 miles RT/Moderate
Elevation: Start at 7,800 feet; total gain 700 feet
Best Season: June to September

If you're a wildflower lover, Lundy Canyon will float your boat. If it's autumn colors you seek, Lundy Canyon will be the pearl in your oyster. If you're a waterfall aficionado, Lundy Canyon is your cat's meow.

There just aren't enough clichés to describe how good Lundy Canyon is. The camping is good. The fishing is good. The backpacking is good. The day-hiking is good. What's not good? The season's not good. It's too short; you can never get enough time here. Lundy Canyon usually isn't snow-free until late June, and it can snow again by October. Plan on July as the best month to see the waterfalls.

It takes 5.4 miles of hiking in Lundy Canyon to reach the spectacular 20 Lakes Basin, but you don't have to go that far to

One of Lundy Canyon's many cascades

see waterfalls. We hiked just over two miles into the canyon, until just before the trail starts to climb in earnest, and we saw more waterfalls than we could keep track of.

The Lundy Canyon Trail leads into the Hoover Wilderness, a remote and rugged land of granite, mountains, lakes, and glaciers. The trail follows Mill Creek, which has two main falls on it in the first two miles of trail. In addition, many smaller streams cascade for hundreds of feet down the surrounding canyon walls, feeding into Mill Creek. Within half an hour of hiking, you are surrounded by falls. As you walk deeper into the canyon, every couple of minutes you have to stop and count how many you can see.

From the trailhead, the path briefly meanders through an aspen grove and then climbs abruptly and steeply on loose shale, but in 15 minutes you're rewarded with your first view of a waterfall on Mill Creek. It's a doozy. In the next 15 minutes, you'll pass two more falls on your right. And so it goes. The trail ascends for the first three-quarters of a mile, then goes completely flat in a forested grove along the stream, where we came upon some Boy Scouts on a camping trip. The route passes a dilapidated trapper's cabin, then opens out to a large clearing, where the vista is wide, expansive, and humbling. You can look around you and see half a dozen cascades dropping along the back and side walls of the canyon.

At two miles out, the trail starts to climb again, slowly working its way off the canyon floor, and shortly you reach my favorite fall on Mill Creek. It has three main cascades, the first being a long stair-stepped drop, which you hike right alongside. The smell of wild spearmint is almost intoxicating near the falls. We were compelled to stop here to spread out a picnic and admire the scenery.

What scenery? You already know about the waterfalls; let's talk wildflowers. They're so good in Lundy Canyon that rangers from nearby Yosemite bring visitors here on guided tours. (And Yosemite is no slacker in the wildflower department.) On our visit, I counted more than 30 different species, including wandering daisies, Indian paintbrush, mariposa lilies, purple vetch, mule's ears, columbine, Sierra daisies, and tiger lilies. And if you're so unlucky as to miss the June to August wildflower season, you can always visit in September or October and watch the quaking aspens do their golden autumnal dance.

It will be difficult, but when you bring yourself to leave Lundy Canyon, you'll have an easy downhill walk back to the trailhead. Along the way, you'll witness the wonders of the canyon all over again, plus a bright spot of blue in the distance that is Lundy Lake.

If you find Lundy Canyon so captivating that you want to see more, consider a hike up the South Fork of Mill Creek. To access the South Fork, you'll need to start hiking at Lundy Resort or farther back at the dam at the east end of Lundy Lake. A seven-mile round-trip from the dam will take you to spectacular Lake Canyon and its historic gold mine. There's plenty of beauty and history to be seen.

Trip notes: There is no fee. For a map of Inyo National Forest, send $4 to USDA-Forest Service, 1323 Club Drive, Vallejo, CA 94592. For more information, contact Inyo National Forest, Mono Lake Ranger District, P.O. Box 429, Lee Vining, CA 93541; (760) 647-3044.

Directions: From Lee Vining, drive 6.8 miles north on U.S. 395 to the Lundy Lake Road turnoff on the left. Drive west on Lundy Lake Road for five miles, past Lundy Lake Resort, to the signed trailhead parking area. (Beyond the resort, the road turns to dirt. It is two miles from the resort to the trailhead.)

100-102. RAINBOW, LOWER, & MINARET FALLS

Devils Postpile National Monument
Off Highway 203 near Mammoth Lakes

Access & Difficulty: Hike-in 2.0 miles RT/Easy (Rainbow Falls)
or Hike-in 8.0 miles RT/Moderate (Rainbow, Lower, Minaret Falls)
Elevation: Start at 7,600 feet; total loss 200 feet to Rainbow Falls
or Start at 7,600 feet; total loss 400 feet to all three falls
Best Season: June to September

Rainbow Falls is one of the prized geologic possessions of Devils Postpile National Monument. The Devils Postpile, of course, is the other. Add in Minaret Falls and Lower Falls, which can be seen with the others in an easy-to-moderate hiking trip, and we're talking about a treasure chest trail filled with natural wonders.

That's three stunning waterfalls, and one intriguing volcanic formation, within four miles of each other. You can see them all in one eight-mile hike, or you can visit just one or two in various shorter trips. Options, you've got plenty of options.

Let's start with the whole enchilada. If you decide to see it all, you can expect a long, pretty hike through wildflower-filled meadows and lodgepole pine forests. You'll get many lingering looks at the Middle Fork of the San Joaquin River, a flyfishing paradise. Plus three waterfalls. Start by getting to the Devils Postpile parking lot, near the ranger station. This is the hub from which all your hiking begins.

Hike south past the ranger station, following the sign for Devils Postpile in four-tenths of a mile. Immediately you are wowed by a pristine meadow filled with purple shooting stars and views of the meandering river. Hang on to your hat; this is just the beginning. Pass by the Postpile, a formation of towering "posts" composed of columnar basalt left from a lava flow nearly 100,000 years ago. Be sure to take either of the trails along the sides of the Postpile that climb to its crest, where you can see that the top of the formation looks like a slightly off-kilter parquet floor.

Continue hiking south past the Postpile. Watch as the thriving pine forest changes to a severely burned area, the result of a 1992 wildfire. The undergrowth has already returned in full force, and the wildflowers bloom like mad in the spring. Keep heading gently downhill until you reach the first overlook of Rainbow Falls, which plummets 101 feet over a volcanic cliff. If you arrive at midday, when

Rainbow Falls (left) and Minaret Falls (right)

direct light rays are passing through water droplets, you'll see the rays be refracted and separated into their component colors. That means the fall's namesake rainbows are dancing through the mist.

Although Rainbow Falls drops over volcanic rock, it's a different volcanic rock than the basalt of Devils Postpile. It's rhyodacite, and it has two extremely hard horizontal rock layers at the top of its cliff, much like Niagara Falls. That keeps the San Joaquin River from eroding the waterfall and eventually beveling it off. Rainbow's been here for a long time, and it's probably going to stick around.

If you're taking pictures, the best spot is at the next overlook, just 30 yards further downstream, where you can also walk down the stairs to the base of the fall. Ferns and moss grow on the rock at the cliff bottom; they benefit from the waterfall's constant mist.

When you're ready, head downstream to often-snubbed Lower Falls. Poor Lower Falls; always in the shadow of big brother Rainbow Falls, it gets little recognition. Rainbow Falls gets its picture taken by hundreds of tourists a day in the summer; it appears on calendars, postcards, promotional brochures, even the cover of this book. Rainbow Falls gets the limelight; Lower Falls doesn't even get an imaginative name.

Beautiful in its own right, Lower Falls is a mere 15-minute walk from Rainbow Falls. The fall is a nearly vertical drop of about 40 feet.

Because its cliff is not as wide as Rainbow Falls', Lower Falls' flow is channeled, creating greater volume as the river drops through a narrow chute. Almost no foliage grows by the fall's cliff, except for a few fire-scarred trees standing on top.

The base of Lower Falls is easily accessible. There are no stair-steps like at Rainbow, just a dirt path, and the descent is less because the falls and the canyon walls are not as tall. Check out the good fishing holes filled with small- to medium-size trout.

After visiting

Lower Falls

Lower Falls, retrace your steps, heading back uphill past Rainbow Falls and the Devils Postpile again. The climb is steady and sustained enough to get your heart working. After passing the Devils Postpile, watch for the trail fork on your left where a scenic footbridge crosses over the San Joaquin River. This is your route to the third waterfall in the park, Minaret Falls.

The surprising thing about Minaret Falls is its size. Whereas Rainbow Falls and Lower Falls are classic river falls—imposingly wide but not immense in height—Minaret Falls drops on Minaret Creek, cascading 300 feet tall and 100 feet wide at peak flow. The fall is composed of a dozen or more long cascades, side by side, streaming down the hillside.

The trail to the waterfall is well-signed and easy to follow. After crossing the river by Devils Postpile, turn right and walk upstream. The route is basically flat, with just a slight uphill as you approach the falls. Watch for a fork a half-mile from the bridge, where you bear right on the Pacific Crest Trail.

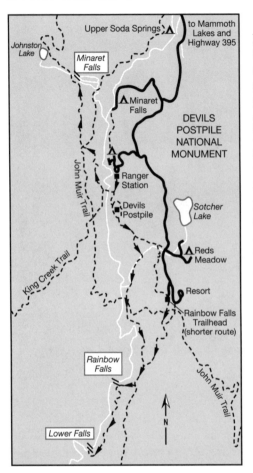

The path brings you near the base of the falls. Then with a short cross-country scramble over rocks and fallen trees, you choose your own viewing spot. Even in July, the fall is so loud that conversation is nearly impossible. Shout a few words to your hiking partner, take some photographs, then retrace your steps back to the bridge, turning left to return to the Devils Postpile ranger station and parking lot.

Now that's my idea of a fine eight-mile day. But if you're not up for the whole trip, try one of these shorter hikes instead: From the Devils Postpile ranger station, hike to Rainbow and Lower falls and back, passing by the Devils Postpile lava formation, for a 5.5-mile round-trip. Or hike out-and-back to Minaret Falls for a three-mile round-trip.

If you want to see Rainbow and/or Lower Falls via an even shorter walk, you can start from the trailhead at Reds Meadow (see the directions that follow) for a two-mile round-trip, plus an extra half-mile round-trip to Lower Falls.

Options; you've got options. And they're all good.

Trip notes: There is no fee, unless you arrive between 7:30 a.m. and 5:30 p.m. and have to take the park shuttle bus (see below). Park maps are available for free at the ranger station in Devils Postpile. For more information, contact Devils Postpile National Monument, (760) 934-2289, or Inyo National Forest, Mammoth Ranger District, P.O. Box 148, Mammoth Lakes, CA 93546; (760) 934-2505 or (760) 924-5500.

Directions: From U.S. 395 in Lee Vining, drive 25 miles south to the Mammoth Lakes/Highway 203 cutoff. Take Highway 203 west for four miles, through the town of Mammoth Lakes, then turn right at Minaret Road (still on Highway 203) and drive 4.5 miles to the Devils Postpile entrance kiosk. Here you must park and ride the shuttle bus, or continue driving for 7.8 miles to an intersection where you turn right for Devils Postpile. From there, it's a quarter-mile to the trailhead and parking lot. The trail begins from the left (south) side of the parking area, just past the ranger station.

For a shorter hike to Rainbow and Lower falls, follow the directions as above but don't take the Devils Postpile turnoff. Instead, continue straight for 1.3 miles past Devils Postpile to the signed Rainbow Falls trailhead, just before Reds Meadow.

If you arrive between the hours of 7:30 a.m. and 5:30 p.m., you must ride the shuttle bus into the park. The cost of the shuttle is $8 for adults, $5 for children ages 5 to 12, and free for children under five. Get off the bus at either the Devils Postpile parking area or Reds Meadow.

---

103. TWIN FALLS

Inyo National Forest
Off Highway 203 in Mammoth Lakes

Access & Difficulty: Hike-in 0.5 mile RT/Easy
Elevation: Start at 8,400 feet; total gain 0 feet
Best Season: June to September

Twin Falls can be seen plainly enough from the bridge between the two campgrounds at Twin Lakes in Mammoth. Plenty of folks stand on that bridge, cast a line into the water, and admire the view of the two lakes, the falls, and the surrounding granite crags. Some of them even hope to catch a fish or two while they're standing there. But if the waterfall interests you more than the fishing, take a little walk and inspect it more closely.

From the bridge, head into the west loop of the campground to the gravel road between sites 36 and 37. Walk down it until you see a trail marked "private road, public trail." The private road to the right leads to some cabins, so follow the single-track trail to the left. The route is only a few hundred yards long, tunneling through a very lush glen. Be careful not to trample any of the columbine blossoms and corn lilies growing at your feet.

In minutes, you're at the base of 250-foot Twin Falls, where the stream pours down the mountainside and drops into Upper Twin

---

Twin Falls and Twin Lakes from above and below

Lake. Late in the summer, you can cross the stream at the waterfall's base by rockhopping. You get a perfect view of the falls on one side of you and the lakes and bridge on the other.

For a different angle on Twin Falls, you can drive two miles further on Lake Mary Road, past the turnoffs for Twin Lakes and Lake Mary, to the Twin Falls Picnic Area across from Lake Mamie. The picnic area is perched at the top of Twin Falls, where Lake Mamie's outlet stream cascades down the hillside. There's a fine view of Twin Lakes from here, although the waterfall view is better from below.

Trip notes: There is no fee. For a map of Inyo National Forest, send $4 to USDA-Forest Service, 1323 Club Drive, Vallejo, CA 94592. For more information, contact Inyo National Forest, Mammoth Ranger District, P.O. Box 148, Mammoth Lakes, CA 93546; (760) 934-2505 or (760) 924-5500.

Directions: From U.S. 395 in Lee Vining, drive 25 miles south to the Mammoth Lakes/Highway 203 cutoff. Take Highway 203 west for four miles, through the town of Mammoth Lakes, to the intersection of Highway 203/Minaret Road and Lake Mary Road. Continue straight on Lake Mary Road for 2.2 miles, then bear right on Twin Lakes Road and follow it for a half-mile to the camp store. Park and walk across the bridge toward the west loop of Twin Lakes Campground (you can see the falls from the bridge).

104. HORSETAIL FALLS

Inyo National Forest
Off U.S. 395 near Lake Crowley

Access & Difficulty: Hike-in 4.0 miles RT/Moderate
Elevation: Start at 8,000 feet; total gain 600 feet
Best Season: June to September

Several waterfalls in California go by the name Horsetail Falls. But the Horsetail Falls in McGee Creek Canyon, just off the McGee Creek Trail, really lives up to its moniker. The instant you see it, you know what it is, because its shape is a perfect inverted V, with a wide drop at the bottom that appears to swish back and forth in the wind. The only question is: Where's the rest of the horse?

But the waterfall is perhaps only a sidelight on this trip. The mountain vista surrounding McGee Creek Canyon is so large and looming, it actually dwarfs the falls. There's Mount Baldwin on the right and Mount Crocker on the left, but what really dominates the canyon is Red and White Mountain straight ahead at 12,816 feet, as colorful as its name implies. One of the most incredible sights I have ever seen in the Eastern Sierra is McGee Creek Canyon at sunset, backed by towering Red and White Mountain. Talk about a range of light.

The view from the trailhead itself is awe-inspiring—the path leads back into a narrow pass, surrounded on both sides by huge peaks jutting straight upward. Reaching Horsetail Falls requires a two-mile walk up this pass, heading into the John Muir Wilderness, climbing the whole way on a slow grade. The trail is a typical Eastern Sierra wilderness trail—rocky and sandy. It's a where-desert-meets-mountains hike, but it's not all sagebrush country. Thick groves of aspens, birches, and cottonwoods create incredible autumn colors. In summer, bright orange paintbrush, white lupine, and huge yellow mule's ears paint the hillsides. The trail gets more lush, and more beautiful, the further you travel.

The McGee Creek Trail does not go right to Horsetail Falls; instead it passes by the waterfall on its way to Steelhead Lake and the McGee Lakes. You can take a rough spur trail that brings you closer. At two miles out from the trailhead, cross the waterfall's creek (it flows right across the trail), then continue walking for two or three more minutes until you spy a crude route on the right. Follow it for a few hundred yards off the main trail and you come to a rock outcrop

Horsetail Falls

with a view of the fall and its dramatic mountain backdrop. We could only see about 50 feet of Horsetail, because the rest of its length is obscured in the foliage.

Ideally you want to see Horsetail Falls early in the day—morning is best—while it is lit from the front by the sun. If you don't see it until later, the fall will be completely shaded. Of course, in the late afternoon you can witness the miracle of the range of light in the colorful peaks. It's as if Mother Nature shines her spotlight on one mountain after another as the sun drops below the horizon. They light up one at a time, on cue, like each member of a jazz band taking turns playing lead. It's a sight you'll never forget.

Trip notes: There is no fee. For a map of Inyo National Forest, send $4 to USDA-Forest Service, 1323 Club Drive, Vallejo, CA 94592. For more information, contact Inyo National Forest, White Mountain Ranger District, 798 North Main Street, Bishop, CA 93514; (760) 873-2500.

Directions: From U.S. 395 in Lee Vining, drive approximately 33 miles south to the McGee Creek Road turnoff on the right. (It's eight miles south of the Mammoth Lakes turnoff and 30 miles north of Bishop.) Drive three miles southwest on McGee Creek Road to the trailhead (past the pack station).

Sequoia, Kings Canyon, & Southern Sierra

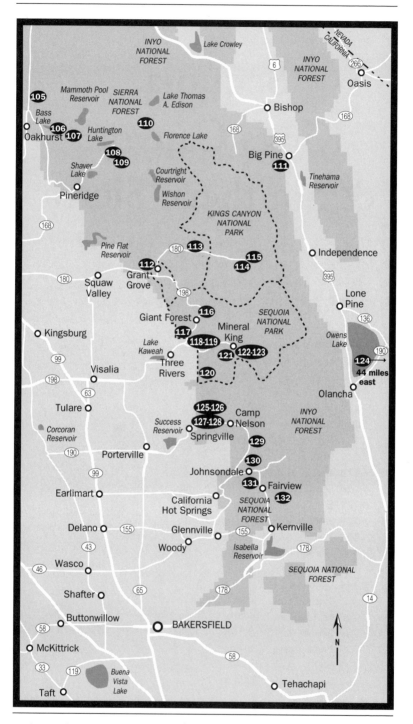

105. CORLIEU & RED ROCK FALLS

Sierra National Forest
Off Highway 41 near Oakhurst

Access & Difficulty: Hike-in & Scramble 4.0 miles RT/Easy
Elevation: Start at 3,900 feet; total gain 200 feet
Best Season: May to October

You don't expect a hiking trail with a trailhead right along a busy highway to be this good. But the Lewis Creek National Recreation Trail, which is accessible from Highway 41 just south of Yosemite and north of Oakhurst, is good. In addition to two excellent waterfalls, Corlieu and Red Rock, the trail offers good trout fishing in Lewis Creek and an interesting historical perspective on the area.

Apparently it's also one of the best trails around for holding hands with your hiking partner, because we passed three different couples, ranging from teenagers to senior citizens, all of them hand-in-hand and smiling. It's just that kind of place.

Although the Lewis Creek Trail has three access points, at both ends and in the middle, most people start from the middle, because that trailhead is right along the highway. From this access point, Corlieu Falls is a mere 10 minutes away. Just follow the trail from the parking pullout, then take the signed right fork and continue to the top of the falls.

You can look down at 40-foot Corlieu Falls from an overlook on the main trail, or follow a use trail that continues to Corlieu's base. It requires some short but steep scrambling to get there. The waterfall has several fallen logs clustered at its base, and a forest of elephant ears growing on tall stalks around its stream. Many rocks and wayward branches have collected below Corlieu, providing a seating gallery for viewing the falls.

When you're ready for the next waterfall, scramble back to the main trail and follow it upstream. You're walking on the path of an old logging route, where the Madera Sugar Pine Company built a section of a 54-mile-long flume

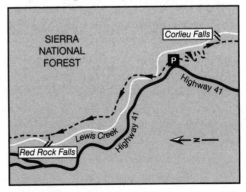

Red Rock Falls

to carry milled boards from the town of Sugar Pine to the railroad in the San Joaquin Valley. The flume operated from 1900 to 1931. Evidence of the old flume—in the form of boards, nails, and metal scraps—can be spotted along the trail, if you look carefully.

To hike upstream to Red Rock Falls, you must cross Lewis Creek, and the footbridge is not always in place. If not, look for a fishermen's trail that travels downstream. It will lead you to a fallen tree that traverses the stream, which makes for convenient crossing.

Colorful wildflowers pepper the banks of Lewis Creek. May apples, big-leaf maples, bear clover, blackberries, and huge ferns proliferate along the stream, all happily growing under a filtered canopy of oaks, ponderosa pines, and incense cedars. If you've been traveling around the stark, higher elevations of Yosemite, it's a pleasant change to be in this lush mixed forest.

In the last half-mile before Red Rock Falls, the trail breaks from its mostly level meandering and begins to climb a bit above the creek. Here your surroundings become drier and more exposed, and at 1.8 miles from Corlieu Falls you see a left spur which descends steeply to the creek. Take it to the base of Red Rock Falls, which is a wide river-type waterfall, about 20 feet high. Unlike Corlieu Falls, Red Rock has almost no foliage or delicate nooks and crannies. Instead, the water pitches over a rock ledge in one bold sheet, creating a loud downpour. We didn't see any red rock, but it is said to appear when the stream level is lower. Several fallen logs have gathered in front of the falls, casualties that washed downstream in a season of harsh storms.

There's not much of a viewing area for Red Rock Falls; you have to sit on the ground alongside it, at an angle to the falls and about 50 feet distant. Although this is a fine spot for picture taking, it's not much of an up-close-and-personal waterfall experience. Of the two falls, Corlieu seems much more intimate.

From Red Rock Falls, you can simply head back 1.5 miles to the trailhead and your car, or you can continue for one mile to the trail's north terminus at Sugar Pine. If you wish to hike the entire length of the Lewis Creek Trail rather than just visit the waterfalls, start hiking at Cedar Valley Road (the trail's south terminus) and walk four miles one-way to Sugar Pine.

Oh, and be sure to bring along a hiking friend, someone you like holding hands with.

Trip notes: There is no fee. For a map of Sierra National Forest, send $4 to USDA-Forest Service, 1323 Club Drive, Vallejo, CA 94592. For more information, contact Sierra National Forest, Mariposa-Minarets Ranger District, 57003 Road 225, North Fork, CA 93643; (559) 877-2218.

Directions: From Oakhurst, drive north on Highway 41 for eight miles to the signed trailhead for the Lewis Creek Trail on the east (right) side of the highway. (The trailhead is four miles south of Westfall Picnic Area.)

---

106. ANGEL & DEVIL'S SLIDE FALLS

Sierra National Forest
Off Highway 41 near Bass Lake

Access & Difficulty: Hike-in 4.8 miles RT/Moderate
Elevation: Start at 3,800 feet; total gain 400 feet
Best Season: May to September

When you hear of waterfalls named Angel and Devil's Slide, you have to wonder what they're going to look like. We wondered; we even debated it some; but when we finally saw them, we understood. Angel Falls looks like an angel's wings, fanning out in thousands of delicate rivulets over light-gray granite. Devil's Slide looks like the place where a laughing devil would play—a series of water chutes, holes, and dips, running for a 200-yard length along Willow Creek.

To hike to Angel and Devil's Slide falls, take Willow Creek Trail from the north end of Bass Lake in Sierra National Forest. The trail is excellent, making for a beautiful walk along its whole route; the only downer is figuring out how to access it. Officially, Willow Creek Trail (also called the McLeod Flat Trail) starts at Road 274 on the east side of the highway bridge over Willow Creek, and there's limited parking on the west side of the bridge. If you can't park there, you must park on North Shore Road between the Bass Lake Dam and Falls Beach Picnic Area. Then walk along the lake for a short distance to the east side of the Willow Creek bridge, and follow an access trail up along the North Fork of Willow Creek. When you reach Road 274, walk 50 feet to your left and access the dirt driveway on the northeast side of the highway bridge, then walk 50 yards on the driveway and take the left cutoff on to single-track. There, finally, you'll find the trail sign and the official start of the Willow Creek Trail. Even so, things are still a bit confusing, because you'll see three different routes—one up high, one right along the creek, and another somewhere in the middle. Take the highest trail above the creek; the lower trails are short spur routes for anglers and swimmers who aren't going all the way to the falls.

The route has many gentle ups and downs, but no steep pitches, if you stay off the side trails which descend to the creek. The main trail has great wildflowers—orange columbine, lavender poppies, white western azaleas, deep purple lupine, wild strawberries, mariposa

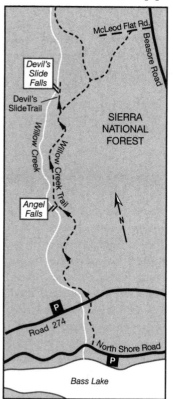

lilies, and even the rare harlequin lupine that has both purple and yellow flowers on the same plant. All of these are tucked in amid ferns, ivies, and a canopy of black and white oaks and mixed conifers. Because of its huge variety of flora, the Willow Creek Trail is an excellent tree and wildflower identification trail.

Hike above the rushing flow of Willow Creek as it carves its way through and around its granite streambed. You reach Angel Falls at nearly one mile from the trailhead, and true to its name, it looks like the gossamer wings of an angel. You can hike to its base on one of several side trails, or follow the main trail to the top of the falls.

Although many other small cascades tumble above and below it, Angel Falls is distinct. Willow Creek's stream runs like latticework over the granite, dropping into granite pockets and then pouring back out. It forms an intricate and beautiful cascade. A small dam controls the water above Angel Falls. Water pipes run by its side. Although these signs of mechanization slightly mar the beauty of Angel Falls, it's only slightly.

Continue hiking upstream of Angel Falls for another 1.5 miles. In between Angel Falls and Devil's Slide, the creek is so quiet and still that it's nearly impossible to believe you will see any more waterfalls. But shortly you'll reach the left fork off the main trail that leads to Devil's Slide. It ends at a chain-link fence designed to keep people

Devil's Slide Falls

off the slippery granite near the cascade. It's wise to stay behind it.

Devil's Slide is not impressively tall, but it is impressively long. It's the perfect water slide for a sea otter or a beaver, or perhaps the Devil himself. The water runs cold, fast, and loud. Watch your step; it could be dangerous here. Stay behind the fence.

On your return trip, watch for views of bright blue Bass Lake as you descend on the trail. And since you've just been visiting the Devil's playground, you might want to stop and pay homage to saintly Angel Falls once more before returning to the trailhead.

Trip notes: There is no fee. For a map of Sierra National Forest, send $4 to USDA-Forest Service, 1323 Club Drive, Vallejo, CA 94592. For more information, contact Sierra National Forest, Mariposa-Minarets Ranger District, 57003 Road 225, North Fork, CA 93643; (559) 877-2218.

Directions: From Oakhurst, drive north on Highway 41 for four miles, then turn right on Road 222. Drive four miles and bear left on Road 274. Drive one mile to the trailhead parking area on the left side of the road, on the west side of the highway bridge over Willow Creek. Or, bear right on the Bass Lake cutoff (Road 222), then bear left on North Shore Road and drive one mile to Falls Beach Picnic Area. Park there or further west in the dirt pullouts along the road, closer to the dam. A use trail begins across the road from the dam; follow it up and across Road 274 to the official start of the Willow Creek Trail.

107. WHISKEY FALLS

Sierra National Forest
Off Highway 41 near Bass Lake

Access & Difficulty: Drive-to/Easy
Elevation: 5,800 feet
Best Season: May to September

Usually the waterfalls you can drive to don't interest me as much as the ones you must hike to. Drive-to falls are often too well known and crowded; hike-in falls are usually more secluded and remote. But Whiskey Falls in Sierra National Forest is the exception. Even though the waterfall drops right along the Whiskey Falls Campground access road, it somehow manages to stay a secret. Maybe the long, unpaved access road keeps it isolated, or perhaps the other campgrounds and attractions around Bass Lake draw the crowds away. Whatever it is, it's a good thing.

You can combine your visit to Whiskey Falls with a camping trip at the adjacent Forest Service camp, where your stay will cost you a

Whiskey Falls

whopping five bucks a night. Then you can get up in the morning and head off on various hiking and fishing adventures in the area. At the end of each day, you return to Whiskey Falls, always running wide and clear, and go to sleep at night with the sound of a waterfall accompanying your dreams.

Whiskey Falls can be found just beyond the campground entrance sign at a bridge over Whiskey Creek. The 40-foot waterfall drops just upstream over two stair-stepped granite slabs, which are framed by big western azaleas blooming brightly white along the creek. The fall's width is almost double its height, and its stream provides excellent flow year-round. Large sheets of granite at the waterfall's base furnish a place to sun yourself and admire the shimmering, lacy cascade. Big conifers nearby offer a shady respite.

Whiskey Falls is two side-by-side cataracts, one wide main drop and one alongside it that's a beautiful narrow stair-step, with large clumps of elephant ears growing between the two. The waterfall's secret is that the larger cascade has a shallow cave behind it, lined with greenery, mosses, and ferns of all variety. My hiking partner insisted on going underneath the spray of water to crawl into the cave. Then, just to prove he'd done it, he took a picture of me on the other side of the running water. It's one of the most unusual photographs I've ever seen, something like Kodachrome crossed with Impressionism.

If you decide to stay at Whiskey Falls Camp, make sure you take the nearby hikes on the Willow Creek Trail and Lewis Creek Trail to see more waterfalls (see the two previous stories).

Trip notes: There is no fee. For a map of Sierra National Forest, send $4 to USDA-Forest Service, 1323 Club Drive, Vallejo, CA 94592. For more information, contact Sierra National Forest, Mariposa-Minarets Ranger District, 57003 Road 225, North Fork, CA 93643; (559) 877-2218.

Directions: From Oakhurst, drive north on Highway 41 for four miles, then turn right on Road 222. Drive four miles and bear left on Road 274, following it approximately 10 miles into North Fork. At the four-way stop sign where roads 274 and 225 intersect, turn left on Road 225. Drive one mile, then turn left on to Cascadel Road (Road 233). Drive two miles, then bear left on Road 8S09. Follow Road 8S09 for about seven miles, then turn right and drive 1.2 miles to Whiskey Falls Camp. The falls drop right along the road.

108. RANCHERIA FALLS

Sierra National Forest
Off Highway 168 near Huntington Lake

Access & Difficulty: Hike-in 2.0 miles RT/Easy
Elevation: Start at 7,760 feet; total gain 350 feet
Best Season: May to September

The Rancheria Falls National Recreation Trail is so well groomed, it's hikeable in tennis shoes—even little four-inch-long

Rancheria Falls at low flow in August

Reeboks made for three-year-old feet. I know, because I found one on the trail, and then a few moments later, I came upon its owner, walking along with one shoe on and one shoe off. She seemed nonplussed by the missing Reebok, but feigned gratitude for its return.

Why worry about footwear when you're hiking to Rancheria Falls? There's so much else to concern yourself with. It's a gorgeous one-mile trail, smooth and wide, that takes a gentle uphill grade to the waterfall. You'll share it with blue butterflies and noisy cicadas flitting by. The route leads through a fir forest with an understory of gooseberry, chinquapin, and colorful wildflowers, mostly hardy lupine and paintbrush.

You don't see or hear water until you're almost on top of the falls. The path delivers you at Rancheria Falls' base, and your first view of it can take your breath away. The waterfall plummets 150 feet over a 50-foot-wide rock ledge, then continues in a long, boisterous cascade that greatly increases its magnitude. As Rancheria Creek's flow hits assorted smaller ledges below its lip, the water pushes off and sprays outward like fireworks exploding. It's the kind of sight you want to watch for a long, long time.

From the end of the trail, you can climb over rocks and pick your viewing spot, either closer to or farther from the voluminous spray. Even if there is a crowd here, as there often is because of the fall's proximity to popular Huntington Lake, you can usually find a private spot downstream. Make sure you check out the vista down-canyon; it's almost as pretty as the waterfall view.

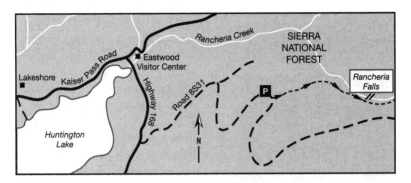

Trip notes: There is no fee. For a map of Sierra National Forest, send $4 to USDA-Forest Service, 1323 Club Drive, Vallejo, CA 94592. For more information, contact Sierra National Forest, Pineridge Ranger District, P.O. Box 559, Prather, CA 93651; (559) 855-5360.

Directions: From Fresno, drive northeast on Highway 168 through Clovis for 70 miles, past Shaver Lake. One-half mile before reaching Huntington Lake, take the right turnoff signed for Rancheria Falls (Road 8S31). Follow the dirt road for 1.3 miles to the signed trailhead at a sharp curve in the road. Park off the road.

109. DINKEY CREEK FALLS

Dinkey Lakes Wilderness
Off Highway 168 near Shaver Lake

Access & Difficulty: Hike-in 0.6 mile RT/Easy
Elevation: Start at 8,590 feet; total gain 0 feet
Best Season: May to September

Don't plan on coming to Dinkey Creek just to see the waterfall. Once you get out of your car and start walking into the Dinkey Lakes Wilderness, there's almost no chance you'll be willing to turn around at the falls, which are only one-third of a mile in. The place is just too good to pass up.

Before you jump in your car and head out, though, make sure you pack along the bug spray. On our July visit, we pulled up in the parking lot, opened the doors of our air-conditioned car, and were immediately attacked by about eight million mosquitos. In the middle of the day, no less. I've never experienced anything like it. We jumped back in the car and armed ourselves with repellent, then tried again, with great improvement.

Dinkey Creek Falls

Another odd fact about the trailhead is that it's located right next to a popular off-highway vehicle area. While we were swatting mosquitos, three guys on all-terrain vehicles roared up to us and asked, "Hey, how far is it to the first Dinkey Lake?" We told them it was just over a mile, but they weren't allowed to ride their motorcycles in the wilderness. They were shocked. "A mile?!? That's way too far to walk." Then they roared off in the other direction. To each his own, I suppose.

Immediately beyond the parking area, the trail crosses Dinkey Creek, which can make things a bit tricky, depending on the stream level. You'll be instantly wowed by the colorful striated rock formations in the creekbed and along the edges of the trail. After hopping across the creek, walk for only about two minutes down the trail, until you see a huge 100-yard-wide rock slab on your left. It looks like a gray lava field. Leave the trail and cross over to it, then walk across it and you'll find the falls on the far side. Total walking time from the parking area? About seven minutes.

Dinkey Creek Falls is only about 20 feet high, dropping through a notch in the fractured granite, then fanning out in a wide horsetail shape and hitting a single wide stair-step below. Except for this one cliff-like section at the waterfall, Dinkey Creek is otherwise flat. The water is very clear, showing off the colorful rock beneath it. Tiny pink and white mountain wildflowers grow out of cracks in the granite alongside the fall, and if you wear enough bug spray you can actually stand still for a minute and enjoy the scene.

But like I said, you won't want to stop here. The trail continues along Dinkey Creek to a right turnoff for Mystery Lake at 1.3 miles. The lake is only a quarter-mile further from this junction. Or, continuing straight along Dinkey Creek brings you to First Dinkey Lake, as it is prosaically named, in three miles. You're sure to have company at these and the more distant lakes. A popular backpacking trail links several of them. The loop trip is flat and short enough for hikers of any level, and the scenery is world-class, replete with verdant meadows, colorful wildflowers, stark granite walls, and deep blue lakes.

Trip notes: There is no fee. For a map of Dinkey Lakes Wilderness or Sierra National Forest, send $4 to USDA-Forest Service, 1323 Club Drive, Vallejo, CA 94592. For more information, contact Sierra National Forest, Pineridge Ranger District, P.O. Box 559, Prather, CA 93651; (559) 855-5360.

Directions: From Fresno, drive northeast on Highway 168 through Clovis for 50 miles to the town of Shaver Lake. Turn right on Dinkey Creek Road and drive nine miles. Turn left on Rock Creek Road (9S09) and drive six miles, then turn right on 9S10 and drive 4.7 miles. Turn right at the sign for Dinkey Lakes on Road 9S62 and drive 2.2 miles to the trailhead. These last two miles are very rough road. (Stay left at the fork to bypass the four-wheel-drive area and go straight to the trailhead.)

You can also reach the trailhead from the northern end of Road 9S09, at Tamarack Winter Sports Area, nine miles north of Shaver Lake. Drive 6.4 miles on 9S09, then bear left on 9S10 and drive 4.7 miles. Follow the rest of the directions as above.

110. BEAR CREEK FALLS

John Muir Wilderness
Off Highway 168 near Mono Hot Springs

Access & Difficulty: Hike-in or Backpack 11.6 miles RT/Moderate
Elevation: Start at 6,900 feet; total gain 1,000 feet
Best Season: June to September

The drive to the trailhead is a big part of this adventure to Bear Creek Falls. Four-wheel-drive or very high clearance is necessary for the final two miles of the trip, but even the paved stretch on narrow, winding Kaiser Pass Road is exciting.

Bear Creek Falls is located in the John Muir Wilderness just outside of Mono Hot Springs in Sierra National Forest. The nearest major development is at Huntington and Shaver lakes, 20 miles to the west. After you leave these recreation areas and set out over Kaiser Pass, all you'll find are a few spartan resorts and campgrounds and the incredible granite landscape of the Central Sierra. The scenery is priceless—a nonstop parade of granite slabs and dome-like structures, both on the drive in and on the trail itself. This is the scenery that defines the word "Sierra" in the minds of so many nature lovers.

Be sure to stop in at the rustic resort at Mono Hot Springs to fill up your day-pack or backpack with supplies, then head for the wilderness boundary and a gorgeous hike along Bear Creek.

Bear Creek Trail leads past Bear Creek Reservoir and along the continually rushing cascades of Bear Creek. If you've ever hiked along the Tuolumne River in Yosemite, you'll find this experience to be similar—the stream is always in close proximity, but its many cascades are partially hidden from the trail. The greenish colored water, clear pools, and nearly non-stop sound of waterfalls will force you to keep leaving the main path to get a closer look. You say you want to swim? Well, be forewarned—the water in Bear Creek is colder than any place I've ever stuck my big toe in. Anglers, take note: there are many good-sized trout in this stream.

You hike with the stream on your right for the entire trip. The trail has a constant, gentle elevation gain. Occasional welcome shade is provided by Jeffrey pines and firs, but much of the route is exposed. Along the streambanks are groves of quaking aspens, which would be a treat to see in October when their leaves turn.

At 5.8 miles out, you'll spot 25-foot Bear Creek Falls from the trail. It is formed where two cascading branches of Bear Creek pour into an enormously wide, shallow pool. Stay on the trail for a few more yards as it leads up and around the huge pool. Take off your shoes and socks and ford the creek where you can. On the far side you'll gain access to a lovely beach near the base of the falls, alongside the pool. The beach is composed of beautiful, tiny, rounded pebbles. Pull out your lunch; you won't be leaving soon.

Trip notes: There is no fee. For a map of John Muir Wilderness or Sierra National Forest, send $4 to USDA-Forest Service, 1323 Club Drive, Vallejo, CA 94592. For more information, contact Sierra National Forest, Pineridge Ranger District, P.O. Box 559, Prather, CA 93651; (559) 855-5360.

Directions: From Fresno, drive northeast on Highway 168 through Clovis for 70 miles to Huntington Lake. Turn right on Kaiser Pass Road and drive 17 miles (narrow and winding) to a fork. Bear left for Mono Hot Springs and Edison Lake. Drive 2.5 miles to the Bear Creek turnoff on the right (it's one mile past the Mono Hot Springs turnoff and before the Mono Creek Campground turnoff). Turn right and drive 2.3 miles on rough dirt road (four-wheel-drive is required) to Bear Creek Reservoir parking area and trailhead. Park on the granite slabs, then follow the trail that leads downhill toward the reservoir.

111. FIRST & SECOND FALLS

Inyo National Forest
Off U.S. 395 near Big Pine

Access & Difficulty: Hike-in or Backpack 3.0 miles RT/Moderate
Elevation: Start at 7,800 feet; total gain 300 feet
Best Season: May to September

Want a perfect beginner-level backpacking trip where you camp on top of a waterfall? How about an easy day-hike near the border of the John Muir Wilderness, visiting two waterfalls on the way? Sign up here for the trip to First and Second Falls, just 10 miles off U.S. 395 in Big Pine.

The trip begins at the trailhead near Glacier Lodge, where you take a stroll down a paved and dirt road in front of some privately owned cabins, paralleling Big Pine Creek. In moments you cross a bridge over First Falls, which is a long, 200-foot cascade that pours down the mountainside. Because its edges are completely overgrown with willows and cottonwoods, you can't see much of it, but it creates a terrific noise even late in the summer.

After the bridge, take the right fork and begin a steep uphill climb, switchbacking up and over First Falls. It takes a dozen or more tight curves in the trail to get above it, and your body feels the elevation if you aren't acclimated. You get great views straight into Big Pine Canyon, though, and the sound of the creek will spur you on.

The trail's surprise is that you're not heading into the great expanse in front of you, which is Big Pine Canyon's South Fork. Instead you're stealing away to a hidden canyon off to your right, the North Fork Canyon of Big Pine Creek, which you can't see until you get on top of First Falls. Cross a bridge to your right, then take a hard left onto a dirt road, staying along the creek. Note that if you turn right instead, you'll reach First Falls Walk-in Camp in 100 yards, with its six campsites, fire rings, and picnic tables. This is a perfect

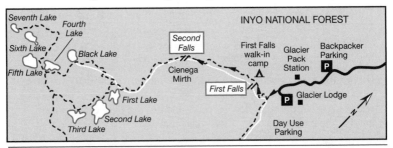

backpacking destination for families, only a mile's hike from the backpackers' parking lot. The camp sits along the stream just above First Falls, nestled in some pine trees. (There's also a single-track trail option at this junction, signed only as "Upper Trail," which is for backpackers heading farther back into the canyon.)

Now that you've made all those switchbacks, you can relax a while and just stroll along the level dirt road, enjoying the proximity of the creek and the canyon and mountain vistas. At 1.2 miles, you'll get your first view of Second Falls, which actually looks more impressive from a distance than it does close up. Like First Falls, Second Falls is a 200-foot cascade, but it delivers much more visual impact than First Falls does. The fall is surrounded by interesting rocks and has a few sparse Jeffrey pines growing on top.

The dirt road you're hiking on eventually narrows to single-track, then switchbacks to the right to join the upper trail in the canyon. But an unmaintained route continues to the left, bringing you closer to the waterfall if you choose to follow it. I scrambled to the fall's edge, fighting my way through low trees and brush, but I was disappointed with the view and quickly retreated a quarter-mile back to a big rock near a lone pine tree. From there, the scenery was superb: In addition to Second Falls and the surrounding mountains, the profusion of plant life in the canyon could be surveyed. In one glance, you can see mountain mahogany, lodgepole pines, aspens along the creek, sagebrush, paintbrush, and even some scrubby cactus growing near the waterfall's edge.

Backpackers staying at First Falls or camping further back in the canyon can continue hiking beyond the falls to Cienega Mirth at three miles, First Lake at 4.5 miles, Second Lake at 4.8 miles, or Third Lake at 5.5 miles. By Second Lake you've climbed to over 10,000 feet, and the lakes are a stunning glacial blue-green color. A popular summer trip is to hike all the way to the edge of the Palisade Glacier, the southernmost glacier in the Sierra, but it's a long, hard pull of nine miles one-way, with a 5,000-foot elevation gain.

Trip notes: There is no fee. For a map of Inyo National Forest, send $4 to USDA-Forest Service, 1323 Club Drive, Vallejo, CA 94592. For more information, contact Inyo National Forest, White Mountain Ranger District, 798 North Main Street, Bishop, CA 93514; (760) 873-2500.

Directions: From Bishop, drive 15 miles south on U.S. 395 to Big Pine. Turn right (west) on Crocker Street, which becomes Glacier Lodge Road, and drive 10.5 miles to Glacier Lodge and the Big Pine Canyon Trailhead at the end of the road. Day-hikers may park in the day-use area near the lodge, but backpackers must park a half-mile east on Glacier Lodge Road in the backpackers' parking lot.

112. ELLA FALLS

Kings Canyon National Park
Off Highway 180 near Grant Grove

Access & Difficulty: Hike-in 4.5 miles RT/Moderate
Elevation: Start at 6,590 feet; total loss 1,000 feet
Best Season: April to August

Ella Falls was the destination of my first hiking trip ever in Kings Canyon National Park. What an introduction. I've been a Kings Canyon believer since.

Ella Falls was also the place where I got my education about exploring off-trail on the slick granite around southern Sierra waterfalls. While looking for a good spot to take a photograph, my hiking boots suddenly and mysteriously lost all traction, and I slid on my backside about 10 feet into a freezing pool. Luckily I landed in a basin, so I didn't tumble further downstream. And luckily I wasn't hurt. I hiked back home feeling very humble, though, and carrying my pants, which were soaking wet. I learned my lesson.

The trail to Ella Falls starts at Sunset Campground, right across the road from Grant Grove Village. The trip is downhill all the way, with a 1,000-foot elevation loss that you must gain back on the return. It's a well-built trail with an even grade and sturdy wooden

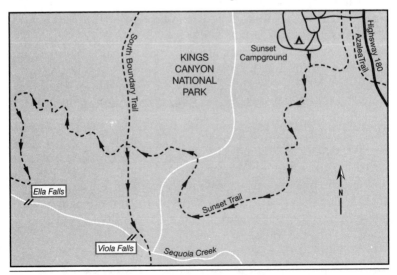

Ella Falls

bridges to carry you across streams. The trail descends through big pines and firs and winds through stands of ceanothus and flowering western azalea. Although the forest is partially burned in places around the trail, incredible foliage and ferns surround all the side streams.

At 1.5 miles from the trailhead, reach a junction where the South Boundary Trail crosses Sunset Trail. Turning left will take you on a quarter-mile side-trip to what the park rather liberally calls Viola Falls. I found Viola to be rather disappointing. Although the area around it is lovely, it's not really tall enough to be considered a waterfall. The cataract is about five feet high, set in a rock garden of sculptured granite pools. The best thing about the side-trip is not Viola Falls at all, but a huge Sequoia tree that grows just upstream of it, with chunks of granite permanently fused in its above-ground roots. The big old tree grew right around the rocks, imprisoning them in its grasp. More cascades drop downstream from Viola Falls and the South Boundary Trail, but they can't be accessed because of the slick, polished granite of the streambed and the steep canyon walls. Take the side-trip to Viola if you choose, or continue straight on Sunset Trail to Ella Falls.

Like Viola, Ella Falls drops on Sequoia Creek. It's a 50-foot-long narrow cascade that shimmers bright white among the gray rocks and dense green foliage along the stream. The granite streambed appears soft, because of being continually rounded and eroded by the coursing stream. Alders and willows grow tightly along the stream's edge. Look for tall cow parsnips and colorful leopard lilies growing along the banks.

If you'd like to continue hiking before making the uphill return trip to Sunset Campground, you can follow Sunset Trail for another quarter-mile to a YMCA camp on Sequoia Lake. Although Sequoia is a privately owned lake and not part of the park, you're allowed to walk along the lake's edge as long as you stay out of the camp area.

Trip notes: There is a $10 entrance fee at Sequoia and Kings Canyon National Parks, good for seven days. Park maps are available for free at the entrance stations. A more detailed map is available for a fee from Tom Harrison Cartography at (415) 456-7940 or Trails Illustrated at (800) 962-1643. For more information, contact Sequoia and Kings Canyon National Parks, Three Rivers, CA 93271-9700; (559) 565-3134.

Directions: From Fresno, drive east on Highway 180 for 55 miles to the Big Stump Entrance Station at Kings Canyon National Park. Continue 1.5 miles and turn left for Grant Grove. Drive 1.5 miles to Grant Grove Village and park in the large parking lot near the visitor center. Cross the road and walk on the paved trail toward Sunset Campground's amphitheater. Continue heading left through the campground to site #179, where the trail begins.

113. GRIZZLY FALLS

Sequoia National Forest
Off Highway 180 near Cedar Grove

Access & Difficulty: Drive-to/Easy
Elevation: 4,400 feet
Best Season: May to September

Most people don't notice the difference, but Grizzly Falls is not in Kings Canyon or Sequoia National Parks, it's in Sequoia National Forest. The national park/national forest boundary line is drawn in such a way that the Kings Canyon Highway enters the national park near Grant Grove, then leaves it, then re-enters it again near Cedar Grove after passing through 27 miles of Sequoia National Forest. Grizzly Falls is in the final few miles of the forest before the winding highway re-enters the park boundary.

But jurisdictions matter little when you're looking at a waterfall as pretty as 80-foot Grizzly Falls, which runs just 50 yards from the road. A small parking lot and picnic area near the base of the falls make Grizzly an easy and fun destination, especially when a stop here breaks up the long and winding drive into the heart of Kings Canyon.

The water from Grizzly Falls starts at Grizzly Lakes, deep in the Monarch Wilderness below the Monarch Divide, and pours all the

Grizzly Falls

way down to the Kings River along the Kings Canyon Highway. The falls are on the edge of the Monarch Wilderness, a roadless land of steep and rugged terrain. Hikers can make their way into the wilderness by way of the Deer Cove Trailhead two miles east of the falls, but limited water and relentless ups and downs keep all but the hardiest of hikers away.

Grizzly is a waterfall for people who have little interest in hiking, or a lot of interest in waterfalls, since the fall is only 50 yards from where you park your car. The waterfall is loud and powerful, dropping 80 feet over a 35-foot-wide granite ledge. The first time you see it, you may have a sense of déja vu, because photos of this fall frequently appear on park brochures and local travel magazines. It's that pretty.

If you're making the drive all the way out here to see Grizzly Falls, you might want to take a look at another natural wonder just five miles away, Boyden Cave. Crystalline stalactites and stalagmites are the primary features of this limestone cavern. Like Grizzly Falls, Boyden Cave is under the Forest Service's jurisdiction, and with the aid of a concessionaire they offer tours daily from May through October. Phone (209) 736-2708 for schedules and information.

Trip notes: Although the waterfall is in Sequoia National Forest, the only way to reach it is by entering Kings Canyon National Park on Highway 180. There is a $10 entrance fee at Sequoia and Kings Canyon National Parks, good for seven days. Park maps are available for free at the entrance stations. A more detailed map is available for a fee from Tom Harrison Cartography at (415) 456-7940 or Trails Illustrated at (800) 962-1643. For more information, contact Sequoia National Forest, Hume Lake Ranger District, 35860 East Kings Canyon Road, Dunlap, CA 93621; (559) 338-2251 or Sequoia and Kings Canyon National Parks, Three Rivers, CA 93271-9700; (559) 565-3134.

Directions: From Fresno, drive east on Highway 180 for 55 miles to the Big Stump Entrance Station at Kings Canyon National Park. Continue 1.5 miles and turn left for Grant Grove and Cedar Grove. Continue 27 miles on Highway 180 to Grizzly Falls on the left, 5.5 miles past Boyden Cave.

114. ROARING RIVER FALLS
Kings Canyon National Park
Off Highway 180 near Cedar Grove

Access & Difficulty: Hike-in or Wheelchair 0.4 mile RT/Easy
Elevation: Start at 4,850 feet; total gain 0 feet
Best Season: May to July

I figured that Roaring River Falls was the cute and clever name for a Kings Canyon waterfall that made lots of noise, but no; Roaring River Falls is a waterfall that falls on the Roaring River. So my next question was: Does the Roaring River actually roar? And the answer is yes, but not as much as the South Fork Kings River, which it drops

Roaring River Falls

into. It just goes to show that in the waterfall business, you can take some things literally, but not everything.

A great feature of Roaring River Falls is that it's the only waterfall in Kings Canyon and Sequoia National Parks that is accessible via wheelchair; the trail is paved, wide, and only four-tenths of a mile round-trip. If able hikers want a longer trip, they can continue upstream on the River Trail to Zumwalt Meadow in 1.6 miles or Road's End in 2.7 miles.

Getting to the falls is a breeze. After leaving your car in the Roaring River Falls parking lot, just follow the trail through the forest and you arrive in about five minutes. At the overlook area, you have a perfect view of the falls, nicely framed by a big Jeffrey pine on the right and two red firs on the left. The river funnels down through a narrow rock gorge, forming two water chutes—one is 40 feet tall; the one behind it is 20 feet tall. You stand directly across from the waterfall, on the north side of the dark, gray, rocky bowl into which the water pounds.

Roaring River Falls' pool is so large—probably 50 feet wide—and the cliffs surrounding it are so tall and sheer, that the falls are somewhat dwarfed. Keep in mind, however, that you are seeing only their final drop. The cascades continue for hundreds of feet upstream, hidden from view and inaccessible. Park officials estimate that from the overlook, you see only one-third of Roaring River Fall's total drop.

Trip notes: There is a $10 entrance fee at Sequoia and Kings Canyon National Parks, good for seven days. Park maps are available for free at the entrance stations. A more detailed map is available for a fee from Tom Harrison Cartography at (415) 456-7940 or Trails Illustrated at (800)

962-1643. For more information, contact Sequoia and Kings Canyon National Parks, Three Rivers, CA 93271-9700; (559) 565-3134.

Directions: From Fresno, drive east on Highway 180 for 55 miles to the Big Stump Entrance Station at Kings Canyon National Park. Continue 1.5 miles and turn left for Grant Grove and Cedar Grove. Continue 35 miles on Highway 180 to the sign for Roaring River Falls and the River Trail, three miles past the Cedar Grove campground and ranger station. The trailhead and parking area are on the right side of the road.

115. MIST FALLS

Kings Canyon National Park
Off Highway 180 near Cedar Grove

Access & Difficulty: Hike-in 8.0 miles RT/Moderate
Elevation: Start at 5,035 feet; total gain 600 feet
Best Season: May to July

The Mist Falls Trail is easily the busiest hiking trail in the Cedar Grove area of Kings Canyon National Park. Although it's an eight-mile round-trip to Mist Falls, they're easy miles, with a well-marked trail and only 650 feet of elevation gain. The route is equally shared by day-hikers heading to the falls and backpackers heading to Paradise Valley and beyond, so if you want to have any solitude on your walk, you must start early in the morning.

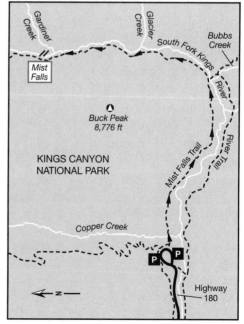

The trail begins level and stays level for the first two miles. It's convenient because the scenery is so spectacular that you won't want to think about anything else. You find yourself craning your neck a lot, always looking up at the imposing canyon walls on both sides of the trail.

The mixed oak, pine, and cedar forest is sparse, sandy, and dry at

Mist Falls from above

first, then becomes increasingly dense. In the spring, a tall, narrow waterfall on Avalanche Creek pours down the right canyon wall. Giant boulders are scattered around the trail, having dropped from the cliffs sometime during the last 100,000 years. The roar of the South Fork Kings River is a pleasant accompaniment.

After a lovely shaded stretch where the forest closes in and ferns grow squeezed in between big boulders, you reach a junction at two miles out. Bear left and climb slightly, rising above the river. As you leave the forest and enter granite country, your views get increasingly spectacular. At three miles out, make sure you turn around and check out the vista of the Kings River canyon behind you, framed by 9,000-foot mountains on both sides. The epitome of classic Sierra drama is the silhouette of The Sphinx (an odd-shaped granite peak that looks remotely like the Egyptian Sphinx) with Avalanche Peak on its right side. It's views, views, views in all directions.

At exactly four miles from the trailhead, after a few switchbacks on exposed granite and some heavy breathing, you're at the river's edge, and a short right spur drops you 100 yards from the base of Mist Falls. Although the fall is not high, only about 45 feet, it exhibits tremendous flair as it fans out over a wide granite ledge and then crashes into a boulder-lined pool. Mist Falls is famous for the mist and spray it exudes, but it's perhaps more impressive for the amount of noise it makes. In springtime, you have to shout at your hiking companions to be heard.

Mist Falls actually looks prettier when the river level is down somewhat; during heavy snowmelt, the details of the cascade can be completely obscured by rushing water and spray. The first time we saw it, in a wet June, it looked like a big white blob. A month later, it showed off its finer points. The best place to view the fall is from a huge flat rock just 100 feet downstream.

Angling is popular below Mist Falls, especially in late spring and early summer. When the river level is just right, many brown and rainbow trout invite themselves to dinner. One fisherman told us that he works this stretch of river every June, and it's not uncommon to catch 50 fish a day between Mist Falls and the trailhead.

If the crowds get too heavy for you on the Mist Falls Trail, there's a less-used alternate route for the homeward trip: When you return to the trail junction at two miles, turn left and cross Bailey Bridge. Walk an eighth of a mile, passing by the Bubbs Creek Trail junction, then turn right, heading back on the River Trail on the south side of the Kings River. In addition to leaving most of the crowds behind, this trail has great views. You'll need to walk slightly downstream of the trailhead to reach a bridge where you can cross the river and head back to your car.

Trip notes: There is a $10 entrance fee at Sequoia and Kings Canyon National Parks, good for seven days. Park maps are available for free at the entrance stations. A more detailed map is available for a fee from Tom Harrison Cartography at (415) 456-7940 or Trails Illustrated at (800) 962-1643. For more information, contact Sequoia and Kings Canyon National Parks, Three Rivers, CA 93271-9700; (559) 565-3134.

Directions: From Fresno, drive east on Highway 180 for 55 miles to the Big Stump Entrance Station at Kings Canyon National Park. Continue 1.5 miles and turn left for Grant Grove and Cedar Grove. Continue 38 miles on Highway 180 to Road's End, six miles past the Cedar Grove campground and ranger station. The trailhead is at the east end of the parking lot, near the wilderness ranger station.

116. TOKOPAH FALLS

Sequoia National Park
Off the Generals Highway near Lodgepole

Access & Difficulty: Hike-in 3.6 miles RT/Easy
Elevation: Start at 6,780 feet; total gain 500 feet
Best Season: April to July

Tokopah Falls is hands-down the best waterfall in Sequoia and Kings Canyon. Accept no substitutes or imitations; if you want the

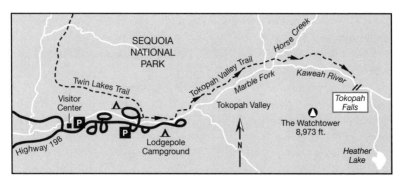

best possible waterfall experience in the two national parks, head to Lodgepole Campground and the Tokopah Falls trailhead.

Sure the trail's crowded—why wouldn't it be? The walk to the falls is only 1.8 miles of level trail through gorgeous High Sierra scenery, consummating at the base of 1,200-foot-high Tokopah Falls. But if you follow the cardinal rule for popular outdoor destinations and start hiking early in the morning, the crowds will still be asleep in their tents. You can be out to the falls and back before most people have finished brushing their teeth.

The trail is almost as awesome as the falls. In a little more than a mile and a half, you get incredible views of the Watchtower, a 1,600-foot-tall glacially carved cliff on the south side of Tokopah Valley. Your perspective on the Watchtower changes with every few steps you take, and it's breathtaking from every angle. Then there's Tokopah Valley itself, with Tokopah Falls pouring down the smooth back curve of its U-shape. Tokopah Valley is similar in geological type and appearance to Yosemite Valley, formed partially by the river in its center but mostly by slow-moving glaciers.

The Tokopah Falls Trail also provides a near guarantee of seeing wildlife. What kind, you ask? Yellow-bellied marmots, the largest and most charming member of the squirrel family. In a completely nonscientific survey, I determined that this area has more marmots per square mile than probably anywhere in the Sierra. Their great abundance is due in part to the proximity of the campground and the marmots' great love of food. (Don't give them any handouts.) You'll have dozens of chances to photograph the cute little guys or to just admire their beautiful blonde coats, as they sun themselves on boulders or stand on their back legs to whistle at you.

The trail is a mix of conifers and granite, always following close to the Marble Fork of the Kaweah River. It leads gently uphill all the way to the falls, and then downhill all the way back. If the route seems rather rocky at the start, don't fret; its surface changes. Sometimes the trail travels on a soft forest floor of conifer needles, other times over bridges that cross tiny feeder creeks, and still other times in meadow areas overflowing with lush ferns, orange columbine, yellow violets, and purple nightshade. The trail passes through so many different habitats, it has 40 different kinds of wildflowers growing along its brief length.

The bottom cascade of Tokopah Falls

The final quarter-mile of the path, which traverses rocky slopes, gives you wide-open views of Tokopah Fall's impressive 1,200-foot height, and increases your anticipation. The trail has been dynamited into granite; in one section you must duck your head as you walk under a ledge. You can proceed right to the edge of the falls, which drop over fractured granite. Choose a rock to sit on and marvel at the cacophony of cascading water, but don't get too close—Tokopah flows fast, and can be dangerous in springtime.

Trip notes: There is a $10 entrance fee at Sequoia and Kings Canyon National Parks, good for seven days. Park maps are available for free at the entrance stations. A more detailed map is available for a fee from Tom Harrison Cartography at (415) 456-7940 or Trails Illustrated at (800) 962-1643. For more information, contact Sequoia and Kings Canyon National Parks, Three Rivers, CA 93271-9700; (559) 565-3134.

Directions: From Fresno, drive east on Highway 180 for 55 miles to the Big Stump Entrance Station at Kings Canyon National Park. Continue 1.5 miles and turn right on the Generals Highway, heading for Sequoia National Park. Drive approximately 25 miles on the Generals Highway to the Lodgepole Campground turnoff, then drive three-quarters of a mile to the Log Bridge Area of Lodgepole Camp. Park in the large lot just before the bridge over the Marble Fork Kaweah River, and walk 150 yards to the trailhead, which is just after you cross the bridge.

117. MARBLE FALLS

Sequoia National Park
Off Highway 198 near Three Rivers

Access & Difficulty: Hike-in 7.0 miles RT/Moderate
Elevation: Start at 2,100 feet; total gain 1,500 feet
Best Season: February to June

Marble Falls is a series of wide cascades that swoop and scatter over white granite on the Marble Fork of the Kaweah River in Sequoia National Park. But the beauty of the falls is only one of its great features; the other is that its trail is open year-round for hiking, even when other trails in Sequoia and Kings Canyon parks are closed down with heavy snow.

The Marble Fork Trail begins on a dirt road at the upper end of Potwisha Campground. After crossing a flume filled with flowing water in springtime, watch for a sign that marks the official start of the trail, which climbs a steep bank to the right.

You're in chaparral country here at 2,100 feet in elevation. It's hard to believe that this dry habitat is in the same park as all those giant Sequoia trees and snowy peaks, but it's true. As the trail leads through hillsides covered with canyon oaks, chamise, poison oak, and yerba santa, you may find yourself wondering if you're in San Diego rather than the Sierra.

After the initial climb, the trail occasionally levels and curves into gullies where you'll find blessed shade and foliage that is more lively than the continual chaparral and oaks. Buckeye trees bloom in springtime in these marginally wet areas. Although you can hear the roar of the river continually as you hike, you are a few hundred feet feet above it. The ascent remains gradual but steady.

Amateur geologists will enjoy the many outcroppings of colorful marble, which increase in number underfoot and alongside the trail as you approach Marble Falls. At 3.5 miles, the trail descends to the river's edge near the falls. Take the short spur trail on your left (before the main trail ends) for a better view. Marble Falls drops in a series of cascades; the tallest is about 40 feet. Many of the cascades are upstream from the trail, in a rocky gorge and out of sight. Trying

Marble Falls

to reach them is dangerous and not recommended. (Beware fast water and slick granite.) Instead, choose a spot on the river bank near the trail's end to watch the action.

Remember, what's good about this trail in winter—that it's located at low elevation and snow-free—can be a curse in summer. With a 1,500-foot climb and little shade along the route, you don't want to be hiking here at midday in August. If you want to see Marble Falls in summertime, head out early in the morning, reach the falls by 9 A.M., and make the downhill return trip before the sun reaches high noon.

Trip notes: There is a $10 entrance fee at Sequoia and Kings Canyon National Parks, good for seven days. Park maps are available for free at the entrance stations. A more detailed map is available for a fee from Tom Harrison Cartography at (415) 456-7940 or Trails Illustrated at (800) 962-1643. For more information, contact Sequoia and Kings Canyon National Parks, Three Rivers, CA 93271-9700; (559) 565-3134.

Directions: From Visalia, drive east on Highway 198 for 44 miles to the turnoff on the left for Potwisha Campground, 3.8 miles east of the Ash Mountain entrance station to Sequoia National Park. The trail begins next to site #16 in Potwisha Campground; park in the day-use parking area in the camp.

118. PANTHER CREEK FALLS

Sequoia National Park
Off Highway 198 near Three Rivers

Access & Difficulty: Hike-in or Backpack 6.0 miles RT/Moderate
Elevation: Start at 3,300 feet; total gain 600 feet
Best Season: February to June

You want to be alone? You don't want to see anybody else on the trail? Okay, just sign up for this trip any time between June and September. We hiked the Middle Fork Trail to Panther Creek Falls on Labor Day Weekend, when every campground in the national park was jammed and every trail was a veritable parade of hikers, and ours was the only car at the trailhead. Of course, the price for solitude is the summer heat, but if you start early enough in the morning, you can beat it.

Don't let the name mislead you. The Middle Fork Trail does indeed parallel the Middle Fork of the Kaweah River, but this is no streamside ramble. You are high, high above the river for the entire length of your trip, traversing steep canyon slopes. The trail is mostly flat to Panther Creek, but there is almost no shade and very little water available. Because the route is so high and open, it often catches breezes blowing through the canyon, making the exposed slopes more comfortable for hiking.

After leaving the trailhead, you cross over Moro Creek, a pretty cascading stream just two minutes down the trail; it's practically a waterfall in its own right. Enjoy the shade around its banks, then say goodbye and put on your sun hat. Hike through chamise, manzanita, yuccas, and scrub oaks—nothing tall enough to obscure the incredible views in all directions. The first two miles of trail provide sweeping vistas of the Upper Middle Fork canyon area, Moro Rock, the Great Western Divide, and Castle Rocks. With all the peaks and ridges in your scope, there's enough stunning geology to keep anyone enthused, even on a hot day.

At three miles, the Middle Fork Trail brings you right on top of the waterfall on Panther Creek, which drops into the Middle Fork Kaweah River. Now's the time to warn anyone in sight to be darn careful if they look over the edge. The view of the Middle Fork Kaweah River below is awesome, with its many green pools and small falls, and the sight of Panther Creek's 150-foot freefall drop is stunning, but the granite you're standing on is extremely slippery. You have to peer very carefully over the edge to see any of Panther Creek Falls' drop, or the scenic and largely untouched river below, and it's hard to do this without endangering yourself. Use extreme caution.

The safer upstream areas of Panther Creek warrant exploration. If you want to swim and see another small fall, head upstream and off-trail for a few hundred feet, where there are several cascades and cold, clear pools for cooling off.

If you'd prefer to hike this trail in the winter, when the air is cool and the foothills are moist and green, you'll have to earn it. The road to Buckeye Flat Campground is closed during winter months, so you must park at Hospital Rock and walk an extra 1.8 miles one-way to the trailhead. If this sounds like a lot of work, take along a backpack and make it an overnight trip. A few campsites are situated along the trail shortly following Panther Creek Falls. One of the many charms of the foothill areas of Sequoia National Park is that the weather is warm enough for backpacking even in January.

Trip notes: There is a $10 entrance fee at Sequoia and Kings Canyon National Parks, good for seven days. A free wilderness permit is required for overnight stays. They are available on a first-come, first-served basis from any ranger station, or in advance by mail or fax. Phone (559) 565-3708 for wilderness permit information. Park maps are available for free at the entrance stations. A more detailed map is available for a fee from Tom Harrison Cartography at (415) 456-7940 or Trails Illustrated at (800) 962-1643. For more information, contact Sequoia and Kings Canyon National Parks, Three Rivers, CA 93271-9700; (559) 565-3134.

Directions: From Visalia, drive east on Highway 198 for 47 miles to the turnoff on the right for Buckeye Flat Campground, across from Hospital Rock. Turn right and drive a half-mile to a left fork shortly before the campground. Bear left on the dirt road and drive 1.3 miles to the trailhead and parking area. (In the winter, both the Buckeye Flat Camp road and the trailhead road are closed to vehicles, but you may begin your hike at Hospital Rock, adding an extra 3.6 miles to your round-trip.)

119. MIDDLE FORK KAWEAH FALLS

Sequoia National Park
Off Highway 198 near Three Rivers

Access & Difficulty: Hike-in 0.5 mile RT/Easy
Elevation: Start at 2,900 feet; total gain 50 feet
Best Season: February to June

Middle Fork Kaweah River Falls

When it's summertime in the foothills region of Sequoia National Park, most people don't feel like hiking in the hot and dry afternoons. Swimming, on the other hand, is a better draw. How about swimming at the foot of a pretty Kaweah River waterfall? Sounds good, honey; don't forget the sunscreen.

Campers at Buckeye Flat Camp have the best access to the Paradise Creek Trail and its spur to Middle Fork Kaweah River Falls. All they have to do is saunter over to site #28, where the trail begins. Day-hikers, on the other hand, must park alongside the road outside the camp or a half-mile back at Hospital Rock, then walk into the campground and pick up the trail.

From the Paradise Creek Trailhead, you hike only a few hundred feet under the shade of blue oaks, buckeyes, and ponderosa pines before reaching a 40-foot-long bridge over the Middle Fork Kaweah River. There's a huge swimming hole on its downstream side that looks nearly Olympic-size. Teenagers sometimes dive off the bridge into the river here.

After crossing the bridge, leave the main trail and make a hard left turn, following the use trail upstream along the river. It's only a tenth of a mile to the falls, which are surrounded by jagged, colorful rocks. Even in late summer, your ears will lead you right to it, because although the fall is only about 20 feet tall, it's 35 feet wide and creates a tremendous volume of water.

When I visited, kids were climbing up on the rocks, walking to the crest of the waterfall, then sliding down its chute. Everyone was wearing jean shorts over their bathing suits, as protection from the sharp edges on the rocks around the water slide.

For tamer swimming, head further upstream to more pools, or walk back to the river bridge and its big downstream basin.

Trip notes: There is a $10 entrance fee at Sequoia and Kings Canyon National Parks, good for seven days. Park maps are available for free at the entrance stations. A more detailed map is available for a fee from Tom Harrison Cartography at (415) 456-7940 or Trails Illustrated at (800) 962-1643. For more information, contact Sequoia and Kings Canyon National Parks, Three Rivers, CA 93271-9700; (559) 565-3134.

Directions: From Visalia, drive east on Highway 198 for 47 miles to the turnoff on the right for Buckeye Flat Campground, across from Hospital Rock. Turn right and drive six-tenths of a mile to the campground. Park in any of the dirt pullouts outside of the camp entrance; no day-use parking is allowed in the campground. (You can also park at Hospital Rock and walk to Buckeye Flat Campground.) The trailhead is near campsite #28.

120. SOUTH FORK KAWEAH FALLS (Ladybug Falls)

Sequoia National Park
Off Highway 198 near Three Rivers

Access & Difficulty: Hike-in or Backpack 3.4 miles RT/Moderate
Elevation: Start at 3,600 feet; total gain 800 feet
Best Season: February to September

It was Labor Day Weekend in the foothills section of Sequoia National Park and we braced ourselves for the worst. We expected swarms of people, no room at the campgrounds, and boiling daytime heat. What could be worse than a national park on a holiday weekend? Combine it with low elevation and a hot day.

Well, we drove out to South Fork Campground and the Ladybug Trailhead, and discovered we were wrong on all counts. The camp still had open campsites—the only available sites in the whole park. Not a single soul was hiking on the Ladybug Trail. And since we started our trip early in the morning, we actually got chilled from swimming in the waterfall pool, and were happy to hike uphill in the sunny foothills.

In short, we starting out dreading and wound up loving our trip to the South Fork Kaweah River Falls, better known as Ladybug Falls.

Why Ladybug? Because of its location below Ladybug Camp, where the little brick-red beetles predominate. Thousands of ladybugs come here by the stream to nest in the winter, but you can find at least a few hundred at any time of the year. We didn't see any until we sat down next to the creek; then we noticed they were all around us, on every rock and blade of grass. There are so many, it's hard not to step on them. I even found a rare yellow one.

The Ladybug Trail starts from the far end of the South Fork Campground, where a sign says that Ladybug Camp is 1.7 miles, Cedar Creek is 3.2 miles, Whiskey Log Camp is 4.0 miles, and the trail dead-ends at 5.1 miles. A few hundred feet from the camp, the route crosses the South Fork Kaweah on the Clough Cave Footbridge.

The hike to Ladybug Falls leads through dry foothill country, but with a surprising amount of shade from canyon oaks and bay trees. The route is only slightly uphill, so the 1.7 miles can be easily covered in about 45 minutes. You travel parallel to the river for the entire trip, with occasional views of tree-covered ridges to the south, and increasingly wider views of the entire canyon as you climb. In spring, look for Putnam Creek across the canyon; it has an excellent but short-lived white-water cascade.

No signs alert you to when you've reached Ladybug Camp and

South Fork Kaweah River Falls (Ladybug)

Falls at 1.7 miles; you'll simply notice a few primitive campsites between the trail and the river, in a level clearing beneath shady incense cedars. If you reach a point where the trail switchbacks to the left and a sign points to Whiskey Log Camp, you've walked right by Ladybug Camp. The falls are hidden from view, downstream.

To reach them, walk the few feet from the camp down to the river and you'll come upon a 10-foot water slide and a narrow, deep swimming hole. Keep walking to your right, on a well-used, short but steep route. In the last few yards, you may have to use your hands to help you descend. The waterfall is tucked into a rocky corner in the river gorge, so the only way to see it is to position yourself at its base. Once there, you'll see that it's a perfect 25-foot freefall, shooting over rocks and ferns.

In the morning, it can be quite shady and cool in this grotto, and the river water is not warm by any stretch of the imagination, so you might want to head back up to the camp to sunnier pools for swimming. But before you do, pause a while to admire the beauty of this sheltered spot.

If you decide to camp at Ladybug, remember to bring a filter for pumping water out of the river, and if you are thinking about catching fish for dinner, forget it. The rules are catch-and-release only from downstream of the Clough Cave Footbridge to an elevation of 7,600 feet. But for catch-and-release angling, or for just a picnic, head upstream of Ladybug Camp, beyond where the trail switchbacks away from the river. There's a marvelous stretch of stream with pristine pools, rounded boulders, and ferns growing in huge clumps, making little rock-and-waterfall gardens. The conifers growing along the river here provide a welcome contrast to the foothills and grasslands along the trail.

There's one more positive and one more negative to the hike to Ladybug Falls. The positive: You don't have to pay a park entrance fee to visit the South Fork section of Sequoia National Park, and although there is a fee for camping at South Fork Campground, there is no fee for camping at Ladybug Camp. The negative: There's poison oak all over the place because of the low elevation. The trail and the camp are usually cleared of it, but be wary if you venture off-trail.

Trip notes: There is no fee for day-use at the South Fork section of Sequoia National Park, but if you are going to other park regions, there is a $10 entrance fee, good for seven days. A free wilderness permit is required for overnight stays. They are available on a first-come, first-served basis from any ranger station, or in advance by mail or fax. Phone (559) 565-3708 for wilderness permit information. Park maps are available for free at the entrance stations. A more detailed map is available for a fee from Tom Harrison Cartography at (415) 456-7940 or Trails Illustrated at (800) 962-1643. For more information, contact Sequoia and Kings Canyon National Parks, Three Rivers, CA 93271-9700; (559) 565-3134.

Directions: From Visalia, drive east on Highway 198 for 35 miles to one mile west of Three Rivers. Turn right on South Fork Drive and drive 12.8

miles to South Fork Campground. (At nine miles, the road turns to dirt.) Day-use parking is available just inside the campground entrance. Walk to the far side of the campground to the Ladybug Trailhead.

121. EAST FORK KAWEAH FALLS

Sequoia National Park
On Highway 198 near Mineral King

Access & Difficulty: Hike-in 2.0 miles RT/Easy
Elevation: Start at 6,500 feet; total loss 600 feet
Best Season: May to August

It's a gentle descent to East Fork Kaweah River Falls, a picturesque cascade that arches gracefully over big boulders. This short trip on the Hockett Trail is one of the few hikes in the Mineral King area of Sequoia National Park that is suitable for families, or people who don't want a long and arduous hike to reach a pretty destination. And it's downright gorgeous every step of the way.

The trail begins between sites 16 and 17 at Atwell Mill Camp, and you take the fork that is signed for Hockett Meadow. Pass by many huge Sequoia stumps, 12 to 15 feet wide, left from the days when people thought it was a good idea to cut down the mammoth

East Fork Kaweah River Falls

trees. In a small meadow, you'll find remains of an 1880s sawmill, where the Sequoias were transformed into fenceposts and shingles.

Be prepared for olfactory bliss, because the scent of mountain misery is ubiquitous on the downhill route to the river. (This shrub is also called bear clover, because bears love to munch on it.) Listen for the tap-tap-tap of woodpeckers as you walk, and look for the large pileated variety with their bright red heads. We spotted two.

Hike through a variety of big conifers, including pines, cedars, firs, and young Sequoias, many with velvety mosses growing on their bark. At one-half mile, you'll start to hear the rumble of the East Fork Kaweah River. Cross a small stream, and in just a few minutes you come to a picture-perfect footbridge over the river. A 20-foot waterfall descends into an aquamarine pool just upstream of the bridge. Many more luxurious pools and cataracts can be seen both up- and downstream, bounded by the bright red berries of currant bushes and lavish fern banks. In springtime, it seems that everywhere you look, cascading white water drops over car-size boulders. What perfects the scene are the giant Sequoias that grow along the river banks; apparently these were just far enough from the mill to escape its giant saw.

Most people set up a picnic right here by the bridge, or just take a few photographs and head back uphill. If you choose to continue, you'll find that the trail climbs uphill through a burned area on its way to the East Fork Grove of Sequoias and Deer Creek, one mile further. Both make good destinations.

Trip notes: There is a $10 entrance fee at Sequoia and Kings Canyon National Parks, good for seven days. Park maps are available for free at the entrance stations. A more detailed map is available for a fee from Tom Harrison Cartography at (415) 456-7940 or Trails Illustrated at (800) 962-1643. For more information, contact Sequoia and Kings Canyon National Parks, Three Rivers, CA 93271-9700; (559) 565-3134.

Directions: From Visalia, drive east on Highway 198 for 38 miles to Mineral King Road, 2.5 miles east of Three Rivers. (If you reach the Ash Mountain entrance station, you've gone too far.) Turn right on Mineral King Road and drive 20 miles to the Hockett Trail parking area on the right, one-third mile past Atwell Mill Camp. Park there and walk into the campground. Take the left fork to sites 16 and 17, where the Hockett Trail begins.

122. FAREWELL GAP FALLS (Tufa, Crystal, Franklin Falls)

Sequoia National Park
Off Highway 198 in Mineral King

Access & Difficulty: Hike-in 4.0 miles RT/Moderate
Elevation: Start at 7,860 feet; total gain 450 feet
Best Season: June to September

You can say "Farewell" when you begin hiking from the Farewell Gap Trailhead, but it doesn't have to be for long. Sure, you can hike

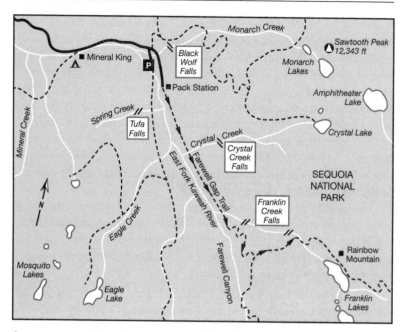

for more than 20 miles from the trailhead and be gone for days, or you can just head out for two miles, visit three waterfalls, and return.

The Farewell Gap Trail begins at the end of the road in Mineral King Valley in Sequoia National Park, one of the most beautiful places in California. The glacial valley, a peaceful paradise of meadows, streams, and 19th-century cabins, is surrounded by 12,000-foot granite and shale peaks that are colored rust, red, white, and black. The headwaters of the East Fork Kaweah River flows through the valley, encouraging aspen groves and wildflowers along its banks. Farewell Gap Trail traces its path.

Ah, paradise. You know you're in it as soon as you park your car at the end of the Mineral King Road, in the Eagle/Mosquito Trailhead parking lot. Don't start walking on the trail that leads south from the lot; walk back up the road you drove in on, cross a bridge over the river, then turn right and walk past the Mineral King Pack Station. All the horses will turn to look at you. If they could talk, they would ask the inevitable question: Do you have any extra apples?

The path officially begins at the trail sign by the pack station, where you continue straight, heading south into a beautiful glacial canyon. You see your first fall almost immediately—it's Tufa Falls on Spring Creek, dashing off the far canyon wall just across from the pack station. The trail you didn't take from the Eagle/Mosquito parking lot leads across the fall's stream on a wooden footbridge, but you get no view from that trail. From close up, the stream is almost completely hidden in foliage. But from your vantage point on the Farewell Gap Trail, you can see and especially hear all of Tufa's remarkable 500-foot cascade, as it flows down from Spring Creek's spring. The spring's porous layer of calcified minerals gives Tufa Falls its name.

Continue walking on the Farewell Gap Trail, which stays level as it wanders up the canyon. At one mile from the trailhead, Crystal Creek Falls surprises you on your left. The falls are hidden around a corner, invisible from the trail until you're practically at their base. A short walk on a spur trail brings you alongside the waterfall, which drops about 50 feet. (The spur can be found just after crossing the stream on the main trail; it leads up the right side of the fall.) Crystal Creek flows downhill from Crystal Lake and the Cobalt Lakes, both at more than 10,000 feet in elevation.

An unmarked right fork just beyond Crystal Creek Falls leads further up the canyon bottom to Aspen Flat, a lovely grove of aspens, and Soda Springs, a bubbling natural spring alongside the river that has colored the nearby earth bright orange. Many people take this fork up the river, visit the little spring and the aspens, maybe fish in the river or have a picnic, and then head back to the trailhead for a level 2.5-mile round-trip. But if you want to see another waterfall, the best one yet on the Farewell Gap Trail, stay on the main trail and begin to climb, gaining 350 feet on your way to Franklin Creek Falls, a little less than a mile away.

Crystal Creek Falls

Your view up Farewell Canyon, which has been stellar all along, keeps getting better as you climb. Your perspective changes as you leave the canyon floor and begin to meet this steep, rocky terrain on its own terms. Colorful Rainbow Mountain at 12,000 feet reveals its rings of pigmented rock on your left, and massive Vandever Mountain looms straight ahead. In a few heart-pumping minutes, you arrive at Franklin Creek at the base of a 15-foot cascade. An impressive series of falls continues hundreds of feet up and down the slope.

Trip notes: There is a $10 entrance fee at Sequoia and Kings Canyon National Parks, good for seven days. Park maps are available for free at the entrance stations. A more detailed map is available for a fee from Tom Harrison Cartography at (415) 456-7940 or Trails Illustrated at (800) 962-1643. For more information, contact Sequoia and Kings Canyon National Parks, Three Rivers, CA 93271-9700; (559) 565-3134.

Directions: From Visalia, drive east on Highway 198 for 38 miles to Mineral King Road, 2.5 miles east of Three Rivers. (If you reach the Ash Mountain entrance station, you've gone too far.) Turn right on Mineral King Road and drive 25 miles to the end of the road and the Eagle/Mosquito Trailhead. (Take the right fork at the end of the road to reach the parking area.)

123. BLACK WOLF FALLS (Black Wall, Monarch Falls)

Sequoia National Park
Off Highway 198 in Mineral King

Access & Difficulty: Hike-in 0.5 mile RT/Easy
    or Drive-to/Easy
Elevation: Start at 7,850 feet; total gain 50 feet
Best Season: May to August

Black Wolf Falls in Mineral King is a waterfall of many names: it's alternately called Black Wolf Falls, Black Wall Falls, or Monarch Falls. The latter moniker is easy to explain, because the waterfall drops on Monarch Creek in the Mineral King Valley. The first two names are related: Black Wolf is apparently a bastardization of Black Wall, the original name of the falls. It was named by miners in the 1870s who weren't as interested in waterfalls as they were in minerals. Black Wall was the name of the copper mine at the base of the falls, clearly designated as such because of the dark-colored, sheer cliff over which the fall drops.

You can drive right by Black Wolf Falls. It's set just 500 feet from the edge of Mineral King Road, shortly before the road ends in the valley. If you want to see it from close up, park at the Sawtooth Trailhead, then walk further up the Mineral King Road toward the Mineral King pack station. Continue past where Monarch Creek flows under the road, about 150 yards before the left fork for the pack station. Look for the "No Parking Any Time" sign. Across the road from the sign is a wide, usually dry wash.

Black Wolf Falls

The best, most well-worn route to the falls is on its left (north) side.

Follow the rough footpath, and shortly it crosses the wash to its south side, taking you up and over the scrubby, sagebrush-covered hillside to the right of the falls. From there you can scramble down to the water's edge. If you do, you'll see what looks like a small cave near the base of the falls, but as you move closer you'll see that it's an abandoned mining tunnel, a leftover from the Black Wall Mine. Do not enter the tunnel, as its walls are unstable.

Black Wolf Falls drops 50 feet over a dark cliff, with a flow that's quite full and lively even as late as July. Big clumps of yellow flowers grow in between the streams of water when the level drops in late summer. During my visit, one of the hundreds of black-tail deer that abound in Mineral King was trying to get near the falls to mow down those tasty yellow blooms.

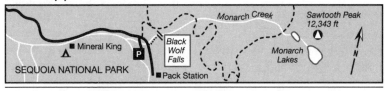

If you time it right, you can take a free ranger-led tour to Black Wolf Falls. These occur periodically over the summer, usually on Saturdays, and a call to the Mineral King ranger station can get you the current schedule. Your short walk to the waterfall is combined with an interesting talk on Mineral King's mining history.

Trip notes: There is a $10 entrance fee at Sequoia and Kings Canyon National Parks, good for seven days. Park maps are available for free at the entrance stations. A more detailed map is available for a fee from Tom Harrison Cartography at (415) 456-7940 or Trails Illustrated at (800) 962-1643. For more information, contact Sequoia and Kings Canyon National Parks, Three Rivers, CA 93271-9700; (559) 565-3134.

Directions: From Visalia, drive east on Highway 198 for 38 miles to Mineral King Road, 2.5 miles east of Three Rivers. (If you reach the Ash Mountain entrance station, you've gone too far.) Turn right on Mineral King Road and drive 24.5 miles to the Sawtooth Parking Area, one-half mile before the end of the road. The waterfall is visible from the road.

124. DARWIN FALLS

Death Valley National Park
Off Highway 190 near Panamint Springs

Access & Difficulty: Hike-in 1.8 miles RT/Easy
Elevation: Start at 2,600 feet; total gain 120 feet
Best Season: February to May

I drove to the desert to see the stars at night and then to watch the sun rise at five in the morning. Both were unforgettable. Then I started looking around for the trailhead to Darwin Falls, but I couldn't find it anywhere. When I stopped in at nearby Panamint Springs Resort—the only sign of civilization for miles—and asked for directions, they told me I was only a mile from the trailhead access road but that it was four-wheel-drive only. They had a good laugh at my tiny Hyundai rental car.

Well, it turns out that occasionally the access road is four-wheel-drive only, but that's only after a storm, and they don't get too many of those in the desert. The dirt road was practically as smooth as glass, except for the last quarter-mile, but I just parked along the road and walked that stretch. The little Hyundai made the drive easily, like a regular desert rat.

To sum up the trip, Darwin Falls is a must-do desert hike. A waterfall in the desert is a rare and precious thing, a miracle of life in a harsh world. If you visit Darwin Falls early in the morning, when no one else is around, your oasis experience may feel spiritual.

Hiking back into the desert canyon, you follow the trail of a tiny trickle of water as it slowly grows into a full-flowing stream. Then at the back of the canyon, the stream drops over a 30-foot-high cliff to form Darwin Falls, a free-falling waterfall tucked into a three-sided gallery of rock.

The hike to the falls is only one mile each way, and although it requires a modest amount of route find-

Darwin Falls

ing, the trip is suitable for families. Just make sure the weather is cool when you go, because after all, this is the desert. And carry water.

The National Park Service prohibits bikes and dogs from making the trip, which keeps the area pristine for hikers and protects the precious water supply. Bathing, wading, and washing are forbidden because the water from Darwin's spring is a domestic water source, used by both humans and wildlife. In the spring, more than 80 species of resident and migrating birds have been sighted here.

The path is not a well-defined trail, more like a well-used route following an old jeep road and some water pipes, then turning into single-track. At several points you must cross the stream to follow the trail, but rocks are conveniently placed for easy rock-hopping. Route-finding is simple because you just walk upcanyon, following the stream. Canyon walls on both sides keep you channeled in the correct route.

The stream flow increases as you approach the waterfall, and the canyon walls narrow, requiring some minor rock scrambling. You'll feel like you're having a real desert adventure. The amount of vegetation also increases as you near the fall; notice the proliferation of willows, cattails, and reeds jockeying for position next to the running water.

You pass a small stream-gauging station right before you reach Darwin Falls, then round a corner and enter a box canyon. The rocks surrounding you have turned more and more colorful as you've traveled; now you are completely surrounded by shades of yellow, coral, orange, and crimson. Darwin Falls drops over a rock cliff, with a large cottonwood tree growing at its lip. The water comes down in two separate streams, one on either side of the tree, giving life to ferns and colorful mosses growing on the rock face.

Stay for a while and savor the miracle of the waterfall and oasis, then retrace your steps back to your car.

Trip notes: There is no fee. For more information and a free park map, contact Death Valley National Park, P.O. Box 579, Death Valley, CA 92328; (760) 786-2331 or fax (760) 786-3283.

Directions: From Lone Pine on U.S. 395, drive east on Highway 136 for 18 miles, then continue straight on Highway 190 for 30 miles. The right (south) turnoff for Darwin Falls is exactly one mile before you reach the Panamint Springs Resort. Look for a small sign that says "Darwin Falls" and a dirt road. (If you reach the resort, turn around and drive west one mile.) Drive 2.5 miles on the dirt road till you reach a fork, then bear right and drive three-tenths of a mile to the parking area. (Or, from Olancha on U.S. 395, drive east on Highway 190 for 44 miles.)

---

125. HIDDEN FALLS

**Mountain Home Demonstration State Forest
Off Highway 190 near Springville**

Access & Difficulty: Scramble 0.25 mile RT/Easy
Elevation: Start at 5,900 feet; total loss 30 feet
Best Season: May to September

It's one heck of a drive to get to Hidden Falls. Maybe that's why they call it Hidden. Or maybe it's because the waterfall is so carefully tucked into a dark and narrow corner of a gorge, you could camp right on top of it and not even know it's there.

Hidden Falls is in Mountain Home Demonstration State Forest, a long 22 miles from Springville. They're slow and winding miles, climbing up and out of the valley foothills, so plan on an hour's drive to make the trip. Also, make sure you follow the directions exactly, because if you just follow the road signs you might be inclined to take Balch Park Road all the way to Hidden Falls, and that makes for an even longer trip on one of the most narrow, winding roads in the Southern Sierra.

Once you get to the state forest, the fun begins. Hey, how come all these big Sequoias are growing outside the national parks? They're an unexpected sight—cool, dark green, and welcoming if you've driven in from the hot Central Valley. In addition to the mammoth trees, which there are thousands of, many young Sequoias are also getting their start here.

Pick up a free map at park headquarters, then drive on paved and dirt roads to the Hidden Falls Recreation Area, where there's a campground and some hiking trails. Hidden Falls is a walk-in camp, which means you must park your car in the lot and then walk a few hundred feet to your campsite. Day-hikers park in a separate lot above the campground, just before where the road crosses the Wishon Fork Tule River. The falls drop on the river, right by the camp, but you can only glimpse the top of them from the camp-ground area. To get a better view and to access the fall's pools for swim-ming, walk through the camp to site #6, where an easy route leads down to the water. From there, you can walk upstream to the falls, which drop in a chiseled gorge just below site #2. (A rough route leads directly down to the falls from site #2, but it's much steeper.)

The waterfall's total height is about 50 feet, falling in a series of pools

Hidden Falls

and drops. The best way to get a look at the whole picture is to climb on top of a giant Sequoia trunk that sits in the streambed. From there you can see three lovely tiers of falling water nestled between giant Sequoias. The tallest drop is 20 feet high, with a wide and shallow pool at its base. Some people swim here, but others prefer the stretch of river upstream of the camp (across the road), where an unmaintained trail leads a short distance to more and deeper swimming holes. The water is downright cold, but refreshing.

One note of great importance: Bears are very hungry at this park and they have gotten used to humans. Two that I encountered didn't even bother running away. Even if you're only day-hiking or exploring, don't leave any food in your car.

Trip notes: There is no fee. A free map/brochure of Mountain Home Demonstration State Forest is available at park headquarters (see directions below). For more information, contact Mountain Home Demonstration State Forest, P.O. Box 517, Springville, CA 93265; (559) 539-2321 (summer) or (559) 539-2855 (winter).

Directions: From Porterville, drive east on Highway 190 for 18 miles to Springville. At Springville, turn left (north) on Balch Park Road/Road 239 and drive 3.5 miles, then turn right on Bear Creek Road/Road 220. Drive 14 miles to Mountain Home State Forest Headquarters, pick up a free map, then continue three-quarters of a mile on Bear Creek Road and turn right. Drive two miles and turn right again, then drive 1.5 miles and turn left. Hidden Falls Campground is a quarter mile farther. (Obtaining a park map is highly recommended.)

126. GALENA CREEK FALLS

Mountain Home Demonstration State Forest
Off Highway 190 near Springville

Access & Difficulty: Hike-in 1.5 miles RT/Easy
Elevation: Start at 5,900 feet; total loss 100 feet
Best Season: May to September

If you've driven all the way to Mountain Home Demonstration State Forest to see Hidden Falls (see the previous story), you should take a little hike to see Galena Creek Falls too. The trail begins from the state forest's other campground, Moses Gulch, just a few miles from Hidden Falls Campground and its waterfall. The nicest thing about Galena Creek Falls is that you have to hike a bit to reach it, and once you're there you may have your own private swimming hole.

Galena Creek Falls in late summer

You'll pass the River Trail on the drive in to campsites 6 to 10 in Moses Gulch. Park in the pullouts at the beginning of the campground loop near the rest rooms (not in any of the campsite spaces), then walk back down the road for about 50 yards to where the trail crosses the road. River Trail leads to the North Fork of the Middle Fork of the Tule River, less complicatedly known as the Wishon Fork of the Tule River.

The hike is only three quarters of a mile from Moses Gulch Campground, heading downstream and downhill through a lovely mixed forest with many big Sequoias. After a quarter mile, you reach the river. Cross it, pick up the trail on the other side and continue hiking, now on more level ground. In another half-mile, you'll spot an old wooden sign stating "Galena Creek." Look for a spur trail to your right near this sign; there are several. Follow any of the spurs and in a few yards you'll be right on top of Galena Creek Falls.

The creek cascades 20 feet into a narrow slot in the Wishon Fork of the Tule River. Use caution climbing down to the base of the falls; the granite is typically slick. You can swim in the skinny, tub-like pool below the falls, or just hang out on the granite alongside the falls. Galena Creek runs dependably even in autumn, but it is best seen in June or July.

On our trip, we encountered an incredible number of ladybugs convening near the falls. Ladybugs galore. More than we could count.

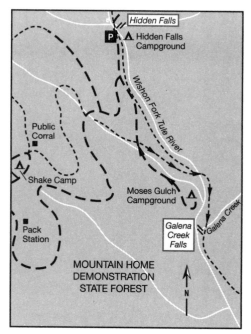

Trip notes: There is no fee. A free map/brochure of Mountain Home Demonstration State Forest is available at park headquarters. For more information, contact Mountain Home Demonstration State Forest, P.O. Box 517, Springville, CA 93265; (559) 539-2321 (summer) or (559) 539-2855 (winter).

Directions: Follow the directions on page 270 to Mountain Home State Forest Headquarters. Pick up a free map, then continue three-quarters of a mile on Bear Creek Road and turn right. Drive two miles and turn right again, then drive 1.5 miles and turn right. Drive one mile to Moses Gulch Campground. Take the fork for sites 6-10.

127. WISHON FORK TULE RIVER FALLS

Sequoia National Forest
Off Highway 190 near Springville

Access & Difficulty: Hike-in or Backpack 6.0 miles RT/Moderate
Elevation: Start at 4,000 feet; total gain 800 feet
Best Season: May to September

You can see plenty of falls and cascades on the Wishon Fork of the Tule River just by driving around, but if you want a good walk and some solitude at a waterfall, the Doyle Trail to Wishon Fork Falls is your ticket.

If you're staying at Wishon Camp, you can start the hike right from your campsite, but if you're a day-visitor, you should drive to the gated trailhead that is signed for the Doyle Trail in a quarter-mile. Start hiking on the paved, gated road, then at the bridge, bear left (just before the "No Trespassing" sign at Doyle Springs, a small community of cabins). The route is clearly signed as "Trail to Upstream Fishing."

The Doyle Trail is a great alternative to the heat of the Springville and Porterville valleys. It's in the transition zone between foothills and conifers, with plenty of shade from tall manzanita, hardwoods (oaks, madrones, and dogwoods), and some pines. Squirrels and lizards are your main trail companions, making plenty of noise as they scurry among the dry leaves and clumps of bear clover on the ground. The path ascends gently but steadily, lateraling along the slopes above the Wishon Fork.

Wishon Fork Tule River Falls

Ignore any side trails leading down to the river. Always stay on the main route, heading uphill.

After 2.5 miles, you'll finally stop climbing and descend to the same level as the river, where you'll find some primitive campsites along the banks and good swimming holes, in case you can't wait for the waterfall. Soon you climb again, and in another half-mile, you reach a surprise clearing along the trail. The trees suddenly open up, and you see huge chunks of jagged, greenish rock lining the river. If you leave the trail and cross the rocks on your right, you'll find yourself on top of Wishon Fork Falls, which is comprised of two tiered cascades hidden in a narrow, angular gorge. The lower fall is the tallest, about 25 feet high. An incredible range of color is visible in the river rock, primarily in shades of red and gray. Multicolored lichens add to the display.

Have a seat on the rocks, and chew on a few sandwiches. If you want to swim, you'll find long, deep pools among the rectangular rocks here, but it's easier to scramble into the river downstream and then wade your way up to the waterfall's pools.

Trip notes: There is no fee. For a map of Sequoia National Forest, send $4 to USDA-Forest Service, 1323 Club Drive, Vallejo, CA 94592. For more information, contact Sequoia National Forest, Tule River Ranger District, 32588 Highway 190, Springville, CA 93265; (559) 539-2607.

Directions: From Porterville, drive east on Highway 190 for 18 miles to Springville. From Springville, continue east on Highway 190 for 7.5 miles to Wishon Drive (Road 208), a left fork. Turn left and drive four miles on Wishon Drive, then take the left fork which is signed for day-use parking (above the campground). Drive a quarter-mile and park off the road, near the gate.

128. MIDDLE FORK TULE RIVER FALLS

Sequoia National Forest
Off Highway 190 near Springville

Access & Difficulty: Hike-in 0.5 mile RT/Easy
Elevation: Start at 4,000 feet; total loss 100 feet
Best Season: May to September

The Middle Fork Tule River has more waterfalls and swimming holes than you can shake a stick at. Its granite bed is as slick and smooth as any you'll find in the Sierra—a shining example of water-sculpted rock. In addition, the river is a spectacular aquamarine color, with deep pools so inviting that it's tempting to jump into every single one you find. Unfortunately, the Tule River canyon is remarkably steep and brushy, so gaining access to many of its pools and falls is a major challenge.

For waterfall lovers, here's one of the best and easiest-to-access spots on this stretch of the Tule, with a 50-foot waterfall and a good trail leading to it. From the roadside pullout 1.7 miles above the powerhouse, begin hiking at the Forest Service signboard. A footpath leads a quarter mile down to the river. (You might want to bring your clippers because it is sometimes a little overgrown.) At a fork in the trail, go right. You'll pass alongside the lip of a spectacular freefalling waterfall, where the Tule River drops in an even, rectangular block over smooth granite. Even in autumn, the fall runs about 15 feet wide and 50 feet high.

If you continue all the way down to the canyon bottom (another 25 yards), you'll wind up at the pool below the falls. Swimming here is as sweet as it gets, with a terrific view of the big fall.

When I visited, teenagers were jumping off the waterfall's 50-foot-high brink. Watching them nearly gave me a heart attack.

Middle Fork Tule River Falls

Trip notes: There is no fee. For a map of Sequoia National Forest, send $4 to USDA-Forest Service, 1323 Club Drive, Vallejo, CA 94592. For more information, contact Sequoia National Forest, Tule River Ranger District, 32588 Highway 190, Springville, CA 93265; (559) 539-2607.

Directions: From Porterville, drive east on Highway 190 for 18 miles to Springville. From Springville, continue east on Highway 190 for 7.5 miles to the powerhouse and highway bridge near the turnoff for Camp Wishon and Wishon Drive (Road 208). Reset your odometer and continue on Highway 190 for another 1.7 miles. Park in the roadside pullout on your right. A use trail leads down to the river.

129. PEPPERMINT CREEK FALLS

Sequoia National Forest
Off Highway 190 near Johnsondale

Access & Difficulty: Scramble 0.5 mile RT/Moderate
Elevation: Start at 5,300 feet; total loss 150 feet
Best Season: May to September

In a word, it's awesome. Peppermint Creek Falls is a classic 150-foot granite waterfall, with wide slabs and ledges, a steady flow of water all summer, and big Jeffrey pines growing along its sides. It's the only waterfall in this book that drops over the edge of a rounded granite dome.

To reach it, take the scenic drive on Road 22S82, the road that parallels the Western Divide Highway in Sequoia National Forest. Try to stay on the pavement and between the lines as you view all the stunning geology of the area. You get views of Sentinel Peak, Elephant Knob, and the Needles, all which look remarkably like their names.

Park your car in Camping Area #6, the informal dispersed camping area shortly past Lower Peppermint Camp. Usually a few families or groups are camped along the creek. Just beyond the campers is where Peppermint Creek plummets over

Peppermint Creek Falls

smooth, rounded granite. In several places, sheets of the granite dome's exterior have peeled off and broken into chunks, creating a pile of rubble at the base of the fall, which the creek cascades over.

Peppermint Creek Falls has a wide pool at its base, just deep enough for wading. The falls are impressive even in late summer, although by then the stream flows more delicately over the granite, rather than pouring down in a thick sheet over the rounded crest.

The route to the base of the fall is a steep drop and not for the faint of heart, mostly because of the brief, breathtaking climb back up. Start by scrambling over the rocks at the top of the cliff, then take any of several use trails down the side of the falls. As much as possible, try to stay off the waterfall's granite and on the dirt paths, because the rock is much more slippery than it looks.

Trip notes: There is no fee. For a map of Sequoia National Forest, send $4 to USDA-Forest Service, 1323 Club Drive, Vallejo, CA 94592. For more information, contact Sequoia National Forest, Hot Springs Ranger District, Route 4, Box 548, California Hot Springs, CA 93207; (661) 548-6503.

Directions: From Kernville on the north end of Lake Isabella, drive north on Sierra Way/Road 99 for 27 miles to one-half mile north of Johnsondale R-Ranch. Turn right on Road 22S82 and drive 11.3 miles to Road 22S82F, signed for Camping Area 6. (It's on the right, one-quarter mile past Lower Peppermint Camp on the left.) Turn right on 22S82F, then drive three-tenths of a mile to a large clearing near a cliff edge.

---

130. NOBE YOUNG FALLS
Sequoia National Forest
Off Highway 190 near Johnsondale

Access & Difficulty: Hike-in & Scramble 1.0 mile RT/Moderate
Elevation: Start at 6,500 feet; total loss 100 feet
Best Season: May to September

Nobe Young is the secret waterfall of Sequoia National Forest; it has no signs, no markers, not even a trailhead. The first time you go to it, you practically need someone to take your hand and show you the way. You'll need route-finding skills and also some scrambling ability, because there's no formal trail to the falls. Even so, the route takes only about 15 minutes from where you leave your car.

Follow the directions at the end of this story exactly, and once you've parked in the dirt pullout, look for sign markers for 22S11 and

304 015. (They're not visible from the road, only from the pullout.) This is the secret code that tells you you're in the right place.

Next, start hiking on the dirt road off to your left. When it forks, follow it to the right. (The fork is signed as 304 186, and the

Nobe Young Falls

left branch is very overgrown.) You're on a real trail at this point, and the going is easy. Pass a makeshift camp and campfire ring, with a short spur trail leading from it to Nobe Young Creek. You'll hear the creek along this stretch, but now start to listen for the change in its sound, going from a steady gurgle to more of a pouring or spraying sound. Keep your eyes peeled for spur routes leading off the main trail to your left. The best route comes up after you walk for about three minutes past the campfire ring, or about five minutes past the fork in the trail.

It's a steep route down to the falls, so be cautious. Anglers and waterfall-lovers have made a pretty good path to Nobe Young Fall's base, but it has some sheer drops. The falls spill and splash for 125 feet over three granite ledges, creating a watery playground. Between the top and middle ledges is a tall, wide cave behind the falling water, where some people like to climb in and look out from behind the waterfall. If you choose to do so, be careful scrambling your way up to it.

Exploring around below the falls, you'll find many little trout in the stream, plus thimbleberries (red berries that look like raspberries), and currants. Big woodwardia ferns and dogwoods grow along the creek, thriving in the abundant shade of surrounding oaks and cedars.

Many big, smooth boulders are situated directly in front of the falls, just a few feet from the spray, perfect for picnicking. Choose your spot, and know that you are in on the big waterfall secret of Sequoia National Forest. Shhh. . . .

Trip notes: There is no fee. For a map of Sequoia National Forest, send $4 to USDA-Forest Service, 1323 Club Drive, Vallejo, CA 94592. For more information, contact Sequoia National Forest, Hot Springs Ranger District, Route 4, Box 548, California Hot Springs, CA 93207; (661) 548-6503.

Directions: From Kernville on the north end of Lake Isabella, drive north on Sierra Way/Road 99 for 27 miles to a half-mile north of Johnsondale R-Ranch. Turn left on Road 50, then in 5.5 miles, turn right on Road 107, the Western Divide Highway. Drive eight miles to the fall's parking pullout on the east (right) side of the road, which is unsigned. Look for a dirt pullout exactly one mile north of the turnoff for Camp Whitsett and Lower Peppermint Camp, and a quarter-mile south of the Crawford Road turnoff.

(If you are coming from Porterville, drive east on Highway 190 for 54 miles to the falls turnoff, 6.7 miles south of Ponderosa Lodge.)

131. SOUTH CREEK FALLS

Sequoia National Forest
Off Highway 190 near Johnsondale

Access & Difficulty: Drive-to/Easy
Elevation: 3,800 feet
Best Season: May to September

As the crow flies, South Creek Falls and Salmon Creek Falls are five miles apart in Sequoia National Forest. But in the roundabout way that humans must travel, South Creek Falls and Salmon Creek Falls are 20 miles apart, and the latter requires some serious work to get to (see the following story). If you want to see a waterfall in the national forest without a long drive and long hike, cruise up Road 99 from Kernville and Lake Isabella and pay a visit to South Creek Falls.

South Creek Falls

At 120 feet tall, South Creek Falls is a spectacular plume of vertical white water. It bears an uncanny resemblance to Cedar Creek Falls in San Diego, hundreds of miles away, except that South Creek Falls drops right along the road. From the side of the pavement, the fall plunges into the bottom of a steep-walled canyon, surrounded by digger pines, sagebrush, and rocks—hallmarks of the hot, dry, rugged land of the Kern River Canyon.

If you drive to South Creek Falls from the north, you'll notice a small sign that says "Caution: Waterfall

300 Yards Ahead," and then you'll see a chain-link fence, but you can't see the fall itself unless you look back over your right shoulder as you drive. A better approach is from Kernville to the south. The waterfall seems to come suddenly and magically into view shortly after you cross the huge Johnsondale highway bridge over the Kern. You can park in one of the pullouts near the fence above the fall, then walk south on the road for about 100 yards to get the best view or to take a few pictures.

Don't get any ideas about hiking down to the big pool at the base of South Creek Falls. The slope is extreme—almost vertical. A sign states "South Creek Falls: Stay alive; stay behind the railing. Extremely dangerous area." For once, obeying authority is a wise idea.

Trip notes: There is no fee. For a map of Sequoia National Forest, send $4 to USDA-Forest Service, 1323 Club Drive, Vallejo, CA 94592. For more information, contact Sequoia National Forest, Cannell Meadow Ranger District, P.O. Box 9, Kernville, CA 93238; (760) 376-3781.

Directions: From Kernville on the north end of Lake Isabella, drive north on Sierra Way/Road 99 for 17 miles to Fairview (a small settlement). Continue north from Fairview for 5.5 miles to South Creek Falls. (The falls drop right alongside the highway, exactly one-half mile north of the Johnsondale Bridge, the highway bridge over the Kern River.) There is a small parking pullout at the chain-link fence just above the falls.

132. SALMON CREEK FALLS
Sequoia National Forest
Off Highway 190 near Johnsondale

Access & Difficulty: Hike-in or Backpack 9.0 miles RT/Moderate
Elevation: Start at 7,600 feet; total loss 600 feet
Best Season: May to July

Don't be fooled by the clearly marked sign on Road 99 north of Kernville that says "Salmon Creek Falls." Just 2.1 miles north of Goldledge Camp, the sign appears on the left and a parking pullout and a trail show up on the right. The next thing you know you're slamming on the brakes and envisioning your upcoming hike to a waterfall. Better think again. There once was a trail from Road 99 to Salmon Creek Falls, but it's now overgrown with encroaching brush. After about three-quarters of a mile, it becomes nearly impassable. All that's left of the real trail is that darn misleading sign, and in the wet season, a long-distance view of the falls.

But the good news is that you can get to Salmon Creek Falls, as long as you're willing to take a long drive to the Salmon Creek Trailhead at Horse Meadow Campground. It's a nine-mile round-trip hike, and unfortunately the trail ends at the top of the falls, where your view is less than optimal. Still, it's a stellar walk through lodgepole pines and white fir, with a chance for fishing, skinny-dipping, and getting close to the lip of a big waterfall—my idea of a perfect day-trip or an easy one-night backpacking jaunt in early summer.

Although the drive to the Salmon Creek Trailhead at Horse Meadow is nearly 20 miles on dirt roads, they're incredibly smooth and well-graded roads, easily passable in a passenger car. The only hazard is logging trucks, which you must be on the lookout for. (When you see one, get out of its way.) Along the drive, check out the small waterfalls on Alder Creek, three-quarters of a mile down Road 22S12.

Hiking to Salmon Creek Falls from Horse Meadow is a vastly different experience than the hot, dusty, brush-laden, cross-country route off Road 99. Once you've made the drive to Horse Meadow, you've gained 4,000 feet in elevation, and you're in granite and big conifer country. The area is much like Mammoth Lakes or Lake Tahoe, with huge old pine and fir trees and very little undergrowth.

The trailhead is well-signed, and the path begins in big trees and then skirts the edge of Horse Meadow, where cattle sometimes graze. When you first meet up with Salmon Creek, it's just a tiny little stream meandering through the meadow, but it quickly gathers a stronger flow and picks up speed as it hits steeper, more rocky terrain.

At the edge of the meadow, you have two choices: You can continue along the north side of Salmon Creek on a well-worn use trail, or you can turn left and cross the creek, hiking on the official Salmon Creek Trail on the stream's south side. The two trails meet up again about two miles downstream, where the official trail crosses back to the north side of Salmon Creek. My suggestion is to take the use trail on the way in to the falls, when your energy level is highest, then return on the main trail. The creekside use trail is more scenic, but it requires careful footing over granite slabs.

Occasionally you may lose sight of the use trail in the huge, football-field-sized sheets of granite lining the creek, but since you're always paralleling the water, the route is simple. Just keep heading downstream and downhill. The shade of tall pines alternates with a few sunny stretches. While in the latter, you may want to dip into some of the many smooth granite swimming holes. Be forewarned—

the water is cold. Trout like it, though; they seem to be present in every deep pool.

At two miles out, the two trails meet. Continue to amble on the smooth downhill path toward the falls. Look for plentiful wildflowers in shady areas tucked among the increasingly drier, sunnier slopes. The trail ends with a bit of a climb to a rocky ridgeline, where you can see the stream ahead of you disappear off what seems like the edge of the earth. Clamber downhill carefully, over more slick granite slabs, to reach the pools above the falls.

If you brought lunch with you, be sure to eat it here, so your pack is lighter for the uphill return trip. If you want to camp, you'll see a few campfire rings in this area, and more at various points along the creekside route.

If you wish to attempt the shorter, unmaintained route to the falls from Road 99, here are some directions to get you started: From the dirt pullout across from the Salmon Creek Falls sign, hike up the dirt road as it narrows to single-track. When the trail meets another dirt road, walk 20 yards to your right and pick up the trail on the far side of the road. Continue for a few hundred yards until you hit yet another dirt road; this time walk about 20 yards to your left and pick up the trail on the far side. You'll notice the path is getting fainter all the time.

By now you should find yourself on the left (north) side of Salmon Creek. Right at the point where the trail gets nearly impossible to follow, near some large jumbled rocks, climb to the highest point and you'll be able to see the falls, still a mile or so ahead. If you want to continue further toward them, you're on your own. It was here that my hair got hopelessly tangled in the choking brush that was all around me, and in frustration I almost pulled out my pocket knife and cut off my ponytail.

Remember to try this lower route only in cool temperatures and after some good rain. When you've had enough, do what I did: Cry "Uncle!" and get in your car to drive to the Salmon Creek Trailhead at Horse Meadow.

Trip notes: There is no fee. For a map of Sequoia National Forest, send $4 to USDA-Forest Service, 1323 Club Drive, Vallejo, CA 94592. For more information, contact Sequoia National Forest, Cannell Meadow District, P.O. Box 9, Kernville, CA 93238; (760) 376-3781.

Directions: From Kernville on the north end of Lake Isabella, drive north on Sierra Way/Road 99 for 22 miles to the right turnoff for Sherman Pass Road (22S05) to Big Meadow and Horse Meadow (before the highway bridge over the Kern River). Turn right and drive 6.1 miles on Sherman Pass Road, then turn right on Road 22S12, the road to Horse Meadow Campground. Drive 6.3 miles on Road 22S12 (it turns to dirt at 5.8 miles but is still manageable for a passenger car) till you reach a fork; stay straight. At 8.0 miles, bear left. At 9.3 miles, turn right at the Horse Meadow Campground sign (Road 23S10). You'll reach the camp at 10.7 miles, but take the right turnoff just before the camp to reach the trailhead. (It's well signed.)

MORE WATERFALLS

in Sequoia, Kings Canyon, & Southern Sierra

•Silver Spray Falls and Blue Canyon Falls, Tehipite Valley, Kings Canyon National Park. Two spectacular waterfalls in a spectacular valley, best accessed from the Rancheria Trailhead near Wishon Reservoir, 35-mile round-trip. For more information, phone Sierra National Forest, Pineridge Ranger District, at (559) 855-5360.

•Ninemile Creek Falls, Golden Trout Wilderness. Accessible via a backpacking trip on Ninemile Creek and Hells Hole trails near the Kern River and Jordan Hot Springs. For more information, phone Sequoia National Forest, Cannell Meadow District, at (760) 376-3781.

•Chagoopa Falls and Hamilton Creek Falls, Sequoia National Park. Accessible via a backpacking trip on the High Sierra Trail out of Bearpaw Meadows. Phone Sequoia National Park at (559) 565-3134.

San Francisco Bay Area

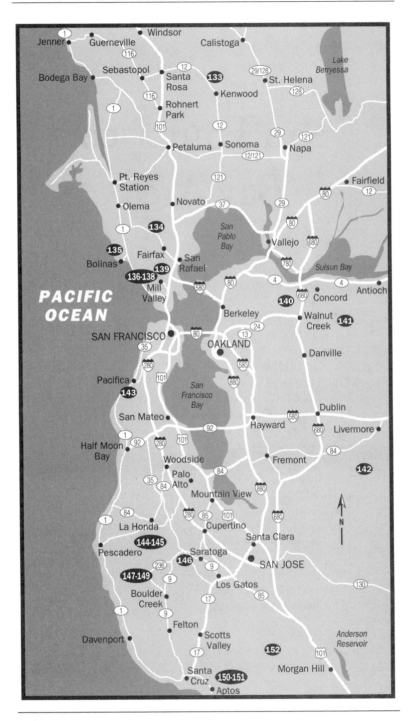

133. SONOMA CREEK FALLS

Sugarloaf Ridge State Park
Off Highway 12 near Kenwood

Access & Difficulty: Hike-in 1.0 mile RT/Easy
Elevation: Start at 1,100 feet; total loss 300 feet
Best Season: December to May

You want a short, pretty trail in a redwood forest? You got it. You want to see a 25-foot waterfall cascading down over rocks, surrounded by big-leaf maples and ferns? Here it is. You want to walk downhill all the way to reach it? No problem. You get all of this on the Canyon Trail in Sugarloaf Ridge State Park when you pay a visit to Sonoma Creek's tumbling waterfall.

The fall is surprising not just because it runs in notoriously dry and warm Sonoma County, but also because it's hidden just off the road, less than a half-mile walk from where you leave your car. Start walking downhill at the Canyon Trail sign from near the entrance kiosk, dropping a steep 300 feet in elevation in four-tenths of a mile. Descend through a dense and shady forest of hardwoods—oaks, bays, madrones, and alders.

When you reach the falls after about 15 minutes of walking, you enter a lush, wet grotto that is piled with huge, rounded, moss-covered boulders. Many of them are more slippery than they look, so use caution. The trail runs along the edge of the creek. You can climb on the rocks and explore quite close to the cascading water.

Huge boulders have tumbled down the canyon to create Sonoma Creek Falls, a stairstepped cascade about 25 feet high. Bigleaf maple vines and plentiful ferns thrive at the water's edge, providing a leafy green contrast to the

Sonoma Creek Falls

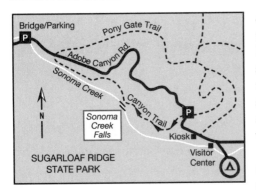

Bridge/Parking
P
Pony Gate Trail
Adobe Canyon Rd.
Sonoma Creek
N
Sonoma Creek Falls
Canyon Trail
P
Kiosk
SUGARLOAF RIDGE STATE PARK
Visitor Center

dark, jagged rock. Although Sonoma Creek Falls is best seen right after a period of rain, this shady glen remains a cool respite even in the summer heat, when the waterfall is nearly dry.

If you want to hike a little more, continue downstream from the falls into a grove of redwoods along Sonoma Creek. When the trail meets up with Adobe Canyon Road, cross the road and follow Pony Gate Trail back to the parking lot where you left your car. This makes a nice 3.5-mile loop.

Trip notes: A $5 day-use fee is charged per vehicle. A park map is available at the entrance kiosk for 75 cents. For more information, contact Sugarloaf Ridge State Park, 2605 Adobe Canyon Road, Kenwood, CA 95452-9004; (707) 833-5712 or (707) 938-1519.

Directions: From U.S. 101 in Santa Rosa, turn east on Highway 12 and drive for 11 miles to Adobe Canyon Road. Turn left and drive 3.5 miles to the park entrance kiosk. Pay the entrance fee, then turn around and head back down the road for about 100 yards to the gravel parking area on your right and the trailhead for the Pony Gate Trail. (You may not park anywhere in the park without paying the entrance fee.) Cross the road to reach the trailhead for the Canyon Trail.

134. STAIRSTEP FALLS

Samuel P. Taylor State Park
Off Sir Francis Drake Boulevard near Fairfax

Access & Difficulty: Hike-in 2.5 miles RT/Easy
Elevation: Start at 140 feet; total gain 350 feet
Best Season: December to May

Samuel P. Taylor State Park gets somewhat overshadowed by its large and famous neighbor, Point Reyes National Seashore, but that's okay with the people who know and love the place. Even when the state park campground is filled with campers on summer weekends, it's rare to find many people on Samuel P. Taylor's hiking trails. This means that Stairstep Falls has managed to remain something of a secret in Marin County, a quiet little place where you can find some solitude at a sparkling waterfall tucked into the back of a shady, fern-filled canyon.

The trailhead isn't at the main Samuel P. Taylor park entrance; rather it's a mile west on Sir Francis Drake Boulevard at Devil's Gulch Horse Camp. Park in the dirt pullout across the road from the camp, then walk up the paved camp road for about 150 yards until you see a trail leading off to the right along Devil's Gulch Creek, paralleling the road. Take it, and immediately you descend into a stream-fed canyon filled with Douglas fir, redwoods, oaks, laurel, and about a million

Stairstep Falls

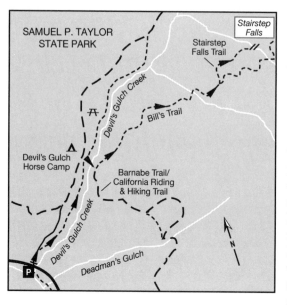

ferns. In April, the ground near the stream is covered with forget-me-nots, buttercups, and milkmaids.

A few minutes of upstream walking brings you to a bridge over Devil's Gulch and an immense, hollowed-out redwood tree. It's the only redwood around, situated among many other kinds of hardwoods. Go ahead, climb inside it. Everybody does. Then turn right and cross the footbridge. Turn left on the far side of the bridge, following the sign marked "Bill's Trail to Barnabe Peak."

Climb gently above the creek, marveling at the walls of ferns and the long limbs of mossy oaks, gaining 350 feet over three-quarters of a mile. After crossing a bridge over a side creek, look for the Stairstep Falls Trail cutting off to the left of the main trail. It's usually signed, but sometimes not. Bear left and in 10 minutes of walking, you'll reach the trail's end near the base of Stairstep Falls.

True to its name, 40-foot-tall Stairstep Falls drops in three main cascades, with a rocky "staircase" at its base producing dozens of rivulets of water. Trail maintenance crews try to keep the area around the falls cleared of fallen trees and branches, allowing you to stand close to the cascading flow. It makes a lovely spot, perfect for quiet contemplation in the tranquil company of ferns, forest, and water.

If you want to take a longer hike, keep following Bill's Trail all the way to the summit of Barnabe Peak. A fire lookout tower on top offers a fabulous view of West Marin County and Point Reyes.

Trip notes: If you park along Sir Francis Drake Boulevard in the parking pullout across from Devil's Gulch Horse Camp, there is no fee. A park map is available for 75 cents from the ranger kiosk at the main park entrance. For more information, contact Samuel P. Taylor State Park, P.O. Box 251, Lagunitas, CA 94938; (415) 488-9897 or (415) 893-1580.

Directions: From San Francisco, drive north on U.S. 101 to Marin County and take the Sir Francis Drake Boulevard exit west, signed for San Anselmo. Drive about 15 miles on Sir Francis Drake Boulevard (through the towns of Ross, Fairfax, and Lagunitas) to the entrance to Samuel P. Taylor State Park. Don't turn here; continue one mile farther past the main entrance and park across the road from Devil's Gulch Horse Camp in the dirt parking pullout. Walk in on the camp access road, then cut off on the trail that parallels its right side.

135. ALAMERE FALLS

**Point Reyes National Seashore
Off Highway 1 near Bolinas**

Access & Difficulty: Hike-in 8.4 miles RT/Moderate
    or Backpack 10.5 miles RT/Moderate
Elevation: Start at 100 feet; total gain 500 feet
Best Season: December to May

Quick—Which California waterfall leaps off high coastal bluffs and cascades gracefully down to the sand and surf below? Most people think of infamous McWay Falls at Julia Pfeiffer Burns State Park in Big Sur, one of the most frequently visited and photographed waterfalls in the state. (See the story on page 336.) But don't forget the other coastal cataract that makes the same dramatic plunge from earth to sea, 150 miles up the coast in western Marin County. That would be Alamere Falls in Point Reyes National Seashore, which is less celebrated but no less dramatic than McWay Falls.

Having hiked in Marin County for more than a decade, I can't think of a finer way to spend a spring day than walking to Alamere Falls. If you time your trip for a clear day on the coast, when the lupine and Douglas iris are in full bloom and the waterfall is running hard, the trailside beauty will knock your socks off.

Start hiking on Coast Trail from the Palomarin Trailhead in Point Reyes, the southernmost trailhead in the national seashore. Despite its off-the-beaten-track location outside the town of Bolinas, the trailhead parking area is often full of cars. The occupants of those cars are usually hiking the entire 15-mile Coast Trail, a spectacular backpacking trip. You'll follow the southern section of that route, where the Coast Trail is a wide dirt road beginning in stands of eucalyptus.

The first mile offers many excellent ocean views, then Coast Trail turns inland, climbing slightly to a junction with Lake Ranch Trail at two miles. Stay on the Coast Trail as it veers left, passing a couple of seasonal ponds that are usually covered with paddling water birds, then skirt the north edge of Bass Lake. Picnic and rest spots abound here; just follow the spur trail amid the Douglas firs.

Reach another trail junction where Crystal Lake Trail heads right to Crystal Lake and tiny Mud Lake, but continue straight on the Coast Trail, now heading back toward the ocean. Prepare yourself for a stunning view of Pelican Lake, which sits smack on a coastal bluff, off to your left. After curving past the lake, reach an unmarked left spur trail that leads to an overlook of the ocean and Stormy Stack, a big offshore rock outcrop. Just beyond the spur turnoff, a sign points straight ahead for Wildcat Camp, and a second unmarked spur leads left, heading for the coastal bluffs and Alamere Falls. Follow this quarter-mile spur trail, which is narrow and frequently overgrown

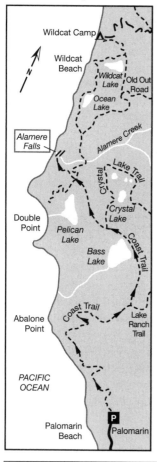

with poison oak and coastal scrub, till it meets up with Alamere Creek near the cliff edge. Although you are now practically on top of the falls, you still have few clues to the watery theatrics ahead.

Scramble downstream, then cross the stream wherever you're able, so that you wind up on the north side of Alamere Creek. At the edge of the bluffs and alongside the falls' lip, you'll find a well-worn route leading down to the beach. A rope is usually tied in place to help you over the most vertical spots. Still, be wary of the loose sandstone and shale.

It's only when you touch down on the beach that the full drama of Alamere Falls unfolds. Although the pristine coastline would be stunning even without the waterfall, it's made even more impressive by the sight of Alamere Creek dropping in a wide, effusive block over the cliff, then running across the sand and into the sea. The fall is 50 feet high, and although its width varies greatly according to how much water is flowing through the creek, it's always beautiful.

Although day-hikers will spend some time on this magical beach and then return to Palomarin Trailhead, backpackers will continue one mile northwest on Coast Trail, passing Ocean Lake and Wildcat Lake, to Wildcat Camp. (You can also leave Coast Trail and take Ocean Lake Trail to reach the camp; the two routes form a conve-

Alamere Falls

nient loop.) If you're camping, make sure you've obtained your permit beforehand and brought a camp stove, because fires are not permitted. Wildcat Beach is just a few steps away, and a network of trails lead north, east, and south from the camp.

Trip notes: There is no fee. Backpackers spending the night at Wildcat Camp must have reservations and a backcountry camping permit. For more information and a free map of Point Reyes National Seashore, contact Point Reyes National Seashore, Point Reyes Station, CA 94956; (415) 663-1092.

Directions: From San Francisco, drive north on U.S. 101 to Marin County and take the Sir Francis Drake Boulevard exit west, signed for San Anselmo. Drive about 20 miles on Sir Francis Drake Boulevard to the town of Olema, then turn left on Highway 1. Drive 8.9 miles south on Highway 1 to Bolinas Road, which is usually not signed. Turn right and drive 2.1 miles to Mesa Road. Turn right and drive 5.8 miles to the Palomarin Trailhead.

136. CARSON FALLS
Marin Municipal Water District
Off Bolinas-Fairfax Road near Fairfax

Access & Difficulty: Hike-in & Scramble 3.5 miles RT/Moderate
Elevation: Start at 1,080 feet; total gain/loss 500 feet
Best Season: December to May

When it flows hard, Carson Falls appears like a miracle. Draining a large and steep canyon, Little Carson Creek drops 150 feet in five tiers, creating a series of rushing cascades that culminate in a 40-foot freefall drop over rugged basalt rock. Most of the year, the fall is only a trickle, but its craggy cliff, which holds a series of basins and pools, remains a fascinating sight to behold.

No signs point the way to Carson Falls, so you have to know where to go. Start at Pine Mountain Road, a gated fire road across from the large parking area on Bolinas Road. Walk up the dirt road, gaining views of Fairfax and San Rafael to the east, then as you climb higher, even wider views of San Pablo Bay, the Richmond Bridge, and the East Bay. Mount Diablo looms in the background. On a clear day, it can be an awesome scene.

Climb for nearly a mile on Pine Mountain Road (watch out for mountain bikers who sometimes come screaming down the hill), then turn left on Oat Hill Road. There's an unsigned cutoff trail about a tenth of a mile before you reach signed Oat Hill Road; you can also take this, because it joins Oat Hill in short order. Walk downhill on Oat Hill Road for a quarter-mile to an area where the road flattens out. Pay attention to the telephone lines that are strung up above your head; they're your indicator of where to look for an unsigned single-track trail on the right, the path to Carson Falls. The telephone lines run in the same direction you're going.

Turn right on the single-track, which is often marked with a "no bikes" symbol, and hike steeply downhill for another quarter-mile to the top of the falls. There, you must scramble down to get a look at the cascades, and to do so, you have a few choices: You can cross over Carson Creek above the falls and follow the route down to various overlooks of the middle and lower falls, or stay on the east side of the falls and scramble down to the upper cascades. (The route on the east side does not go all the way to the fall's base; to see the lowest drop, you must cross the creek.)

Carson Falls reveals its pleasures slowly, one cascade at a time. There are a total of five cascades and pools, with the largest at the bottom, and it's worth climbing all the way down to see each one.

The route on the west side of the falls leads to the base of the final 40-foot drop, set in a dark and shady grotto. It also leads to my favorite viewing spot for the entire fall, a rock outcrop just above the final drop. You can sit on this rocky perch and look upward at three gorgeous tiers of Carson Falls, then peer over the edge at the big cascade below. The greenstone basalt rock is a beautiful shade of gray and green. The surrounding grasslands are peppered with ferns and bright red toyon bushes in winter. In early summer, the buckeye trees

Carson Falls

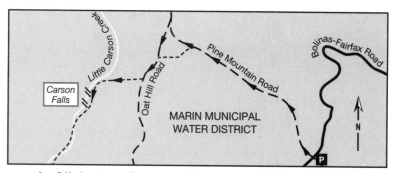

near the falls begin to flower, producing an enticing aroma.

Even in summer, when Carson Falls is reduced to a mere trickle, sitting beside it can be a great experience, like relaxing in a Zen garden with the sound of the wind and the tinkling of water as your only companions. But then, shortly after a hard rain, Carson Falls roars. For visitors who are accustomed to the fall's usually placid state, the effect is stunning.

Trip notes: There is no fee. For more information and a $2 map, contact Marin Municipal Water District, 220 Nellen Avenue, Corte Madera, CA 94925; (415) 945-1195. Or phone Sky Oaks Ranger Station at (415) 945-1181. A more detailed map of the area is available for a fee from Olmsted Brothers Map Company, P.O. Box 5351, Berkeley, CA 94705; (510) 658-6534.

Directions: From San Francisco, drive north on U.S. 101 to Marin County and take the Sir Francis Drake Boulevard exit west, signed for San Anselmo. Drive six miles on Sir Francis Drake Boulevard to the town of Fairfax, then turn left by the "Fairfax" sign (on unsigned Pacheco Road), then right immediately on Broadway. Drive one block and turn left on Bolinas Road. Drive 3.8 miles on Bolinas Road, past the golf course, to the trailhead parking area on the left side of the road. Walk across the road to the trailhead.

137. CASCADE FALLS

Marin County Open Space District
Off Bolinas-Fairfax Road near Fairfax

Access & Difficulty: Hike-in 2.0 miles RT/Easy
Elevation: Start at 280 feet; total gain 80 feet
Best Season: December to May

Quiz question: Name three waterfalls located on or nearby Mount Tamalpais, all within six miles of each other, all with names that begin with the letter C.

Answer: Cataract Falls on the back side of Mount Tamalpais (see page 299), Carson Falls in Marin Municipal Water District (see page 294), and Cascade Falls in Marin County Open Space District.

Too easy? Okay, now describe which is which. Carson Falls? Isn't that the one with the trail that starts at Alpine Dam and climbs the whole way? Nope, that's Cataract. Cataract Falls? Isn't that the one that falls in a long chain of pool-and-drop stairsteps into rocky pools? No, that's Carson. Cascade Falls? Isn't that the one that's just outside the Fairfax suburbs? Well, you got one right.

Cascade Falls

Of the three neighboring waterfalls, Cascade Falls is by far the easiest to reach. While Cataract and Carson require some up-and-down hiking, Cascade Falls is reachable by a nearly flat two-mile round-trip. It's a perfect waterfall to take small children to, or a great place to go for a walk after work.

Because the trail begins at the end of a house-lined street, be careful where you park your car, so you're not blocking driveways or infringing on private property. Start walking on the gated fire road, then veer off it on to single-track. The trail stays close to San Anselmo Creek, which can look rather unpromising, even stagnant, at this end of the preserve. (Don't be fooled—in periods of heavy rain, San Anselmo Creek can run like a river, as much as 30 feet wide and dark brown from sediment pouring off the hillsides. But this is a rare occurrence; mostly the creek is tranquil.)

A half mile in, cross a wooden footbridge and head to your right, now heading upstream along Cascade Creek. Quickly the stream's flow picks up. The trail leads you into a lovely oak and laurel forest, and as you travel, the anticipation builds.

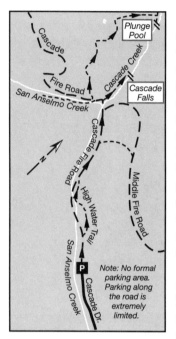

Cascade
Cascade Creek
Plunge Pool
Fire Road
San Anselmo Creek
Cascade Falls
N
Cascade Fire Road
High Water Trail
Middle Fire Road
San Anselmo Creek
P
Note: No formal parking area. Parking along the road is extremely limited.
Cascade Dr.

In a quarter mile, you'll round a bend and hear the sound of falling water, then get your first look at Cascade Falls, tumbling 18 feet down a rough rock face. The trail leads up and over its lip, where you'll find many rock seats. Or you can drop down to the large boulder at the fall's base, a favored spot for waterfall-watching. On my first of many visits here, I was surprised to find two musicians sitting cross-legged on this rock, playing a duet on the violin and guitar. I stayed and listened to their music, and the music of the falls, for an hour or more.

Those who desire a longer hike can continue on to see Upper Cascade Falls, also known as the Plunge Pool or the Ink Well. Although a rough footpath travels along Cascade Creek to the upper falls, it is extremely steep in places and overgrown with poison oak. A better option is to retrace your steps to the footbridge, then turn right (west) on Cascade Fire Road. Walk 100 yards, then turn right on a single-track trail signed as "no bikes." This trail leads another 1.5 miles to a point just 150 feet north of Upper Cascade Falls. When you near the creek again, turn right to reach the cataract.

Trip notes: There is no fee. A detailed map of the area is available for a fee from Olmsted Brothers Map Company, P.O. Box 5351, Berkeley, CA 94705; (510) 658-6534. For more information, contact Marin County Open Space District, Parks and Recreation Department, Marin Civic Center, 3501 Civic Center Drive, Room 417, San Rafael, CA; (415) 499-6387.

Directions: From San Francisco, drive north on U.S. 101 to Marin County and take the Sir Francis Drake Boulevard exit west, signed for San Anselmo. Drive six miles on Sir Francis Drake Boulevard to the town of Fairfax, then turn left by the "Fairfax" sign (on unsigned Pacheco Road), then right immediately on Broadway. Drive one block, and turn left on Bolinas Road. Drive three-tenths of a mile on Bolinas Road, then bear right on Cascade Drive (the middle road of three roads). Drive 1.5 miles on Cascade Drive to the end of the road and the gated trail. Park alongside the road, being careful to obey the "no parking" signs in the last 100 yards before the trailhead.

138. CATARACT FALLS

Marin Municipal Water District
Off Bolinas-Fairfax Road near Fairfax

Access & Difficulty: Hike-in 3.2 miles RT/Moderate
Elevation: Start at 680 feet (Bolinas) or
    1,940 feet (Ridgecrest); total gain/loss 800 feet
Best Season: December to May

Before you set out for Cataract Falls, you must do two things. First, check your calendar, because the falls only run in the wet half of the year. Second, decide whether you prefer to hike up and then down, or down and then up. There are two separate trailheads for reaching Cataract Falls, one from Alpine Lake leading uphill to the falls; the other from Mount Tamalpais leading downhill to the falls. The latter is a somewhat easier route, with less of a steep grade, as long as you don't travel the entire length of the trail.

Both routes are gorgeous. I've hiked them both many times, and the only factor that matters is which trailhead I'm closer to when I want to hike. The trailhead at Alpine Lake requires a winding drive on Bolinas Road to reach, but it's more convenient if you're in northern Marin. The trailhead on Mount Tamalpais also requires a winding drive, but it's easier to reach if you're coming from San Francisco or southern Marin.

If you start hiking from the Alpine Lake trailhead, you're

Cataract Falls

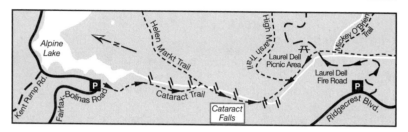

treated to pretty lake views for the first quarter-mile of trail, then
dense redwood forest as you head steeply uphill, often walking on
rock stair-steps. You can hike as much or as little as you like, because
Cataract Falls is a series of cascades that are spread out over 1.6 miles
of the Cataract Trail. As soon as the trail leaves the lake and starts to
climb, you start seeing waterfalls. Half a dozen of them cascade in the
first three-quarters of a mile, from the edge of the lake to a signed
turnoff for the Helen Markt Trail, just after a narrow footbridge
where the trail crosses to the east side of Cataract Creek.

Most of the cascades are between 20 and 30 feet high, but their
shapes and appearances are all completely different. The common
element they share, besides the life-giving flow of Cataract Creek, is
that each one is completely surrounded by ferns. After a good rain,
the hike is truly breathtaking, with the continual sound and sight
of waterfalls providing nonstop excitement through every curve of
the trail.

If you hike from the trailhead on West Ridgecrest Boulevard,
northwest of the big parking area at Rock Springs, you descend on a
fire road to a clearing by Laurel Dell, three-quarters of a mile away.
Cataract Creek often floods across this road in winter and spring,
making your crossing a bit tricky. In summer, the route is dry, but of
course that means no waterfalls.

After rock-hopping across the creek, head to your left into Laurel
Dell, a grassy flat. Walk through it, pick up the Cataract Trail at its far
end, then begin a steep descent through redwoods and Douglas firs.
Watch for an intersection with the High Marsh Trail on the right;
continue straight and shortly you'll be at the uppermost cascade of
Cataract Falls. The Cataract Trail curves in tightly, bringing you right
by the stream, and you'll see the water tumbling over huge boulders
as it rushes downhill. Pick a rock and watch the show.

From this first fall, the magic continues as you head downhill,
past one cascade after another, for another full mile of waterfall-
watching. Just remember that if you're hiking in this direction, all
your elevation loss will need to be regained on the return trip. The

trail's slope gets steeper the further you go; the last three-quarters of a mile before Bolinas Road are mostly rock stair-steps. At any point, you can cut your trip short and save yourself some of the climb back.

Trip notes: There is no fee. For more information and a $2 map, contact Marin Municipal Water District, 220 Nellen Avenue, Corte Madera, CA 94925; (415) 945-1195. Or phone Sky Oaks Ranger Station at (415) 945-1181. Or contact Mount Tamalpais State Park, 801 Panoramic Highway, Mill Valley, CA 94941; (415) 388-2070. A more detailed map of the area is available for a fee from Olmsted Brothers Map Company, P.O. Box 5351, Berkeley, CA 94705; (510) 658-6534.

Directions: For the Bolinas Road Trailhead: From San Francisco, drive north on U.S. 101 to Marin County and take the Sir Francis Drake Boulevard exit west, signed for San Anselmo. Drive six miles on Sir Francis Drake Boulevard to the town of Fairfax, then turn left by the "Fairfax" sign (on unsigned Pacheco Road), then right immediately on Broadway. Drive one block and turn left on Bolinas Road. Drive 7.8 miles on Bolinas Road to the dam at Alpine Lake. Cross the dam, and continue one-tenth mile further on Bolinas Road, to the hairpin turn in the road. Park in the pullouts along the turn; the trailhead is on the left.

For the West Ridgecrest Road Trailhead: From San Francisco, drive north on U.S. 101 to Marin County and take the Mill Valley/Stinson Beach/Highway 1 exit. Continue straight for one mile until you reach a stoplight at Shoreline Highway, then turn left and drive uphill for 2.5 miles. Turn right on Panoramic Highway and drive for nine-tenths of a mile to an intersection where you can go left, right, or straight. Take the middle road (straight), continuing on Panoramic Highway for 4.3 more miles to Pantoll Road. Turn right and drive 1.4 miles to Pantoll Road's intersection with Ridgecrest Boulevard. Turn left on West Ridgecrest Boulevard, and drive 1.6 miles to a small parking area on the right. Park there and hike on the trail marked "Laurel Dell."

139. DAWN FALLS

Marin County Open Space District
Off U.S. 101 near Larkspur

Access & Difficulty: Hike-in 2.4 miles RT/Easy
Elevation: Start at 160 feet; total gain 240 feet
Best Season: December to May

For years, I made the classic error that I should know better than to make: I didn't go visit Dawn Falls, because I thought that any waterfall located in the midst of a Marin County suburb couldn't be that good. It was a big mistake, a huge omission in my collection of

---

Dawn Falls

waterfalls. Dawn Falls is better than good; it's gorgeous. Now that I've seen it, I plan to return again and again.

One of the nicest things about the easy stroll to Dawn Falls is that your dog can accompany you. Like nearby Cascade Falls in Fairfax, the land around Dawn Falls is managed by the Marin County Open Space District, so leashed dogs are permitted. On our trip, almost everyone on the trail had either a puppy or a child with them, and they were all having an excellent time.

From the end of Madrone Avenue, cross Larkspur Creek on a wooden footbridge and then turn right to head to the falls. Walking upstream, you head deeper and deeper into Baltimore Canyon, a gorgeous basin filled with redwood trees. Ignore the many spur trails and stay along the creek. The main trail winds through dark and shaggy redwoods, which are best seen when they're dripping with moisture after a rain or heavy fog. Don't hesitate to make this trip if it's raining or misting—that just makes the hike more beautiful.

The trail climbs slowly and gently. As it does, the forest changes to somewhat drier terrain, including oak and laurel trees. The falls are set in mixed hardwoods, and because this section of the forest is not dense, you get many excellent waterfall views from the trail. The single-track leads to the top of the falls, which cascades 30 feet over a sheer rock ledge, beautifully framed by a garden of ferns. The stream above the waterfall is almost as scenic as the fall itself, nourished by a little feeder creek coming in from the side.

Larkspur Creek often dries up by late summer, and the waterfall loses much of its appeal by late spring. For the best experience, visit

Dawn Falls in winter or early spring, preferably early in the morning or during the week, when fewer people are out walking in the canyon.

An even shorter route to Dawn Falls begins at the end of Crown Road in Kentfield. From the start of the gated fire road (Northridge Trailhead), it's only a quarter mile to the Dawn Falls Trail cutoff on the left. It's a nice, easy stroll.

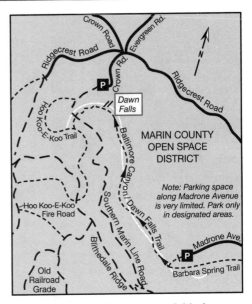

Trip notes: There is no fee. A detailed map of the area is available for a fee from Olmsted Brothers Map Company, P.O. Box 5351, Berkeley, CA 94705; (510) 658-6534. For more information, contact Marin County Open Space District, Parks and Recreation Department, Marin Civic Center, 3501 Civic Center Drive #417, San Rafael, CA; (415) 499-6387.

Directions: From San Francisco, drive north on U.S. 101 to Larkspur. Take the Tamalpais Drive exit, then head west on Tamalpais Drive to Corte Madera Avenue. Turn right and drive a half-mile, then turn left on Madrone Avenue. When it forks, stay left, and follow it to its end where it intersects with Valley Way. The trailhead is at the end of Madrone, on the left side of the road. (There is parking for about six cars, and more parking further down Madrone. Obey the "no parking" signs.)

140. ABRIGO FALLS

Briones Regional Park
Off Highway 24 near Orinda

Access & Difficulty: Hike-in or Bike-in 2.6 miles RT/Easy
Elevation: Start at 400 feet; total gain 100 feet
Best Season: December to May

People who live in the East San Francisco Bay Area watch the skies carefully, keep their day-packs packed, and make sure there's always gas in the car. That way, when conditions are just right, they can head out to see Abrigo Falls. Because water is not exactly plentiful

Abrigo Falls

in the East Bay, any waterfall is a big deal, even the thin-streamed cascade on Abrigo Creek in Briones Regional Park.

Having previously hiked in arid Briones only in summer, I had a hard time believing Abrigo existed before I saw it with my own eyes. But like many places in the San Francisco Bay Area, Briones comes to life with winter rain, and tiny Abrigo Creek starts to run, feeding larger Bear Creek. Although the waterfall is not large—it drops only 15 feet over a rock face—it's set in a cave-like canyon, creating an unusual, prehistoric-looking scene. It's the kind of place you might expect a brontosaurus to show up and start munching on the oak and bay leaves.

The big downer at Abrigo is that the waterfall is hard to see; the trail leads above and alongside the fall, not to its base. The creek and falls are set in a deep and narrow canyon, so it's hard to get a good perspective on the drop, even in the rare times when the waterfall is flowing hard.

The hike to Abrigo Falls is most pleasant in late winter and spring, preferably the day following a good rain. It's an easy route for families, with the creek meandering pleasantly alongside. Because the trail is really a ranch road, it can be heavily pocketed and eroded from cow traffic, making hiking boots necessary. In April and May, wildflowers bloom in the meadows.

Start hiking at the Abrigo Valley Trailhead, just past the kiosk at Briones' Bear Creek entrance, walking an easy 1.3 miles up the dirt road. Mountain bikes, horses, and dogs are allowed on the route. Pass two group camping areas after the first mile, Maud Walen and Wee-ta-chi, and you'll find the waterfall shortly past the latter. The fall is located at the point where the road makes a short, steep climb, the first noticeable ascent along the route. (If the road makes a hairpin turn to the left and moves away from the creek, you've gone too far.)

From the trail, you can see two small streams of water pouring over an exposed rock face, surrounded by ferns on the canyon walls.

If you've come this far and want to keep walking, continue another quarter-mile to where the Abrigo Valley Trail meets up with the Briones Crest Trail. Turn right and hike for a half-mile along Briones Crest for stellar views of Mount Diablo, Suisun Bay, San Pablo Bay, and Point Pinole. Then retrace your steps or loop back to Abrigo Valley on the Mott Peak Trail.

Trip notes: A $3.50 day-use fee is charged per vehicle. Free trail maps are available at the entrance kiosk. For more information, contact East Bay Regional Park District, 2950 Peralta Oaks Court, P.O. Box 5381, Oakland, CA 94605-0381; (510) 635-0135 or (510) 562-7275.

Directions: From Interstate 580 in Oakland, take the Highway 24 exit east. Go through the Caldecott Tunnel and exit at Acalanes Road/Mount Diablo Boulevard. Follow the signs to get on Upper Happy Valley Road (you'll be on El Nido Ranch Road, then turn left on Upper Happy Valley Road). Drive one mile on Upper Happy Valley Road, then turn left on Happy Valley Road and drive two miles. Turn right and drive three-tenths of a mile on Bear Creek Road. Don't turn left into the Bear Creek Staging Area; turn right into the Briones Park entrance just beyond it. Pay at the kiosk, then turn left and park just to the left of the kiosk. Start hiking on the Abrigo Valley Trail.

141. DIABLO FALLS (Donner Creek Falls)

Mount Diablo State Park
Off Interstate 680 near Clayton

Access & Difficulty: Hike-in 6.5 miles RT/Moderate
Elevation: Start at 100 feet; total gain 900 feet
Best Season: December to May

Waterfalls? On Mount Diablo? I know, it seems pretty unlikely. But a trip to Clayton in the rainy season and a hike along the back side of the 3,849-foot mountain reveals half a dozen cascades, each about 30 feet tall. Scattered along the hillsides on two forks of Donner Creek, the falls drop in a canyon that is notoriously dry, steep, and hot as Hades most of the year. Pick the right day, soon after a good winter rain, and it's water, water everywhere, and it's cool and comfortable to boot.

The closest trailhead to Diablo Falls, which is also called Donner Creek Falls, is at the end of Regency Drive, a suburban neighborhood

One of Diablo Falls' cascades

in Clayton. It's an unlikely start for an unlikely hike. Where the road ends, walk to your left along a gated dirt road, one of three possible trails, signed as "Donner Canyon Road to Cardinet Oaks Road." Right away, you're hiking along Donner Creek, so you can gauge how good the falls will be by how much water is flowing in the creek.

Keep walking upstream, and in six-tenths of a mile take the single-track route signed as "Trail to Donner Cabin Site." You'll stay along the creek and pass the remains of the Donner Cabin (a stone foundation and an old bathtub). Cross Donner Creek and reach a junction with Hetherington Loop Trail, which eventually leads back to Donner Canyon Road. Although you can stay on Donner Canyon Road for the whole distance, it's a steep and tedious climb. Hetherington Loop Trail, in contrast, is a longer, meandering route along Donner Creek, which adds only a half-mile and much enjoyment to your trip.

Where Hetherington Loop Trail and Donner Canyon Road meet up again, continue to the left and uphill on the dirt road to Cardinet Junction, where Donner Canyon Road and Cardinet Oaks Road join. Bear left, then shortly later cross the creek (if you're in luck, it will be widely flooding the road, which means good waterfalls). Then prepare to gain about 500 feet in elevation in five tight switchbacks on the dirt road. With these completed, you'll see the signed turnoff on the right for Falls Trail. You'll also gain some wide-reaching views of Clayton and far-off Suisun Bay.

Falls Trail is pleasant single-track, lateraling along the left side of the steep canyon. In moments, you begin to spot waterfalls coming into view. The first is a 20-foot cascade, across the canyon on your right. Then, moments later, you see another 20-footer straight ahead. Keep walking and you spot two more, including one perfect freefall about 30 feet high. The trail is about 100 yards distant from the falls, so you never get the pleasure of standing at their bases or alongside them, but you do get the extraordinary experience of seeing as many as five waterfalls at once, in a very small area. (If you choose to scramble off-trail to get a closer look at any of the falls, be very careful. This canyon is remarkably steep.)

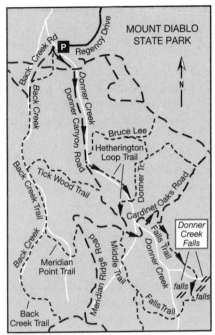

Note the occasional gray pines along Falls Trail; their cones are extremely dense and can weigh up to four pounds.

Falls Trail leads you right across the two forks of Donner Creek, the source of the falls, then loops back to Cardinet Junction. You can walk the entire loop if you wish, or just turn back and retrace your steps.

An even longer loop (seven miles round-trip) is possible by taking Falls Trail to Middle Trail, Meridian Ridge Road, and Meridian Point Trail, then hiking into Back Canyon. The Back Creek Trail will return you to your starting point at the Regency Drive trailhead.

Trip notes: There is no fee at the Regency Drive Trailhead. A park map is available at the main park gates and the visitor center for $1. The Mount Diablo Interpretive Association publishes a more extensive map, which is available for $5. For more information, contact Mount Diablo State Park, 96 Mitchell Canyon Road, Clayton, CA 94517; (925) 837-2525 or (925) 837-0904. Website: www.mdia.org

Directions: From Interstate 680 heading north in Walnut Creek, take the Ygnacio Valley Road exit. Drive east on Ygnacio Valley Road for 7.5 miles to Clayton Road. Turn right on Clayton Road and drive 2.9 miles (it becomes Marsh Creek Road, but don't turn right at the sign for Marsh Creek Road) to Regency Drive. Turn right and drive a half-mile to the end of the road and the trailhead. (Or, from Interstate 680 heading south in Walnut Creek, take the Treat Boulevard Road exit and go east. In one mile, turn right on Bancroft Road. In another mile, turn left on Ygnacio Valley Road and drive five miles to Clayton Road. Continue as above.)

142. MURIETTA FALLS

Ohlone Regional Wilderness
Off Interstate 580 near Livermore

Access & Difficulty: Hike-in or Backpack 12.0 miles RT/Strenuous
Elevation: Start at 750 feet; total gain/loss 3,500 feet
Best Season: January to April

Everybody loves a waterfall, but do you love waterfalls enough to be willing to grunt out a 3,500-foot elevation change? Think it over. If your answer is yes, you're heading for a fine adventure in Ohlone Regional Wilderness, culminating in a visit to 100-foot Murietta Falls.

If your answer is "not sure," the first half-hour on this trail will be challenging enough to make up your mind, one way or the other.

Ohlone Regional Wilderness is one of the Bay Area's special places. No public roads lead through it or even near it. You have to hike to reach its boundary, starting either from Sunol Regional Wilderness to the west or Del Valle Regional Park to the north. To be more specific, you have to hike uphill.

In the same vein, Murietta Falls is one of the Bay Area's most special waterfalls. That's partly because it's much taller than other area falls and partly because it's hard enough to reach that most people never make the trip. The difficulty doesn't just lie in the trail's many steep ups and downs, its sunny exposure, and its 12-mile-long round-trip distance. The real difficulty is that the waterfall has an extremely short season and must be seen immediately following a period of rain. More than a few hikers have made the long trip to Murietta and then been disappointed to find only a trickle of water. March is often the best month to see the fall flowing, but it depends on the current year's rain pattern. Depending on when the rains come, Murietta's top flow could happen anywhere from January to April. Keep your eyes on the skies.

One thing to remember: this trail is absolutely not suitable for a warm or hot day. It offers very little shade and a ton of climbing.

A single element makes the trip easy. The trail is remarkably well signed. Just pay attention at all junctions and keep following the red markers for Ohlone Wilderness Trail in the first five miles. Also, you must purchase a wilderness permit in order to hike on the Ohlone Wilderness Trail. With your permit you get a free map, which comes in quite handy.

The trail starts by climbing and stays that way for 2.4 miles. (Don't forget to stop and sign in at the wilderness register one mile in.) There are only a very few spots where the wide dirt road levels off. Otherwise, it's up, up, up all the way to the top of Rocky Ridge, a 1,670-foot gain from the trailhead. Then all of a sudden you start an incredibly steep descent—steep enough so that you'll wish you'd brought your trekking poles. You drop 530 feet in about a half mile. The good news is that you're heading for water; you can hear its welcoming sound. The wide fire road narrows to single-track for the first time all day as you descend into the beautiful stream canyon of Williams Gulch. The sound of the cascading creek is so refreshing and inviting that you may suddenly remember why you are doing this hike after all. The half-mile stretch of path that cuts through the stream canyon is pure, refreshing pleasure.

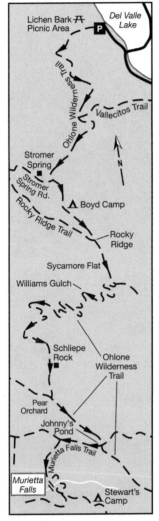

You might as well enjoy it, because next you're going to climb out of the canyon in a 1,200-foot ascent. The single-track trail is surprisingly well graded with some good switchbacks, however, so this climb isn't nearly as bad as some of the dirt road stretches. The path is fairly well shaded. Prolific miner's lettuce and pink shooting stars grow alongside it.

You'll get a hint that you're nearing the falls when you start to notice rock outcrops along the trail. For the first four miles, you see mostly grasslands and massive oak trees, some with diameters that rival the size of giant redwoods. (The only exception to the oak savannah terrain is in riparian Williams Gulch.) But suddenly large rock outcrops start to pop up out of nowhere. One of these, on the left side of the trail, is signed as Schliepe Rock, with no explanation.

The trail also levels out substantially as you near the falls. At this 3,000-foot elevation, you'll gain some wonderful views to the north

Murietta Falls

and west. (On our trip, we were amazed to see snow on the high ridges around us, and even a few lingering white patches right along the trail.)

Seven-tenths of a mile beyond Schliepe Rock you'll reach Johnny's Pond. Just beyond the small pond turn right at the sign for Murietta Falls (signpost 35). Hike a quarter mile farther, then turn left and start paying close attention to your surroundings. In just under a half mile, you'll reach a hairpin turn in the road. If you've timed your trip well, you'll note a few streams of water crossing the road. Leave the trail and follow the main stream downhill to your right; it will deliver you to the brink of the falls in a few hundred feet.

A good use trail makes a steep descent to the base of the falls. Follow it carefully—you've come this far, you might as well get the full effect. The waterfall's cliff, an incredible rocky precipice with a 100-foot drop, is composed of greenstone basalt. At its base is a wide, round, shallow pool. Many good picnicking spots are found nearby. If you made it this far, you deserve to eat well. Pull out that turkey and avocado sandwich.

Birdwatchers, take note: The trailside oak savannah is home to many residents and migratory birds. I counted more western bluebirds on this walk than I had seen in my entire life previously.

Trip notes: A $4 day-use fee is charged per vehicle from October to March ($5 from April to September). Hikers on the Ohlone Wilderness

Trail must purchase a $2 wilderness permit, which includes a detailed trail map. (You may purchase a permit in advance by mail at the address below, or on the day of your hike at the park entrance station.) For more information, contact East Bay Regional Park District, 2950 Peralta Oaks Court, P.O. Box 5381, Oakland, CA 94605-0381; (510) 635-0135 or (510) 562-7275.

Directions: From Interstate 580 in Livermore, take the North Livermore Avenue exit and turn right (south). Drive south through the town of Livermore for 3.5 miles (North Livermore Avenue becomes Tesla Road) and turn right on Mines Road. Drive 3.5 miles on Mines Road to its junction with Del Valle Road. Continue straight at the fork, now on Del Valle Road. Drive 3.2 miles to the entrance kiosk at Del Valle Regional Park. Purchase a wilderness permit at the entrance kiosk, then continue three quarters of a mile to the dam and cross it. Turn right and drive a half mile to the Lichen Bark Picnic Area. Take the signed Ohlone Trail.

143. BROOKS FALLS

San Pedro Valley County Park
Off Highway 1 near Pacifica

Access & Difficulty: Hike-in 1.6 miles RT/Easy
Elevation: Start at 200 feet; total gain 400 feet
Best Season: December to May

If you live or work in San Francisco or on the San Mateo coast, Brooks Falls is the closest waterfall you can reach. It's a mere five-minute drive off Highway 1 in Pacifica, less than half an hour from downtown San Francisco. You could leave your office job, drive to San Pedro Valley County Park, hike to the waterfall, and be back in your cubicle before anyone's suspicions get aroused. Just be careful not to leave your muddy shoes under your desk.

But keep in mind that if you prefer your waterfalls up close and personal, you're not going to get your desires fulfilled at Brooks Falls. You'll have many chances along the trail to see and hear the waterfall, but you're always at least a half-mile from the cascading stream. No matter how much rain there is, Brooks Falls never appears as anything but a delicate silver strand pouring down a lush, foliage-congested canyon, because you just can't get close enough to see more.

The hike around the Brooks Creek canyon is excellent, though, and it can be made into an easy 3.5-mile loop trip that provides numerous views of the waterfall and also of the wide, blue Pacific Ocean. Or, if you're short on time, an out-and-back trip to a bench

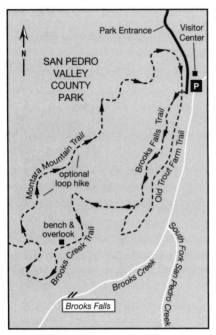

San Pedro Valley County Park map showing Park Entrance, Visitor Center, Montara Mountain Trail, Brooks Falls Trail, Old Trout Farm Trail, South Fork San Pedro Creek, Brooks Creek Trail, optional loop hike, bench & overlook, Brooks Creek, and Brooks Falls.

overlooking Brooks Falls takes only 1.6 miles of hiking.

Locate the trailhead for the Montara Mountain Trail alongside the rest rooms in San Pedro Valley County Park. A few feet past the trailhead, the trail splits, with the Montara Mountain Trail heading right and Brooks Creek Trail heading left. Follow Brooks Creek Trail as it leads uphill through a eucalyptus grove, eventually breaking out to wide views of the canyon. At trail junctions, look for small signs stating: "To Waterfall Viewing Area." Remain on Brooks Creek Trail, bearing right at two forks, and keep heading uphill.

Twenty minutes of well-graded climbing delivers your first glances of the waterfall, far off in the canyon on your left. Look for a narrow plume of water cascading down the mountainside, dropping in three tiers that total 175 feet. Brooks Falls' narrow, wispy length is reminiscent of the tropical waterfalls of Hawaii, especially since it's frequently viewed through the misty haze of coastal fog. The best viewing spot is at a conveniently placed bench right along the trail, where after a hard rain, you can hear as well as see the water crashing down the slopes, a quarter-mile across the canyon.

By this point on the Brooks Creek Trail, you've climbed above the eucalyptus trees and are surrounded by manzanita and coastal brush. Your options are to turn around and head back, or continue on an excellent 3.5-mile loop trail. If you choose the latter, you get continual views of Brooks Falls as you continue upward, switchbacking to a trail junction and an overlook of the Pacific Ocean and Pacifica Beach. Here, turn right on the Montara Mountain Trail, then start your descent back down the slope.

Trip notes: A $4 day-use fee is charged per vehicle. Free park maps are available at the entrance kiosk. For more information, contact San Pedro Valley County Park, 600 Oddstad Boulevard, Pacifica, CA 94044; (650) 355-8289.

Directions: From San Francisco, take Highway 1 south for 10 miles to Pacifica. Turn east (left) on Linda Mar Boulevard, and follow it for two miles until it dead-ends at Oddstad Boulevard. Turn right and drive 50 yards to the park entrance on the left. Park in the upper parking lot (to the right of the visitor center as you drive in), and locate the trailhead marked "Montara Mountain Trail," next to the restrooms.

144. TIP TOE FALLS

Portola Redwoods State Park
Off Highway 35 near La Honda

Access & Difficulty: Hike-in 2.0 miles RT/Easy
Elevation: Start at 425 feet; total gain 100 feet
Best Season: December to May

The name says it all. Tip Toe Falls is no loud watercourse thundering down over house-sized granite boulders. Rather, it's a petite little cataract, short and sweet, tip-toeing down a tiny cliff into a rounded rock pool. It's the smallest waterfall in this book, but there's something special about it, a kind of *je ne sais quoi* that makes you draw in your breath and say, "Wow, look at that."

Tip Toe is one of the many jewels of Portola Redwoods State Park, a dark and shady redwood park that's tucked into the hillsides of the Santa Cruz Mountains. The park is like a smaller, less visited version of nearby Big Basin Redwoods State Park, set in a canyon filled with big trees and ferns, although the majority of the redwoods here are second-growth. Biking, hiking, camping, and picnicking are all popular activities.

To hike to Tip Toe Falls, start your trip by the park office and visitor center. It's a good idea to ask a few questions inside, because rangers remove many of the footbridges over Pescadero Creek in the winter, which may affect your trail options. Although Tip Toe Falls is on Fall Creek, you need to cross Pescadero Creek to reach it.

You have a couple of trailhead choices, all which eventually put you on the Iverson Trail, a two-mile loop that leads to Tip Toe Falls' canyon. You can start from the Iverson Trail on the north side of the visitor center, the Sequoia Nature Trail on the south side of the visitor center, or you can walk or drive an eighth of a mile past the visitor center to the group campgrounds and campfire center, where there's another trailhead for the Iverson Trail. If winter storms have ruled out all three routes, you can do what we did one rainy December day:

Tip Toe Falls

Walk three-quarters of a mile down the gated park service road, then turn right and pick up the Iverson Trail from there. It's not the prettiest way to go, but if you're determined to see the waterfall, it might just do the trick.

No matter how you do it, you'll eventually connect to the Iverson Trail on the far side of Pescadero Creek. It's easy streamside walking under dense redwoods and conifers, on a maze of well-signed and well-maintained trails. When Iverson Trail meets up with Fall Creek, a sign points to a spur trail leading upcanyon to Tip Toe Falls. A few steps on the spur trail take you to the narrow canyon's end, where two rock walls join and Tip Toe pours over a low notch. What's remarkable is the large and deep pool in front of the diminutive, six-foot waterfall, and the strong breeze the stream creates when it's running hard. If you look carefully, you can see another cascade about 50 feet behind Tip Toe. The entire scene is bordered by cascade-loving ferns.

While you're in Portola State Park, take a walk on the short Old Tree Trail to see a fascinating, 12-foot-wide, fire-scarred redwood.

Trip notes: A $5 day-use fee is charged per vehicle. A park map is available at the visitor center for $1. For more information, contact Portola Redwoods State Park, 9000 Portola State Park Road, La Honda, CA 94020; (650) 948-9098 or (408) 429-2851.

Directions: From Interstate 280 in Palo Alto, take the Page Mill Road exit. Turn west and drive 8.9 miles to Highway 35 (Skyline Boulevard). Cross Highway 35, and continue on Alpine Road for 3.2 miles. Turn left on Portola Redwoods State Park Road and drive 3.3 miles to the main park entrance. (Note: Do not take the Alpine Road exit off Interstate 280; this section of Alpine Road dead-ends.)

145. POMPONIO FALLS

Memorial County Park
Off Highway 35 near La Honda

Access & Difficulty: Hike-in 0.25 mile RT/Easy
Elevation: Start at 450 feet; total gain 0 feet
Best Season: December to May

Pomponio Falls is a 25-foot-tall cataract that drops just outside of Sequoia Flat Campground in Memorial County Park. It's simple, easy to reach, and worth a look. The waterfall cascades into wide, river-like Pescadero Creek, in a dense forest of ferns and redwoods.

To see it, you can follow the trail by site #12 in Sequoia Flat Camp, but that only takes you to a footbridge above the falls. To reach its base and get the best view, look for the gated road just to the left of the camp entrance. Hike down the road for about 100 yards to a concrete apron where Pescadero Creek streams across the road. Don't cross the creek, just look to your right: there's Pomponio Falls. If Pescadero Creek isn't running too high, you can pick your way downstream on an old broken concrete trail. In about 30 yards, you're at the base of the waterfall. Five-finger, deer, maidenhair, and sword ferns grace its cliff. It drops onto the smooth rounded rocks along Pescadero's streambanks. To sum up: a nice waterfall, near a fine family campground, in a pretty county park.

Pomponio Falls

Trip notes: A $4 day-use fee is charged per vehicle. A park map is available for $1 at the ranger station. For more information, contact San Mateo County Parks,

455 County Center, Fourth Floor, Redwood City, CA 94063; (650) 363-4020 or Memorial Park Visitor Center at (650) 879-0212.

Directions: From Interstate 280 at Woodside, take Highway 84 west for 13 miles to La Honda. Turn left (southeast) on Pescadero Road and drive one mile, then bear right to stay on Pescadero Road. Continue 4.5 miles farther to the entrance to Memorial County Park on the left. Park at Sequoia Flat Campground or the amphitheater parking lot.

146. CASTLE ROCK FALLS

Castle Rock State Park
Off Highway 35 near Saratoga

Access & Difficulty: Hike-in 1.6 miles RT/Easy
Elevation: Start at 2,650 feet; total loss 200 feet
Best Season: December to May

It's hard to say which is better at Castle Rock State Park: the waterfall, the sandstone formations, or the views. It's a three-way tie for scenic beauty; the hikers who visit the park are the real winners.

To make the trip, set out on Saratoga Gap Trail from the far side of the parking lot, heading right. (The trail is signed as "To Campground.") The pleasure begins immediately as you hike downhill, walking along rocky, fern-lined Kings Creek through a mixed forest of Douglas fir, black oaks, and madrones. The stream begins as a trickle at the parking lot, then picks up flow and intensity as it heads downhill alongside the trail.

It's a mere eight-tenths of a mile to Castle Rock Falls. After 15 minutes of trail time, you find yourself standing on a large wooden viewing deck, perched on top of the waterfall. Although the fall is

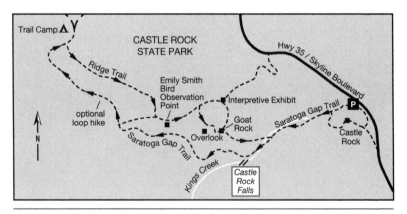

tricky to see because you're at its brink, you'll be torn between searching for the best view of the 50-foot water drop and gazing outward at the miles of uninhabited Santa Cruz Mountains' wildlands. It's hard to say whether the park built this deck for viewing the waterfall or the canyon vista. Both are incredible.

At Castle Rock Falls, Kings Creek leaps 50 feet off a vertical sandstone slab, then cascades onward, eventually joining the San Lorenzo River. Although you can't see the river from the overlook, you can gaze far off to its final destination in Monterey Bay and the Pacific Ocean.

From the observation platform, you can return to the parking lot or continue on a five-mile loop around the park, following Saratoga Gap Trail and then looping back on Ridge Trail. You'll pass by many beautiful sandstone displays, including the local rock climbers' favorite, Goat Rock. If you must turn back, be sure to take the short connector trail that leads a quarter-mile to Castle Rock, the park's namesake sandstone formation. It has many shallow caves that are fun to photograph or just climb around in.

Trip notes: A $5 day-use fee is charged per vehicle. A park map is available at the trailhead for 50 cents. For more information, contact Castle Rock State Park, 15000 Skyline Boulevard, Los Gatos, CA 95020; (408) 867-2952 or (831) 429-2851.

Directions: From Saratoga, take Highway 9 west to its junction with Skyline Boulevard (Highway 35). Turn left (south) on Skyline and drive 2.5 miles to the Castle Rock State Park parking area on the right. The trailhead is on the west side of the parking lot, opposite the entrance. Or, from Interstate 280 in Palo Alto, take Page Mill Road west for 8.9 miles to Skyline Boulevard. Turn left (south) on Skyline and drive 13 miles, past Highway 9, to the Castle Rock parking area on the right.

147. BERRY CREEK FALLS
Big Basin Redwoods State Park
Off Highway 1 near Davenport

Access & Difficulty: From Highway 1 Trailhead—Hike-in, Bike-in, or Backpack 12.0 miles RT/Moderate
Elevation: Start at 50 feet; total gain 600 feet
Best Season: December to May

Berry Creek Falls is easily the most photographed waterfall in the San Francisco Bay Area. The first time you lay eyes on it, you may

Berry Creek Falls

feel like you've seen it before. Its picture has graced calendars, greeting cards, and magazine covers, creating an eerie sense of *déjà vu* for many first-time visitors. But even being familiar with its image doesn't prepare you for the way the fall's beauty touches you. Berry Creek Falls can truly take your breath away.

You can reach the waterfall from two different trailheads, practically a world apart—one at the coast near Davenport, and the other at park headquarters in Big Basin Redwoods State Park near Felton. The route from the coast allows bicyclists to ride the first 5.2 miles of the trip along with hikers, but then everybody must walk the final three-quarters of a mile to the waterfall on foot. (The park has set up a bike rack at the spot where bikers must dismount, so don't forget to bring your lock.) The route from park headquarters is for hikers only, and is detailed in the following story on Silver Falls and Golden Falls Cascade. It's a nine-mile round-trip to Berry Creek Falls, but most people hike a mile further to Silver and Golden Falls as well.

Which route should you take? Both, if you get the chance. They're both first-class adventures in a beautiful, stream-fed redwood forest, leading to a destination that is as spectacular as any you'll find in the Bay Area. Why should you have to choose between them?

When you take the trip from Waddell Beach to Berry Creek Falls, a mountain bike can make the 12-mile trail length seem short and easy. Of course you could always hike it, but most people use two wheels at this trailhead. Even beginning bike riders and children can ride the 5.2 miles on Skyline to the Sea Trail, a wide and smooth ranch road, usually covering the distance in about an hour. Along the way, your head is continually turned by beautiful scenery, including flowing Waddell Creek, fields of ferns, alders, Douglas firs, and, of course, big redwoods.

The ranch road ends at a stream crossing. If you're riding, lock up your bike at the bike rack and set out on foot, still on Skyline to the Sea Trail but now paralleling Berry Creek. A mere 15 minutes of walking on meandering single-track brings you to the fork where Skyline to the Sea heads east (right) to park headquarters, and you head left for Berry Creek Falls, now only moments away.

A large viewing platform with a bench is placed in front of the fall's large pool, so you can sit for a long, long time staring at the 70-foot cataract, which pours over a near-vertical drop. Berry Creek Falls creates a strong wind in peak flow, blowing and twisting the five-finger ferns growing at its edges. On sunny days, you can watch as light filters through the redwoods and makes beautiful patterns on the streams of water.

Berry Creek maintains a decent flow even in summer, making this one of the few waterfalls in the Bay Area that you can see outside of the rainy season. Still, late winter and spring are usually best.

If you have energy to spare, you can hike up and over Berry Creek Falls, following Berry Creek Falls Trail for one more mile and a 400-foot gain to Silver Falls and Golden Falls Cascade. Then it's an easy downhill hike back to the bike rack, and a coasting ride (or hike) homeward. Backpackers have the option of staying at Sunset Trail Camp near Silver Falls, or at one of three trailside camps along the first three miles of Skyline to the Sea Trail. If you're planning an overnight stay, contact the park for advance reservations and a permit. Not surprisingly, on summer weekends Skyline to the Sea Trail is a popular route.

Trip notes: If you hike or bike from the Rancho del Oso entrance at Highway 1, there is no fee. If you hike from Big Basin park headquarters, a $6 day-use fee is charged per vehicle. A park map is available at the Rancho del Oso visitor center, and at other park kiosks, for $1. Backpackers spending the night at park trail camps must have reservations and a trail camping permit. For more information, contact Big Basin Redwoods State Park, 21600 Big Basin Way, Boulder Creek, CA 95006; (831) 338-8860 or (831) 429-2851.

Directions: From Santa Cruz, drive north on Highway 1 for 18 miles to Waddell Beach (on the west side of the highway) and Big Basin Redwoods State Park/Rancho del Oso (on the east side of the highway). Park in either of the parking areas, and start hiking or biking from the Rancho del Oso Trailhead. (Rancho del Oso is exactly 7.5 miles north of the town of Davenport on Highway 1.)

148. SILVER FALLS & GOLDEN FALLS CASCADE

Big Basin Redwoods State Park
Off Highway 9 near Felton

Access & Difficulty: From Park Headquarters Trailhead—Hike-in
or Backpack 10.4 miles RT/Moderate
Elevation: Start at 1,000 feet; total gain/loss 1,600 feet
Best Season: December to May

Even though Silver Falls and Golden Falls Cascade are less than
a mile from Berry Creek Falls, they seem like a world apart. For
starters, the two falls are vastly different in appearance from downstream Berry Creek Falls. Also, they're a little further away from park
trailheads, so they get fewer visitors. Furthermore, both of these falls
are best visited not on a day-hike, but on a spectacular overnight
backpacking trip to Sunset Trail Camp.

Although you can get to Silver Falls and Golden Falls Cascade
by taking the Skyline to the Sea Trail from the coast near Davenport
(see the preceding story on Berry Creek Falls), you'll be traveling on a
dirt ranch road for much of the trip, and sharing the trail with horses
and mountain bikers. The hikers-only route is on Skyline to the Sea
Trail from Big Basin State Park Headquarters near Felton, where you
can pick up a trail map and overnight permit if you're planning to
backpack. Starting from park headquarters, you get a long and pleasant stroll on single-track through stands of old-growth redwoods, and
a visit to all three waterfalls on Berry Creek—Berry Creek Falls, Silver
Falls, and Golden Falls Cascade.

The trail starts out good and stays that way, as it meanders
among the big trees. After climbing 250 feet up a ridge in the first
mile, the route drops down the other side to follow first Kelly Creek

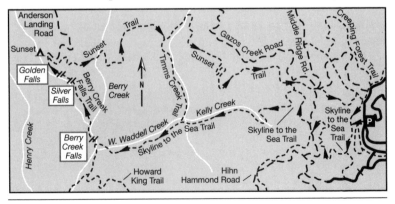

Silver Falls (left) and Golden Falls Cascade (right)

and then West Waddell Creek. The only thing you need to watch out for are the huge yellow banana slugs that slowly cross the trail and the colorful newts that always seem to be right under your boots.

At 4.3 miles, just before the Skyline to the Sea Trail meets up with the Berry Creek Falls Trail, you get your first glimpse of Berry Creek Falls. It's enough to make you quicken your pace. Turn right on Berry Creek Falls Trail, and in moments you'll be standing in front of the tremendous 70-foot cataract. Berry Creek Falls is truly awe inspiring as it tumbles over a fern-lined cliff surrounded by big redwoods. Many people go this far and no further.

But if you want more, you get more. Follow the trail up the left side of Berry Creek Falls, reaching some interesting overlooks above it, then climb for another 20 minutes until you're standing at the base of Silver Falls. The stream changes completely above Berry Creek Falls, becoming narrower, tamer, and more channeled. The streambed also changes, and nowhere is this more apparent than at Silver Falls. The 60-foot freefall spills over colorful sandstone and limestone rock, painted a bright tan, gold, and orange in contrast to Berry Creek Fall's dark cliff. There's no viewing platform holding you back from Silver Falls, so in summer, you can walk right up to its flow and stick your head in. Several redwoods have fallen around the fall's base, and they make good spots to sit down and take it all in.

Get accustomed to the orange glow of the rock underneath white water, because as you climb the wooden steps around the right side of Silver Falls, you'll see plenty more. The trail takes you to the top of the falls, where you walk on rocky sandstone steps. The park has put cables in place here, and in high water, it's wise to use them.

In moments, you're looking at the lower drop of Golden Falls Cascade, which is a long series of slippery orange sandstone, like a water slide for sea otters. There's one spot where the water funnels and plunges in a cascade, but most of Golden Falls Cascade is just a big orange slip-and-slide. The color of the rock is so striking, and the shape of the falls is so unusual, that you'll find it hard to believe you're still in Big Basin State Park, less than a mile from classic-looking, postcard-like Berry Creek Falls.

At Golden Falls Cascade, day-hikers may want to consider retracing their steps for a 10.4-mile round-trip. The other option is to hike back on a loop, following Berry Creek Falls Trail for another quarter-mile then turning right on Sunset Trail, making a 12-mile round-trip. Backpackers need continue only another quarter-mile to Sunset Trail Camp, where they can spend a peaceful night alongside Berry Creek, then visit the waterfalls all over again the following day. Now that's my idea of a good camping trip.

Trip notes: A $6 day-use fee is charged per vehicle. A park map is available at the entrance station for $1. Backpackers spending the night at Sunset Trail Camp must have reservations and a trail camping permit. For more information, contact Big Basin Redwoods State Park, 21600 Big Basin Way, Boulder Creek, CA 95006; (831) 338-8860 or (831) 429-2851.

Directions: From the junction of highways 35 and 9 at Saratoga Gap, drive six miles west on Highway 9 to Highway 236. Turn west on Highway 236 and drive 8.4 winding miles to Big Basin Redwoods State Park Headquarters. Park in the lot across from park headquarters, then begin hiking from the west side of the lot on a signed connector trail to the Skyline to the Sea Trail.

149. SEMPERVIRENS FALLS

Big Basin Redwoods State Park
Off Highway 9 near Felton

Access & Difficulty: Hike-in 3.6 miles RT/Easy
Elevation: Start at 1,000 feet; total gain 200 feet
Best Season: December to May

Berry Creek Falls, and its neighbors Silver Falls and Golden Falls Cascade, are indisputably the prime destinations of hikers in Big Basin Redwoods State Park. Why? They're incredible, that's why. But not everybody has the time or energy required to make the trip to see Berry Creek's three waterfalls. If you're in that category, you can go find another, easier-to-reach cataract at Big Basin State Park, arriving at its side in less than two miles of nearly level hiking.

That would mean a trip to Sempervirens Falls, named for the many *Sequoia sempervirens,* or coast redwood trees, that surround its creek. The Sequoia Trail leads to the waterfall in 1.8 miles from park headquarters, and from there you can just turn around and head back,

Sempervirens Falls

or make a pleasant five-mile loop by returning on Shadowbrook Trail.

The route is well-marked all the way. You don't even have to remember that you're on the Sequoia Trail, because all the trail signs read "Sempervirens Falls" on your way in and "Park Headquarters" on your way out. Without trail directions to worry about, you can spend your time admiring the huge redwoods along the way, which reach more than 300 feet tall in Big Basin. Mixed in with the big guys are Douglas fir, tanoak, and laurel trees, as well as thousands of ferns lining the forest floor. Springtime brings wild ginger, trillium, and azalea blooms, especially near the feeder streams to Sempervirens Creek. Although portions of the Sequoia Trail are routed near a park road, it gets little traffic and shouldn't disturb your hike.

To see the waterfall, you must leave the Sequoia Trail and cross the park road, a half-mile after passing Wastahi Camp. Sempervirens Falls is a 25-foot drop that can be as wide as four feet at the top, with two miniature cascades flowing into it from above. The waterfall is perfectly framed by standing and fallen redwood trees on either side of its drop, and a large, clear pool at its base. From your position on the wooden viewing deck above the fall, you look straight down into its six-foot-deep pool.

A nice bonus is that if you're staying in Big Basin State Park at Sky Meadow Group Camp, Wastahi Camp, or Huckleberry Camp, you can access the waterfall directly from your tent on either Sequoia or Shadowbrook trails, rather than hiking from park headquarters.

Trip notes: A $6 day-use fee is charged per vehicle. A park map is available at the entrance station for $1. For more information, contact Big Basin Redwoods State Park, 21600 Big Basin Way, Boulder Creek, CA 95006; (831) 338-8860 or (831) 429-2851.

Directions: From the junction of highways 35 and 9 at Saratoga Gap, drive six miles west on Highway 9 to Highway 236. Turn west on Highway 236 and drive 8.4 winding miles to Big Basin Redwoods State Park Headquarters. Park in the lot across from park headquarters, then begin hiking on the Sequoia Trail from the right side of the building.

150. MAPLE FALLS

**Forest of Nisene Marks State Park
Off Highway 1 near Aptos**

Access & Difficulty: Hike-in & Scramble 9.0 miles RT/Moderate
Elevation: Start at 300 feet; total gain 600 feet
Best Season: December to May

Part of what makes Maple Falls so good is that it's just not easy to get there. It's a four-mile hike from George's Picnic Area, the winter season trailhead in Forest of Nisene Marks State Park, followed by a half-mile stream scramble. By the time you complete the long walk through second- and third-growth redwoods, then squeeze your way upstream through a narrow canyon, you feel like you've earned a reward. Luckily, Maple Falls repays you for your effort.

In summer, you can hike from Porter Picnic Area, which cuts two miles off your round-trip. But Maple Falls should really be seen in winter or spring, when you can only drive as far as the trailhead at George's Picnic Area, where the road is gated off. To shorten your trip, bring along your mountain bikes and ride the first two miles on the dirt road to the Mill Pond Trail cutoff. Then lock up your bikes anywhere you can, and start walking on single-track.

Whether you're hiking or biking, everyone starts off on the Aptos Creek Fire Road, passing through the Mary Easton Picnic Area

and Porter Picnic Area and traveling under a thriving canopy of
second-growth redwoods. A
quarter-mile past Porter Picnic
Area, the Loma Prieta Grade Trail
takes off on the left, and hikers
can cut off Aptos Creek Road
there or continue with bikers to
the Mill Pond Trail cutoff, also
on the left. Mill Pond Trail soon
joins with the Loma Prieta Grade,
where you turn right and continue upcanyon.

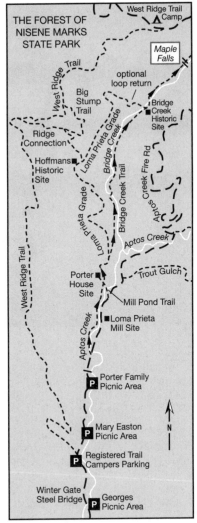

As soon as you're on single-
track, what was good becomes
gorgeous. Looking at the lush
green forest around you, it's hard
to imagine the park's past, when
the Loma Prieta Lumber Company teamed up with Southern
Pacific Railroad in 1881 to log
the winding canyon. They built
the Loma Prieta railroad grade
you're walking on, and worked
the winding canyon with trains,
oxen, skid roads, inclines, horses,
and as many men as they could
get. In 1922, when they put their
saws down, they had removed
140 million board feet of lumber.
No trees were left.

Now, 75 years later, the
forest has recovered, and it's prospering with young trees, both redwoods and Douglas firs. You hike among them, alongside Aptos
Creek and then Bridge Creek. At a fork signed for Bridge Creek
Historic Site, bear right for a shorter, more direct route to Maple
Falls. (Loma Prieta Grade makes a loop, with the left fork following
a longer, more meandering route to the historic site and the fall's
canyon. Save it for the return trip, if you still have the energy.)

At four miles out, you reach Bridge Creek Historic Site, the
scene of a former logging camp. Get ready for a half-mile stream

Maple Falls

scramble up Bridge Creek to Maple Falls, the most fun part of the trip. The trail quickly disappears and the canyon walls narrow. When Bridge Creek is running strong, you must walk in the creekbed and cross the stream numerous times, so wear your waterproof boots.

The canyon is decorated with millions of ferns and mini-waterfalls dropping among the rocks and crevices. Keep going until you reach the back of it, where the walls come together and 40-foot Maple Falls rushes over a rock wall, blocking any further progress upstream. Here, at last, is your reward.

Trip notes: A $3 day-use fee is charged per vehicle. A free park map is available at the entrance kiosk. For more information, contact Forest of Nisene Marks State Park, 201 Sunset Beach Road, Watsonville, CA 95076; (831) 763-7063 or (831) 429-2851.

Directions: From Santa Cruz, drive south on Highway 1 for six miles to the Aptos exit. Bear left at the exit, then turn right on Soquel Drive and drive a half-mile. Turn left on Aptos Creek Road. Stop at the entrance kiosk, then continue up the road and park at George's Picnic Area or Porter Picnic Area. (Porter Picnic Area is closer to the falls, cutting two miles off your round-trip, but it's closed in winter.)

151. APTOS CREEK FALLS (Monte Vista, Five Finger Falls)

Forest of Nisene Marks State Park
Off Highway 1 near Aptos

Access & Difficulty: Hike-in & Scramble 12.0 miles RT/Strenuous
or Bike-in 5.0 miles & Hike-in /Scramble 7.0 miles RT/Strenuous
Elevation: Start at 300 feet; total gain 700 feet
Best Season: December to May

If you've hiked to Maple Falls in Forest of Nisene Marks State Park and you're looking for an even bigger adventure, Aptos Creek Falls is your ticket. Plan on a whole day for the 12-mile trip, and make sure you're properly dressed for some serious stream scrambling, with waterproof boots and dry clothes to change into. Then fill up your day-pack with lunch and a water filter, and set out for a trip to a rarely visited waterfall.

As with Maple Falls, you can shorten your time and energy expended by riding your bike part of the way to Aptos Creek Falls. Starting from George's Picnic Area, you can bicycle 2.5 miles one-way along Aptos Creek Fire Road, then lock up and walk the Aptos Creek Trail for two miles until it ends, then scramble for the final 1.5 miles up Aptos Creek.

The trip starts out following the Aptos Creek Fire Road, passing Mary Easton and Porter picnic areas. The trail is wide, hard-packed, and smooth the whole way, with an almost imperceptible climb through the second-growth redwood canyon. Ride or hike on the road, passing several single-track cutoffs, for a total of 2.5 miles to the large Loma Prieta earthquake sign. The placard marks the area of the epicenter of the October 17, 1989 earthquake, which shook the San Francisco Bay Area and nearly destroyed Santa Cruz. Bicyclists lock up here (there's a bike rack), and all waterfall seekers must cross Aptos Creek and pick up the trail on the other side. This can require wading in the winter months, so be prepared to remove your shoes and socks.

Once on the far side of Aptos Creek, follow the single-track Aptos Creek Trail. You must cross the creek again, back to the north side, then in a half-mile you reach the exact center of the Loma Prieta quake. Another 1.5 miles of streamside travel brings you to an intersection with the Big Slide Trail, coming in from the left. The Aptos Creek Trail abruptly ends, but you can see a decent route leading up the side of the creek. Follow it, and in about a mile you'll have to cross the creek again, because the north side becomes too steep to negotiate.

Sooner or later you'll have to give up the route along the bank and just slog along in the streambed. The canyon walls narrow, and after 1.5 slow miles from where the Aptos Creek Trail ended, you'll reach the base of Aptos Creek Falls, tucked into the back of a fern-lined grotto. The fall looks surprisingly different than nearby Maple Falls; it's taller and wider with a large, deep pool at its base. It drops in a jagged cascade over the back of the canyon wall. In addition to the plentiful sword ferns around it, you'll see many delicate five-finger ferns, the source of the cascade's common nickname, Five Finger Falls. I think of those ferns as pointing the way to Nirvana.

Trip notes: A $3 day-use fee is charged per vehicle. A free park map is available at the entrance kiosk. For more information, contact Forest of Nisene Marks State Park, 201 Sunset Beach Road, Watsonville, CA 95076; (831) 763-7063 or (831) 429-2851.

Directions: From Santa Cruz, drive south on Highway 1 for six miles to the Aptos exit. Bear left at the exit, then turn right on Soquel Drive and drive a half-mile. Turn left on Aptos Creek Road. Stop at the entrance kiosk, then continue up the road and park at George's Picnic Area or Porter Picnic Area. (Porter Picnic Area is closer to the falls, cutting two miles off your round-trip, but it's closed in winter.)

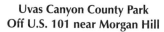

152. UVAS PARK FALLS—Black Rock, Uvas, Triple, Upper, & Basin

Uvas Canyon County Park
Off U.S. 101 near Morgan Hill

Access & Difficulty: Hike-in 1.0 to 3.5 miles RT/Easy
Elevation: Start at 1,100 feet; total gain 700 feet (3.5-mile RT)
Best Season: December to May

Uvas Canyon County Park is a little slice of waterfall heaven on the east side of the Santa Cruz Mountains. Although the drive to reach it is a long route from the freeway through grasslands and oaks, it ends in a surprising redwood forest at the park entrance. Suddenly, you've entered another world.

Uvas is a small park, offering camping and picnicking facilities and a short length of hiking trails in its 1,200 acres, but it's living proof that good things come in small packages. You can walk the one-mile Waterfall Loop Trail and see Black Rock Falls and several smaller cascades on Swanson Creek, or you can add on an eighth-mile side trip to see Basin Falls and Upper Falls. If you're in the mood to stretch your legs, you can make a larger loop out to Alec Canyon, then take the uphill trail a half-mile to Triple Falls on Alec Creek. Or, if you've truly got waterfall fever, you can take another short hike to Uvas Falls, behind park headquarters on Uvas Creek.

There are enough waterfalls to make your head spin. Start your trip at the Black Oak Group Picnic Area, by the gated dirt road. Head straight (not uphill on the road) to connect to the short loop trail in the canyon. Cross Swanson Creek on a footbridge, then bear right at

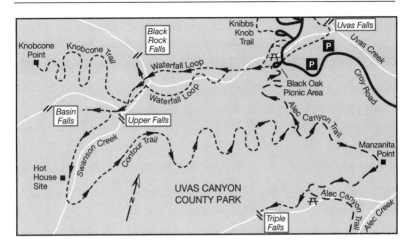

the fork, and head directly for Black Rock Falls, a quarter-mile away. You'll find it on your right, pouring 30 feet down a side canyon over —you guessed it—black rock.

Take a few pictures, then continue back in the canyon, heading for Basin Falls (20 feet tall, surrounded by moss-covered rocks and making a lovely S-curve at it carves its way downcanyon) and Upper Falls (15 feet tall with a fallen tree in front of it). Water pours down the canyon walls on all sides, creating a good deal of noise. The canyon is filled with oaks, laurels, and Douglas firs, all thriving in the wet environment around Swanson Creek.

At Upper Falls, it's decision time: Either head back and take the other side of the Waterfall Loop Trail for a short and flat trip, or continue up Swanson Creek and follow the winding Contour Trail to Alec Canyon and Triple Falls. The latter adds 2.5 miles and a good hill climb to your mileage. If you're heading for Triple, follow Contour Trail until it meets up with Alec Canyon Fire Road, then turn right and hike for a half-mile, passing Manzanita Point, where you get far-reaching views on clear days. Then turn right again on the spur trail to Triple Falls. True to its name, Triple Falls is a series of three cascades, totalling 40 feet in height. You can climb off-trail and sit right alongside the cascading fall, and maybe munch on a sandwich and think about how great it is to be alive. Then make a short return trip by following the fire road back to Black Oak Picnic Area, a steep three-quarter mile descent.

If after all this, you're still in a waterfall mood, walk down to the restrooms on the west side of the ranger station, near the family campground, and take the steep trail that leads down to Uvas Creek, where Uvas Falls drops in the back of a canyon.

So which waterfall at Uvas Park is the best? At one time, Uvas Falls was considered the largest and prettiest waterfall in the park, but now it rarely gets visited because a landslide filled it in, spoiling its beauty. Uvas rangers say that if you're only going to see one cataract in the park, see Upper Falls, which is the widest of the bunch. My favorite was Basin Falls. My hiking partner's favorite was Triple Falls. Your favorite? Better go see them all and decide.

Trip notes: A $4 day-use fee is charged per vehicle. Free maps are available at the park visitor center. For more information, contact Uvas Canyon County Park, 8515 Croy Road, Morgan Hill, CA 95037; (408) 779-9232 or (408) 358-3741.

Directions: From U.S. 101 heading south in Morgan Hill, take the Bernal Road exit. At the stoplight, turn right, then right again, to access Monterey Highway. Turn left (south) on Monterey Highway. Turn right on Bailey Avenue and drive 2.8 miles to McKean Road. Turn left on McKean Road and drive six miles (McKean Road becomes Uvas Road). Turn right on Croy Road and drive 4.5 miles to the park (continue past Sveadal, a private camp/resort). Park near park headquarters or in one of the picnic area parking lots. The trail is the gated dirt road at Black Oak Picnic Area.

MORE WATERFALLS

in San Francisco Bay Area

•Cascade Falls, Mill Valley. It's a pretty little 20-foot fall, accessible via an easy 100-foot walk off Cascade Drive, near Cascade's junction with Throckmorton Avenue. For more information, phone (415) 388-9700.

•Big Carson Creek Falls, Marin Municipal Water District. Requires a 14-mile round-trip on Pine Mountain Road, best done on a bike. For more information, phone Sky Oaks Ranger Station at (415) 945-1181.

•Golden Gate Park Falls. More wedding photographs have been taken in front of these falls than probably anywhere else in San Francisco. So what if they're man-made? They flow even in summer. For more information, phone (415) 831-2700.

Monterey &
Central Coast

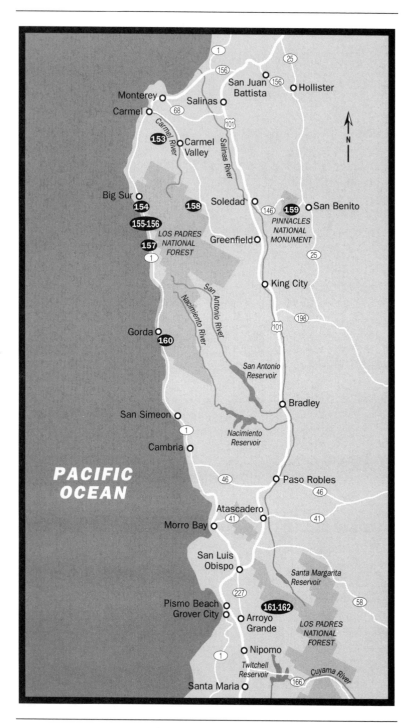

153. GARLAND RANCH FALLS

Garland Ranch Regional Park
Off Highway 1 in Carmel Valley

Access & Difficulty: Hike-in 1.6 miles RT/Easy
Elevation: Start at 200 feet; total gain 200 feet
Best Season: December to May

Garland Ranch Regional Park is the perfect place to take your kids to see a waterfall or to walk with a friend on a clear winter day in Carmel. The park has an excellent nature center that is dedicated to educating budding naturalists, and the riverside grasslands support a fine display of wildflowers. The park's waterfall is ephemeral, however, so you need to time your trip for just after a rain.

From the parking area alongside Carmel Valley Road, cross the Carmel River on either of two bridges and walk to the visitor center. After taking a look inside at some of their excellent pamphlets on park plants and animals, walk to the left on the Lupine Loop, a wide hiking and equestrian trail. In addition to the blooming lupine, you'll see many bunches of purple statice, monkeyflower, and paintbrush growing in the flood plain along the river.

In a half-mile, leave the Lupine Loop and continue straight on the Waterfall Trail. The trail climbs a bit as it enters an oak and laurel forest, an abrupt vegetation change from the grasslands in the river valley. The path changes to single-track, and horses aren't allowed on this short section of trail. In 10 minutes you'll reach Garland Ranch Falls. Watch for a footbridge just before the falls; if the stream underneath it is running full, you're in luck. Garland Ranch Falls pours (or cascades, or trickles, depending on when you visit) over a 70-foot-high sandstone cliff.

If you want a bit of a workout, you can continue uphill on the Waterfall Trail, climbing for another three-quarters of a mile to its end at a high meadow with views in all directions. You can return by taking the Mesa Trail to the Lupine Loop, then walk either side of the loop back to the nature center.

Trip notes: There is no fee. Free park maps are available at the visitor center. For more information, contact Garland Ranch Regional Park, Monterey Peninsula Park District, 700 West Carmel Valley Road, Carmel Valley, CA 93924; (831) 659-6063 or (831) 659-4488.

Directions: From Highway 1 at Carmel, turn left (east) on Carmel Valley Road. Drive 8.6 miles on Carmel Valley Road to the Garland Ranch parking area on the right side of the road. Walk across the river bridge to get to the visitor center and the trailhead for the Lupine Loop.

154. PFEIFFER FALLS

Pfeiffer Big Sur State Park
Off Highway 1 near Big Sur

Access & Difficulty: Hike-in 0.8 mile RT/Easy
Elevation: Start at 350 feet; total gain 250 feet
Best Season: December to June

The key factor to remember when you visit Pfeiffer Falls is that Pfeiffer Big Sur State Park is a busy place, especially on weekends. Unlike the other nearby state parks on the Big Sur Coast, Pfeiffer Big Sur has all the amenities—campground, lodge, restaurant, gift shop—so it gets more visitors. It's critical to time your trip carefully so you can see pretty Pfeiffer Falls without getting stuck in a long line of cars at the entrance kiosk.

Pfeiffer Falls

Your best bet is to visit during the week or on a rainy day, but you can always sneak in early in the morning, even on weekends. I visited one Saturday morning in June when the park campground and lodge were full to the brim, but most park visitors were still snug in their beds and sleeping bags. In the early dawn, I walked to Pfeiffer Falls in solitude. But on my return trip an hour or so later, I passed more than a dozen hikers on the trail.

The Pfeiffer Falls Trail leads from the north side of the nature center. It's well-signed and easy to follow. You'll pass trail junctions for Valley View and Oak Grove trails, but simply keep heading straight, following Pfeiffer Redwood Creek. The trail crosses the creek four times on wooden footbridges, making a fair little climb in its short distance. Stairsteps carry you up the steepest parts. The entire walk is shaded by giant redwoods. This is one of the oldest groves in Big Sur.

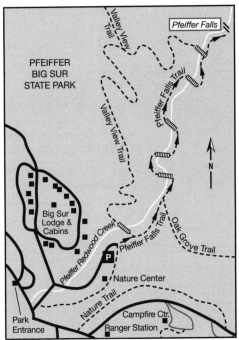

The trail ends at a viewing platform in front of Pfeiffer Falls, where Pfeiffer Redwood Creek drops 60 feet over a dark granite face. Most often, the fall flows in two skinny cascades, but after a big rain, the entire rock face can be covered with a wide sheet of white water. If you look carefully, you can spot another cascade above the main drop, set further back in the canyon. Very large ferns grow on the plateau between the two drops.

Pfeiffer Falls' pool is shallow and wide, largely due to a man-made check dam that shores it up. Five-finger and maidenhair ferns grow on the granite around the fall, giving the damp grotto a tropical feeling. The fall can be difficult to photograph because its surroundings are so dark in contrast to the white cascade.

After visiting Pfeiffer Falls, you have many options for further hiking, including walking the Valley View Trail from the junction near the waterfall's base. It leads uphill through chaparral and oaks to an expansive overlook of Point Sur and the Big Sur Valley, then it returns to the trailhead by the nature center, where you began.

Trip notes: A $7 state park day-use fee is charged. A park map is available at the entrance kiosk for $1. For more information, contact Pfeiffer Big Sur State Park, Big Sur, CA 93920; (831) 667-0158, (831) 667-2315, or (831) 649-2836.

Directions: From Carmel, drive 26 miles south on Highway 1 to Pfeiffer Big Sur State Park, on the east side of the highway. (It's two miles south of Big Sur.) Drive through the entrance kiosk, turn left and pass the lodge, then turn right, following the signs to Pfeiffer Falls Trailhead and Nature Center. Park just beyond the nature center. The trail is on the left side of the parking lot, signed as Oak Grove Trail, Valley View Trail, Pfeiffer Falls Trail.

---

155. McWAY FALLS

Julia Pfeiffer Burns State Park
Off Highway 1 near Big Sur

Access & Difficulty: Hike-in or Wheelchair 0.5 mile RT/Easy
Elevation: Start at 200 feet; total gain 0 feet
Best Season: December to June, but good year-round

Next to Yosemite Fall and Bridalveil Fall, McWay Falls is probably the waterfall that appears most often on family snapshots of California vacations. Although most people can't remember its name, no one can forget the image of the 80-foot waterfall leaping off a rugged ocean bluff and pouring gracefully into the Pacific.

Consider the setting. First, we're on the Big Sur coast, one of the most beautiful stretches of sand, sea, and sky in the West. Here, McWay Creek intersects the beach, tumbling year-round through a pristine canyon of redwoods and over tall granite cliffs. Long, rolling ocean waves dissolve along the shoreline and crash against rock out-

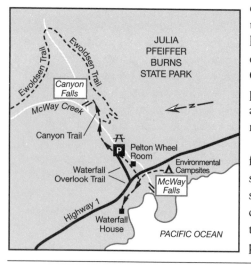

crops protruding from the sea. Seals and sea lions bask on the sands of McWay Cove, and California gray whales parade past on their annual winter and spring migrations.

The viewing point for the waterfall is on a short, flat, paved trail, so it's suitable for wheelchairs. The trail leaves the parking area and parallels the park access

McWay Falls

road as it heads west, then it enters a pedestrian tunnel that leads underneath the highway. Once on the coast, the path carves a few curves around the steep and craggy cliffs, and wooden railings keep you from venturing too near the edge.

Suddenly you see the waterfall, streaming down the cliff to your left, pouring to the sand like milk from a pitcher. Dropping into a perfect little pocket beach, McWay Falls is just like all those pictures you've seen, only better. Although its cliff is sheered off at an unforgiving right angle, McWay Falls leaps gracefully over the abrupt pitch.

A bench is situated along the trail for relaxing while you view the fall, but actually the best overlook is just 20 feet further along the paved trail, where you get a better perspective. The path continues for another 50 yards, out of sight of the waterfall, to the ruins of the stone Waterfall House, which was the home of Lathrop and Helen Hooper Brown in the 1940s. In 1962, Helen Hooper Brown gave this land to the state of California for a park, with the stipulation that it be named after her friend Julia Pfeiffer Burns, a Big Sur pioneer and cattle ranch owner.

If the last time you visited McWay Falls was 20 years ago, you might be surprised that the waterfall isn't exactly as you remember. The cataract used to drop directly into the sea, but a major landslide in the winter of 1983 deposited so much earth and sand in McWay Cove that the waterfall now lands on the beach. Unfortunately, there's no access to the cove's strip of sand, due to the constantly eroding coastal bluffs.

A little known fact about McWay Falls is that a backpacking camp is located just south of it. Although you can't see the falls from the primitive camp, you do get a spectacular view of the Big Sur coast. Contact the park for reservations; the camp has only two sites.

Trip notes: A $6 state park day-use fee is charged. A park map is available at the entrance kiosk for $1. For more information, contact Julia Pfeiffer Burns State Park, c/o Pfeiffer Big Sur State Park, Big Sur, CA 93920; (831) 667-0158, (831) 667-2315, or (831) 649-2836.

Directions: From Carmel, drive 37 miles south on Highway 1 to Julia Pfeiffer Burns State Park, on the east side of the highway. (It's 13 miles south of Big Sur.) Drive through the entrance kiosk, then park near the restrooms. The Waterfall Overlook Trail starts across the pavement from the restrooms, on a series of wooden stairs. Wheelchair users can ride over a bridge to bypass the stairs.

156. CANYON FALLS

Julia Pfeiffer Burns State Park
Off Highway 1 near Big Sur

Access & Difficulty: Hike-in 0.75 mile RT/Easy
Elevation: Start at 200 feet; total gain 200 feet
Best Season: December to June

After you've visited the famous McWay Falls at Julia Pfeiffer Burns State Park, don't be in a rush to drive down Highway 1 in search of your next waterfall. The state park harbors another cataract, far less renowned than McWay Falls on the coast. Your next trip need only be as far as the inland side of the parking lot, to the trailhead for the Canyon and Ewoldsen trails.

If you've just walked the paved Waterfall Overlook Trail along the wide-open, windswept coast, it's something like culture shock to head into the dense, dark redwood forest along the Ewoldsen Trail. Your eyes have to adjust to the filtered light and the silent woods, a major contrast to the bright horizon and the crashing of the sea.

Immediately you're taken by the beauty of fast-running McWay Creek, gurgling past tall redwoods and leafy, clover-like sorrel. After passing through a picnic area, cross the creek and follow the Ewoldsen

Trail for less than a quarter-mile until you reach the turnoff for Canyon Trail. Bear left, and a few more minutes of streamside rambling brings you to the back of the canyon, where a 30-foot waterfall drops in a hurried cascade. It carves two tiers, makes a smooth turn and drop, then forms another 10-foot cascade. You can sit at a bench at Canyon Trail's end, a few feet from the foot of the falls, and marvel at the incredible setting of ferns, huge trees, rocks, and cascading, musical white water.

Canyon Falls

You'll have a chance of privacy at Canyon Falls because most park visitors are at the coast marveling at the other waterfall on McWay Creek, and most day-hikers who make their way up the Ewoldsen Trail don't realize what lies at the end of the Canyon Trail fork. Ewoldsen is considered by many to be the finest day-hiking trail in Big Sur, and if you have the time, you should hike some or all of it. The trail makes a 4.3-mile loop, climbing 1,600 feet in the process. In the rainy season, you'll find many small cascades along its path.

Trip notes: A $6 state park day-use fee is charged. A park map is available at the entrance kiosk for $1. For more information, contact Julia Pfeiffer Burns State Park, c/o Pfeiffer Big Sur State Park, Big Sur, CA 93920; (831) 667-0158, (831) 667-2315, or (831) 649-2836.

Directions: From Carmel, drive 37 miles south on Highway 1 to Julia Pfeiffer Burns State Park, on the east side of the highway. (It's 13 miles south of Big Sur.) Drive through the entrance kiosk, then turn left, following the signs for the Canyon Trail and picnic area. Park in the parking lot by the restrooms. The trail starts from the inland side of the parking lot, signed as Canyon Trail/Picnic Area/Ewoldsen Trail.

157. LIMEKILN FALLS

Limekiln State Park
Off Highway 1 near Big Sur

Access & Difficulty: Hike-in & Scramble 1.0 mile RT/Moderate
Elevation: Start at 250 feet; total gain 200 feet
Best Season: December to June

Don't tell everybody, but the waterfall at Limekiln State Park is more spectacular than Pfeiffer Falls at Pfeiffer Big Sur State Park. Heck, Limekiln's fall is so good, it even gives ocean-bound McWay Falls at Julia Pfeiffer Burns State Park a run for the money.

But while getting to Pfeiffer Falls or McWay Falls is an easy walk in the park, so to speak, getting to Limekiln Falls requires some rock hopping. You might get your feet wet. You have to tango with the stream gods, tap-dance over some slippery boulders, and take your chances on an intimate watery encounter.

Limekiln Falls

Of course, if you mention Limekiln State Park to most Big Sur visitors, they'll stare at you with blank faces. That's because Limekiln is a relatively new state park, and so far, it hasn't been developed much. It has a small and pleasant drive-in campground, one hiking trail, and that's about it. May it always stay that way. Limekiln State Park is just fine as is.

The hiking trail leads a half mile to the park's namesake lime kilns, which were used to manufacture limestone bricks and cement in the 1880s. This gives you a clue as to what the waterfall is going to look like. Rather than dropping over a granite or basalt cliff, it fans out over a limestone face. The waterfall trail is undeveloped, but well used, and it branches off the lime kiln trail.

To make the trip, start hiking from the end of the campground on the signed path through the redwoods. The route appears similar to other coastal trails here in Big Sur, as it parallels a stream that's surrounded by big trees, ferns, rocks, and sorrel. Cross a bridge over Limekiln Creek immediately past the campground, then in another quarter-mile, cross a second bridge.

Immediately past the second bridge is the unsigned spur trail to the falls. It's on the right, across the stream, and to reach it you must boulder-hop. Once that's accomplished, you're heading up the canyon toward Limekiln Falls. Plan on a stream scramble of about 15 minutes, covering about a quarter mile. You'll need to cross and recross the creek several times, and in winter and spring when it's flow is strong you should be prepared to get wet.

Your scramble ends at the base of the waterfall, where Limekiln Falls pours 100 feet down a nearly vertical sheet of limestone. When I visited in May, it fanned out to 25 feet wide at the bottom. The light is surprisingly bright by the waterfall, in contrast to the dark and shady forest you've been traveling in. The rock cliff prevents any trees from growing near the falls and blocking out the sun.

Limekiln is the northernmost limestone fall that I discovered in my waterfall travels, although there are plenty of them to the south: Rose Valley Falls in Ojai, Nojoqui Falls near San Luis Obispo, and several of the waterfalls in the Santa Monica Mountains.

After being appropriately awed by the falls, head back to the main trail and turn right to visit the limekilns. You'll cross one more footbridge, then see four kilns on your right, looking like giant smokestacks with mossy, brick bottoms. After the kilns, a sign marks the end of the trail, although an unmaintained route continues up the creek.

Trip notes: A $7 state park day-use fee is charged. A park map is available at the entrance kiosk for 50 cents. For more information, contact Limekiln State Park, c/o Pfeiffer Big Sur State Park, Big Sur, CA 93920; (831) 667-2315, (831) 667-2403, or (831) 649-2836.

Directions: From Carmel, drive 52 miles south on Highway 1 to Limekiln State Park, on the east side of the highway. (It's 2.5 miles south of Lucia, and 14.8 miles south of Julia Pfeiffer Burns State Park.) The trailhead is at the far side of the inland campground.

158. PINE FALLS

Ventana Wilderness
Off Highway 1 near Carmel Valley

Access & Difficulty: Hike-in or Backpack 10.6 miles RT/Moderate
Elevation: Start at 4,260 feet; total loss 1,500 feet
Best Season: December to June

Lots of people want to explore the Ventana Wilderness, but they don't know where to start. Pine Falls on the Carmel River is the perfect place. You can make a long day trip to Pine Falls, or take it easy and go for a one-night backpacking trip, either out-and-back for 10.6 miles or on a loop of 13 miles. Either way, you're heading for a great journey into the rugged Ventana, one of the largest Forest Service wilderness areas in California.

Your route is on the Pine Ridge Trail, and although its western end from Highway 1 is one of the most well-used paths in the wilderness, up here things are a little more peaceful. That's especially true in winter or spring, which are the best seasons to see the waterfall. Keep in mind that the trailhead access roads can be impassable after heavy rain, however, so call to check on road conditions before setting out.

The Pine Ridge Trail leaves the parking area just south of the campground, at the signed trailhead on the west side of the road. It starts with a half-mile climb through a tanoak forest, reaches a ridge, then follows an up-and-down course, lateraling along the grassy hillsides with wide-open views of the wilderness. You'll see evidence of the 1977 Marble Cone Fire in the tall blackened trees that stand among the regenerated chaparral.

The trail begins to drop more steeply, till at 3.5 miles you reach a trail junction at Church Creek Divide. You have three choices: Pine Ridge Trail continues straight, eventually heading down to the redwoods at Big Sur; the Church Creek Trail heads left (south); and the Carmel River Trail heads right (north). Turn right on the Carmel River Trail, which descends gently as it meets the meager headwaters of the Carmel River. Your surroundings get more beautiful as you go: The stream picks up speed and flow, and the forest becomes more dense with firs and ponderosa pines in this two-mile stretch.

At 5.3 miles from the trailhead, you reach Pine Valley Camp, an established wilderness camp in lush Pine Valley, a spacious high meadow lined with ferns, ponderosa pines, and rocky sandstone formations. The camp is surprisingly large, with many campfire rings,

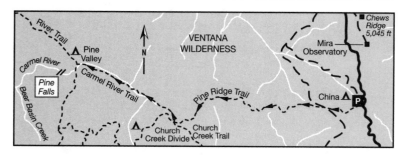

but it's often unused in wintertime, especially during the week. Water is dependable from a spring and the nearby Carmel River, which by this point on the trail is truly a river, no longer a stream.

To see Pine Falls, follow the well-worn route downstream for a little over a half-mile. The waterfall has an inviting pool below its drop, but getting to it is tricky, especially when the river is flowing hard. A route leads from the fall's brink, but is nearly vertical and often extremely muddy. Proceed slowly. If you can make it to the fall's base, this is the best spot for taking photographs.

From the waterfall and camp, you have the option of retracing your steps for a 10.6-mile round-trip or taking the trail from the upper end of the camp, which climbs steeply to the south and then southeast to meet up with the Pine Ridge Trail. From this junction, turn left on Pine Ridge Trail and hike back to Church Creek Divide, making an excellent 13-mile loop trip.

The Ventana Wilderness is rife with waterfalls, both named and unnamed. If the trip to Pine Falls whets your appetite, try a longer hike to the waterfalls on Pick Creek, Ventana Mesa Creek, or the Little Sur River. Contact the Monterey Ranger District for details.

Trip notes: There is no fee. A free wilderness permit is required for overnight stays; they are available at the district office in King City. For a map of the Ventana Wilderness or Los Padres National Forest, send $4 to USDA-Forest Service, 1323 Club Drive, Vallejo, CA 94592. For more information, contact Los Padres National Forest, Monterey Ranger District, 406 South Mildred Avenue, King City, CA 93930; (831) 385-5434.

Directions: From Greenfield on U.S. 101, take the G-16/Monterey County Road exit and drive west for 29 miles. Turn south on Tassajara Road and drive 1.3 miles to Cachagua Road. Turn left and drive nine miles to the trailhead, located just past the turnoff for China Campground. (The road turns to dirt; high-clearance vehicles are recommended. The county sometimes closes the road during bad weather; phone the Monterey Ranger District before traveling.)

159. BEAR GULCH & CONDOR GULCH FALLS

**Pinnacles National Monument
Off Highway 25 near King City**

Access & Difficulty: Hike-in 3.0 miles RT/Easy
Elevation: Start at 1,260 feet; total gain 500 feet
Best Season: December to April

Pinnacles National Monument is not known as a watery place. Much of the year, it's darn hot here and dry as a bone. But when the rains come in winter, a magical change occurs amid the spires, crags, and caves of the rocky park: The creeks in Bear and Condor gulches start to run, creating short-lived but beautiful waterfalls.

Pinnacles is a hiker's park. You can tell right away because there are no roads going through the place, although you can hike from one side to the other. It's a perfect setup, ideal for people who like their national parks to seem, well, natural. But it also means that if you don't have the time or energy to hike the four miles one-way across the park, you better make sure you drive to the proper park entrance, east or west. To see the waterfalls in Bear and Condor gulches, you want the east entrance to the Pinnacles, by the park visitor center at Bear Gulch.

Start hiking right by the visitor center, heading downstream along Bear Gulch. After passing some park residences, cross the stream and walk parallel to the park access road. It's only a quarter-mile from the visitor center parking lot to the waterfall. The path is nearly flat until you reach the falls, then it steepens as you drop to its jumbled, bouldery base.

Although the trail doesn't go right beside the 25-foot waterfall, it offers some good views of it and of the many cascades along the stream. The water snakes around big volcanic boulders, winds circuitously through the canyon bottom, and even pours through arches formed by rocks.

After you get a good look at Bear Gulch Falls, retrace your steps to the visitor center, and pick up the trail across the road, signed as the Condor Gulch Trail to the High Peaks Trail and Overlook. It's a good 30-minute climb up the hill to the overlook, which gives you some aerobic exercise on a nice, smooth trail with good switchbacks. You can hear the cascades as you climb, because the stream parallels the trail, but you can't always see the water. The scent of wild sage and rosemary is encitingly aromatic, and your eyes will be drawn to the fascinating colorful lichen growing on the equally colorful rocks. That is until you start getting views of the high pinnacles and of the cascades flowing down the hillside, which will surely divert your attention.

At the overlook, which is simply a metal railing on a ledge, you're standing on a huge, round boulder. In the wet season, the headwaters of Condor Gulch's creek flow over the top of it. Its drop results in a narrow falls that pours a graceful 100 feet.

There are myriad hiking options at Pinnacles, especially in winter and spring when the weather is good and the wild-

Bear Gulch Falls

flowers are in bloom. If this is your first visit to the park's east side, be sure to hike the Moses Spring Trail to (and inside) Bear Gulch Caves. Children and adults equally adore this trip. Just remember: Bring a flashlight for the caves, preferably one for each person.

Trip notes: There is a $5 entrance fee at Pinnacles National Monument, good for seven days. Park maps are available for free at the entrance stations. For more information, contact Pinnacles National Monument, 5000 Highway 146, Paicines, CA 95043; (831) 389-4485.

Directions: Note—No roads traverse Pinnacles National Monument. To access the eastern trailheads, you enter from Highway 25 and head west. To access the western trailheads, you enter from U.S. 101 and head east.

From the south: From King City on U.S. 101, take the First Street exit and head east. First Street turns into Highway G13/Bitterwater Road. Follow it for 15 miles to Highway 25, where you turn left (north). Follow Highway 25 for 14 miles to Highway 146. Turn left on Highway 146, and follow it for 4.8 miles to the park entrance and visitor center. The trailhead is at the visitor center.

From the north: From Gilroy, drive south on U.S. 101 to the Highway 25/Hollister exit. Take Highway 25 south to Hollister, then continue 32 miles south on Highway 25 to Highway 146, where you turn right (west). From Highway 146, follow the directions above.

160. SALMON CREEK FALLS

Los Padres National Forest
Off Highway 1 near Gorda

Access & Difficulty: Hike-in & Scramble 1.0 mile RT/Moderate
Elevation: Start at 270 feet; total loss 50 feet
Best Season: December to June

What's the best waterfall on the Big Sur Coast? It's impossible to choose. How about a three-way tie for McWay Falls, Limekiln Falls, and Salmon Creek Falls? They're about as different from each other as any waterfalls could be, but all of them have the capacity to make you rejoice in your existence on this planet. That good? Yes, they're that good.

Salmon Creek Falls is the only one of the three that's located on national forest land, and it is visible from the highway. Sort of. Driving north on Highway 1 from San Simeon, you go right past Salmon Creek Falls without noticing; it's over your right shoulder and set back in the canyon. But heading south on Highway 1 from Gorda, you can't miss the sudden splash of white along the hillside. More than a few travelers have slammed on the brakes and pulled off the highway to get a better look.

Salmon Creek Falls

From the large pullouts along the road, it's a short walk to reach Salmon Creek Falls, following the Salmon Creek Trail partway. The trick is to know where to exit the trail and scramble up the creek, because the trail leads high above the fall, without going to its base.

Start from the south end of the guardrail at the

signed trailhead. Immediately you'll see several cutoffs on the left; don't take the first one, which is right by an old wooden gate. If you do, you'll have an unnecessarily long and difficult upstream scramble. (Guess how I know?) Instead, walk up the Salmon Creek Trail for about five minutes, and when you hear the falls loud and clear, take one of the left cutoffs, and head down to the stream. You can climb over the huge boulders at the fall's base to get up high and obtain a good vantage point.

Salmon Creek is a "wow" waterfall, the kind that when you stare at it, not much else comes to mind but the word "wow," so you say it over and over. The fall drops about 120 feet in a huge crash of water, with three big chutes plummeting down to join at the bottom. A gigantic boulder is balanced at the top, separating the streams.

I visited the waterfall in May and was soundly impressed, but when I told a forest service ranger about it the next day, he sniffed, "Well, it doesn't have as much water as it did a few weeks ago." Wow.

Trip notes: There is no fee. For a map of Los Padres National Forest, send $4 to USDA-Forest Service, 1323 Club Drive, Vallejo, CA 94592. For more information, contact Los Padres National Forest, Monterey Ranger District, 406 South Mildred Avenue, King City, CA 93930; (831) 385-5434.

Directions: From Big Sur, drive 33 miles south on Highway 1 to Gorda, then continue 7.6 miles south of Gorda to the trailhead for the Salmon Creek Trail on the east side of the highway, at a hairpin turn. (The trailhead is 70 miles south of Carmel on Highway 1.) Park in the large parking pullout along the road. You can see the waterfall from the pullout. Salmon Creek Trail leads from the south end of the guardrail.

161. BIG FALLS

Santa Lucia Wilderness
Off U.S. 101 near Arroyo Grande

Access & Difficulty: Hike-in 3.0 miles RT/Moderate
Elevation: Start at 800 feet; total gain 350 feet
Best Season: December to June

As remarkable as Big Falls Canyon is, the thing that people remember most about it is the drive. That's because the trailhead is 17 miles from the freeway on pavement, the last several miles of which are quite narrow and have frequent rockslides. That's the easy part. Then, it's another 3.5 miles on a dirt road that gets crossed by

Lopez Creek dozens of times, and I don't mean via bridges or culverts. The stream crosses the road, and your vehicle must cross the stream. Along one stretch, the stream simply becomes the road, and you just keep driving.

On my first trip here in June, I drove my low-clearance, two-wheel-drive Toyota, but I was foiled at the second stream crossing, which was more than a foot deep. I knew there were at least a dozen more crossings to negotiate, so my chances of making it weren't good. Two weeks later I showed up with a high-clearance truck and made it through easily, although the stream level hadn't dropped much. A Big Falls Canyon hiker told me he came here once in wintertime, but the only way into the canyon during the wettest weather is on horseback. He and his friends spent the entire trip trying to convince the horses not to lay down in the stream.

Once you get to the trailhead, the rest is easy. The trail is well built and smooth, and it sees plenty of use. It winds through a dense wooded canyon, crossing and recrossing Big Falls Creek. Many people just hike a half-mile in, to the first waterfall in the canyon, which they assume is Big Falls. It's really only Medium Falls (don't quote me—I made this up); the real Big Falls is another mile farther down the trail. Medium Falls is a 30-foot limestone fall that is completely covered with greenery when the stream flow drops. It has many small trout swimming in its pool. There's another, much deeper rock pool above the fall's lip, with a 20-foot cascade flowing into it. It's called "The Slide." Only the very brave or very foolish ride the cascading chute, and even they wear something thick on their backsides.

Going down "The Slide" in Big Falls Canyon

The trail continues above this fall to Big Falls, located off a short left spur. It's an excellent one-mile walk, making easy switchbacks uphill, heading through some open chaparral as you climb a ridge. We passed a huge pile of quartz and many bunches of monkeyflower growing in the crevices between the rocks. The canyon has lovely wildflowers in spring but also a good crop of poison oak, so use caution.

Medium Falls is just right for people who like water play, and Big Falls is for true waterfall aficionados. Big Falls is much bigger, an easy 80 feet tall,

"Medium Falls" in Big Falls Canyon

but it can have less water than the downstream falls because it doesn't have the benefit of the lower feeder streams. If you want to see Big Falls roar, go see it early in the year or just after a rain.

Trip notes: There is no fee. For a map of Los Padres National Forest, send $4 to USDA-Forest Service, 1323 Club Drive, Vallejo, CA 94592. For more information, contact Los Padres National Forest, Santa Lucia Ranger District, 1616 North Carlotti Drive, Santa Maria, CA 93454; (805) 925-9538.

Directions: From San Luis Obispo, drive 15 miles south on U.S. 101 to Arroyo Grande and the Highway 227/Lopez Lake exit. Head east on Highway 227, then Lopez Drive, following the signs toward Lopez Lake for 10.3 miles. Turn right on Hi Mountain Road (before Lopez Lake's entrance station). Drive eight-tenths of a mile, then turn left on Upper Lopez Canyon Road. Drive 6.3 miles, passing a Boy Scout Camp, then turn right. In one-tenth mile, the pavement ends, and you pass a Christian camp. Continue for 3.5 miles on the dirt road, crossing the stream dozens of times, to the trailhead for Big Falls. (It's not always marked, so set your odometer and look for a small waterfall on the left side of the road. The trail is directly across the road on the right.) Four-wheel drive or high-clearance is necessary if the road is wet.

162. LITTLE FALLS

Santa Lucia Wilderness
Off U.S. 101 near Arroyo Grande

Access & Difficulty: Hike-in 1.0 mile RT/Easy
Elevation: Start at 650 feet; total gain 50 feet
Best Season: December to June

Little Falls Canyon is the next-door neighbor of Big Falls Canyon in the Santa Lucia Wilderness. Getting to the trailhead requires the same rugged drive as the trip to Big Falls, but less of it, because it's only 1.6 miles from the pavement. That means that even if your car can't manage the stream-crossed dirt access road, you can walk in and visit the falls anyway, adding 3.2 miles to your one-mile hike (if you don't mind wading through the stream). Not only that, but later in the summer, as the water level drops, Little Falls actually becomes a prettier waterfall than Big Falls.

Little Falls is an easy walk from the trailhead, following the creek on a well-used trail into the Santa Lucia Wilderness. The trail stays close to the cool, shady stream, which is teeming with small trout and lined with oaks, sycamores, bays, and maples. Maidenhair and giant woodwardia ferns line the rocky pools of Little Falls Creek, and wildflowers bloom in patches.

After 15 minutes of hiking, you'll reach an unsigned junction where a spur trail leads off to the left, and the main trail heads up and away from the creek. Keep to the left and scramble upstream for a few hundred feet until you reach 50-foot-high Little Falls. You'll need good hiking boots to keep your feet dry, but the scramble is easily accomplished in about five minutes.

Little Falls' stream pours down between giant sheets of limestone, which look like freshly poured concrete that has frozen in mid-pour. A maple tree grows about halfway up the fall, and others hang over its lip. The fall's pool is about three feet deep, perfect for wading amid the reeds and ferns.

If you scramble back to the main trail, you can continue up and above Little Falls, where you'll find deeper, water-carved pools, perfect for cooling off. If the sculptured basins don't invite you to continue, the wildflowers should—they're stunning along the next mile of trail as you climb out of the canyon.

Trip notes: There is no fee. For a map of Los Padres National Forest, send $4 to USDA-Forest Service, 1323 Club Drive, Vallejo, CA 94592.

Little Falls

For more information, contact Los Padres National Forest, Santa Lucia Ranger District, 1616 North Carlotti Drive, Santa Maria, CA 93454; (805) 925-9538.

Directions: Follow the same directions as for the preceding listing, Big Falls, but drive only 1.6 miles on the dirt road. There's parking alongside the road, and the trail leads from the right side. Four-wheel drive or high-clearance is necessary if the road is wet.

MORE WATERFALLS

in Monterey & Central Coast

•Pico Blanco Camp Waterfall, Ventana Wilderness. Waterfall is on the Little Sur River, accessible via the Pico Blanco Trail or Little Sur Trail. For more information, phone Los Padres National Forest, Monterey Ranger District, at (831) 385-5434.

•Ventana Mesa Creek Waterfall, Ventana Wilderness. On Ventana Mesa Creek near the Carmel River, accessible via the Carmel River Trail out of Pine Valley Camp (see story on page 342). For more information, phone Los Padres National Forest, Monterey Ranger District, at (831) 385-5434.

•Pick Creek Falls, Ventana Wilderness. Near South Fork Camp on the Big Sur River. Accessible via the South Fork Trail. For more information, phone Los Padres National Forest, Monterey Ranger District, at (831) 385-5434.

Santa Barbara & Santa Monica Mountains

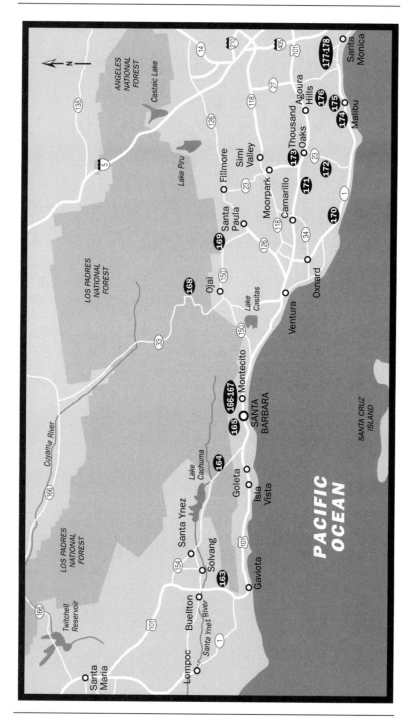

163. NOJOQUI FALLS

Nojoqui Falls County Park
Off U.S. 101 near Gaviota

Access & Difficulty: Hike-in 0.6 mile RT/Easy
Elevation: Start at 950 feet; total gain 50 feet
Best Season: December to May

Let's start with the right pronunciation. The waterfall is "No-Ho-Wee," not "No-Jokey," and if you don't say it properly, the locals will mock you without mercy. Once you've got it right, you're ready to make the trip, and you can do it any time you're cruising U.S. 101, either heading south from San Luis Obispo or north from Santa Barbara.

One of the best things about Nojoqui Falls is that it's only a couple of miles off the highway, nestled in the back of a canyon in Nojoqui Falls County Park. It's an easy side trip from the road. The walk to the falls is short and sweet, requiring a mere 15-minute commitment on a smooth, wide trail through a canopy of 200-year-old California laurels and oaks. Small footbridges carry you over the wet parts, so you can leave your hiking boots at home. Even Fido is allowed to make the trip, as long as he is on a leash and can appreciate a good waterfall.

Nojoqui Falls

Nojoqui Falls is stunning, dropping 80 feet over a sandstone cliff that is almost completely covered with delicate

Venus maidenhair ferns. This is one of the few places in Santa Barbara County where maidenhairs thrive; they require acidic, calcium-rich soil and plenty of moisture, which are rarities in this arid coastal climate. A sign at the falls explains that Nojoqui is an unusual waterfall, situated where the shale of the lower canyon meets the sandstone of the upper canyon. Rather than being continually eroded by its stream flow like most waterfalls, Nojoqui Falls is continually built up. Calcium deposits from the sandstone of the upper canyon trickle over the face of the waterfall, adding layer upon layer to its cliff.

There's a stair-stepped rock perch right by the fall's pool, where you can sit in the shade of big-leaf maples and have a picnic lunch, or just gaze in admiration at the falls' long, moss- and fern-covered drop.

Trip notes: There is no fee. For more information, contact Santa Barbara County Parks, 610 Mission Canyon Road, Santa Barbara, CA 93105; (805) 568-2461.

Directions: From Santa Barbara, drive 40 miles north on U.S. 101 to the signed turnoff for Nojoqui Park, north of Gaviota State Beach. Drive one mile on the Old Coast Highway, then turn east on Alisal Road. Drive eight-tenths of a mile, then turn right into the park entrance. Drive a quarter-mile down the park access road to the parking lot and trailhead. The trail starts from the far end of the parking lot loop.

164. WELLHOUSE FALLS (Lewis Canyon Falls)

Los Padres National Forest
Off U.S. 101 near Santa Barbara

Access & Difficulty: Hike-in & Scramble 3.5 miles RT/Strenuous
Elevation: Start at 2,960 feet; total loss 800 feet
Best Season: December to May

Knapp's Castle has something to offer for everyone. It's one of the historical oddities that give Santa Barbara its character; the stone ruins of Knapp's mansion have the ability to intrigue visitors much in the same manner as Hearst Castle. It also has the capacity to awe; the site's 180-degree views of the Santa Ynez River canyon and Lake Cachuma are downright inspiring. Finally, it gives waterfall collectors a cataract with a good story; a downhill walk leads to Wellhouse Falls, a natural waterfall that was once an integral part of Knapp's luxurious estate.

George Knapp was the former chairman of the board of Union Carbide, and in 1916 he built a five-bedroom sandstone mansion, complete with a pipe organ, on this mountain site. In addition to the main house, Knapp built servants' quarters, a groundskeeper's house, and a road that led down to Lewis Canyon below his home, where a cascading waterfall flowed in winter and spring. Not content with the natural seasonal changes of the waterfall, Knapp installed a pumphouse and system of locks in Lewis Creek, so he could store up water and make the waterfall run at his leisure or for the entertainment of guests. Going completely over the top, he installed an observation deck for the falls, a bath house, spotlights for nighttime viewing, and a speaker system so organ music could be piped down from the main house. It may seem obsessive, but the guy liked his waterfall.

Knapp's mansion burned in a canyon fire in 1940. Wellhouse Falls still flows after winter rains, but it no longer does so at Knapp's (or anyone's) beck and call.

The ruins of Knapp's Castle are located near the top of the Snyder Trail, a well-maintained Forest Service route that runs from Santa Ynez Canyon six miles uphill to East Camino Cielo. Although the property around Knapp's Castle is private, you can hike Snyder Trail 1.4 miles downhill, and take a short cutoff to see the falls. At present, you can also take another short cutoff and visit the castle ruins, although this is completely at the landowner's discretion. The dirt road to reach the castle ruins is public, but the ruins are privately owned.

Start hiking at the gated dirt road on East Camino Cielo that is signed "Private Property Ahead." Where the road reaches another gate, bear left and head downhill on the unsigned Snyder Trail. (The main road continues to the castle ruins, which you should visit on your return trip.)

Snyder Trail quickly turns to well-graded single-track as it drops below the Knapp's Castle site. Follow it for 1.4 miles from the road, about 35 minutes of downhill walking, enjoying tremendous views of the Santa Ynez River canyon over the entire distance. A terrific display of wildflowers, including purple nightshade and pink wild roses, is found in the grasses in springtime.

As you descend, keep watching for some gray metal electrical towers and power lines. (There are power lines at the start of the trail as well, but you'll move away from these and reach a second, more prominent set.) One-quarter mile beyond where the power lines cross the trail, look for a side trail on the right, the unsigned route to Lewis Canyon and Wellhouse Falls. (At this fork, the Snyder trail is marked with a rusted "Trail" sign.)

Now things get a bit dicey. The route gets progressively more eroded, and the chaparral closes in, but if you're willing to scramble for a third of a mile, you'll come out to several points where you can view Wellhouse Falls. Just keep your fingers crossed that it's running full of water, because Lewis Canyon drains quickly. Time your trip for immediately after a good rain, preferably the following day. Otherwise, you'll find yourself wishing that Lewis Creek still had Knapp's pumphouse and locks on it, so you could flip the switch and make the waterfall pour.

Trip notes: There is no fee. For a map of Los Padres National Forest, send $4 to USDA-Forest Service, 1323 Club Drive, Vallejo, CA 94592. For more information, contact Los Padres National Forest, Santa Barbara Ranger District, Los Prietos Station, 3505 Paradise Road, Santa Barbara, CA 93105; (805) 967-3481.

Directions: From U.S. 101 in Santa Barbara, take the Highway 154/State Street exit and drive north for 10.5 miles. Turn right on East Camino Cielo and drive 2.9 miles to the parking pullout on the right, across from a locked gate and dirt road on the left. The gate is signed "Private Property Ahead."

165. SEVEN FALLS

Los Padres National Forest
Off U.S. 101 near Santa Barbara

Access & Difficulty: Hike-in & Scramble 2.8 miles RT/Moderate
Elevation: Start at 950 feet; total gain 350 feet
Best Season: December to May

Seven Falls is a perfect springtime day-trip in Santa Barbara. It has a little bit of everything: waterfalls, swimming holes, vistas, wildflowers, and a good trail. The only problem is that the route to Seven Falls, one of the most popular paths in Santa Barbara, is also one of the most poorly signed. You've got to know where you're going before you set out.

From the parking area at the end of Tunnel Road, there are three possible roads to follow; you want the middle one, which is the continuation of Tunnel Road. Walk past a water tank and around a gate, continuing uphill on pavement for three-quarters of a mile. On any given day, you may pass any or all of the following characters on this road: Families coming to splash around in the lower pools of Mission Creek, serious power-walkers on training hikes on the fire roads, an old guy who leads a three-horse pack train up and down the canyon, and college kids going to explore the falls. It's a busy trail, but the ocean views are awesome.

At a bridge over Mission Creek, look for Fern Falls, which drops below the foot-bridge in winter and early spring only. It has a lovely pool below it, but there were no ferns that I could see. From the bridge, look up at the rocky peaks ahead and admire the sandstone jutting upward. Yes, Virginia, this is water-fall country. Some-

Four of Seven Falls' seven pools

times you'll spot hang gliders soaring above the cliffs.

Cross the bridge and continue walking uphill on the deteriorating paved road. When the pavement ends, a dirt road leads straight ahead and also to the right. Go straight, hiking among red wild fuchsias and peach-colored monkeyflowers. In a few hundred yards, you'll see a sign on your left: Jesusita Trail to Inspiration Point and San Roque Road are straight ahead; Tunnel Trail is the single-track to your right. Walk 100 yards straight ahead, then bear left on Jesusita Trail, cutting downhill to parallel Mission Creek. You reach small cascades and rocky pools almost immediately, and families with small children usually stop here and choose a pool to play in.

To see Seven Falls, cross the creek, but on the far side, don't continue on Jesusita Trail, which leads up the slope to Inspiration Point. Instead, follow the well-worn use trail a quarter-mile upstream, on the left (west) side of Mission Creek. It takes only 15 minutes of scrambling on fairly good trail to reach the sandstone-carved cascades of Seven Falls. The trail paralleling the creek is well defined, but

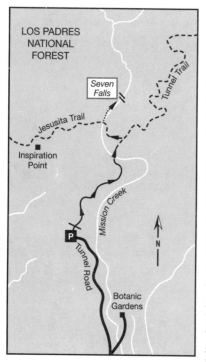

which spur you take to descend to the falls is up to you—there are several of them, all steep. The first cutoff leads you to a rocky overlook near the main set of falls; the rest take you to various swimming holes and other cascades.

The Seven Falls designation is a little nebulous; it's more like "Nearly Seven Falls" because there are five falls right in a row and then a couple more sprinkled up- and downstream. None of them are huge, but they're all beautiful. Their pools are as much as eight feet deep, perfect for swimming when there's enough water in Mission Creek. (If you do swim, don't step on the newts.) Fervent believers of Truth in Advertising would say that after about May 15th, this place should be called Seven Pools, not Seven Falls, because the water flow dwindles as soon as the rains stop. If this happens to you, just head back to the path and continue on Jesusita Trail to Inspiration Point, elevation 1,750 feet, a fine overlook of the Santa Barbara coast and Channel Islands.

Trip notes: There is no fee. For a map of Los Padres National Forest, send $4 to USDA-Forest Service, 1323 Club Drive, Vallejo, CA 94592. For more information, contact Los Padres National Forest, Santa Barbara Ranger District, Los Prietos Station, 3505 Paradise Road, Santa Barbara, CA 93105; (805) 967-3481.

Directions: From U.S. 101 in Santa Barbara, take the Mission Street exit and follow it east for just over a mile, crossing State Street. When Mission Street ends, turn left on Laguna Street and drive past the Santa Barbara Mission, turning right on Los Olivos directly in front of the Mission. As you pass the Mission, bear left on Mission Canyon Road for eight-tenths of a mile. Turn right on Foothill Boulevard. In one-tenth of a mile, turn left onto the continuation of Mission Canyon Road. Then bear left on Tunnel Road, and follow it for 1.1 miles until it ends. Park alongside the road, on the right.

166. WEST FORK COLD SPRINGS FALLS
(Tangerine Falls)

Los Padres National Forest
Off U.S. 101 near Santa Barbara

Access & Difficulty: Hike-in & Scramble 2.0 miles RT/Strenuous
Elevation: Start at 750 feet; total gain 700 feet
Best Season: December to May

West Fork Cold Springs Falls is a locals-only waterfall, so don't tell everybody that I told you about it. Also known as Tangerine Falls due to the peach-colored tint of its sandstone face, it's the kind of place they'll probably never build a "real" trail to reach. To see the falls, you must be willing to hike off-trail, scramble a bit, get a little muddy, and rub elbows with a fair amount of poison oak. The payoff is incredible, however, with West Fork Cold Springs being the most beautiful fall in the Santa Barbara area.

West Fork Cold Springs Falls

The trail starts in a suburban neighborhood, then it leads away from the road into Cold Springs Canyon. In a quarter-mile, the East and West Forks of Cold Springs Creek converge at a small waterfall, where there's a bench for viewing the little cascade. Here you must cross the creek at a sometimes-signed trail junction, now heading up the less-maintained West Fork Trail on the West Fork of Cold Springs Creek. At your feet are millions of ferns,

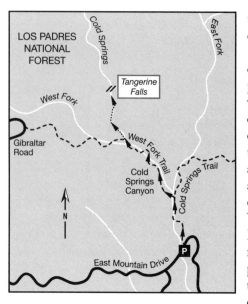

thriving in the leafy shade of the canyon.

As the trail starts its climb above the canyon, pay attention to the point where your view suddenly opens up, about three-quarters of a mile from the junction. Look ahead and slightly to the right and you'll catch a glimpse of Tangerine Falls, a.k.a. West Fork Cold Springs Falls. Hike 100 yards farther, watching for the point where the main trail turns away from the creek, curving to the left. Keep your eyes peeled on this stretch for a narrow spur trail that leads right, continuing along the creek.

Take the spur and follow the water pipes up the creek canyon, partly on a use trail and partly bushwhacking along the banks. Be prepared to climb over a lot of rocks, and be wary of eroded slides and the ubiquitous poison oak. In about 20 minutes of scrambling, you'll reach a series of small sandstone falls about 15 feet tall, each with a lovely pool at its base. Admire them, then keep heading farther back in the canyon.

Finally you'll reach the base of West Fork Cold Springs Falls, a sandstone monolith more than 100 feet tall. The reason for its nickname "Tangerine" is readily apparent in the peach- and green-colored moss and lichen on the fall's white cliff. The waterfall has a giant pool, from which the stream cascades down the hillside in a series of pools and drops.

As if all this isn't enough to thrill your senses, you can stand at the waterfall's base, turn your back to it, and look to the south for an exquisite view of the coastline beyond Montecito.

Trip notes: There is no fee. For a map of Los Padres National Forest, send $4 to USDA-Forest Service, 1323 Club Drive, Vallejo, CA 94592. For more information, contact Los Padres National Forest, Santa Barbara Ranger District, Los Prietos Station, 3505 Paradise Road, Santa Barbara, CA 93105; (805) 967-3481.

Directions: From Santa Barbara, drive south on U.S. 101 for four miles and exit on Hot Springs Road. Turn left on Hot Springs Road and drive 2.5 miles to Mountain Drive. Turn left and drive 1.2 miles to the Cold Springs Trailhead. Park off the road, near where the creek runs across the road.

167. SAN YSIDRO FALLS

Los Padres National Forest
Off U.S. 101 near Santa Barbara

Access & Difficulty: Hike-in 3.6 miles RT/Moderate
Elevation: Start at 600 feet; total gain 1,200 feet
Best Season: December to June

If you like running water, San Ysidro Canyon is your chance at seeing some, even long after the last rain. Other streams in the Santa Barbara area are often nearly dry by May, but San Ysidro keeps on flowing year-round, creating two lovely waterfalls and many small cascades that are accessible by an easy walk.

Not only that, but the falls in San Ysidro Canyon win an award: They're the only waterfalls in Santa Barbara that you can actually walk to on a well-maintained trail! No bushwhacking or rock scrambling required. But there's a price to be paid—a healthy climb of 1,200 feet over 1.8 miles, so get ready to give your heart and lungs a workout.

Start hiking on the signed San Ysidro Trail by the stables at San Ysidro Ranch, a popular playground of the rich and famous. You'll pass blooming lantana, bougainvillea, and geraniums along this trail stretch, not exactly wildflowers but certainly flowers that have gone wild. In the first mile, your route goes from single-track to pavement to wide fire road and then finally back to single-track, following San Ysidro Creek the whole way, passing a continual series of rushing cascades. Sandstone outcrops rise above the stream; rock climbers are often seen practicing their craft on them. The canyon is almost completely shaded by oaks and bays, making it cool even in summer.

At 1.5 miles from the trailhead, just before the trail climbs a steep slope on a series of rocky stairs lined with a guide rail, take the left cutoff which leads to the stream and a small, five-foot-tall waterfall and sculpted sandstone pool. (They're easily visible from the trail.) If you don't mind a little scrambling, you can take the side trail upstream of this cascade for about 100 feet to a much larger and prettier waterfall about 25 feet high. Two cascades come together over sandstone boulders, with a plethora of ferns and mosses growing in between. The fall has a great swimming hole, and is just hidden enough so that many people miss it.

After this little side trip, continue up the trail on the rock stairway, which the trail-builders have scored deeply so the surface isn't too slippery. (Still, watch your footing and use the handrail on your downhill return.) You move away from the creek, heading for another fork of it.

At 1.75 miles a stream, which sometimes rushes wildly and sometimes seeps slowly, crosses the trail. A few hundred feet beyond it, just before the trail curves right and moves away from the creek, take the left cutoff for 30 yards to see a sandstone waterfall set in the back of a canyon. It's 60 feet tall and completely different from the canyon's other cascades. The waterfall exhibits an incredible array of colors, much like nearby West Fork Cold Springs Falls. Lichen, mosses, and ferns appear yellow, green, peach, and gold against the cascade's gray sandstone cliff. The stream flow can be thin or wide, depending on recent rains, but the cliff and its fern-filled grotto are stunning any time.

Trip notes: There is no fee. For a map of Los Padres National Forest, send $4 to USDA-Forest Service, 1323 Club Drive, Vallejo, CA 94592. For more information, contact Los Padres National Forest, Santa Barbara Ranger District, Los Prietos Station, 3505 Paradise Road, Santa Barbara, CA 93105; (805) 967-3481.

Directions: From U.S. 101 in Montecito, take the San Ysidro Road exit and head east for one mile to East Valley Road/Highway 192. Turn right on East Valley Road/Highway 192 and drive a mile, then turn left on Park Lane. Drive a half mile on Park Lane, then bear left on East Mountain Drive. Follow East Mountain Drive to its end in a quarter-mile. Park alongside the road; the trail is on the right.

168. ROSE VALLEY FALLS

Los Padres National Forest
Off Highway 33 near Ojai

Access & Difficulty: Hike-in 0.6 mile RT/Easy
Elevation: Start at 3,400 feet; total gain 50 feet
Best Season: December to May

Rose Valley Falls is the kind of place where you take your kids when they want to have an adventure, but they're not quite old enough for adventures. The trip to the waterfall is like a Shirley Temple cocktail—colorful and exciting, but with no possible hazard in it.

Start your hike at the signed trail by site #4 in Rose Valley Campground. Head into the woods, cross Rose Creek, then cross it again a few more times. From a clearing in the canyon, you get a glimpse of the falls far off in the distance—a tall, narrow, awesome stream pouring through a notch between two small peaks. If that sight doesn't motivate your four-year-old to keep walking, nothing will. The path is smooth

The bottom tier of Rose Valley Falls

and nearly flat, bordered on both sides by oaks and fragrant bays, and it parallels the stream all the way. Several side trails on the left head down to small cascades and pools on Rose Creek, which are good swimming spots on a warm day. You'll continue to get little peek-a-boo glances at the falls as you head upcanyon.

In 15 minutes you're standing at Rose Valley Falls' base, which, surprisingly, looks nothing like what you saw coming up the canyon. That's because this is only the very bottom of the huge, 300-foot fall, which drops in two tiers. The upper tier is accessible only by climbing, and shouldn't be attempted without proper equipment and skills.

The lower tier is an immense 100-foot slab of sandstone and limestone, with that strange molten-rock look that is characteristic of this type of fall. It appears as if the cliff has melted down the hillside in sheets of sand-colored lava, then become completely encased in moss. Water cascades over the limestone in separate, thin streams. Children and adults alike feel compelled to reach out and touch the strange-looking surface. Many large boulders are sprawled at the waterfall's base, where you can sit and marvel.

Trip notes: There is no fee. For a map of Los Padres National Forest, send $4 to USDA-Forest Service, 1323 Club Drive, Vallejo, CA 94592. For more information, contact Los Padres National Forest, Ojai Ranger District, 1190 East Ojai Avenue, Ojai, CA 93023; (805) 646-4348.

Directions: From Ojai, drive north on Highway 33 for 16 miles to Rose Valley Road and the sign for Rose Valley Recreation Area. Turn right, drive three miles, then turn right again at the sign for Rose Valley Camp. Drive six-tenths of a mile to the campground. The trail starts by site #4.

169. SANTA PAULA CANYON FALLS
Los Padres National Forest
Off Highway 150 near Ojai

Access & Difficulty: Hike-in or Backpack 6.0 miles RT/Moderate
Elevation: Start at 1,050 feet; total gain 800 feet
Best Season: December to May

High-quality, easy backpacking trips that are brief in length are few and hard to find, but Santa Paula Canyon makes a perfect destination for a one-night camping trip. It has waterfalls, swimming holes, small trout, and a shady campground that's perfectly situated for fun adventures. It's the kind of place you hike to late in the afternoon, make a big dinner, get a good night's sleep, then play all the next day in the river before heading home.

The trail starts out unpromisingly by following an easement around Thomas Aquinas College and Ferndale Ranch, passing school buildings, ranch buildings, oil-drilling grasshoppers, and too much pavement. Posted signs keep hikers on the proper route until in three-quarters of a mile, you finally reach the single-track trail along Santa Paula Creek. Sadly, there's graffiti and often some litter in the canyon, mixed in among the streamside wildflowers—purple nightshade, yellow phlox, purple vetch, lupine, and brodiaea. It's difficult to imagine how anyone could despoil this flower-filled canyon.

In a quarter-mile, you cross the creek and turn right, joining the double-wide Santa Paula Canyon recreation trail, which runs flat for another mile, getting prettier all the time. After a second creek crossing, the wide trail heads uphill, switchbacking through a tunnel of ceanothus as it curves around Hill 1989. The path moves up and away from the creek, but eventually descends to join it again. When it drops down, you reach a pristine-looking, grassy flat, surrounded by oaks and a few big cone spruce. This is Big Cone Campground,

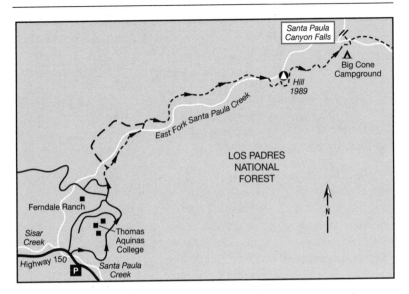

with six sites and fire rings. In late winter and spring, you can hear the sound of nearby waterfalls from the camp, although the creek is a few hundred feet away.

The site on the far left of the camp is set on a bluff above Santa Paula Creek, and a spur trail leads from it to an overlook, where you glimpse one of the largest falls on the stream. You can clearly see the pool above the fall, and the top of its narrow, 30-foot chute, funneled through sandstone. Santa Paula's waterfalls have earned their nickname "the Punchbowls," because they plummet from one perfectly rounded rock pool to the next.

Follow a more well-used path from the edge of the campground to the creek, where you'll find a narrow sandstone gorge and numerous swimming holes in summer. Small waterfalls are located up and down this stretch, but their accessibility depends on how low the stream is running.

Trip notes: There is no fee. For a map of Los Padres National Forest, send $4 to USDA-Forest Service, 1323 Club Drive, Vallejo, CA 94592. For more information, contact Los Padres National Forest, Ojai Ranger District, 1190 East Ojai Avenue, Ojai, CA 93023; (805) 646-4348.

Directions: From Ojai, at the junction of highways 33 and 150, drive east on Highway 150 for 11.5 miles to Thomas Aquinas College on the left (look for iron gates and stone buildings). Drive 100 yards further to the parking pullout on the right side of the road, just beyond the highway bridge over Santa Paula Creek. Park there and walk back across the bridge to the paved road on the right side of the college.

170. LA JOLLA CANYON FALLS

Point Mugu State Park
Off Highway 1 near Oxnard

Access & Difficulty: Hike-in 1.6 mile RT/Easy
or Backpack 3.8 miles RT/Easy
Elevation: Start at 100 feet; total gain 150 feet
Best Season: December to May

Of all the parks in the Santa Monica Mountains, Point Mugu State Park wins hands down. Maybe it's because Point Mugu is a little further north on the highway, closer to Oxnard than it is to Los Angeles, or maybe it's the park's proximity to the ocean, but this place seems more wild, and more pristine, than the others. Things are just plain better up here at Point Mugu.

The park has two waterfalls—Sycamore Canyon and La Jolla Canyon, and although the former is better accessed from a Santa Monica Mountains National Recreation Area site near Newbury Park (see the following story), the latter is an easy walk from the state park trailhead on Highway 1, near Thornhill Broome Beach. You can also walk an extra mile and spend the night at the La Jolla Canyon Trail

La Jolla Canyon Falls

Camp, turning the day-hike into a perfect family backpacking trip.

There are two trails at the Ray Miller Trail-head in La Jolla Canyon, so make sure you take the right one, which is the wide dirt road signed as La Jolla Canyon Trail. Walk through a wide-open valley, which is continually freshened by cool ocean breezes blowing up the canyon. Cross the stream, then at eight-tenths of a mile from the trailhead, reach the water-fall at a second stream crossing.

Although La Jolla Creek runs most of the year, the fall is exciting only shortly after a rain. The rest of the time it's just a moderate trickle, about 15 feet high with a shallow pool at its base. The cascade continues below the trail, but the lower portion is obscured by dense willows and sycamores.

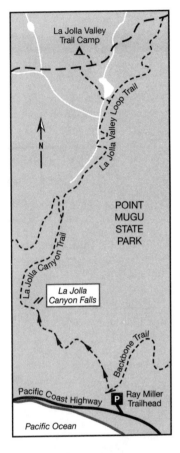

If you have the time, don't end your trip here. Keep heading deeper into La Jolla Canyon. As you climb, the canyon gets narrower and rockier, and hidden amid the chaparral you'll see rock caves that were once used by Native Americans. If you're backpacking, take the left fork at the junction with the Mugu Peak Trail. The trail levels and brings you to an area of native grasses. The La Jolla Canyon Trail Camp is located there, shortly beyond a cattail-bordered pond. Water and restrooms are provided.

Although the wildflowers are excellent in La Jolla Canyon in late March and April, an even more colorful happening occurs in January and February: Monarch butterflies who winter here begin to mate and leave for their return migration to Canada and the northern United States. The monarchs cluster in both La Jolla Canyon and next-door Sycamore Canyon in Point Mugu State Park. Each year, generation after generation of butterflies return to these same ancestral sites. If your timing is good, you can see the waterfall and the monarchs in the same trip.

Trip notes: A $2 state park day-use fee is charged for parking at the Ray Miller Trailhead. A trail map is available for $1 from the ranger kiosk at Sycamore Canyon Campground, one mile south on Highway 1. Backpacking campsites are available on a first-come, first-served basis; backpackers must register at the Sycamore Canyon Campground. For more information, contact Point Mugu State Park, 9000 W. Pacific Coast Highway, Malibu, CA 90265; (805) 488-5223 or State Parks, Angeles District, 1925 Los Virgenes Road, Calabasas, CA 91302; (818) 880-0350.

Directions: From U.S. 101 in Camarillo—Take the Los Posas Road exit and drive south through Oxnard. Follow Los Posas Road for eight miles to Highway 1, then turn south on Highway 1. Drive five miles to the La Jolla Canyon trailhead parking area on the left, across from Thornhill Broome State Beach.

From Highway 1 in Malibu—Drive west on Highway 1 for 22 miles to the La Jolla Canyon trailhead parking area on the right.

171. SYCAMORE CANYON FALLS (Rancho Sierra Vista Falls)

Satwiwa Site/Point Mugu State Park
Off U.S. 101 near Newbury Park

Access & Difficulty: Hike-in 2.4 miles RT/Easy
Elevation: Start at 800 feet; total loss 350 feet
Best Season: December to May

The Santa Monica Mountains National Recreation Area Rancho Sierra Vista/Satwiwa Site is the very long name for the back entrance to Point Mugu State Park. It's a mouthful to say, but all you need to remember is Satwiwa, which means "the bluffs," the name of the

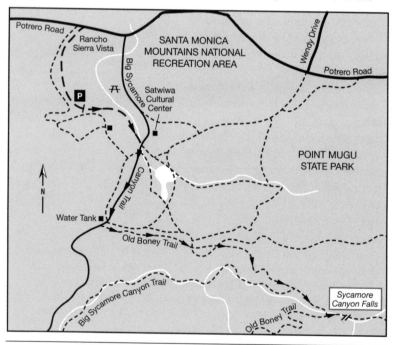

Chumash Indian village that existed here. That's what people call this trailhead, because many come here to visit the park's Native American cultural site.

You know the hike will be good when at the trailhead parking lot you're greeted by two friendly roadrunners and half a dozen small bunnies, the local welcoming committee. Pick up a trail map at the signpost and walk up the gated road from the parking lot. Pass the Satwiwa Culture Center on your left with its dome-shaped stick dwelling, which was built to exhibit traditional Native American life.

Keep heading straight ahead on the paved Big Sycamore Canyon Trail, following the signs toward Point Mugu State Park. When you reach a water tank on your right, a half-mile from the parking lot, turn left on a dirt road and follow it to the canyon bottom. The route is not always signed, but it's the Old Boney Trail. (If you don't like walking on pavement, you can take the west side of the Satwiwa Loop Trail from just beyond the Satwiwa Culture Center, which joins the Old Boney Trail in a quarter-mile. The paved road provides you with views, wildflowers, and chaparral. Satwiwa Loop gives you grasslands and a small pond. Take your pick.)

Where Old Boney Trail makes a sharp switchback uphill and out of the canyon, take the left spur that leads a few hundred feet to Sycamore Canyon Falls. You'll reach the first cascades in a minute or two. If you have to do a little boulder-hopping, congratulate yourself on your good luck. That means the falls will be flowing strong.

Sycamore Canyon Falls

Sycamore Canyon Falls is one of the most dramatic in the Santa Monica Mountains, consisting of a half dozen pool-and-drop cascades that are carved into a soft sandstone cliff and completely surrounded by lush foliage. When running full, the water cascades more than 100 feet from top to bottom, pouring from one sandstone tier to the next. Big-leaf maples, immense woodwardia ferns, and smaller sword ferns thrive in this shady glade. Even in low water, the fall is a serene and scenic place, a shelter from the exposed slopes and the heat of the inland sun.

Trip notes: There is no fee. For more information and a free park brochure, contact Santa Monica Mountains National Recreation Area, 401 West Hillcrest Drive, Thousand Oaks, CA 91360; (805) 370-2300. Maps are also available at the trailhead.

Directions: From U.S. 101 in Newbury Park, exit on Wendy Drive and head south for 2.6 miles to Potrero Road. Turn right on Potrero Road and head west for 1.8 miles to the park entrance at the corner of West Potrero Road and Pine Hill Avenue. Turn left into the park and drive four-tenths of a mile to the main parking lot. Walk up the paved road that leads from the parking lot to a gate at the Big Sycamore Canyon Trail (also a road).

172. THE GROTTO FALLS
Circle X Ranch
Off Highway 1 near Malibu

Access & Difficulty: Hike-in 3.5 miles RT/Moderate
or Hike-in 0.5 miles RT/Easy
Elevation: Start at 1,700 feet; total loss 550 feet
or Start at 1,200 feet; total loss 50 feet
Best Season: December to May

Is it a waterfall or a boulder playground? It just depends on when you show up. Circle X Ranch's "the Grotto" is a rugged jumble of volcanic rocks, many bigger than your average Volkswagen, over which the West Fork of Arroyo Sequit tumbles (or sadly dribbles, in summer). Perhaps they should call this rock garden the Playground instead of the Grotto, because in low water you can spend all day climbing around it, making use of the millions of possible handholds and toeholds. In high water, don't even attempt exploring; just stand back and listen to the water roar.

You can reach the Grotto the easy way, by driving down to Happy Hollow Campground, then walking a few hundred yards through the camp. Or you can go the more strenuous way, by hiking the Grotto Trail 1.7 miles from the group campground near the park entrance. The trail makes a steep descent with a 550-foot elevation loss that must be gained back on the return trip, so save the hike for a cool day.

Circle X Ranch is a different ball of wax from the coastal parks in the Santa Monica Mountains. It's much warmer, it's at a higher elevation, and it has a tremendous backdrop of rocky peaks looming behind it. These include Boney Mountain and Sandstone Peak, which is the highest mountain in the Santa Monica Mountains at 3,111 feet. But down at Happy Hollow Campground and the Grotto lies a lush riparian environment, overgrown with oaks, willows, sycamores, and ferns. Even on the hottest days of summer, a pleasant breeze often blows through the shady sites at Happy Hollow.

If you elect to drive instead of hike, park just outside the camp, then walk through the camp. Beyond the tent sites, you'll pass the Grotto Trail coming in from the left, then reach the first giant boulders of the Grotto. Several use trails lead down the right side of the stream.

Even in low water, hidden in the Grotto's many caves and recesses are secret waterfalls. When I visited in June, I stood knee-deep in a pool, the source of which was a cascade concealed behind large boulders. The noise of running water is incredibly loud along the stream. The waterfalls are often surrounded on three sides by rock, resulting in great echoing sounds.

If you plan to camp near the Grotto, remember that Happy Hollow is a walk-in campground, which means you leave your car at a parking area, then carry your stuff a short distance to your campsite. It's like car camping, only better, because your car isn't right next to your tent, making you feel like you're at a tailgate party. You can choose your site depending on how far you want your walk to be, but the best sites are about 200 yards from the parking area, in the shady area closest to the Grotto.

Trip notes: There is no fee. For more information and a free park brochure, contact Santa Monica Mountains National Recreation Area, 401 West Hillcrest Drive, Thousand Oaks, CA 91360; (805) 370-2300. Or contact Circle X Ranger Station at (310) 457-6408.

Directions: From Malibu, drive west on Highway 1 for 15 miles to Yerba Buena Road, 1.5 miles past Leo Carrillo State Beach. Turn right and drive 5.3 miles up Yerba Buena Road to the entrance to Circle X Ranch on the right. Park at the ranger station and hike downhill on the Grotto Trail, which starts at the group campground, for a 3.5-mile round-trip. Or drive 1.5 miles down the narrow dirt access road to Happy Hollow Campground, and walk in to the Grotto from there. (No trailers or vehicles over 25 feet long are allowed on this road.)

173. PARADISE FALLS (Wildwood Falls)
Wildwood Park
Off U.S. 101 near Thousand Oaks

Access & Difficulty: Hike-in 2.4 miles RT/Easy
Elevation: Start at 640 feet; total loss 260 feet
Best Season: December to May

I have seen Paradise, and it's in Los Angeles. I spent a lot of time searching all over the globe for it, when I could have just driven down U.S. 101.

Well, to be more precise, I have seen Paradise Falls, and it's located in Thousand Oaks, a Los Angeles suburb. But hey, Paradise Falls seems like Paradise, a little slice of protected wilderness in a tangle of freeways and subdivisions. A visit to the waterfall and its surroundings in Wildwood Park can change your perspective on things, make you feel like there's still plenty of good in the world, even if you're sitting in 101 gridlock on your commute to downtown.

One of the amazing things about Paradise Falls is that it's so easy to reach. Just drive a few miles off the freeway and take a short walk on fire roads. From Wildwood Park's Arboles parking lot, hike due west on the Mesa Trail for a half-mile to the North Tepee Trail, then turn left and head down to the falls. (This is one of several possible routes; you have many options, including driving a half-mile beyond the Arboles parking lot to a lower lot, cutting some distance off your hike. Check out the park trail maps at the Arboles lot.)

Shortly, you'll drop into the canyon, where you'll see many signs directing you to Paradise Falls, or sometimes Wildwood Falls, the cascade's less imaginative name. The best approach is via the Wildwood Canyon Trail, hiking in from the east so you can see the stream just before it makes its tremendous hurtle over a basalt lip. The trail parallels the creek downhill to the fall's base. A chain link fence keeps you from tumbling down the hillside at the steepest dropoffs.

Even in low water, Paradise Falls makes a frothy white stream, with a startlingly wide pool at the bottom, more like a large pond, about 50 yards wide. You can't get directly in front of the fall without getting your feet wet, so most people view it from the side. From this angle, the middle section is obscured by a large rock, but that just makes it look more interesting.

If you have trouble imagining a 70-foot waterfall in Thousand Oaks, you should lace up your sneakers and see for yourself. At the

Paradise Falls

parking lot, you may rate this place as "Least Likely Spot for a Good Waterfall," but hey, prepare to be surprised.

Trip notes: There is no fee. For more information and a free park brochure and map, contact Wildwood Park, c/o Conejo Recreation and Park District, 155 East Wilbur Road, Thousand Oaks, CA 91360; (805) 495-6471.

Directions: From U.S. 101 in Thousand Oaks, take the Lynn Road exit and head north. Drive 2.5 miles to Avenida de los Arboles, then turn left. Drive nine-tenths of a mile and make a U-turn into the Arboles parking lot on the left side of the road.

174. ESCONDIDO FALLS

Santa Monica Mountains Conservancy
Off Highway 1 near Malibu

Access & Difficulty: Hike-in 4.2 miles RT/Easy
Elevation: Start at 200 feet; total gain 300 feet
Best Season: December to May

This is a strange and wonderful waterfall hike.

Strange? You have to walk a mile just to reach the trailhead, through an opulent neighborhood of truly mammoth Malibu homes. It feels weird walking by these houses dressed in hiking clothes, like you're hoping for a job raking leaves or pulling weeds.

Wonderful? The payoff is access to a gorgeous footpath into Escondido Canyon, where a huge, multi-tiered limestone waterfall awaits you.

Begin your trip at the well-signed hikers' parking lot at the start of Winding Way. Walk up the paved road, gaining ocean views as you climb. Try not to gawk at the affluence. When you reach the end of the road and the sign for the Santa Monica Mountains Conservancy, take the trail to the left, heading into the canyon.

Escondido Falls

Walk upstream, ignoring any trail junctions and staying along the creek, which you'll cross a few times. The trail is nearly level, extremely well-maintained, and beautiful to boot, mixing shade, sun, wildflowers, and views. In a half mile, you'll glimpse a big waterfall far ahead, and one look will be enough to spur you onward. Fifteen minutes later you'll be standing at the base of Escondido Canyon's limestone fall, oohing and aahing at the 50-foot length of streaming water pouring over an incredible growth of ferns and moss. You'll want to kick off your shoes and wade into its shallow pool.

But if your scrambling skills are good, don't stop here. This is only the lower tier of Escondido Falls. That big fall you saw back in the canyon is still waiting above this one, and a steep 10-minute climb will get you there. On the way up, you'll pass a pretty cascade about 15 feet high, then you'll suddenly find yourself at the foot of an immense limestone tier, at least 150 feet high. Now you'll definitely want to go wading in the fall's three-foot-deep pool. If you do, be careful not to step on the giant newts who make their home here. They are unusually large water babies, appropriately oversized to match this amazing cataract.

Trip notes: There is no fee. For more information, contact the Santa Monica Mountains Conservancy, 5750 Ramirez Canyon Road, Malibu, CA 90265; (310) 589-3200.

Directions: From Malibu, drive west on Highway 1 for 5.5 miles to Winding Way on the right, and the large sign for the Winding Way Trail. (If you reach Kanan Dume Road, you've gone 1.5 miles too far.) Turn right, then left immediately into the well-signed parking lot.

175. SOLSTICE CANYON FALLS (Roberts Ranch Falls)

Santa Monica Mountains National Recreation Area
Off Highway 1 near Malibu

Access & Difficulty: Hike-in 2.0 miles RT/Easy
Elevation: Start at 100 feet; total gain 250 feet
Best Season: December to May

You're tired of getting poison oak. You're tired of scrambling upstream over slippery boulders. Maybe you're just plain tired. You want to see a waterfall in the Santa Monica Mountains and you want it to be easy. If that's your story, show up at Solstice Canyon, where all you have to do is take a one-mile stroll on a paved road.

From the old park office building (a small cottage), walk up the paved road, paralleling Solstice Creek and passing by El Alisar picnic area. Where the road reaches a T junction, bear right, and hike up the canyon to the Roberts Ranch site. Solstice Creek makes fine company along the way, as do the many bunches of orange sticky monkeyflower and sweet hot mustard. The walk is similar to other canyon hikes in the Santa Monica Mountains, but it is made about a million times easier by the wide paved road and the nearly level grade.

Solstice Canyon Falls at Roberts Ranch

Pass by the 1865 Keller house, a lovely stone house that's the oldest in Malibu. It's now a private residence, located about halfway to the falls. Continue to the ruins of Tropical Terrace, the 1950s home of the Fred and Florence Roberts family. The beautiful home and its exotic terraced gardens were destroyed by a fire in 1982, but its natural waterfall remains. Walk past the stone ruins of the house, following the stream as it makes a 90-degree turn around the property. First you'll see a small eight-foot fall, then, on the right side of the house foundation, you'll come to 30-foot Solstice Canyon Falls. You can reach the cataract's base fairly easily by following the remains of the stone stairways and paths that were built here. In places, the paths have washed out, but there are plenty of rocks to step on, keeping your feet dry and out of the stream.

Solstice Canyon Falls is surprisingly beautiful, often flowing with more volume than other falls in the area. It cascades over huge sandstone boulders, with maidenhair ferns clinging to the rocks around the fall's edges. It's fun to sit by the waterfall and imagine what it was like here when Roberts Ranch was in its splendor.

Solstice Canyon has a few other waterfalls, but most of these are caused by artificial dams on Solstice Creek, so they don't count. There is a big fall up Dry Canyon, accessible via the Dry Creek Trail, which begins across the road from the old park office building. The maintained trail leads six-tenths of a mile to a decent overlook of the fall, which only runs after a rain. It was dry when I visited in May, even though the fall at Roberts Ranch was flowing strong. The trail is lovely, however, and it is only slightly marred by a couple of monolithic homes high on the hillside above. A use trail continues from the end of the maintained trail, but it gets quickly overgrown.

Trip notes: There is no fee. For more information and a free park brochure which includes Solstice Canyon, contact Santa Monica Mountains National Recreation Area, 401 West Hillcrest Drive, Thousand Oaks, CA 91360; (805) 370-2300.

Directions: From Malibu, drive west on Highway 1 for three miles and turn right on Corral Canyon Road. Drive two-tenths of a mile to the park entrance on the left. Turn left, and drive to the Caballero Picnic Area and old park office building. Park there and continue walking up the paved road, past the picnic area.

176. ZUMA & NEWTON CANYON FALLS
Santa Monica Mountains National Recreation Area
Off Highway 1 near Point Dume

Access & Difficulty: Hike-in & Scramble 2.0 miles RT/Moderate
Elevation: Start at 1,500 feet; total loss 600 feet
Best Season: December to May

Three waterfalls, one short trip. That's what you get when you visit Zuma and Newton canyons in the Santa Monica Mountains National Recreation Area. The adventure starts from a roadside pullout along Kanan Dume Road, where a trail drops down to a little slice of watery paradise below the road. This brief path, an uncompleted section of the proposed Backbone Trail that may someday run the entire length of the Santa Monicas, leads to two shaded and thickly vegetated canyons, and to the waterfalls hidden within.

Trails lead from both ends of the parking pullout, so make sure you take the one on the east side, which is signed as the Backbone Trail. It switchbacks confidently downhill into Newton Canyon, then peters out in one-half mile. But never mind. Just before the trail ends, you cross above a 25-foot waterfall, where Newton Creek slides down a vertical, moss-covered limestone face. To reach the fall's base, take one of the left cutoff trails just beyond the fall's crest, then head upstream a few yards. The scene is set in a rounded rock grotto, where little sandstone caves surround the fall. With all the leafy trees, winding vines, and thick moss, you might think this was someplace in the tropics, not the near-desert of Los Angeles.

Newton Canyon Falls

If you want to see more waterfalls, prepare to do some stream scrambling, because there's no more trail to follow. (The scramble can be easy or difficult, depending on how much water is in the stream.) Working your way downstream from the first fall, you'll descend over an eight-foot cascade which drops in a narrow chute, then continue to a second, larger fall. It's similar to the 25-footer, but by late spring, every inch of it is covered with greenery, like a Rose Parade float. You can hardly see the water through the leaves.

It's difficult climbing down to the base of the second waterfall because the slope is nearly vertical and muddy. But if you can manage it, you'll gain access to Zuma Canyon. Zuma and Newton creeks join here, and you can head to the right (east) for five more minutes of stream scrambling to Zuma Falls. Although it's only 20 feet tall, it has a spectacular setting, dropping over a sandstone ledge surrounded by small caves and ferns, with a double pool—two basins divided by a rock ledge—at its base. In high water, the waterfall's flow spills from one pool to the next. When the stream warms up, swimming is best in the lower, deeper pool.

Trip notes: There is no fee. For more information and a free park brochure, contact Santa Monica Mountains National Recreation Area, 401 West Hillcrest Drive, Thousand Oaks, CA 91360; (805) 370-2300.

Directions: From Malibu, drive west on Highway 1 for seven miles to Kanan Dume Road. Turn right and drive 4.4 miles to a large dirt parking pullout on the left, immediately after passing through the southern tunnel on Kanan Dume Road.

From Agoura Hills on U.S. 101, take the Kanan Road exit and drive eight miles to the parking pullout on the right side of the road, near a road sign marked "Newton Canyon Road, Private." It's just before you enter the third tunnel on Kanan Road.

177. SANTA YNEZ CANYON FALLS

Topanga State Park
Off Highway 1 near Pacific Palisades

Access & Difficulty: Hike-in & Scramble 2.4 miles RT/Moderate
Elevation: Start at 600 feet; total gain 250 feet
Best Season: December to May

Topanga State Park is a park with nebulous borders, or rather a park with such an odd perimeter surrounding its irregular shape that it's hard to tell where it starts and where it ends. With the exception of the main park entrance at Trippet Ranch on Topanga Canyon Road, the rest of the park seems like a patchwork of wilderness set among continually growing housing developments. You drive through a neighborhood, park your car in front of somebody's house, walk 20 feet, and wham—you're in the state park. It's kind of weird, but you get used to it.

Don't be put off by the glitzy homes and substantial concrete by the Santa Ynez Canyon trailhead. You may drive up and wonder if you're going to a waterfall or a cocktail party. But once you're on the hiking trail in the canyon, the world becomes a different place: Santa Ynez Canyon is a natural sanctuary for foliage and wildlife, a swath of dense vegetation bordering a life-giving stream, miraculously encased within the city limits of Los Angeles. Not only that, Santa Ynez harbors a surprising sandstone waterfall.

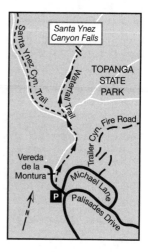

The start of the trail is a little roughed up, with some graffiti on a concrete apron and culvert, but keep going—things get better. The canyon bottom makes remarkably level walking, pleasantly shaded by oaks, willows, and sycamores. In between the patches of poison oak, look for a wide variety of spring wildflowers, including five-foot-tall tiger lilies.

Santa Ynez Canyon Falls

At a half mile from the trailhead you reach a metal gate (it was once across the trail but is now off to the side). Ignore the narrow, unmarked right spur by the gate, and instead bear left and cross the creek. Fifty yards past the creek crossing, there's an unsigned junction. The left fork leads to Trippet Ranch, but head right to stay along the creek.

From here, it's only 15 to 20 minutes to the falls, which are accessible either by following the route on the right side of the creek or by wading in to it. (The latter may be easier.) In the last few hundred yards, the sandstone walls squeeze in tightly and you have no choice but to enter the stream. It's great fun walking up the sandstone narrows and climbing over miniature waterfalls, but the fun is somewhat tarnished by the sight of graffiti on the walls near the back of the canyon. The route ends at a 15-foot fall, dropping over prehistoric-looking sandstone slabs. In summer, a rope is usually in place here for experienced climbers, who scramble up and over this fall to more waterfalls, farther back in the canyon. If you choose to explore them, exercise caution on the slippery climb.

Trip notes: There is no fee. For more information and a park brochure, contact Topanga State Park, 20825 Entrada Road, Topanga, CA 90290; (310) 455-2465, (310) 454-8212, or (818) 880-0350.

Directions: From Santa Monica, drive north on Highway 1 and turn right on Sunset Boulevard in Pacific Palisades. Drive a half-mile and turn left on Palisades Drive. Drive 2.4 miles, then turn left on to Vereda de la Montura. The trailhead is at the intersection of Camino de Yatasto, a private road, and Vereda de la Montura. Park alongside the road.

178. TEMESCAL CANYON FALLS

**Temescal Gateway Park/Topanga State Park
Off Highway 1 near Pacific Palisades**

Access & Difficulty: Hike-in 2.4 miles RT/Easy
Elevation: Start at 400 feet; total gain 300 feet
Best Season: December to May

Even in summer, Temescal Canyon Falls is a sweet little spot, where the sound of tinkling water transports you far from the hustle and bustle of Los Angeles. So what if it's not exactly Yosemite Falls? In the morning, when sunlight hits the cascade's pool, you can watch rippling reflections on the underside of an overhanging maple tree's branches, and on the wide face of the rocks beside the pool. If you're lucky, a bright green hummingbird will accompany you in the shade of the grotto or on the trail to reach it.

You can access the fall by way of Temescal Gateway Park in Pacific Palisades. But don't get any ideas about bringing your dog on the trip, because the hike leaves the city park and enters Topanga State Park, where dogs are *ixnay.*

The signed trail leads from the parking lot, to the left of the kiosk where you pay your fee and pick up a free map, and heads north through a camp and conference center. All the trails are well-signed to keep you off the camp's private property. If it's noisy there, don't fret, you'll soon be beyond it all.

In a quarter-mile, you'll reach a junction of three trails. The left path is unsigned but leads to the lower parking areas, the middle trail is the Temescal Ridge Trail, which can be the return leg of a possible loop trip, and on the right is the Temescal Canyon Trail—the direct route to the waterfall.

Following Temescal Canyon Trail, you'll cross a paved road leading out of the conference center. Bunnies and lizards scurry by. In a half-mile, there's a state park boundary sign, then the trail starts to climb. Although the route is bordered by rock walls and dry chap-arral, leafy maples and sycamores grow along the stream beside you.

Shortly you'll hear the waterfall, which you cross over via a footbridge on the trail. If you like, you can take the steep left cutoff that leads to the fall's base, where you get a close-up view of the huge boulders, clearly volcanic in origin, that form the falls. The rocks look like they're made of cobblestones embedded in cement.

You can simply turn around at the falls for a 2.4-mile round-trip, or continue hiking, crossing over to the west side of the canyon to climb to an intersection with the Temescal Ridge Trail, then turn left to return. This 3.5-mile loop trip provides far-reaching views of the coast in addition to some good exercise.

Trip notes: A $6 day-use fee is charged. A free trail map is available at the park kiosk. For more information, contact Temescal Gateway Park, 15601 Sunset Boulevard, Pacific Palisades, CA 90272; (310) 454-1395.

Directions: From Santa Monica, drive north on Highway 1 to Temescal Canyon Road in Pacific Palisades. Turn right and drive 1.1 miles to the entrance to Temescal Gateway Park. Cross Sunset Boulevard, then continue up the park road for a quarter-mile to the park office and trail information kiosk.

MORE WATERFALLS

in Santa Barbara & Santa Monica Mountains

•Cold Spring Tavern Falls, on Stagecoach Road off Highway 154 in Santa Barbara. Scramble up the creek alongside Cold Spring Tavern for three-quarters of a mile to reach a 50-foot waterfall. It only flows in the wettest weather. For more information, phone Los Padres National Forest, Santa Barbara Ranger District, at (805) 967-3481.

•Mission Falls, on Mission Creek in Santa Barbara. No access except by scrambling up the creek for about a mile past Seven Falls (see the story on page 358). Very rough going, climbing skills required. For more information, phone Los Padres National Forest, Santa Barbara Ranger District, at (805) 967-3481.

•Circle Bar B Ranch Waterfall, near Refugio Beach. See a waterfall by horseback at this privately run ranch. Horse rentals and trail rides are available for a fee. For more information, phone (805) 968-1113.

•Indian Creek Falls, Dick Smith Wilderness. Accessible via day-hike from Indian Creek Trailhead. For more information, phone Los Padres National Forest, Santa Barbara Ranger District, at (805) 967-3481.

•Sisquoc River Falls, San Rafael Wilderness. Near Lower Bear Camp, accessible via backpacking trip on Sisquoc River Trail. For more information, phone Los Padres National Forest, Santa Lucia Ranger District, at (805) 925-9538.

•Rattlesnake Falls, San Rafael Wilderness. Near Cottonwood Camp, accessible via backpacking trip on Sisquoc River Trail. For more information, phone Los Padres National Forest, Santa Lucia Ranger District, at (805) 925-9538.

San Gabriel & San Bernardino Mountains

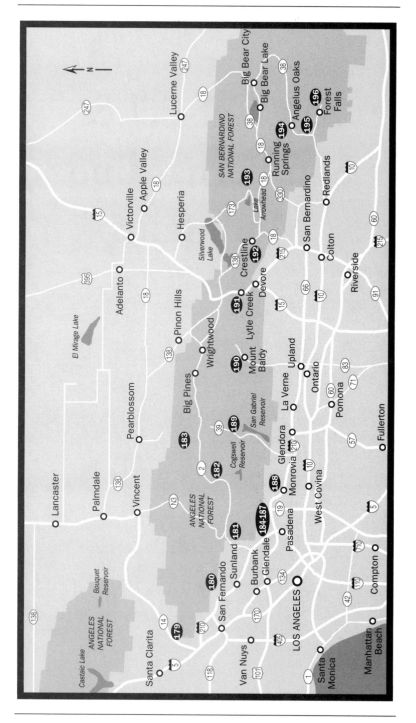

179. PLACERITA CREEK FALLS

Placerita Canyon County Park
Off Highway 14 near Newhall

Access & Difficulty: Hike-in 5.5 miles RT/Easy
 or Hike-in 2.4 miles RT/Easy
Elevation: Start at 1,550 feet; total gain 250 feet
Best Season: December to May

Placerita Canyon County Park is a perfect destination for a family outing. It's just far enough out of the Los Angeles basin that it feels like someplace different, and it offers hiking, picnicking, and horseback riding opportunities in a rural, wilderness-like setting. Even dogs are allowed in the park. And best of all, the area is the home of Placerita Creek's waterfall, accessible by an easy 5.5-mile hike along the creek.

Start your trip by the park's nature center, where you should stop in and learn a thing or two about the flora and fauna of the area. Then, start hiking on the Canyon Trail, which leads from the southeast side of the nature center parking lot and crosses Placerita Creek. The trail leads through Placerita Canyon, passing many shady canyon oaks and sycamores and chunks of colorful igneous granite, to Walker Ranch picnic area. Walk all the way through the picnic area to its far end, then turn right and look for a trail sign for "Waterfall Trail." (Ignore the right turn about 30 yards before this one, which is the Los Piñetos Trail and doesn't go to the falls.)

The trail gets more interesting the further back you go, as it narrows and curves its way deeper into the canyon. Along the way, you can smell the sulphur from underground springs, as well as the springtime fragrance from great bunches of blooming ceanothus. In

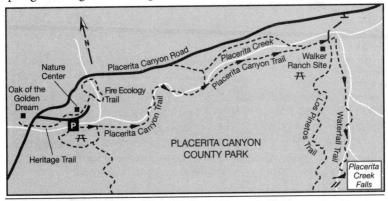

San Gabriel & San Bernardino Mountains—Map page 386   387

Placerita Creek Falls

April, we munched on tiny leaves of edible miner's lettuce near the creek. The trail crosses the stream a few times, making it advisable to wear hiking boots in high water, although we saw people walking along in everyday shoes. In the final 100 yards before the waterfall, the trail ends and you simply hike up the streambed. When we got there, we found four happy-looking kids and their mom sitting near the waterfall's base on a fallen tree, chewing on sandwiches.

Placerita Creek Falls is about 25 feet high with a narrow stream that cascades down the cliff face. It forms a lovely shaded grotto, with only enough room for a few people in its cloister. Some people attempt to climb above the falls, but the cliff face is quite steep and muddy, so it's a bad idea. On our trip, we witnessed a helicopter rescue in progress as paramedics carried out a woman who had broken her shoulder upstream of the falls. It served as a good wake-up call about the potential dangers of climbing around waterfalls.

If you have small children with you who can't manage the 5.5-mile round-trip from the nature center, you can drive two miles past the park entrance on Placerita Canyon Road to the Walker Ranch gate (a dirt road). Park near the gate, walk through it and into the Walker Ranch area. From there, head straight on the Waterfall Trail for a round-trip of 2.4 miles.

Trip notes: A $3 access fee is charged. Free maps of Placerita Canyon County Park are available at the nature center. For more information, contact Placerita Canyon County Park, 19152 Placerita Canyon Road, Newhall, CA 91321; (661) 259-7721.

Directions: From the San Fernando Valley, drive north on Interstate 5 to Highway 14. Follow Highway 14 northeast for four miles to Newhall, then exit on Placerita Canyon Road. Turn right (east) and drive two miles to the park entrance on the right. Park in the nature center parking lot. (For the shorter hike, drive two miles east of the park entrance on Placerita Canyon Road to the Walker Ranch gate on the right.)

180. TRAIL CANYON FALLS

Angeles National Forest
Off Interstate 210 near Sunland

Access & Difficulty: Hike-in 4.0 miles RT/Moderate
Elevation: Start at 1,800 feet; total gain 600 feet
Best Season: December to June

You have to hike on the Trail Canyon Trail to reach Trail Canyon Falls, and although it sounds redundant, it's not a typographical error. That's just what they call it.

Trail Canyon is on the western side of the San Gabriel Mountains, an area that is less visited than the more glamorous eastern side. The trail to the waterfall begins with a ford, and has several more along the way, so make sure you're wearing good boots or are willing to get your feet wet. Except for the stream crossings, the Trail Canyon Trail is a breeze to follow, and it's pretty along the whole route. You'll see many wildflowers (both chaparral and streamside varieties), get some excellent views, and follow a well-maintained path to a big waterfall. What more could you ask for?

Trail Canyon Falls

After parking your car in the lot at Trail Canyon, walk on the dirt road into a community of cabins, then follow the road past them, winding around the canyon. At three-quarters of a mile where the road makes a hairpin left turn, look for a single-track trail leading off to the right. Take it and shortly you'll leave the chaparral and cactus and enter a densely shaded riparian area lined with sycamores, alders, and cottonwoods. Then, in turn, you'll leave the shade and climb back out to sparsely vegetated, exposed slopes. You get a little bit of everything in Trail Canyon.

I took my big sister on this trip. Because this was our first waterfall hunt together, I was a little nervous about whether or not we'd actually find one. Although the stream runs year-round in Trail Canyon, Trail Canyon Falls can be less than ebullient by early summer. While my sister happily counted wildflowers along the trail—orange paintbrush, purple nightshade, yellow phlox, hooker's onions, scented ceanothus, tiny purple violets, sagebrush—I silently prayed to the waterfall gods. We hiked steeply out of the canyon, turned a sharp left curve in the trail, and then hey!—we could see the falls up ahead, about a half-mile away. They made a stunning show of white, as they thundered down the canyon. Few waterfalls look this good from so far away.

Trail Canyon Trail, which climbs almost continually up to this point, suddenly levels out after you round the turn and behold the falls. From there, it's an easy stroll to the fall's crest. Trail Canyon Falls spills over a smooth granite precipice in a rectangular block of water. Rather than being funneled through a notch, its stream is given a wide berth over its rounded lip, making it appear far different, and grander, than other Los Angeles waterfalls. Its breadth can be close to 15 feet when the fall is flowing hard.

The fall's height is 50 feet, but it's impossible to tell from the top. To reach the base of the falls and its big pool, you must take a steep spur trail (before the main trail reaches the waterfall's crest). It's very slippery going down, so be careful. A couple more spur trails lead you to rocks right above the falls, good spots for picnicking or laying in the sun.

Trail Canyon Trail continues above the falls, crossing its stream and heading onward to Tom Lucas Trail Camp. We hiked only a few hundred feet past the falls, to the stream crossing where you can examine the colorful granite streambed, then turned around. The trip back is even better than the route in, with excellent views of the canyons below. Plus it's downhill all the way—just the way we like it.

Trip notes: There is no fee. For a map of Angeles National Forest, send $4 to USDA-Forest Service, 1323 Club Drive, Vallejo, CA 94592. For more information, contact Angeles National Forest, Tujunga Ranger District, 12371 North Little Tujunga Canyon Road, San Fernando, CA 91342; (818) 899-1900.

Directions: From Interstate 210 in Sunland, exit on Sunland Boulevard which becomes Foothill Boulevard. Drive east for one mile to Mount Gleason Avenue. Turn left (north), drive 1.3 miles, then turn right on Big Tujunga Canyon Road. Drive 3.4 miles on Big Tujunga Road to a sign for Trail Canyon Trail on the left. Drive a quarter-mile to a fork, then bear right and drive a quarter-mile on rough road to a large parking lot. The trailhead is on the left side of the lot as you drive in.

181. SWITZER FALLS

Angeles National Forest
Off Highway 2 near La Cañada

Access & Difficulty: Hike-in or Backpack 2.5 to 5.0 miles RT/Easy
Elevation: Start at 3,400 feet; total loss 600 feet
Best Season: December to June

Your trip to Switzer Falls can be as little as 2.5 miles round-trip or as many as five miles round-trip, and it's a choice that's not entirely up to you. The mileage is partly based on how you decide to view the falls (your choice), and partly based on whether the Forest Service has opened the gate to Switzer picnic area (not your choice). If the gate's closed, you have to park along Highway 2 and hike steeply downhill on pavement for an extra third-mile, then steeply back up on the return trip.

At first you may curse the holders of the gate key, like we did, but shortly you'll forget all about the inconvenience as you hike deep into Arroyo Seco Canyon along the Gabrielino National Recreation

Switzer Falls

Trail. Pass through the picnic area, then continue hiking downstream on the smooth dirt trail. The route is pleasantly shaded by willows, alders, oaks, and maples—all water-loving trees. A few creek crossings and one mile of trail brings you to Commodore Switzer Trail Camp, an easy backpacking destination with a few primitive sites along the creek. You can't see it from here, but you're perched above 50-foot Switzer Falls.

Cross the creek by the camp and head uphill, climbing above the canyon, still on the Gabrielino Trail. The trail passes Switzer Falls, affording an excellent view of it from across the canyon. The stone building ruins you see are the remains of the Switzer chapel, where visitors at Switzer's Camp, a popular trail resort in the early 1900s, would attend

---

Sunday services above the falls. This attracted even the not-so-devout.

If you're traveling with children, it's wise to be content with the view from here, where you can see the falls dropping vertically through a narrow chute in the gorge. You can also see the pool above the falls, and a smaller waterfall that leads into it. A chain-link fence separates you from the steep dropoff into the canyon.

If you want to see more of Switzer Falls, a few steps further takes you to a junction where the Gabrielino Trail heads right and uphill, and the Bear Canyon Trail heads left and downhill. (If the campsites at Commodore Switzer are taken, you can hike two miles on either trail to reach trail camps at Oakwild and Bear Canyon.) Take the left fork for Bear Canyon and descend steeply for one mile, being wary of the steep dropoffs. When you reach the creek, walk a quarter mile upstream toward Switzer Falls, but resist the temptation to climb around the lower, smaller falls to reach the large drop. There have been too many accidents here.

Should you wish to explore further, more water slides and falls can be found downstream along Bear Canyon Trail. Trout fishing is surprisingly good, and the continual roar and splash of mini-cascades along Arroyo Seco can keep you entertained for hours.

Trip notes: There is no fee. For a map of Angeles National Forest, send $4 to USDA-Forest Service, 1323 Club Drive, Vallejo, CA 94592. For more information, contact Angeles National Forest, Arroyo Seco Ranger District, 4600 Oak Grove Drive, Flintridge, CA 91011; (818) 790-1151.

Directions: From Interstate 210 in La Cañada, take Highway 2 north and drive 9.8 miles to Switzer Picnic Area on the right. (At 9.3 miles you reach Clear Creek Information Station; bear right and reach Switzer Picnic Area in a half-mile.)

182. DEVIL'S CANYON FALLS
San Gabriel Wilderness
Off Highway 2 near Mount Waterman

Access & Difficulty: Hike-in or Backpack 10.0 miles RT/Strenuous
Elevation: Start at 5,300 feet; total loss 2,000 feet
Best Season: December to June

When you've tired of the front country, it's time to make a trip to the rugged San Gabriel Wilderness. Just be prepared to pay for your pleasure, because this is an upside-down hike—down on the way in and up, up, up on the way out. It's a trail of extremes. There's chaparral on some slopes, then tall pines and big-cone spruce on others. There's sun, then shade. It's dry for the first two miles, then you reach a tributary creek and follow its meander.

The area surrounding Devil's Canyon burned in a wildfire in 1998, causing extensive damage. Miraculously, the trail to Devil's Canyon and the canyon itself were barely touched by the fire. Fortunately, the overstory of big-cone spruce was spared.

It doesn't take long to hike down into the canyon, about an hour and a half for most people. When you come upon an obvious camping area above the creek at 3.5 miles, where there are a few fire rings and flat sleeping spots, you're at the canyon floor and the official end of the trail. From there, you can make your way downstream along Devil's Creek, partly on a fishermen's trail and partly rockhopping, wading, and scrambling. The stream is completely cloaked in alders, and largely choked with willows; occasionally you must bushwhack your way through them. The canyon gets narrower as you go; it's slow travel but not treacherous. Pools are surprisingly deep, and if you're lucky you catch sight of little trout. The canyon walls keep squeezing in tighter and steeper until you are in a series of small cascades, two to five feet high. Soon these increase to full-size waterfalls. Some of the nicest are on side streams pouring into Devil's Creek.

If you can reach it, the highlight of the trip is a 20-foot fall on Devil's Creek at about 1.5 miles from the trail camp. The 1.5 miles can take an hour or more, depending on how high the stream is running, and you'll probably get wet. But the waterfall is a stunner, a well-deserved reward for your hard work, dropping over beautiful light-colored granite. It forms a fine, clear pool, and if you're brave enough, you can wade into it. There are sunny areas around the falls where you can warm up after you get out.

This fall blocks any further travel downstream, so turn around and head back for the long uphill climb to the trailhead. Or better yet, spend the night at the trail camp, maybe invite a few Devil's Creek trout for dinner, then hike back out of the canyon early the next morning. Just remember: the 3.5 miles from the camp back up to the trailhead seems at least twice as long as the trip down.

Trip notes: There is no fee. For a map of Angeles National Forest, send $4 to USDA-Forest Service, 1323 Club Drive, Vallejo, CA 94592. For more information, contact Angeles National Forest, Arroyo Seco Ranger District, 4600 Oak Grove Drive, Flintridge, CA 91011; (818) 790-1151.

Directions: From Interstate 210 in La Cañada, take Highway 2 north and drive 27 miles to Chilao Campground on the left. Continue a quarter-mile beyond the camp on Highway 2 to a parking lot on the left (west) side of the highway. Park there and walk across the road to the trailhead. (If you reach the Chilao Visitor Center, you've gone too far.)

183. COOPER CANYON FALLS

Angeles National Forest
Off Highway 2 near Mount Waterman

Access & Difficulty: Hike-in 4.0 miles RT/Moderate
Elevation: Start at 6,400 feet; total loss 850 feet
Best Season: April to June

Once the snow is gone, most people don't think there's much reason to drive 34 miles to the summit of Mount Waterman. But then again, they probably don't know about Cooper Canyon Falls. The best thing about the waterfall, besides the fact that it's set in a gorgeous 6,000-foot-elevation forest, is that it's just far enough away so that it doesn't get heavily visited. To see it, you have to drive a long way, and then you have to hike a couple miles.

Cooper Canyon Falls

Start off from Buckhorn Campground, an hour's drive from LaCañada, at the trailhead for the Burkhardt Trail. Although some campers make use of the swimming holes and small waterfalls in Buckhorn Creek, within a quarter-mile of the campground, most of them don't hike the full distance to Cooper Canyon. You'll soon be on your own, wandering through a dense forest of big firs, cedars, and pines. There is almost no undergrowth in these woods, only conifers and big rocks. It feels as if you might be in the southern Sierra Nevada, but no, this is the San Gabriels.

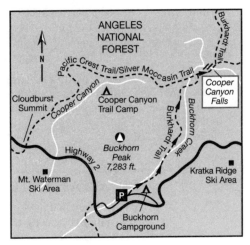

The Burkhardt Trail laterals along the canyon slopes, high above Buckhorn Creek. Just when it seems like you're keeping too high above the stream to be able to see a waterfall, the route makes a left turn into another canyon (Cooper), and traces a long switchback downhill. Look for a group of five young cedar trees, an unusual set of quintuplets, growing together near a tiny stream crossing.

At 1.75 miles from the campground, you'll reach a junction with the Pacific Crest Trail and Silver Moccasin Trail. A sign points left to Cooper Canyon Camp, but you want to head right toward Burkhardt Saddle and Eagle's Roost. It's only one-tenth of a mile to the waterfall, which drops just below the trail's edge.

From the top, Cooper Canyon Falls doesn't look like much, but continue another 30 yards to a cutoff trail that leads steeply to the waterfall's base. A rope near the bottom helps you get down (and up) the last few feet. Once you climb down, you can stand in the middle of the stream, on an island of large boulders, for a perfect view. The fall spills into a steep rock bowl with a big pool at its base, which would be perfect for swimming if it wasn't so cold and shady here. The wide, main section of the waterfall's drop is 35 feet tall, but there's also a 15-foot cascade above it.

On your return hike, you may want to pay a visit to the small falls that are just 10 to 15 minutes' walk from Buckhorn Campground. As you head back on the Burkhardt Trail, look for a huge rock formation across the canyon, a half-mile before you reach the camp. Two nice sets of pools and 10-foot-high falls are along the stream between the rock outcrop and the camp, accessible via short but steep spur trails. They make great swimming holes in summer.

Trip notes: There is no fee. For a map of Angeles National Forest, send $4 to USDA-Forest Service, 1323 Club Drive, Vallejo, CA 94592. For more information, contact Angeles National Forest, Arroyo Seco Ranger District, 4600 Oak Grove Drive, Flintridge, CA 91011; (818) 790-1151.

Directions: From Interstate 210 in La Cañada, take Highway 2 north and drive 34 miles to Buckhorn Camp on the left. (It's 1.5 miles past the Mount Waterman ski lift, just beyond Cloudburst Summit.) The Burkhardt Trail starts at the far end of the camp near the restrooms (bear left at site #18).

184. MILLARD FALLS

Angeles National Forest
Off Interstate 210 near Pasadena

Access & Difficulty: Hike-in 1.0 mile RT/Easy
Elevation: Start at 1,900 feet; total gain 200 feet
Best Season: December to June

If you want to guarantee your kids a good time, take them to Millard Campground for the short hike and scramble to Millard Falls. If it's winter or spring, make sure they're outfitted with hiking boots or shoes they can get wet, because you're on a trail only part of the time, and the rest of the time you pick your way up the creek. It's a perfect family adventure, short enough even for little ones to accomplish, but with beautiful scenery that will impress hikers of all ages.

The only minus to the Millard Falls Trail is the abundance of carvings found on the smooth-barked alder trees. The carvings desecrate almost every tree trunk as high as human hands can reach. Take this opportunity to teach your children never, ever to carve their initials (or anything) into the trunks of trees. Many people don't realize that over time this kills the tree. Spread the word, especially to children.

The route is a half-mile walk up the stream canyon, but because you're in the creek much of the time, it takes a bit longer than a normal half-mile hike. Start walking at the edge of the campground, just beyond the camp host's site. The trail leads to the right, past a couple of private cabins. After the first few yards, the trail disappears into the creek (when the stream flow is high), but keep heading upstream, rockhopping as you go.

The canyon gets progressively narrower as you travel. Finally its walls come together at 60-foot Millard Falls. The fall drops over a rugged cliff face; its stream splits in two at the top, forced to detour around two boulders which are stuck in the waterfall's notch. (Those boulders won't last forever; another earthquake or two and Millard Falls will look completely different.) The two streams rejoin about two-thirds of the way down, creating a tremendous rush of water in springtime.

If you're in the mood for more of an adventure than this easy jaunt to the falls provides, consider taking a cross-country ramble to the site of

Millard Falls

the old Dawn Mine tunnel, located farther back in Millard Canyon. You can't get there from the falls; instead, head back to your car and drive back to the fork on Chaney Trail. Turn east and park near the gate for Sunset Ridge Fire Road. Take the fire road a quarter mile to a trail on the left, then follow that trail to the canyon bottom (bear left where the trail forks). Rockhop your way upstream (there is no formal trail) for about two miles to the old mine site and boarded up tunnel.

Trip notes: There is no fee. For a map of Angeles National Forest, send $4 to USDA-Forest Service, 1323 Club Drive, Vallejo, CA 94592. For more information, contact Angeles National Forest, Arroyo Seco Ranger District, 4600 Oak Grove Drive, Flintridge, CA 91011; (818) 790-1151.

Directions: From Interstate 210 in Pasadena, exit on Lake Avenue and drive north for 3.5 miles to Loma Alta Drive. Turn west (left) on Loma Alta Drive and drive one mile to Chaney Trail at the flashing yellow light. Turn right and drive 1.5 miles on Chaney Trail, keeping left at the fork, to Millard Campground. Park in the parking lot, then follow the fire road on the right (as you drove in) that leads into the campground.

185. EATON CANYON FALLS

Eaton Canyon County Park
Off Interstate 210 in Pasadena

Access & Difficulty: Hike-in 3.0 miles RT/Easy
Elevation: Start at 1,000 feet; total gain 350 feet
Best Season: December to June

Eaton Canyon's waterfall would be rated a 9 or a 10 if it weren't for the ingrates who have defiled the canyon with graffiti. The waterfall is excellent, the hike to it is enjoyable, and despite the spray-paint assault on the canyon, it's an area that's well-loved by local hikers of all ages. During my hike I passed two elementary school groups as well as several hikers of retirement age walking in Eaton Canyon.

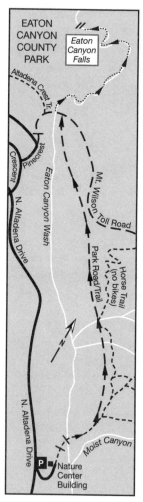

Part of the problem is that the waterfall is accessible via a shortcut from the Mount Wilson Toll Road, so troublemakers can access the waterfall without having to hike the three-mile round-trip. In urban areas, a short walk to a stellar destination is often a recipe for trouble. Outdoor lovers, however, will want to hike the park's main trail because it follows an interesting route along Eaton Canyon's wash, passing cactus, chaparral, willows, and oaks. A waterfall this good should be earned with a pretty walk. Eaton Canyon provides it.

Eaton Canyon Falls is similar in appearance to nearby Millard Falls, although it's not as tall. It pours over a rock wall that has eroded into a low, jagged V-shape; a large rounded boulder lies perched in its notch. The falls are about 40 feet high, with exceptional flow in springtime.

To reach the waterfall, park by the Eaton Canyon nature center, then head inside to pick up a free park map. Don't be shocked if you hear the sound of gunfire. On certain weekdays, the noise from the neighboring police officers' firing range is like fireworks going off. In a few minutes of walking, you'll be far from the blitz.

Walk to the far end of the parking lot and take the dirt road that leads to the right. Cross the wash and hike along the wide canyon trail with the creek on your left. You'll pass a right cutoff for Henninger Flats Trail, then reach a bridge where your trail intersects with Mount Wilson Toll Road. Cross the bridge and take the steep right cutoff trail on its far side down to the streambed.

Now you're mostly off-trail and in the stream, crossing it several times as you work your way upcanyon. The route is different each time you hike it, depending on how much water is flowing. After about 20 minutes of stream scrambling, the canyon makes a sharp left turn, and suddenly you're facing the waterfall. It's a great surprise.

Eaton Canyon Falls

Eaton Canyon Falls and its trail are incredibly popular, even on weekdays. On my trip, I passed by several older hikers picking their way down the stream canyon, and they all remarked on how pretty Eaton Falls looked. It just goes to show that a beautiful waterfall can overcome even the venal efforts of vandals.

Trip notes: There is no fee. A free map of Eaton Canyon County Park is available at the nature center. For more information, contact Eaton Canyon County Park, 1750 North Altadena Drive, Pasadena, CA 91107; (626) 398-5420.

Directions: From Interstate 210 in Pasadena (heading east), take the Altadena Drive exit and drive north on Altadena Drive for 1.6 miles. Turn right into the entrance for Eaton Canyon County Park.

186. STURTEVANT FALLS

Angeles National Forest
Off Interstate 210 near Arcadia

Access & Difficulty: Hike-in 3.2 miles RT/Easy
Elevation: Start at 2,100 feet; total loss/gain 600 feet
Best Season: December to June

Ah, Sturtevant Falls. For many, the name is evocative, mixing images of memory and desire. Sturtevant is the crown jewel of Big Santa Anita Canyon—a lush, almost magical gulch just a handful of miles from the Pasadena Freeway. Day-hikers (myself included) can't help but covet the small summer cabins in Big Santa Anita Canyon, perched as they are in the same beautiful ravine where Sturtevant Falls drops. My idea of the good life in Los Angeles would be to live in one of those cabins and take a daily stroll to the waterfall.

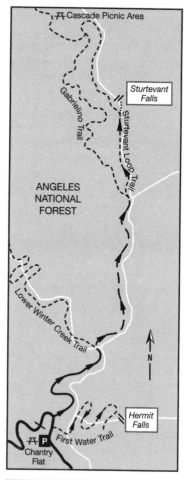

But for now, I must be content to leave my car at Chantry Flat and hike down into the canyon, following the Gabrielino Trail for an easy 3.2-mile round-trip. Since Gabrielino is a national recreation trail, it's open to bikes, horses, and dogs (up to the waterfall cutoff), giving you several options for making the trip. Unfortunately, the path is paved for six-tenths of a mile heading down to the canyon, but the surroundings are so gorgeous, you won't mind. When you reach the canyon bottom, cross Roberts Footbridge over Winter Creek and note the left turnoff for the Winter Creek Trail. Then head to your right on the wide dirt path, going upstream to see Sturtevant Falls, which is only one mile away.

A sign near the footbridge

informs you of the area's history. It tells of the days when the confluence of Winter and Big Santa Anita creeks was the home of Roberts Camp, a popular weekend resort from 1912 to 1936. A stone lodge, dining area, and various cabins and tents once stood here—enough buildings to accommodate 180 guests at a time. The trail leads past some remaining cabins, under the shade of oaks and alders and along Big Santa Anita Creek. The stream is tamed somewhat by a series of small check dams, forming oddly pretty artificial waterfalls and glassy pools.

Sturtevant Falls

At the next junction, the Gabrielino Trail forks to the left and heads uphill, but you continue straight along the creek, heading a quarter-mile further to Sturtevant Falls. Cross the creek and curve around a leftward bend in the canyon, then cross again. Look up as you cross—surprise! Sturtevant Falls suddenly reveals itself, dropping 60 feet over a granite cliff into a perfectly shaped rock bowl.

Like the Grace Kelly of waterfalls, Sturtevant is a classy, elegant act. Set in the back of the shady canyon, it's gracefully framed by alders and has a large pool at its base. If you stand on the right side of the falls, you can see its flow making an S-turn down a chute above the main drop, adding another 15 feet to the falls' total height.

If you want to linger a little longer in Big Santa Anita Canyon after visiting Sturtevant Falls, you can backtrack to the junction where the Gabrielino Trail heads uphill, then follow it out and back to Cascade Picnic Area, a shady spot alongside the creek. This will add 2.5 greenery-filled miles to your round-trip.

Trip notes: There is no fee. For a map of Angeles National Forest, send $4 to USDA-Forest Service, 1323 Club Drive, Vallejo, CA 94592. For more information, contact Angeles National Forest, Arroyo Seco Ranger District, 4600 Oak Grove Drive, Flintridge, CA 91011; (818) 790-1151.

Directions: From Interstate 210 in Pasadena, drive seven miles east to Arcadia. Exit on Santa Anita Avenue and drive six miles north to the road's end at Chantry Flat. The trail begins across the road from the first parking area as you drive in.

187. HERMIT FALLS

Angeles National Forest
Off Interstate 210 near Arcadia

Access & Difficulty: Hike-in 4.0 miles RT/Easy
Elevation: Start at 2,100 feet; total loss 800 feet
Best Season: December to June

Sturtevant Falls is the undisputed queen of the waterfalls in Big Santa Anita Canyon, but don't let that dissuade you from making the trip to see nearby Hermit Falls as well. Although your vision of Hermit Falls is hampered by the fact that the trail leads you to its lip rather than its base, you'll be so pleased with the excursion that you probably won't mind an impeded view.

The trail to Hermit Falls begins on the paved Gabrielino National Recreation Trail, the same route as the trip to Sturtevant Falls. To get to Hermit Falls, however, you must take the right fork off the Gabrielino Trail and on to the First Water Trail, less than a quarter-mile from the parking lot. This is the forté of the Hermit Falls trip—you get off the pavement, away from the crowds, and on to a gorgeous single-track dirt trail that switchbacks gently down into Big Santa Anita Canyon, then heads southward along the North Fork of Santa Anita Creek.

As on the trip to Sturtevant Falls, you'll pass many artificial waterfalls made by small dams on Santa Anita Creek, and dozens of adorable cabins, leftovers from the area's colorful past as a vacation resort. Just before the third of these dams, First Water Trail crosses the creek, and it does so twice more before Hermit Falls. These crossings are easy in summer but can be difficult earlier in the year, like when it's pouring down rain, you're tired and hungry, and your rain gear has long since given out. Just ask me, I'm an expert.

Descend some more as you head downstream to the waterfall,

through a canyon so lush it seems to contain every imaginable type of foliage. In addition to the tall oaks and alders, the ground is covered with huge chain ferns, slender sword ferns, tiny maidenhair ferns, and half a dozen other fern varieties. The constant shade of the narrow canyon, combined with the presence of the year-round stream, makes it possible for every inch of ground to spring forth plant life. Since you're on single-track, the greenery is close enough to touch, and in the morning, dew on the leaves glances off your skin.

When the trail reaches a short spur to the top of Hermit Falls, follow it and take your pick of granite boulders to sit on and have a picnic. You can just barely glimpse the top of the falls as it drops over a rounded ledge, then freefalls about 30 feet. The stream shoots out from a notch as if from a fire hose, then gets wrested downward by gravity.

The First Water Trail ends just beyond the waterfall at one more cabin, so after viewing Hermit Falls, retrace your steps and climb back out of Big Santa Anita Canyon.

Trip notes: There is no fee. For a map of Angeles National Forest, send $4 to USDA-Forest Service, 1323 Club Drive, Vallejo, CA 94592. For more information, contact Angeles National Forest, Arroyo Seco Ranger District, 4600 Oak Grove Drive, Flintridge, CA 91011; (818) 790-1151.

Directions: From Interstate 210 in Pasadena, drive seven miles east to Arcadia. Exit on Santa Anita Avenue and drive six miles north to road's end at Chantry Flat. The trail begins across the road from the first parking area as you drive in.

188. MONROVIA CANYON FALLS

Monrovia Canyon Park
Off Interstate 210 in Monrovia

Access & Difficulty: Hike-in 1.4 miles RT/Easy
Elevation: Start at 1,300 feet; total gain 100 feet
Best Season: December to June

Everything about Monrovia Canyon Falls is a great experience, except if you try to visit it on a Tuesday. That's when the local police have target practice in Monrovia Canyon Park, and they lock the gates and close the whole place down for the day. It's a bummer for waterfall-lovers. Of course, it's better to be safe than be a target.

Time your trip for any day but Tuesday, and get ready for a perfect walk in the woods. The waterfall trail is an ideal hike for

Monrovia Canyon Falls

youngsters because it's nearly level the whole way and less than a mile in length. Start at the picnic area near the park nature center and museum at the far end of the park road. Walk through the picnic area and look for the signed single-track trail to Monrovia Canyon Falls. At the first junction, head to the right.

Almost immediately you pass several check dams, which make small waterfalls of their own, but hey—they're not the real thing. Accept no imitations; keep walking. The canyon is lush and shaded, like a smaller version of nearby Big Santa Anita Canyon, crowded with alders, oaks, and ferns. It's the kind of place that would be unforgettable in a light rain.

In less than half an hour of slightly uphill walking, you're at the falls, which are 50 feet tall, and split in the middle by a granite ledge. There are many big rocks in front of it, perfectly situated for gazing in admiration, and pleasant shade from oaks and bays.

Because access is so easy, Monrovia Canyon Falls is a popular place. For the best experience, visit on a weekday (but not Tuesday).

Trip notes: A $2 access fee is charged. A free park map is available at the nature center. For more information, contact Monrovia Canyon Park, 1200 North Canyon Boulevard, Monrovia, CA 91016; (626) 256-8282. Or contact Public Works, City Hall, 415 South Ivy Avenue, Monrovia, CA 91016; (626) 932-5562.

Directions: From Interstate 210 in Monrovia, take the Myrtle Avenue exit and drive north on Myrtle Avenue for 1.8 miles. Turn right on Scenic Drive, then drive 200 yards and turn right on Encinitas Drive, then turn left again immediately, back on Scenic Drive. Continue on

Scenic Drive as it turns into Canyon Boulevard, then turn right at the sign for Monrovia Canyon Park. Park at the far end of the park road, near the picnic area and nature center.

189. SOLDIER CREEK FALLS (Lewis Falls)

Angeles National Forest
Off Highway 39 near Crystal Lake

Access & Difficulty: Hike-in 1.25 miles RT/Easy
Elevation: Start at 4,000 feet; total gain 300 feet
Best Season: December to June

The thing about the Crystal Lake Recreation Area is that you either know about it or you don't. Many Los Angeles families vacation here year after year, staying in the campground, hiking on the trails, and fishing in small Crystal Lake, the only natural lake in the San Gabriel Mountains. But if you take an informal poll on the streets of nearby Azusa or Glendora, at least half the people will have never heard of Crystal Lake.

Why? Beats me. Crystal Lake Recreation Area is a great outdoor destination, at an elevation high enough to be out of the smog and much cooler than the valley. It is home to a dense forest of large cedars and pines. What makes it even better is the proximity of Soldier Creek Falls, also called Lewis Falls, a 50-foot drop over a mossy double ledge. Since the trailhead is unmarked, and technically there is

Soldier Creek Falls

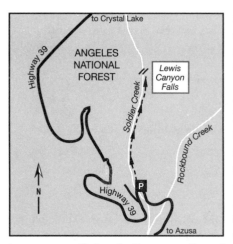

no real trail, the waterfall doesn't get frequented by every weekend visitor to Crystal Lake.

Begin by hiking from the parking pullout on Highway 39 at Soldier Creek, walking with the stream on your left. (There's a route on the other side of the creek as well, but it's much rougher and eventually you'll have to cross over.) The start of the trail has some graffiti and often some litter (mutter a few curses at the perpetrators), but as you head back from the road, conditions will improve.

Pass a few cabins and hike upstream under the shade of oaks and firs. When the trail vanishes, start walking up the streambed, rockhopping over small boulders and climbing over big ones. Your scramble can last anywhere between 200 and 500 yards, depending on how high the water level is and how much of the trail is submerged. Just keep going until you can't go any further, where the canyon walls close in. There, in a rocky grotto, Soldier Creek Falls pours in from the left. The waterfall holds court in this narrow space, surrounded by big trees and many verdant ferns and mosses. Just to remind you that you're still in Southern California, desert plants such as yuccas and chollas cling to the sunnier cliffs above the fall.

Trip notes: There is no fee. For a map of Angeles National Forest, send $4 to USDA-Forest Service, 1323 Club Drive, Vallejo, CA 94592. For more information, contact Angeles National Forest, San Gabriel River Ranger District, 110 North Wabash Avenue, Glendora, CA 91741; (626) 335-1251.

Directions: From Azusa on Interstate 210, drive north on Highway 39 for 18 miles to Coldbrook Camp on the left. From Coldbrook Camp, continue 2.4 miles up Highway 39 to a dirt pullout on the right, where Soldier Creek crosses under the highway. (If you reach the turnoff for Falling Springs Resort, you've gone two-tenths of a mile too far.) Park in the pullout and begin hiking from the far right side, heading up the right side of the creek.

190. SAN ANTONIO FALLS

Angeles National Forest
Off Highway 83 on Mount Baldy

Access & Difficulty: Hike-in 1.5 miles RT/Easy
Elevation: Start at 6,200 feet; total gain 250 feet
Best Season: March to July

When I was a college student in Claremont, I would eagerly await December when the Inland Empire air would clear and the first snows would frost the rounded top of 10,064-foot Mount Baldy. From our dormitory rooms in the valley, we could look out our windows and see the wondrous sight of a nearby snowcapped mountain, even though it might be 70 degrees and balmy at school.

In more recent years I've looked forward to those winter days on Mount Baldy for another reason: December snows lead to springtime snowmelt, and that's when I can go see San Antonio Falls, dropping 80 feet over a steep granite and talus slope.

San Antonio Falls has a short season. Because it has a small drainage area and is fed primarily by snowmelt, you've got to time your trip for the first warm days after winter, sometimes as early as March. The hike to the falls is easy, following the Mount Baldy ski lift maintenance road, which is paved to the falls and has only a slight uphill grade. If they are busy working on the ski lift, you may share the road with a vehicle or two.

At seven-tenths of a mile, you round a sharp curve and see and hear the waterfall. If you wish, you can scramble down to its base on a well-worn route of a few hundred feet. Be

San Antonio Falls

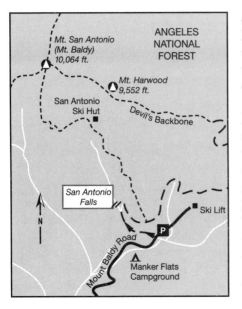

careful on the loose gravel, however. A large landslide to the left of the waterfall testifies to the instability of the slope.

San Antonio Falls has three tiers. The first is a large freefall drop and the second and third are curved cascades over granite. In a good snow year, some white patches will frame the waterfall as late as April. The peak of Mount Baldy, high above the falls, can be crowned with snow until Memorial Day after big storm years.

So why is it called San Antonio Falls? Because its home, Mount Baldy, is really called Mount San Antonio. Few people ever call it that, and many people who live in its shadow don't even know its proper name. The mountain was named for Saint Anthony of Padua, a Franciscan priest and miracle worker. But let's face it, the peak's rounded, exposed summit looks more like a Baldy than a saint.

You may see other people on the waterfall trail heading up the road carrying ropes and ice axes. They're heading for Baldy's summit, and if there is much snow, they need special equipment to get there. After San Antonio Falls, the maintenance road switchbacks to the right, and most summit hikers follow it to a trail junction at Baldy Notch. From there, they head left to the top of the ski lift, then hike along the rather treacherous Devil's Backbone to the south side of Mount Harwood at 9,552 feet and finally to the peak of Mount Baldy at 10,064 feet, a total of six trail miles from San Antonio Falls.

If you opt to make the short return trip to the parking lot instead, check out the great views of the San Gabriel basin far below. On clear days, the hike back to your car is nearly as good as the falls.

Trip notes: There is no fee. For a map of Angeles National Forest, send $4 to USDA-Forest Service, 1323 Club Drive, Vallejo, CA 94592. For more information, contact Angeles National Forest, San Gabriel River Ranger District, 110 North Wabash Avenue, Glendora, CA 91741; (626) 335-1251.

Directions: From Interstate 10 near Upland and Ontario, exit on Euclid Avenue (Highway 83) and drive north for six miles till Euclid Avenue joins Mount Baldy Road. Drive nine miles north on Mount Baldy Road to Manker Flats Camp, then continue three-tenths of a mile further to Falls Road on the left. Park in the dirt pullouts by Falls Road and begin walking on the gated, paved road.

191. BONITA FALLS

San Bernardino National Forest
Off Interstate 15 near Lytle Creek

Access & Difficulty: Drive-to/Easy
    or Scramble 1.0 mile RT/Moderate
Elevation: 3,200 feet
Best Season: December to June

When I read the San Bernardino National Forest's newspaper, I was amazed to see the following in large, bold type: "Bonita Falls, a 90-foot waterfall, is visible from Lytle Creek Road in the South Fork area." What? A 90-foot waterfall? Near Lytle Creek? And I had never heard of it?

It wasn't long before I was heading up Interstate 15 in search of Bonita Falls. I followed the directions exactly, drove up and down Lytle Creek Road about 20 times, stopped at several likely spots and looked around. No waterfall. A visit to the Lytle Creek Ranger Station solved the mystery: If you don't bring your binoculars, Bonita Falls is pretty hard to see from Lytle Creek Road. Guess that means they exaggerated a little in the national forest newspaper.

The waterfall is hard to see because it's located directly behind Bonita Trailer Park, which is closed to non-paying customers. If you turn off Lytle Creek Road on to South Fork Road, you can get a little better view. You have to stop before South Fork Road enters the trailer park, but from this vantage point you can look up and plainly see Bonita Falls about halfway up the mountainside. Binoculars will greatly improve your view. From South Fork Road, the waterfall appears as only a white sliver, but its height is obvious and impressive.

Rangers at Lytle Creek say that informal trails lead from Lytle Creek Wash back to the falls, but the only ones I found required some serious bushwhacking. There's also the danger of straying onto private property—you don't want to run into any mobile home owners who are vigilant about property rights.

The Lytle Creek Ranger Station is one mile south of Bonita Falls on Lytle Creek Road, so check with them for updated information about access to the falls. Another option is to stay overnight at the trailer park, because they allow camping for a few RVs and tents in addition to their live-in community. If you pay your fee for the night, you're entitled to step right out the door of your Winnebago and make your way up to Bonita Falls. Phone Bonita Ranch Trailer Park at (909) 887-3643.

Trip notes: There is no fee. For a map of San Bernardino National Forest, send $4 to USDA-Forest Service, 1323 Club Drive, Vallejo, CA 94592. For more information, contact San Bernardino National Forest, Cajon Ranger District, 1209 Lytle Creek Road, Lytle Creek, CA 92358; (909) 887-2576.

Directions: From Ontario, drive east on Interstate 10 for seven miles to Interstate 15. Drive north on Interstate 15 for 11 miles and take the Sierra Avenue exit, then turn left (north) at the stop sign. Drive 6.2 miles (the road becomes Lytle Creek Road) to South Fork Road. Turn left on South Fork Road and drive to where it intersects with Melody Lane on the right. (You can't continue on South Fork Road, because you reach a "no trespassing" sign for Bonita Ranch Trailer Park.)

192. HEART ROCK FALLS

San Bernardino National Forest
Off Highway 138 near Crestline

Access & Difficulty: Hike-in 2.0 miles RT/Easy
Elevation: Start at 3,800 feet; total loss 250 feet
Best Season: January to June

Of all my collected memories of ecstatic first glances at water-falls, the one that stands out is the way I felt when I first laid eyes on Heart Rock Falls. The cataract was a complete surprise, more beautiful and unusual than I ever could have imagined. Yes, Heart Rock stole my heart.

Heart Rock Falls is really Seeley Creek Falls, because it spills along Seeley Creek near Lake Silverwood. But the distinguishing feature of the waterfall is not its stream, but rather the heart-shaped rock at its crest. Not a rock shaped like a heart, mind you—that's what we falsely assumed from reading the Forest Service brochure. Instead, Heart Rock is a smooth granite boulder in which nature has carved a perfect, heart-shaped bowl, about three feet deep and five feet wide. A 25-foot waterfall spills to the right of the heart, and when Seeley Creek's flow is high, the stream pours into the heart's crown, then flows out the bottom and freefalls downward.

Heart Rock Falls

The striking thing is that the heart bowl is so perfectly shaped. Plenty of rock formations are named after figures or animals that they roughly resemble, but Heart Rock has a deep imprint that could be the mold for Valentine candy boxes. With or without water sliding through it, it's unique.

The trail to reach the fall starts out ingloriously, but it gets better. The trailhead is opposite the buildings of Seeley Camp, a Los Angeles Parks and Recreation camp, where there is often a crowd. But once you get past the swimming pool, things quiet down. The forest is thick with cedars and Jeffrey pines, and the trail descends gently to the creek. In a short mile, you near the trail's end, and a right spur leads to granite stair-steps climbing to an overlook above the creek. Peer over the edge, and you'll see the top of the waterfall and heart-stopping Heart Rock. This one of very few waterfalls that is best seen from above—only from an on-top perspective can you get a full view of the heart and the falls.

Be sure to walk the last few yards of trail, which lead downstream of Heart Rock to a series of pretty waterslides and pools below the falls.

Trip notes: There is no fee. For a map of San Bernardino National Forest, send $4 to USDA-Forest Service, 1323 Club Drive, Vallejo, CA 94592. For more information, contact San Bernardino National Forest, Arrowhead Ranger District, 28104 Highway 18, Skyforest, CA 92385; (909) 337-2444.

Directions: From Crestline at the junction of highways 18 and 138, turn north on Highway 138 and drive 2.5 miles to the sign for Camp Seeley, just past the town of Valley of Enchantment. Turn left at the camp sign on Road 2N03, then take the left fork in the road (don't park in the camp parking lot). Cross the creek, which usually flows over the road, then look for the double-track trail on the right, near a sewer pipeline sign. Park alongside the road. (You will be directly across the creek from the main parking lot for Camp Seeley, near the playground area.)

193. DEEP CREEK FALLS

San Bernardino National Forest
Off Highway 18 near Lake Arrowhead

Access & Difficulty: Hike-in & Scramble 2.0 miles RT/Moderate
Elevation: Start at 5,100 feet; total gain 200 feet
Best Season: April to July

Deep Creek has many personalities. It's a geologically active creek sporting hot springs and pools, where warm-water lovers flock to bathe. It's a wild trout stream, filled with pockets of moss and algae, the start of a plentiful food chain for the fish. Technically, it's a branch of the Mojave River, and eventually it disappears in desert sand. But best of all, it's a year-round creek with many waterfalls, accessible only to those willing to work a little.

A Deep Creek cascade

First, there's the drive from Lake Arrowhead, mostly on dirt roads. We made it almost all the way to the trailhead in our rental car, but in the final eighth of a mile, the rutted road won and we walked. (The ranger told us that sometimes the stream crossings on the road can be as deep as three feet; when we visited in late April, they were only a few inches, but the potholes were deep.) Then, this section of the Deep Creek Trail is vastly different from the downstream section, which is the well-graded Pacific Crest Trail. It's not really a trail at all, more of an anglers' route, and can be in various states of repair and disrepair.

Whatever it takes, you should make the trip. The falls on Deep Creek are not tall, but they are unusually beautiful, dropping on a pristine stream amid granite, cottonwoods, and conifers. In spring, you can see little six-inch trout in the clear green-yellow waters of Deep Creek. Every turn of the stream seems to be home to a water ouzel flitting among the cascades and pools.

When you reach the trailhead, start hiking upstream on the signed trail, scrambling more than walking. Take your time, making use of the many good handholds in the rock and admiring the canyon as you go. Big boulders seem to pop up at every turn of Deep Creek. Cottonwood leaves float down from the trees and drift on the surface. We saw a pair of ducks swimming in one pool; they seemed pleased to have discovered their own private duck pond.

After about 30 minutes of scrambling, you'll get your first peek at Deep Creek's falls, as the canyon narrows and the rocks get more massive. The waterfall looks small when you first see it, appearing as a narrow chute of water over big rocks—no big deal. But as you get closer, you start noticing more, and when you're right on top of the fall, you realize that the chute is only part of it. The main fall is a long cascade of ultra-clear water sliding down over granite. It's a 25-foot-long cascade, but with only about 10 feet of height. You can sit right alongside it on the smooth rock and watch the water go by; if you do, you'll be struck by the clarity of the water. It looks like liquid glass.

You may find a cable strung across the stream at this waterfall for people who choose to cross and continue upstream. More falls are above, but they are treacherous to reach. Use caution if you proceed.

A better bet is to use the downstream pools as swimming holes; there are hundreds of places to wade in and even some small sandy beaches to lay on. If you choose to do any fishing, remember that Deep Creek is a wild trout stream; the limit is two, minimum size is eight inches, and only artificial lures with barbless hooks are allowed.

Trip notes: There is no fee. For a map of San Bernardino National Forest, send $4 to USDA-Forest Service, 1323 Club Drive, Vallejo, CA 94592. For more information, contact San Bernardino National Forest, Arrowhead Ranger District, 28104 Highway 18, Skyforest, CA 92385; (909) 337-2444.

Directions: From Crestline at the junction of highways 18 and 138, drive east on Highway 18 for 10 miles to the left turnoff for Highway 173. Drive north on Highway 173 to Lake Arrowhead, then continue for 1.5 miles to Hook Creek Road. Turn right on Hook Creek Road, and follow it until it turns to dirt and becomes Road 2N26Y. Continue on Road 2N26Y for one mile, then bear right on Road 3N34. In seven-tenths of a mile, you'll reach T-6 Crossing, where the road crosses Deep Creek. Park before the crossing and begin walking on the fishermen's trail upstream.

194. MILL CREEK ROAD FALLS

San Bernardino National Forest
Off Highway 38 near Angelus Oaks

Access & Difficulty: Hike-in 1.2 miles RT/Easy
or Drive-to/Easy
Elevation: Start at 5,800 feet; total loss 200 feet
Best Season: March to June

We were staying at Angelus Oaks Lodge in a cute little cabin in San Bernardino National Forest, having a fine time on a research trip. When one of the owners casually mentioned that there was a waterfall about a mile away from the lodge, we couldn't believe our luck. Off we went to see Mill Creek Road Falls.

You can drive to it, but you might as well hike to it, because Mill Creek Road Falls drops along a dirt road that gets very little traffic. In fact, we nicknamed this waterfall "Closed Road Falls," because when we were there, they'd closed the road on both ends so the road grader could smooth out the potholes from winter storms.

Mill Creek Road Falls is not a show-stopper, just a pretty little 30-foot waterfall dropping down a rock face. If you're heading down-hill on Mill Creek Road from Highway 38, you can drive by the waterfall and miss the whole thing, because it's over your right shoulder as you pass. If you're walking, or if you drive back in the other direction, you'll have no trouble finding it. There's a small clearing at the foot of the falls, so you can get off the road while you take a look.

Trip notes: There is no fee. For a map of San Bernardino National Forest, send $4 to USDA-Forest Service, 1323 Club Drive, Vallejo, CA 94592. For more information, contact San Bernardino National Forest, San Gorgonio Ranger District, 34701 Mill Creek Road, Mentone, CA 92359; (909) 794-1123.

Directions: From Interstate 10 at Redlands, take the Highway 38 exit and drive northeast for 14 miles to the junction with Forest Home Road.

Continue past this junction on Highway 38 for five more miles to Angelus Oaks Lodge on the right. One hundred yards past the lodge, look for a dirt road on the left side of the road, signed as Mill Creek Road. The waterfall is six-tenths of a mile down Mill Creek Road, on the right side. (You can walk or drive.)

---

195. MONKEYFACE & RIM OF THE WORLD HIGHWAY FALLS

San Bernardino National Forest
Off Highway 38 near Forest Falls

Access & Difficulty: Drive-to/Easy
Elevation: 3,800 feet (Monkeyface) & 4,800 feet (Rim of the World)
Best Season: February to May

The Rim of the World Scenic Byway is hands-down the most spectacular drive in Southern California, from its start near Forest Falls to its middle near Big Bear Lake and its end near Cajon Pass. It highlights much of the gorgeous high-mountain scenery of San Bernardino National Forest. If you're going to take a driving tour anywhere, this should be at the top of your list.

If you want to stop along the byway and see a couple waterfalls, you're in luck. Start with Monkeyface Falls; simply turn off Highway 38 toward Forest Falls and you're alongside it in about 100 yards. It's on your left, about a quarter-mile from the road, and there are pullouts where you can stop your car. Unfortunately, the fall is difficult to see unless it's flowing hard, because it's set deep in a crevice on the hillside. It drops an estimated 200 feet through a narrow, twisting canyon.

When it does flow, does it look like the face of a monkey? Good question, but the answer's no. They call it Monkeyface Falls simply because it flows on Monkeyface Creek. It's also on private property, so don't make any plans to hike to it. Yup, somebody's got his or her own private waterfall and isn't interested in sharing it.

If Monkeyface isn't flowing, don't fret; there's another drive-to waterfall to see. From the junction of Highway 38 and Forest Home Road, set your odometer and drive north on Highway 38 for two miles to a pullout on the left (north) side of the road. The pullout is between mileage markers 17.05 and 17.10 and has a very angular, pointed rock formation right next to it. Park by the rock, then walk to the edge and look down into Mountain Home Canyon below.

There you'll see a perfect freefall cataract, funneled through a narrow, 10-foot-wide chute in the rock, then free-leaping about 50 feet into a pool below. It's distant, but very beautiful. A pair of binoculars greatly enhances your view.

The canyon walls are dangerously steep and loose, so don't attempt to climb down to the falls. People have died trying. If you want to see a waterfall from closer up, drive four miles up Forest Home Road to the Falls Recreation Area where you can walk to or drive by Big Falls (see the following story).

Trip notes: There is no fee. For a map of San Bernardino National Forest, send $4 to USDA-Forest Service, 1323 Club Drive, Vallejo, CA 94592. For more information, contact San Bernardino National Forest, San Gorgonio Ranger District, 34701 Mill Creek Road, Mentone, CA 92359; (909) 794-1123.

Directions: From Interstate 10 at Redlands, take the Highway 38 exit and drive northeast for 14 miles to the junction with Forest Home Road. Bear right and continue for 100 yards. Monkeyface Falls is on the left (north) side of the road.

---

196. BIG FALLS
San Bernardino National Forest
Off Highway 38 near Forest Falls

Access & Difficulty: Hike-in 0.6 mile RT/Easy
Elevation: Start at 5,960 feet; total gain 80 feet
Best Season: March to September

Big Falls has earned its name. At 500 feet, it's the tallest waterfall in the San Bernardino Mountains, and most folks claim it's the largest year-round waterfall in all of Southern California. Big Falls is also the centerpiece of the Falls Recreation area, just outside of the town of Forest Falls, and get this—it's located on Valley of the Falls Drive. Everything around here is called "falls" this or "falls" that. It's my kind of place.

For hardy backpackers, the Falls Recreation Area has plenty to offer. Several trails lead to the San Gorgonio Wilderness, including the shortest and steepest route to the summit of Mount San Gorgonio on the Vivian Creek Trail. But for the average visitor, Big Falls is the only easily accessible destination in the area, reached by a 20 minute round-trip walk from the parking lot. Since Big Falls is the big draw around here, you'd expect there to be a well-marked trailhead and maybe an information sign for the Big Falls hike. But no; when we arrived at the huge Big Falls picnic area and parking lot, we met four other hikers who were wandering around, trying to figure out where Big Falls was. We hiked in the wrong direction for a mile before we figured it out.

It turns out that Big Falls is northwest of the parking lot, hidden in a side canyon, and to reach it you must walk downstream on Mill Creek Wash, below the Big Falls picnic area. It's a

Big Falls

rocky walk through the wash, so sturdy shoes or hiking boots are a good idea. (We saw a woman who made the trip in sandals, but she wasn't having a good time.) Mill Creek must be crossed by rockhopping, so plan your trip for when the stream isn't raging, which varies greatly from year to year depending on the snowmelt. Usually, the best place to cross is just after you pass a small private cabin alongside the wash. On the far side, look for a trail leading uphill on the right side of Falls Creek, which is a feeder stream to Mill Creek. There's a small cascade at the bottom of Falls Creek; hike past it and uphill for about five minutes to the overlook area for Big Falls.

Now for the bad news. From the overlook, you peer uphill at the falls and see surprisingly little of it. Much of the waterfall is hidden back in the canyon and out of view; all you can glimpse is the top 40 feet of a very Yosemite Falls-type freefall, complete with what appears to be a hanging valley, and some cascading water down below. The huge middle part of the fall is missing, making it a less impressive sight than you'd expect from the tallest waterfall in Southern California. Don't consider scaling the cliffs for a better perspective, however; many people have died in the attempt.

Want a better look at Big Falls? The easiest and best view is actually from your car window, as you drive up the road between the town of Forest Falls and the Big Falls parking area. Look toward Mill Creek just east of the last few houses along Forest Home Road/Valley of the Falls Drive, and west of the sign for Falls Recreation Area. In this 300-yard stretch, you get excellent views of the fall, in which you can see all 500 feet of its drop. Even though you're almost a half-mile from the waterfall, the vista is impressive. (This is the view of Big Falls that you usually see on postcards.)

Like me, you may find yourself wondering how often those Forest Falls homeowners sit out on their back porches, drink their morning coffee, and watch the waterfall pour.

Trip notes: There is no fee. For a map of San Bernardino National Forest, send $4 to USDA-Forest Service, 1323 Club Drive, Vallejo, CA 94592. For more information, contact San Bernardino National Forest, San Gorgonio Ranger District, 34701 Mill Creek Road, Mentone, CA 92359; (909) 794-1123.

Directions: From Interstate 10 at Redlands, take the Highway 38 exit and drive northeast for 14 miles to the junction with Forest Home Road. Bear right and continue for 4.5 miles to the Falls Recreation Area, past the town of Forest Falls. (The road's name changes to Valley of the Falls Drive.) Park in the first parking lot on the left, just past the sign that says Falls Recreation Area.

MORE WATERFALLS

in San Gabriel & San Bernardino Mountains

• Bouquet Canyon Falls, Angeles National Forest. A 30-foot waterfall called "The Falls" drops right along Bouquet Canyon Road south of Bouquet Reservoir. Unfortunately, this is a popular swimming hole and partying spot. Litter abounds. Boom boxes roar. What a pity. For more information, phone the Santa Clara Ranger District at (661) 296-9710.

• Fish Canyon Falls, Angeles National Forest. This 75-foot waterfall near Azusa is an old favorite, but access to its trail has been cut off because of a private quarrying operation. Shortly before the quarry gate, a sign reads "Fish Canyon Trail Closed Due to Construction." Maybe with increased public pressure, they'll find a way to open it. For more information, phone the San Gabriel River Ranger District at (626) 335-1251.

San Diego, Orange County, & Palm Springs

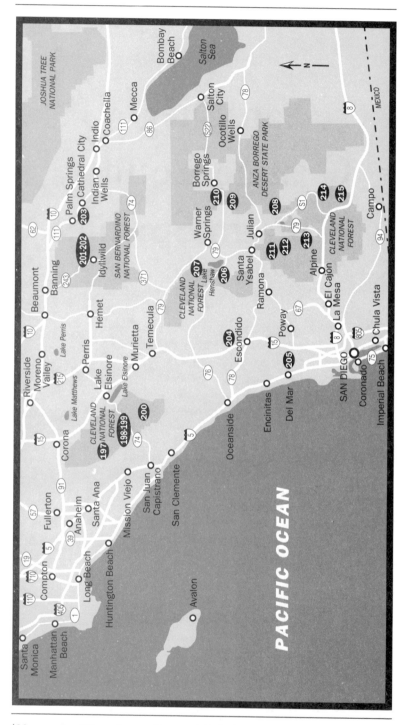

197. HOLY JIM FALLS

Cleveland National Forest
Off Interstate 5 near Trabuco Canyon

Access & Difficulty: Hike-in 2.5 miles RT/Easy
Elevation: Start at 1,000 feet; total gain 350 feet
Best Season: December to June

Holy Jim Falls has one of the finest names, and one of the finest histories, of any waterfall in Southern California. The fall and its canyon were named for a beekeeper who lived here in the 1890s, James T. Smith, better known as "Cussin' Jim." Apparently he had a temper and a colorful way with language, and since honey-loving grizzly bears were plentiful in those days, a beekeeper had a lot to be mad about. But conservative mapmakers who plotted Trabuco Canyon in the early 1900s found Smith's nickname in bad taste, and arbitrarily changed it to "Holy Jim." So it remains.

The waterfall has made its own name for itself. It seems that everybody in Orange County knows about, and likes to visit, Holy Jim Falls. On one April Saturday, we hiked the route with a troop of Boy Scouts, several families with small children, a group of teenagers, and a few older couples.

Holy Jim Falls

The drive can be a bit of a challenge (five miles on a rocky dirt road, usually manageable in a passenger car), but the hike is a breeze. It's a 2.5-mile round-trip stroll through shady oaks, keeping close company with Holy Jim Creek. The only tricky part is that the waterfall isn't right along the trail; you have to take

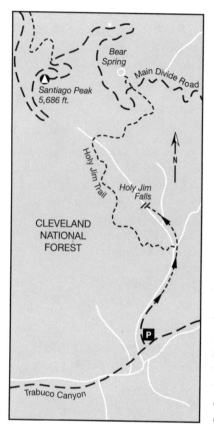

a spur trail and then make an easy 300-yard scramble to reach it. More than a few of us spent some time wandering around before we figured this out.

Start by walking down the dirt road that leads to some leased cabins, past big cactus and succulents, till you reach the official trailhead. (Some people drive this half-mile stretch and park near the cabins; technically, you're supposed to leave your car in the hiker's parking lot.) Once you're off the dirt road and on single-track, you're surrounded by a lush canyon filled with oaks, vine maples, wildflowers, and even a few ferns, all thriving in the shade alongside Holy Jim Creek. The trail crosses the creek several times, passes by many small check dams, and gently gains elevation as it heads upstream.

After nearly 30 minutes of walking, the trail steepens noticeably, and you'll pass a large, old oak tree on your left. From here, use trails branch off in various directions, and it's hard to discern the main route. The answer? Forty yards beyond the oak tree, you must cross the creek again (on your left), then immediately take the right fork, which continues deeper into the stream canyon. The left fork, which is the main trail, switchbacks uphill all the way to 5,687-foot Santiago Peak in seven miles.

Now you have only a 10-minute scramble to get to the falls, as the canyon quickly narrows around you. Holy Jim Falls is only 20 feet high, but it's set in a terrific little grotto—a circular rock amphitheater in the back of the canyon. Several streams of water join at the top and form a chute over the rock, with maidenhair ferns clinging to the side walls. If you look up and above this damp grotto, it's surprising to see that the higher canyon walls are very dry and exposed. Here at the waterfall, it's pleasantly cool, dark, and wet.

Trip notes: There is no fee. For a map of Cleveland National Forest, send $4 to USDA-Forest Service, 1323 Club Drive, Vallejo, CA 94592. For more information, contact Cleveland National Forest, Trabuco Ranger District, 1147 East Sixth Street, Corona, CA 92879; (909) 736-1811.

Directions: From Laguna Hills (north of San Juan Capistrano) on Interstate 5, exit on El Toro Road and drive east for six miles. Turn right on Live Oak Canyon Road and drive for about four miles (two miles past the entrance to O'Neill Regional Park). Turn left on Trabuco Canyon Road, which is an often unsigned, rocky, dirt road, just past the paved Rose Canyon Road turnoff. Drive five miles on the dirt road to the well-signed parking area for Holy Jim Trail. (The road is usually suitable for passenger cars.) The trail leads from the left side of the parking lot.

198. SAN JUAN FALLS

Cleveland National Forest
Off Highway 74 near Lake Elsinore

Access & Difficulty: Hike-in 1.0 mile RT/Easy
Elevation: Start at 1,800 feet; total gain 100 feet
Best Season: December to April

San Juan Falls is one of the many fine features of the San Juan Loop Trail, an easy and informative walk that serves as a good introduction to the Santa Ana Mountains. The only stipulation? Make sure you take this walk in winter or early spring. The rest of the year, it's too darn hot, and the waterfall doesn't last long past April.

If you hike the loop trail from its start on the north side of the parking lot, you reach the falls in less than a half-mile. Beware of the sign at the trailhead, which warns in doomsday-style of mountain lions, rattlesnakes, poison oak, and rugged terrain. Forge ahead, brave explorers.

You walk slightly uphill, passing a surprising variety of plant life, considering the dry and exposed slopes. I call this terrain "lush desert"—extremely arid but thriving nonetheless. It's filled with chaparral-type wildflowers, including deep red monkeyflowers, purple nightshade, and tall, spiky yuccas with their silky, milk-white flowers. Many lizards dart among the foliage, including a large variety with a noticeable horn on its head.

The trail is sandy but well-maintained. The only downer is the sound of the road, which is a little too close on the first section of trail. As the loop curves to the left, a railing and overlook alerts you to the presence of 15-foot San Juan Falls, which is situated below the trail. The view from above is only fair, so take the short spur trail leading from the left side of the railing down into the creek canyon. Standing in the creekbed, looking eye to eye with the falls and its narrow, rock-walled gorge, is your best view. The light gray, polished granite and ultra-clear stream pools invite exploration.

From the waterfall, you can return the way you came (for a one-mile round-trip) or continue hiking the loop, which is a total of two miles long and ends at the other side of the parking lot. Along the way, you pass the turnoffs for the Chiquito Basin Trail and for Upper San Juan Campground, and you walk through a lovely grove of ancient oaks.

Trip notes: There is no fee. For a map of Cleveland National Forest, send $4 to USDA-Forest Service, 1323 Club Drive, Vallejo, CA 94592. For more information, contact Cleveland National Forest, Trabuco Ranger District, 1147 East Sixth Street, Corona, CA 92879; (909) 736-1811.

Directions: From Interstate 5 at San Juan Capistrano, take the Ortega Highway (Highway 74) exit and drive north. In 21 miles, you'll reach the Ortega Oaks store on the right (three-quarters of a mile past Upper San Juan Campground). The trailhead is across the road from the store; turn left and park in the large parking lot. Start the loop trail on the right (north) side of the parking lot.

199. ORTEGA FALLS

Cleveland National Forest
Off Highway 74 near Lake Elsinore

Access & Difficulty: Hike-in 0.5 mile RT/Easy
Elevation: Start at 1,900 feet; total loss 100 feet
Best Season: December to April

A few years back, *Sunset* magazine ran a story about springtime waterfalls in Orange County, and Ortega Falls was one of their picks. When they mentioned that the fall was located just off Highway 74 and accessible by an easy walk from a highway turnout, I knew I had to make the trip.

Well, everything they said was true. Located in between the small villages of Ortega Oaks and El Caruso on the scenic Ortega Highway, the unsigned parking turnouts for the falls make an inconspicuous beginning to a great waterfall visit.

In springtime when you pull off the highway, you can hear the falls roar, and the cascading water is visible from the western turnout. Several short use trails lead from this side of the road down into San Juan canyon.

Ortega Falls

The easiest way to hike to the falls is to stay to your right along the canyon wall, following a well-worn path as it winds around boulders and brush. As you get closer, you see there are actually several falls, with marvelously clear pools in between them, dropping over polished granite. Most people stop by the 35-foot drop which is only a 15-minute walk from the parking pullout. It's a fascinating study of rock and water: The stream splits into two distinct tongues as it splashes its way over a large, block-shaped granite outcrop, then stills momentarily in a wide and shallow pool at its base. You can also visit the smaller cascades below this fall, where you're certain to find the perfect poolside rock for lounging on.

Intrepid hikers can continue scrambling upstream, heading above the 35-foot fall to more falls and pools. Be forewarned that the route is less well-used and the scrambling gets more challenging the farther you go. If you have children with you, don't climb above the first falls.

Trip notes: There is no fee. For a map of Cleveland National Forest, send $4 to USDA-Forest Service, 1323 Club Drive, Vallejo, CA 94592. For more information, contact Cleveland National Forest, Trabuco Ranger District, 1147 East Sixth Street, Corona, CA 92879; (909) 736-1811.

Directions: From Interstate 5 at San Juan Capistrano, take the Ortega Highway (Highway 74) exit and drive north. In 21 miles, you'll reach the Ortega Oaks store on the right. Reset your odometer there, and continue for 1.6 miles north on Highway 74 to the large, unmarked turnouts on both sides of the highway. There are a few trash cans and usually a few cars parked there. The trail leads from the left (west) side of the highway. (If you are coming from Lake Elsinore, the turnouts are three miles south of the village of El Caruso.)

200. TENAJA FALLS

San Mateo Canyon Wilderness
Off Interstate 15 near Murietta

Access & Difficulty: Hike-in 1.5 miles RT/Easy
Elevation: Start at 1,300 feet; total gain 300 feet
Best Season: December to May

For us, Tenaja Falls will always be Ha-ha-ha Falls, or maybe Tee-hee-hee Falls. It was on our trip to Tenaja Falls that we parked our car at the trailhead, loaded up our day-packs, and set out on the trail, except somehow we managed to miss the trail altogether. We ended up bushwhacking upstream through a veritable forest of poison oak, then scrambling, slipping, and scaling our way to the top of the falls, only to find a pack of teenagers with coolers of beer hanging out there. They had been watching our slow progress up the canyon.

Us: "Hey, how'd you manage to carry a cooler up here?"

Them: "We took the trail."

Us: "Trail? What trail?"

To make a long story short, we took the trail on the way back. It turns out it's not just a trail that leads to Tenaja Falls, but a wide dirt road, easy enough for a three-year-old to walk. Did we feel like idiots.

If you do it right, the only hard part in reaching Tenaja Falls is the long drive to the unsigned trailhead. But if you follow the directions exactly, that should be no problem. Then, after parking, head for the metal fence that blocks the road/trail into the San Mateo Wilderness to vehicles, and cross the creek on a concrete apron. If it's flooded, as it was on our trip, you can follow a use trail and cross the creek where it's narrower, but be sure to join up with the main trail again. If you stay on the use trails next to the creek, you'll wind up

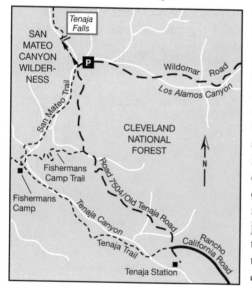

making the same mistake we did and working a lot harder than you have to.

Hike northward, rising out of the canyon and along slopes of sage and chaparral, and in a few minutes you'll round a curve and be treated to a partial view of the waterfall ahead. Keep walking toward it; the trail deposits you at the falls' lip.

Tenaja Falls is surprisingly large compared to other waterfalls in Orange County—dropping 150 feet in five tiers. Unfortunately, you never get to a vantage point where you can see the whole thing at once. Most of the time, you're looking

Tenaja Falls

at two tiers, totalling about 80 feet in height. When the water level is low enough, you can cross over the top of the falls to the other side of the creek, and gain a different perspective. Some people jump off the rocks and into the fall's deep pools, but this is probably only a good idea if you're young and foolhardy. Remember that the granite is even more slippery than it looks.

Tenaja Falls' season is short, so you must visit early in the year. Average annual rainfall in the San Mateo Canyon Wilderness is only 15 to 20 inches per season, and it's usually all over by March. When we visited the falls in mid-April, the stream's flow was already greatly reduced.

By the way, the teenagers at the waterfall departed shortly after we joined them. But when we walked the easy trail back to the parking lot, we saw two of them again. As I passed by, I heard them say to each other, with a certain amount of awe, "Hey, is she the rock climber we saw?" Yeah, right.

Trip notes: There is no fee. For a map of Cleveland National Forest, send $4 to USDA-Forest Service, 1323 Club Drive, Vallejo, CA 94592.

For more information, contact Cleveland National Forest, Trabuco Ranger District, 1147 East Sixth Street, Corona, CA 92879; (909) 736-1811.

Directions: From Lake Elsinore, drive south on Interstate 15 for about 12 miles to the Clinton Keith Road exit. Drive south on Clinton Keith Road for five miles, which will become Tenaja Road, although you won't see any signs. At a signed intersection with Tenaja Road, turn right and drive west for 4.5 miles. Turn right on Rancho California Road; drive one mile to the Tenaja Trailhead. Reset your odometer here and drive 4.4 miles on the dirt road (7S04) to a hairpin turn and the parking area.

201. FULLER MILL CREEK FALLS
San Bernardino National Forest
Off Highway 243 near Idyllwild

Access & Difficulty: Hike-in 0.5 mile RT/Easy
Elevation: Start at 5,600 feet; total gain 0 feet
Best Season: April to June

Idyllwild is a fine, unspoiled town in the magnificent San Jacinto Mountains, with easy access to many excellent trailheads. But after you've hiked around a while and worn a few holes in your boots, a laid-back trip to Fuller Mill Creek and its waterfall could be just what you need. Effort required? Almost none. Driving time? Ten minutes from town. Is it good? You bet.

Park your car at the Fuller Mill Creek Picnic Area, a nice place to have a barbecue or to do a little fishing, especially in springtime when the creek is stocked with trout. Then walk across the highway and take the trail that leads along the right (south) side of the stream. Don't take the trail on the left; it's much more rough.

Five minutes of walking upstream brings you to a 10-foot waterfall, but push on for less than 100 yards to a 25-foot fall that is set in a theater of rock and foliage. The creek has cut deeply in granite bedrock to form this perfect slice of white water, surrounded by big boulders and cottonwoods.

If you want more, you get more. Trails continue on both sides of the creek, with more falls continuing up the canyon. We were content to remain by the waterfall in the rock theater, where my hiking partner posed the all-important question: "So, how do you tear yourself away from these places?"

That's always been a hard one to answer.

Trip notes: There is no fee. For a map of San Bernardino National Forest, send $4 to USDA-Forest Service, 1323 Club Drive, Vallejo, CA 94592. For more information, contact San Bernardino National Forest, San Jacinto Ranger District, 54270 Pinecrest, Idyllwild, CA 92549; (909) 659-2117.

Directions: From Idyllwild, drive north on Highway 243 for 7.5 miles to the left turnoff for Fuller Mill Creek Picnic Area. Park there and walk across the road to mile marker 12 on Highway 243. A trail leads from the south end of the guardrail alongside Fuller Mill Creek.

Fuller Mill Creek Falls

202. DARK CANYON FALLS

San Bernardino National Forest
Off Highway 243 near Idyllwild

Access & Difficulty: Hike-in & Scramble 2.0 miles RT/Moderate
Elevation: Start at 5,800 feet; total gain 300 feet
Best Season: May to July

You can work as hard or as little as you want when you visit Dark Canyon Falls. The falls are a series of drops and cascades on Dark Canyon Creek, which makes its way through pine and fir forest and over polished granite into the San Jacinto River. It's plain from the state of the use trail that most people only hike a half-mile to the first set of falls, then find a rock to sit on and hang out for the afternoon. After that, the trail gets fainter, but the waterfalls continue. How far you go and how much you see is up to you.

Getting to the falls requires an upstream scramble from Dark Canyon Campground, located less than 10 miles from the town of Idyllwild. A use trail starts by the camp rest rooms near sites 15 and 16. If you're not staying in the camp, you must park outside its entrance and walk in to access the trail.

Beginning at the far end of the campground loop, follow the obvious route for a quarter-mile along the left (north) side of the stream. When the path ends, resort to easy scrambling up the rocky streambed.

The first falls you see are noisy, but only about 10 feet high— silvery ropes of water splashing against age-old rock. Continue a few yards farther and you reach an impressive 25-foot drop, a narrow chute rushing through granite. Along its entire length, the fall has chiseled a distinct crevice in the rock, as if forming aqueduct walls for its stream. It also has two pretty cascades, one on either side of the main fall. If you edge closer to the one on the right side, you see it conceals a small but deep cave. Inside, moss and tiny ferns grow.

One of Dark Canyon's falls

Upstream of this fall, the scrambling gets a little rougher, but it's worth the trouble to continue. We were able to get away from some boisterous campers by simply heading farther upstream. There we came across three cascades in the 10- to 15-foot range, with excellent granite swimming pools at their bases. If you want to go for a dip, be forewarned: this canyon is aptly named. It is dark and shady, and as a result the water is bitterly cold. The icy pools warrant the kind of "swimming" where you jump in, then promptly jump out and exclaim, "I'm alive!"

Trip notes: There is no fee. For a map of San Bernardino National Forest, send $4 to USDA-Forest Service, 1323 Club Drive, Vallejo, CA 94592. For more information, contact San Bernardino National Forest, San Jacinto Ranger District, 54270 Pinecrest, P.O. Box 518, Idyllwild, CA 92549; (909) 659-2117.

Directions: From Idyllwild, drive north on Highway 243 for 5.5 miles to the right turnoff for Stone Creek, Fern Basin, Marion Mountain, and Dark Canyon campgrounds. Turn right and drive two-tenths of a mile, then bear left, following the signs for Dark Canyon Camp. Drive eight-tenths of a mile, turn left and proceed 1.5 miles further to the campground. If you're not staying in the camp, you must park in the dirt pullouts along the road before the camp entrance.

---

203. MURRAY CANYON FALLS

Agua Caliente Indian Reservation
Off Highway 111 near Palm Springs

Access & Difficulty: Hike-in 4.0 miles RT/Moderate
Elevation: Start at 450 feet; total gain 300 feet
Best Season: October to May

If you think Palm Springs is all tennis courts, golf courses, and beauty parlors, you haven't been to the Indian Canyons off South Palm Canyon Drive. The Indian Canyons—Palm, Andreas, and Murray—are what's left of the old Palm Springs. They're wide-open vistas of red rock, fan palms, sulphury streams, barrel cactus, and bighorn sheep. Oh, and just our luck, there's even a desert waterfall.

Leave the shopping malls and hotel swimming pools behind, and head for the canyons. Needless to say, winter is the best time to visit, although we made the trip on an unusually cool day in June. Although it costs a few bucks to enter the Agua Caliente Reservation and the Indian Canyons area, it's completely worth it.

Your adventure begins from the east side of the picnic grounds in between Murray and Andreas Canyons, at a sign that states "Murray Canyon, 20 minutes." It's accurate, sort of. Twenty minutes doesn't get you to the good stuff, merely to the start of the canyon and the first palms in the oasis. We passed a guy who had made only the 20-minute trip, and was obviously disappointed. He told us: "Nothing much down there. Not even much water." Don't make his mistake. Have faith and keep hiking.

The trail is well-packed sand, and it's clearly marked along the way. After an initial wide-open desert stretch, you enter Murray

Murray Canyon Falls

Canyon, which narrows and twists and turns, so you never see where you're going until you come around the next bend. It keeps your anticipation high. Very slowly, the stream you've been following starts to exhibit more water. The streamside reeds, palms, and wild grape intensify their growth accordingly. If you're a fan of red rock, you'll love Murray Canyon, with its 100-foot-high slanted rock outcrops that jut out toward the sky. The colorful canyon is a delight for photographers.

As you near the falls, you'll pass the left turnoff for the Kaufmann Trail, then reach what seems like the back of the canyon. It has a small waterfall running down its cliff, but it's tucked back in a cave, difficult to see. Look for the trail continuing on the canyon's left side, climbing up and over this waterfall. Keep hiking for another 10 to 15 minutes until you suddenly come upon a much more accessible and beautiful fall, this one sculpted out of fine, polished granite. It has two 18-foot cascades set about 50 yards from each other, each with a mirror-like pool at its base. You can swim in these, or in the larger pool in front of them, which has only a two-foot fall but offers the deepest area for swimming. You'll want to spend some time here, playing in the pools, taking photographs, or spreading out a picnic.

Trip notes: A $6 entrance fee is charged per adult; $1 for children 6 to 12. A free map/brochure is available at the entrance kiosk. For more information, contact Agua Caliente Band of Cahuilla Indians, Tribal Council Office, at (760) 325-5673; or Indian Canyons Information at (760) 325-1053.

Directions: From Palm Springs, drive south through the center of town on Highway 111/Palm Canyon Drive, and take the right fork signed for South Palm Canyon Drive. Drive 2.8 miles on South Palm Canyon Drive, bearing right at the sign for Palm Canyon/Andreas Canyon. Stop at the entrance kiosk, then drive about 200 yards, and turn right for Murray Canyon. Drive past the Andreas Canyon trailhead, and continue to the Murray Canyon picnic area, one mile from the entrance kiosk.

204. JACK CREEK FALLS
Dixon Lake Recreation Area
Off Interstate 15 near Escondido

Access & Difficulty: Hike-in 0.5 mile RT/Easy
Elevation: Start at 1,100 feet; total loss 100 feet
Best Season: December to May

There are several spectacular waterfalls in the San Diego area that are moderate to challenging to reach, but only a few that are just plain easy. Jack Creek Falls, a bouldery cascade in Dixon Lake Recreation Area near Escondido, is a waterfall that's just right for those who have no interest in route finding, rock scrambling, or long hikes on exposed slopes. It's perfect for children, likely to turn them into waterfall aficionados at a young age.

Keep in mind that this is San Diego, where more than a foot of rain a year is a big deal, and if it rains for two days straight, people start drawing up ark blueprints. Make sure you visit Jack Creek immediately following a wet spell, or better yet, during a wet spell. Otherwise, you could be gazing at a pile of dry (but interesting-looking) boulders.

First, a few words about Dixon Lake. The reservoir looks more natural than you might expect, set in a deep canyon with lots of foliage surrounding it. The fishing is not bad, either, for largemouth bass, rainbow trout, catfish, and bluegill. If shoreline angling isn't your bag, you can rent a boat or launch your own. It's an excellent place to bring your family for a day (or evening) of fishing.

The Jack Creek Nature Trail begins by the park entrance station, and it ends a half-mile later at Dixon Lake. It's a self-guided trail, with interpretive brochures you can pick up at the ranger station or Lakeshore Picnic Area. Start walking by the entrance station, crossing through the Hilltop picnic area and passing two large wooden picnic shelters. Head for the shady area behind the shelters, where Jack Creek flows. Cross a small footbridge over the creek and voilà—you're right on top of the waterfall. You can't really see it from here, but when it's running, you can definitely hear it.

Continue down the trail a few yards further and take the right spur, which leads to the fall's base. If you walk upstream beyond the trail's end for about 30 feet, you reach the tallest cascade. Huge cattails block some of the view, so scramble around till you find the best spot to sit and admire the falls. The creek drops (sometimes furiously, but most of the time gingerly) over gray- and tan-colored boulders of various sizes. The total length of the cascade is about 20 feet.

If you decide to keep hiking, you'll soon get a fine view of Dixon Lake, then arrive right at the water's edge. At the lake, the Jack Creek Trail connects to the Shoreline Trail and the Grand View Trail, giving you more options for continuing your walk.

Trip notes: A $2 access fee is charged by the park on weekends only. For more information and a map, contact Dixon Lake Ranger Station, 201 North Broadway, Escondido, CA 92025; (760) 741-4680.

Directions: From Escondido, drive north on Interstate 15 and take the El Norte Parkway exit. Drive 3.1 miles east on El Norte Parkway, then turn left (north) on La Honda Drive, and drive 1.3 miles to the Dixon Lake entrance on the right. The trailhead is located directly across from the park entrance. Park by the playground/picnic area to the right of the park entrance, signed as Hilltop Picnic Area.

205. LOS PEÑASQUITOS FALLS
Los Peñasquitos Canyon Preserve
Off Interstate 15 near Poway

Access & Difficulty: Hike-in or Bike-in 6.5 miles RT/Moderate
Elevation: Start at 300 feet; total loss 200 feet
Best Season: December to April

Even if your Spanish is limited, you won't have a hard time guessing what "Los Peñasquitos" means when you visit the preserve and the waterfall. If you guessed "big boulders" or "huge chunks of rock," you're pretty close. It means "little cliffs."

Whether you would call Los Peñasquitos a boulder field or a

waterfall depends on when you visit. Although the canyon supports a year-round stream, its level fluctuates wildly, depending on the season. When we visited in May, it was already looking more like a boulder field. But show up in January or February after a good rain, and you'll see a splashy display of white water tumbling over a constricted stretch of tan-colored, volcanic rocks.

Los Peñasquitos boulders and cascades

The hike requires a big leap of faith, because from the trailheads at either end of Los Peñasquitos Canyon Preserve, the place appears flat, and covered with oaks, grasslands, and chaparral. It's unlikely terrain for a waterfall. The preserve is long and narrow, with the waterfall situated practically in the center, so you can hike to it from either side on a dirt road that traverses the park. The road serves as a multi-use path for hikers, bikers, and equestrians. Most people hike from the east end, because it provides more shade along the route. It's a nearly level, 6.5-mile round-trip to the falls from there.

Be sure to bring a friend along on this trip; because the path is wide, there's plenty of opportunity for side-by-side walking and good conversation. But remember not to get so engrossed in your company that you forget what you're looking for. The waterfall isn't clearly visible from the trail; you have to locate and take the spur trails that reach it. Coming from the eastern trailhead, you'll find the right-hand waterfall cutoff located a few hundred yards past mileage marker 3.0. (Coming from the western trailhead, it's past marker 4.0, and on the left.) Look for a long wooden railing, which runs just above the falls. If you're biking, this is where you'd lock up and walk.

A short climb down and over boulders brings you to a 100-yard stretch of peñasquitos and pools. Although each cascade is only five to ten feet tall, the continual series of them is what makes the scene impressive. The "little cliffs" look like a mix of basalt, sandstone, and limestone, giving them unusual colors ranging from pink coral to green to gray. Some are as large as small houses. They're remnants of a volcanic island chain formed underwater 140 million years ago.

In between the largest peñasquitos lay limpid pools, reflecting the rocks' polished pastel colors. In the late afternoon light, those colors become richly saturated, making the small cascades look beautiful even with little water in the stream. Have a seat on a boulder near one of the falls' reflecting pools, and watch the magic interplay of water, rock, and sunlight.

Trip notes: There is no fee. For more information and a map, contact Los Peñasquitos Canyon Preserve, c/o San Diego County Parks and Recreation Department, 5201 Ruffin Road, Suite P, San Diego, CA 92123; (858) 694-3049.

Directions: From Escondido, drive south on Interstate 15 for 16 miles to the Mercy Road exit. Turn right (west) on Mercy Road and follow it for one mile, crossing Black Mountain Road, to the trailhead parking area.

206. PRISONER CREEK FALLS
Cleveland National Forest
Off Highway 76 near Lake Henshaw

Access & Difficulty: Scramble 3.0 miles RT/Strenuous
Elevation: Start at 2,300 feet; total gain 400 feet
Best Season: December to April

Sometimes you have to make sure you really want a destination before you set out to reach it. Such is the case with Prisoner Creek Falls, a terrific waterfall that comes with a big price tag, including a long stream scramble, neck-high poison oak, and the fastest biting ticks I've ever seen.

And lest I forget, a very short season. If you don't make it here before May, you're likely to miss all the action, unless San Diego has an unusually wet year.

Prisoner Creek Falls is located across the road from a San Diego Schools' outdoor learning center, where kids from all over the county come on field trips to learn interesting stuff about their natural world. The creek and waterfall were named years ago, when the outdoor school buildings were part of a prison camp, a place for well-behaved prisoners who worked on road crews. When I visited, the outdoor school principal told me that this is the only school around where kids can say they're in prison and have it be true.

Start hiking from the wooden railing across the road from the school, where a path leads down to and crosses the San Luis Rey River on a makeshift bridge.

After crossing, walk to your left for about 50 yards, paralleling the river, until you reach Prisoner Creek, which empties into it. Stay on the west (right) side of the creek, and head upstream on the use trail, keeping as close to the creek as possible. (Another trail heads up the east side of the creek, but it rises high above the streambed and then drops steeply back down, only halfway to the waterfall. It's quite steep and overgrown with manzanita. Someday this trail may be extended and maintained, but for now, no such luck.)

When the use trail you've been following peters out, you're on your own to make tracks up the streambed. Scramble up and over the millions of rocks, doing your best not to turn your ankle; and bushwhack through the hanging branches and vines that adorn the creek. You should make it to the waterfall in just under an hour, as long as you keep plodding. If the water is high in the creek, your travel may be slower. Waterproof boots can be an asset.

When you finally arrive, you see that Prisoner Creek Falls is a 60-foot cascade, dropping in three tiers over dark gray granite. It blocks the back of the canyon, making further travel impossible. A narrow channel of water cuts straight down the middle of the fall's cliff. If you're lucky enough to see this waterfall at full flood, it's a tremendous sight.

After enjoying the falls and resting a while, make your way back down the canyon over the now familiar route. When you get back to your car, be sure to check for ticks. I didn't do this, and a few hours later I was bitten by two of them, escapees from Prisoner Creek.

Trip notes: There is no fee. For a map of Cleveland National Forest, send $4 to USDA-Forest Service, 1323 Club Drive, Vallejo, CA 94592. For more information, contact Cleveland National Forest, Palomar Ranger District, 1634 Black Canyon Road, Ramona, CA 92065; (760) 788-0250.

Directions: From Escondido, drive north on Interstate 15 for 16 miles to the Highway 76 exit. Turn east on Highway 76, and drive approximately 26 miles to the Denver C. Fox Outdoor Education School on the left (north) side of the road. (If you reach Lake Henshaw, you've gone too far.) Park across the road from the school, in the turnout with a wooden railing marked "no trespassing." The trail leads from there.

207. BARKER VALLEY FALLS

Cleveland National Forest
Off Highway 79 near Warner Springs

Access & Difficulty: Hike-in & Scramble 8.2 miles RT/Moderate
Elevation: Start at 5,150 feet; total loss 1,200 feet
Best Season: December to June

If the combination of a peaceful valley, soaring hawks and eagles, grazing deer, and a 90-foot waterfall appeal to you, you'll love Barker Valley. The hike is a pleasant ramble even in the dry season, but if you go after the Warner Springs area has received a fair amount of rain or snow, Barker Valley Falls is a sight to behold.

The trailhead is 7.9 miles off Highway 79 on Forest Service Road 9S07. This road is also referred to on maps as Palomar Divide Road and it's easy to miss. Look for a left (southern) turnoff 6.5 miles west of Warner Springs. The unpaved road doesn't require four-wheel-drive but high clearance is imperative. A gate 5.7 miles in may be locked during and after severe storms, so check with the Forest Service before making the trip in winter and spring. The trailhead is located 2.2 miles beyond the gate.

At the trailhead, you're provided with great views of Lake Henshaw to the southeast and Palomar Observatory just a few miles to the west. Park off the road and follow the trail signs as you descend gradually on switchbacks. The path is a three-mile downhill beginning in chaparral and manzanita and dropping into oak-lined Barker Valley, where the west fork of the San Luis Rey River runs year-round. Keep in mind that downhill is also the way the cold mountain air flows; the coolness may be a comfort in the summer months but not so in winter. Although we hiked on a day that was sunny and warm at the trailhead, ice had formed on the placid stretches of the river.

If you've timed your trip for the wet season, you'll cross a few running creeks as you near the lower part of the trail. No signs direct you to the river's falls, but just before you reach the river you'll notice a few spur trails leading left. Follow any of them along the river's northern bank. The spur trails converge in a pleasant, oak-shaded camping area (a free camping permit from the Forest Service is required). A rough footpath continues from the campsites for another three-quarters of a mile downstream along the West Fork San Luis Rey River. (Many people get confused in this area and head upstream in search of the falls. Make sure you go downstream!) Sooner or later, depending on how high the water level is, you'll face a scramble through brush and over smooth and slippery rocks.

Eventually you'll come out above Barker Valley Falls. If you continue your cautious scramble along the steep northern bank to your left, you'll be rewarded with a terrific view of the 90-foot cataract as it drops to the pools below. Pick a rock—any rock—pull out your picnic lunch, and enjoy the sound of the water pulsing rhythmically through the otherwise

Barker Valley Falls (lower)

silent valley. If you continue downstream, you'll find more waterfalls. On a warm day, you won't need any encouragement to try a dip in the river's alluring pools.

Of course, after that lovely downhill walk, you'll face an ascent on your way home. Fortunately the climb is gradual; be sure to reward yourself with frequent stops to admire the scenery.

(Author's note: Special thanks to Justin Cunningham for his help in compiling these trail notes.)

Trip notes: There is no fee. For a map of Cleveland National Forest, send $4 to USDA-Forest Service, 1323 Club Drive, Vallejo, CA 94592. For more information, contact Cleveland National Forest, Palomar Ranger District, 1634 Black Canyon Road, Ramona, CA 92065; (760) 788-0250.

Directions: From Ramona, drive 15.3 miles east on Highway 78 to Santa Ysabel. Turn left on Highway 79 and drive north for 35 miles. Turn left (west) on Forest Service Road 9S07 (6.5 miles west of Warner Springs) and drive 7.9 miles to the trailhead on the left side of the road.

208. ORIFLAMME CANYON FALLS

Anza-Borrego Desert State Park
Off Highway S2 near Julian

Access & Difficulty: Hike-in 2.6 miles RT/Moderate
Elevation: Start at 2,700 feet; total gain 400 feet
Best Season: December to May

Oriflamme Canyon is in the desert, but it doesn't look much like the rest of Anza-Borrego. As the crow flies, it's much closer to Lake Cuyamaca and the Laguna Mountains than it is to the main part of Anza-Borrego. Yet it's still a part of Anza-Borrego Desert State Park— a part worth exploring, not just for its spring-fed stream and 20-foot waterfall, but also for its unexpected riparian beauty.

To visit the canyon, begin by parking anywhere near the old primitive camping area in Oriflamme Canyon. Start hiking upstream, following a narrow use trail with the creek on your left. You're hiking under the shade of leafy cottonwoods that grow in profusion along the streambanks. You may notice several use trails; they all converge at an old roadbed on the right side of the stream. Sooner or later you'll wind up high above the creek, following the old road. This obvious trail makes the first part of the hike quite easy.

Oriflamme Canyon Falls

After three quarters of a mile, you begin to cross and re-cross the stream repeatedly on a less obvious track. Keep hiking back in the canyon until you reach the falls, which are only a few yards from the trail but hidden below it and completely invisible. Use your ears to guide you. (On our trip, the short spur to the falls was marked with a trail cairn, but we missed it completely. If you hike to the point where the stream becomes very narrow and minimal in its flow, you've passed the waterfall. Turn around and try again.)

The waterfall drops about 20 feet into a large pool that is completely surrounded by willows. It's difficult to work your way to the front of the pool because the foliage is quite dense, but that's the best spot to get the full visual effect.

One caveat: wearing pants and long sleeves is a good idea for this trail. This is a very brushy hike with a ton of vegetation, from chaparral to cactus such as beavertails, catclaw, and spiky chollas. You can go home with quite a few scratches if you're not dressed right.

Trip notes: There is no fee at the Oriflamme Canyon trailhead. Free maps and brochures are available at the park visitor center. For more information, contact Anza-Borrego Desert State Park, 200 Palm Canyon Drive, Borrego Springs, CA 92004; (760) 767-5311 or (760) 767-4205.

Directions: From Julian, drive east on Highway 78 for about 12 miles to Highway S2. Turn right (south) on Highway S2 and drive about nine miles to the Oriflamme Canyon turnoff located one mile past Box Canyon Historic Site. Turn west on the dirt road to Oriflamme Canyon (high-clearance is required). At a quarter mile in, bear right, then at two miles in, bear left. At three miles in, bear left again and continue a quarter mile to the bright green cottonwood trees near an old primitive camping area. Begin hiking upstream on the right bank of the creek.

209. MAIDENHAIR FALLS

Anza-Borrego Desert State Park
Off Highway S22 near Borrego Springs

Access & Difficulty: Hike-in & Scramble 5.0 miles RT/Moderate
Elevation: Start at 850 feet; total gain 800 feet
Best Season: December to May

I had heard of Maidenhair Falls in Hellhole Canyon in Anza-Borrego Desert State Park, but I was told that it was darn near impossible to reach and only suitable for experienced desert hikers. So one spring day I got up my courage, filled up my day-pack with supplies, and headed for the Hellhole trailhead, only to find dozens of parked cars and dozens of people hiking up the trail. Hard to reach? Not really. Hard to get away from the crowds? Yes indeed, at least on spring weekends. This is one of the most popular hikes in Anza-Borrego.

Well, no wonder. Hellhole Canyon is home to desert foliage galore—lavender, chuperosa, creosote, ocotillos, teddy bear chollas, California fan palms, cottonwood trees, and even ferns and mosses at Maidenhair Falls. Wildlife, too, is prolific—from bighorn sheep and jackrabbits to Costa's hummingbirds, road runners, and ladder-back woodpeckers. And best of all, Hellhole Canyon is the site of Maidenhair Falls, a 20-foot-tall waterfall framed by a wall of delicate ferns. That should be enough to inspire you to make the trip.

As with most desert hikes, it's wise to wear long pants and long sleeves on this trail, to help avoid the pitfalls of walking among plants with names like "cat claw acacia."

From the trailhead on the west side of Highway S22, hike west on the wide, obvious trail, heading up a sandy alluvial fan. The canyon mouth can be seen straight ahead, and you reach it in a mile of hiking. As you enter Hellhole Canyon, listen for the sound of flowing water. The canyon walls gradually narrow and the hiking slowly transitions to mild scrambling and boulder-hopping. Keep listening for the sound of falling water; both Maidenhair Falls and a smaller waterfall called Lower Falls are invisible from the main path. Lower Falls is only about 10 feet high; you'll find it in a secluded grotto on the left side of the stream amid a stand of fan palms. Maidenhair Falls is found about 100 yards farther, also in a secluded grotto on the left side of the stream.

What is extraordinary about Maidenhair is not the flow or shape of the cascade, but rather the wall of maidenhair ferns growing alongside it. Who would expect to find this delicate plant growing prolifically in one of the West's hottest deserts? In between the ferns you'll find a variety of mosses soaking up water like sponges.

If you get confused as to the best path to follow, remember this: after the first cluster of fan palms, follow the footpath uphill on the steep right side of the canyon. This will drop you back down to a big stand of a dozen palms and put you back on track to the falls.

Trip notes: A $5 entrance fee is charged per vehicle. Free maps and brochures are available at the park visitor center. For more information, contact Anza-Borrego Desert State Park, 200 Palm Canyon Drive, Borrego Springs, CA 92004; (760) 767-5311 or (760) 767-4205.

Directions: From Julian, drive east on Highway 78 for 19 miles to Highway S3/Yaqui Pass Road. Turn left (north) on Highway S3/Yaqui Pass Road and drive for 12 miles to Borrego Springs. Turn left on Highway

S22/Palm Canyon Drive and drive one mile to the park visitor center. Pick up a map/brochure on Hellhole Canyon and Maidenhair Falls, then drive south on Highway S22 (Montezuma Valley Road) for three-quarters of a mile to the trailhead on the right side of the road.

Or, from Warner Springs on Highway 79, drive south on Highway 79 four miles to the Highway S2 turnoff. Turn east, drive five miles, then bear left on Highway S22 and drive 18 miles to the trailhead on the left.

210. BORREGO PALM CANYON FALLS

Anza-Borrego Desert State Park
Off Highway S22 near Borrego Springs

Access & Difficulty: Hike-in 3.0 miles RT/Easy
Elevation: Start at 600 feet; total gain 500 feet
Best Season: October to May

The walk from the Anza-Borrego Desert State Park campground to Borrego Palm Canyon Falls is only 1.5 miles in length, but it feels like a trip from the desert to the tropics. You start out in a sandy, rocky, open plain, sweating it out with the cacti and ocotillo plants, and you end up in a shady oasis of fan palms, dipping your feet in the pool of a fern-covered waterfall.

It's incredible but true; water flows year-round from springs in this part of Anza-Borrego, forming a cool stream and a 15-foot waterfall that drops over big boulders in the back of Borrego Palm Canyon. For true desert rats, more and larger falls lie beyond this one, but they require climbing skills (and desert survival skills) to reach them. But even families with small children can walk the nearly flat route to the palm oasis and first waterfall.

The trip begins on the Borrego Palm Canyon Trail from the campground of the same name. They've marked the sandy route clearly, so if your water bottles are filled, just start walking. Be sure to bring along an interpretive brochure from the park visitor center so you can identify the array of desert plants that grow along the trail, including cheesebush, brittlebush, catclaw (ouch!), and chuparosa. All these bushes mean one thing—no shade anywhere.

In a half-mile, when you pass interpretive post 20, you're suddenly rewarded with the sight of hundreds of bright green, leafy palm trees ahead. After walking amid brown bushes, brown sand, and brown rocks, it's more exciting than you might expect. Borrego Palm Canyon has over 800 mature native palms, the largest of over 25 groves in the park. It's one of the largest oases in the United States.

Wading in the pool of Borrego Palm Canyon Falls

Head toward the fan palms and in a few minutes you're nestled in their shade, listening to the desert wind rustle their leafy fronds. Immediately you forget the hot, dry, rocky walk you took to get here. Keep heading farther back in the canyon, passing by more palm trees and climbing up and over a few boulders along the stream.

Another quarter hour of hiking gets you to the waterfall, which streams down over giant boulders framed by palms. Tiny maidenhair ferns grow at the water's edge. The palms and rocks form a perfect arena for the cascade. At its base is a marvelously clear pool with a sandy bottom, where you can wade in and cool off your feet. On our trip, a bright green hummingbird flitted about the scene.

If you stand back a few feet from the waterfall, you can look above it and between the palms to get a peek into the rocky canyon beyond. Sit for a while and listen to the croaking of frogs and the wind in the palms.

Trip notes: A $5 entrance fee is charged per vehicle. Free maps and brochures are available at the park visitor center. For more information, contact Anza-Borrego Desert State Park, 200 Palm Canyon Drive, Borrego Springs, CA 92004; (760) 767-5311 or (760) 767-4205.

Directions: From Julian, drive east on Highway 78 for 19 miles to Highway S3/Yaqui Pass Road. Turn left (north) on Highway S3/Yaqui Pass Road and drive for 12 miles to Borrego Springs. Turn left on Highway S22/Palm Canyon Drive, and drive one mile to the signed junction just before the park visitor center. Turn right and drive one mile to Borrego Palm Canyon Campground. The trailhead is at the west end.

211. CEDAR CREEK FALLS

Cleveland National Forest
Off Highway 79 near Julian

Access & Difficulty: Hike-in 4.0 miles RT/Moderate
Elevation: Start at 1,950 feet; total loss 1,000 feet
Best Season: December to May

You want spectacular? Okay, get ready. Cedar Creek Falls is one of San Diego's best waterfalls. It plummets 100 feet over a granite lip in a steep and treacherous canyon, then crashes into a huge pool. After a rain, it fairly roars with water and can appear truly frightening in its power.

For the best viewing, hike the trail to Cedar Creek Falls well before Memorial Day. Although Cedar Creek flows year-round, "flows" is a relative term. Also, the trail is mostly open fire road and completely exposed, so it's not a good path for the heat of summer. The hike is an easy two miles downhill, then a slightly more difficult two miles back up. Make sure you have some water for the return trip uphill.

The trailhead for Cedar Creek Falls is one of the access points for the California Riding and Hiking Trail, the noncontiguous multi-use trail that crisscrosses much of San Diego County. Begin your walk by heading to the right and downhill on the wide fire road. Be sure to look over your right shoulder for a view of the reported largest waterfall in San Diego, Mildred Falls. What? You don't see any water? Right. Almost no one ever does, which is why the fall doesn't get its own listing in this book. Usually you can make out two big sandstone ledges with algae and moisture streaks, followed by an "S" turn down the back of the canyon, but that's about it. The fall only runs immediately after a hard rain, and the trailhead access road is not easily passable then.

Keep walking downhill, enjoying the excellent views of the San Diego River canyon far away and the many spring wildflowers close by. The slopes along the

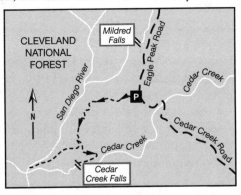

The brink of Cedar Creek Falls

road are colored with paintbrush, monkeyflower, bush lupine, and huge white morning glories. If you time it right, you may even seen the cacti bloom.

At 1.2 miles, look for a left fork off the main trail. It's unsigned, but it's the first and only left turnoff you'll see. Follow it up and over a small hill, then when you come down the other side, you'll see three possible trail options: The right-hand trail takes you uphill to an overlook, the other two trails bring you downhill to Cedar Creek. The middle trail is the shortest route to the stream and the falls, but if you want something less steep, take the left trail, which gets you there on a longer and gentler grade. (The left trail also leads to a smaller waterfall upstream of the big drop, but it only runs during wet weather.)

When you reach the creek, simply walk downstream under the shade of oaks and cottonwoods, hopping over the tops of boulders and around beautiful clear pools for about 50 yards till you reach the lip of the falls. Here's where the drama, and the danger, comes in. While all is placid above the waterfall, its drop is sheer and extremely slippery. It's one of those edge-of-the-world waterfalls, and because you're at its brink, it's difficult to position yourself for a good view. Forget scrambling to the bottom; besides being extremely dangerous, the land at the fall's pool is private property. If you're comfortable off-trail, you can make your way around the right side of the fall to a rocky ridge where your view is more complete.

After peeking at Cedar Creek's big drop, settle in at one of the gorgeous upstream pools for sunning and swimming. In very low water, you can even swim in the pool right before the fall's brink, but of course you should do this only when the stream is not billowing over the edge.

Trip notes: There is no fee. For a map of Cleveland National Forest, send $4 to USDA-Forest Service, 1323 Club Drive, Vallejo, CA 94592. For more information, contact Cleveland National Forest, Palomar Ranger District, 1634 Black Canyon Road, Ramona, CA 92065; (760) 788-0250.

Directions: From Julian, drive two miles west on Highway 78/79, then turn left (south) on Pine Hills Road. In 1.5 miles, bear right on Eagle Peak Road. In 1.4 miles, bear right again, staying on Eagle Peak Road. Continue for eight miles on partly paved, partly dirt road to the signed Forest Service trailhead for the California Riding and Hiking Trail. (The road gets rough after the first four miles, but it's usually suitable for a passenger car.)

212. THREE SISTERS FALLS

Cleveland National Forest
Off Highway 79 near Julian

Access & Difficulty: Hike-in 3.2 miles RT/Moderate
Elevation: Start at 2,900 feet; total loss 1,100 feet
Best Season: December to May

A few years back I heard a rumor that they finally built a real trail in to Three Sisters. As soon as I could, I got on an airplane, flew down to San Diego, and drove up to Julian to check out the new trail to one of my favorite waterfalls. Turns out the rumor was only partly true. You see, they built a new trail that runs the first mile to the waterfall, but then it joins with the old, steep, unmaintained footpath for the last stretch to Three Sisters. Still, the trail is an improvement. The first mile is now a wide, easy-grade path that saves a lot of wear and tear on your knees compared to the old path. The last two miles are still on the rough side, but accessing lovely Three Sisters feels quite a bit easier than it used to.

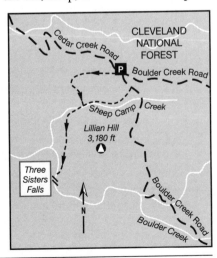

To see it, park at the "new" signboard for Cedar Creek Trail. Follow this good trail for about a mile, heading

Three Sisters Falls

slightly uphill and then switchbacking down to the left until it meets up with tiny Sheep Camp Creek. You'll see the old footpath coming in on your left. Cross Sheep Camp Creek and pick up the good trail on its far side, heading right. Ascend slightly to a low saddle, from which you should spot Three Sisters below. It's good to have some incentive, because now you have some remarkably steep downhill scrambling to negotiate in order to cross the canyon to the waterfall. I hope you wore your good boots; the footing is loose and lousy in places.

When you reach Boulder Creek, hike upstream for a few hundred yards to get to the base of the falls. Take any of several possible routes, but stay off the slick granite as much as possible. It's deadly.

A triple set of waterfalls on Boulder Creek, Three Sisters creates an impressive display of white water on smooth granite. The middle fall is the tallest at about 50 feet. Its flow may not always be wide and full, but its setting is spectacular, and its pools are ripe for swimming if the day is warm. Just use caution on the slippery granite slabs.

Trip notes: There is no fee. For a map of Cleveland National Forest, send $4 to USDA-Forest Service, 1323 Club Drive, Vallejo, CA 94592. For more information, contact Cleveland National Forest, Palomar Ranger District, 1634 Black Canyon Road, Ramona, CA 92065; (760) 788-0250.

Directions: From Julian, drive two miles west on Highway 78/79, then turn left (south) on Pine Hills Road. In 1.5 miles, bear right on Eagle Peak Road. In 1.4 miles, bear left (south) on Boulder Creek Road and drive 8.4 miles to a hairpin turn and junction with another dirt road. A

Forest Service signboard for Cedar Creek Trail is located there. Park and take the trail from the signboard.

213. GREEN VALLEY FALLS

Cuyamaca Rancho State Park
Off Highway 79 near Julian

Access & Difficulty: Hike-in 0.5 mile RT/Easy
Elevation: Start at 3,950 feet; total loss 80 feet
Best Season: December to May

Green Valley Falls is a perfect campground waterfall. It's an easy walk from one of Cuyamaca Rancho State Park's pleasant family camps, a great place to cool off from the spring and summer heat, and a fine picnicking destination. If you're camping for the weekend in the state park, Green Valley Falls is where you'd want to spend your afternoons.

The falls are accessible for day-use visitors, too; all you do is drive to the Green Valley Falls picnic area and walk a quarter-mile along the Sweetwater River. Campers can walk from their tents, making their trip just over a half-mile to the falls. The falls drop on the river, and although they're not tall, they constitute a series of wide and pretty cascades with enough ledges and pools to allow plenty of room for everybody. It's the kind of place where you can find your

A cascading stretch of Green Valley Falls

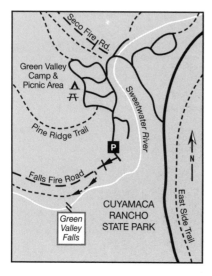

own spot to spread out a blanket or lounge around on a rock.

From the picnic area parking lot, you walk only one-tenth of a mile on the Falls Fire Road (also called the Sweetwater River Fire Road) to the Green Valley Falls Trail, then turn left and head downhill to the falls. You reach them in a few hundred yards, then pick your spot and settle in. Because the cascades and boulders are so large, it's difficult to scramble up- or downstream along the river. If you want to explore around, take any of the several spur trails off the fire road to reach the pools above and below the falls.

Trip notes: A $5 entrance fee is charged per vehicle. Various maps of Cuyamaca Rancho State Park are available for a fee at the park visitor center. For more information, contact Cuyamaca Rancho State Park, 12551 Highway 79, Descanso, CA 91916; (760) 765-0755.

Directions: From San Diego, drive east on Interstate 8 for 40 miles to the Highway 79 exit. Drive north on Highway 79 for seven miles, then turn left (west) at the sign for Green Valley Campground. Follow the signs to the picnic area. One sign points either straight ahead or to the left for the picnic area; continue straight to reach the trailhead.

214. COTTONWOOD CREEK FALLS

Cleveland National Forest
Off Highway S1 near Mount Laguna

Access & Difficulty: Hike-in 2.0 miles RT/Easy
Elevation: Start at 4,400 feet; total loss 400 feet
Best Season: December to June

From the start of the trail, Cottonwood Creek Falls looks like it's going to be a pain in the neck to reach. But don't be fooled. The trail is the steepest, and the brush is the thickest, in its first 100 yards. After that, the trail just keeps getting flatter and wider as you descend. It turns out to be an easy hike.

One of Cottonwood Creek Falls' cascades and pools

To start things off on the right foot, so to speak, make sure you park in the right spot. You'll often see cars parked in the pullout on the east side of the Sunrise Highway, but if you do this, you have to walk along the road for a few hundred yards to the start of the trail. Instead, park on the west side of the highway, in the turnout with the large rock wall, then just cross the road.

Pick up the unsigned trail at the north end of the guardrail, and make your way steeply downhill through the chaparral. When you reach the bottom of the canyon, which takes about 15 minutes, turn sharply left and walk along Cottonwood Creek, heading upstream. You can't see anything yet, but you're only five minutes from the falls.

The trail gets narrower, passing by many spiny cacti, beautiful rock formations, and a terrific show of spring wildflowers. Shortly beyond a makeshift campsite, you start passing one rock-lined cascade after another. There are three main drops, each about 12 feet high, and several smaller ones. The final fall you reach is a gorgeous freefall, and it's the most impressive of the group. It has a nice pool for swimming, which has been dammed by rocks to deepen it.

Trip notes: There is no fee. For a map of Cleveland National Forest, send $4 to USDA-Forest Service, 1323 Club Drive, Vallejo, CA 94592. For more information, contact Cleveland National Forest, Descanso Ranger District, 3348 Alpine Boulevard, Alpine, CA 91901; (619) 445-6235.

Directions: From San Diego, drive east on Interstate 8 for 47 miles to the Highway S1/Sunrise Scenic Byway turnoff. Drive north on Highway S1 for about two miles to the large pullout on the west side of the road, between mileposts 15.0 and 15.5. (It has an obvious, graffiti-covered rock wall.) Cross the road on foot, and locate the unmarked trail at the north end of the guardrail.

215. KITCHEN CREEK FALLS

Cleveland National Forest
Off Interstate 8 near Pine Valley

Access & Difficulty: Hike-in & Scramble 4.5 miles RT/Moderate
Elevation: Start at 3,100 feet; total gain 500 feet
Best Season: December to May

In a word—awesome. To sum up Kitchen Creek Falls in one word is to say, "Wow." Although I have many favorite waterfalls in San Diego and Orange counties, Kitchen Creek at a good flow tops them all.

As with many of the streams and falls in the dry and arid Southland, perfect timing is crucial to your visit. Kitchen Creek runs year-round, but the 150-foot fall is a show-stopper only from December to May, or when there's wet weather. The trail to reach it is a shadeless two miles through classic chaparral country, and uphill to boot. It's not the kind of place you want to find yourself at high noon in mid-August.

The trailhead is only a few short miles from the Mexican border, so don't be surprised by the sudden appearance of border patrol vehicles and uniformed officers along the road where you leave your car. That's just what they do around here. After stocking up on snacks and drinks at the Boulder Oaks Store, take the Pacific Crest Trail (PCT) access route that begins directly across from Boulder Oaks.

The trail has a rather inglorious start as it crosses underneath Interstate 8, but the views improve as you climb upward. The sight and sound of the highway doesn't stop till you drop down to the falls, but you'll be pleasantly distracted by the colorful ceanothus, paintbrush, and peach-colored monkeyflowers along the trail. If you're hiking in the right wind conditions, you may see colorful paragliders soaring high above your head.

It's extremely easy to miss the left-hand spur trail off the PCT to reach the falls. There's no visual indication of a waterfall or even a stream, just the sandy, cactus-lined trail, and your ears can detect water only if it has recently rained. Start paying close attention after about 45 minutes of trail time; keep looking to your left for a side trail. We reached the turnoff in exactly two miles, which for most people is 50 to 60 minutes of hiking. On our trip, small rocks were lined along the PCT where three separate spur trails led off within 15 feet of each other. If you take any of the spurs, you reach a distinctly-shaped pointed rock sticking up from the ground, about six feet tall and 25 feet down the trail. This means you're in the right place. From the rock, follow any of several use

The base of Kitchen Creek Falls

trails (there's a network of them), descending until you hear the sound of water and reach an overlook with a view of Kitchen Creek.

From the overlook, you'll see some small, pretty cascades, but still, no big waterfall in sight. That's because you're upstream of the main drop. Cut down the hillside on any of the use trails, heading generally downstream. In a few more minutes you'll be standing at the top of the falls. If you choose to continue to the waterfall's base, use caution. The polished granite is slippery when dry and treacherous when wet. To make your descent, stay off the rock and keep to the dirt routes alongside the falls.

Kitchen Creek's drop is 150 feet of cascading water sliding off slick granite. The tiered cascades twist and turn over an extended series of rounded ledges in the bedrock, creating a myriad of places to throw down a towel or a blanket and listen to the music of the falls.

Trip notes: There is no fee. For a map of Cleveland National Forest, send $4 to USDA-Forest Service, 1323 Club Drive, Vallejo, CA 94592. For more information, contact Cleveland National Forest, Descanso Ranger District, 3348 Alpine Boulevard, Alpine, CA 91901; (619) 445-6235.

Directions: From San Diego, drive east on Interstate 8 for 50 miles to the Buckman Springs Road turnoff. Drive south on the frontage road for 2.3 miles to the Boulder Oaks store and campground. (Stay on the frontage road; do not turn on to Buckman Springs Road.) Park across the road from the store, at the signed trailhead for the Pacific Crest Trail.

INDEX

ABOUT THE AUTHOR

Ann Marie Brown is an outdoor writer and waterfall lover who lives in Marin County, California. She is the author of eight books on the California outdoors, all published by Foghorn Press:

California Waterfalls
Day-Hiking California's National Parks
California Hiking (with Tom Stienstra)
101 Great Hikes of the San Francisco Bay Area
Easy Hiking in Northern California
Easy Biking in Northern California
Easy Camping in Southern California
Easy Hiking in Southern California

FOGHORN ✖ OUTDOORS

Founded in 1985, Foghorn Press has quickly become one of the country's premier publishers of outdoor recreation guidebooks. Foghorn Press books are available throughout the United States in bookstores and some outdoor retailers.

101 Great Hikes of the San Francisco Bay Area, 1st ed.1-57354-068-4	$15.95
Alaska Fishing, 2nd ed. 0-935701-51-6	$20.95
America's Wilderness, 1st ed. 0-935701-47-8	$19.95
Arizona and New Mexico Camping, 3rd ed. 1-57354-044-7	$18.95
Atlanta Dog Lover's Companion, 1st ed. 1-57354-008-0	$17.95
Baja Camping, 3rd ed. 1-57354-069-2	$14.95
Bay Area Dog Lover's Companion, 3rd ed. 1-57354-039-0	$17.95
Boston Dog Lover's Companion, 2nd ed. 1-57354-074-9	$17.95
California Beaches, 2nd ed. 1-57354-060-9	$19.95
California Camping, 11th ed. 1-57354-053-6	$20.95
California Dog Lover's Companion, 3rd ed. 1-57354-046-3	$20.95
California Fishing, 5th ed. 1-57354-052-8	$20.95
California Golf, 9th ed. 1-57354-091-9	$24.95
California Hiking, 4th ed. 1-57354-056-0	$20.95
California Recreational Lakes and Rivers, 2nd ed. 1-57354-065-x	$19.95
California Waterfalls, 2nd ed. 1-57354-070-6	$17.95
California Wildlife: The Complete Guide, 1st ed. 1-57354-087-0	$16.95
Camper's Companion, 3rd ed. 1-57354-000-5	$15.95
Colorado Camping, 2nd ed. 1-57354-085-4	$18.95
Day-Hiking California's National Parks, 1st ed. 1-57354-055-2	$18.95
Easy Biking in Northern California, 2nd ed. 1-57354-061-7	$12.95
Easy Camping in Northern California, 2nd ed. 1-57354-064-1	$12.95
Easy Camping in Southern California, 1st ed. 1-57354-004-8	$12.95
Easy Hiking in Northern California, 2nd ed. 1-57354-062-5	$12.95
Easy Hiking in Southern California, 1st ed. 1-57354-006-4	$12.95
Florida Beaches, 1st ed. 1-57354-054-4	$19.95
Florida Camping, 1st ed. 1-57354-018-8	$20.95
Florida Dog Lover's Companion, 2nd ed. 1-57354-042-0	$20.95
Montana, Wyoming and Idaho Camping, 1st ed. 1-57354-086-2	$18.95
New England Camping, 2nd ed. 1-57354-058-7	$19.95
New England Hiking, 2nd ed. 1-57354-057-9	$18.95
Outdoor Getaway Guide: Southern CA, 1st ed. 1-57354-011-0	$14.95
Pacific Northwest Camping, 7th ed. 1-57354-080-3	$19.95
Pacific Northwest Hiking, 3rd ed. 1-57354-059-5	$20.95
Seattle Dog Lover's Companion, 1st ed. 1-57354-002-1	$17.95
Tahoe, 2nd ed. 1-57354-024-2	$20.95
Texas Dog Lover's Companion, 1st ed. 1-57354-045-5	$20.95
Texas Handbook, 4th ed. 1-56691-112-5	$18.95
Tom Stienstra's Outdoor Getaway Guide: No. CA, 3rd ed. 1-57354-038-2	$18.95
Utah and Nevada Camping, 1st ed. 1-57354-012-9	$18.95
Utah Hiking, 1st ed. 1-57354-043-9	$15.95
Washington Boating and Water Sports, 1st ed. 1-57354-071-4	$19.95
Washington Fishing, 3rd ed. 1-57354-084-6	$18.95
Washington, DC Dog Lover's Companion, 1st ed. 1-57354-041-2	$17.95

For more information, call 1-800-FOGHORN
email: travel@moon.com
or write to: Avalon Travel Publishing, Foghorn Outdoors
5855 Beaudry St., Emeryville, CA 94608